A Practitioner's Guide to Rational-Emotive Therapy
SECOND EDITION

Susan R. Walen
Raymond DiGiuseppe
Windy Dryden

New York   Oxford
OXFORD UNIVERSITY PRESS
1992

Oxford University Press

Oxford   New York   Toronto
Delhi   Bombay   Calcutta   Madras   Karachi
Kuala Lumpur   Singapore   Hong Kong   Tokyo
Nairobi   Dar es Salaam   Cape Town
Melbourne   Auckland

and associated companies in
Berlin   Ibadan

Published by Oxford University Press, Inc.,
200 Madison Avenue, New York, New York 10016

Oxford is a registered trademark of Oxford University Press

Library of Congress Cataloging-in-Publication Data
Walen, Susan R.
A practitioner's guide to rational-emotive therapy
Susan R. Walden, Raymond DiGiuseppe, Windy Dryden. —2nd ed.
p. cm.   Includes bibliographical references and index.
ISBN 0-19-507168-9
ISBN 0-19-507169-7 (ppk.)
1. Rational-emotive psychotherapy.
I. DiGiuseppe, Raymond. II. Dryden, Windy. III. Title.
[DNLM: 1. Psychotherapy.
2. Psychotherapy, Rational-Emotive.
WM420 W171p]   RC489.R3W34   1992
616.89'14—dc20 DNLM/DLC
for Library of Congress
91–46377

9 8 7 6 5 4 3 2 1

Printed in the United States of America
on acid-free paper

Preface

The literature on Rational-Emotive Therapy (RET) has burgeoned since the first edition of this text. At the time of the first edition, the majority of the works were by Albert Ellis, the founder of RET and still its most articulate spokesman, and a large percentage of those works were written for the patient or the general public as self-help books. (In fact, RET holds a unique place among schools of psychotherapy, in part because of its early and generous dissemination of principles and procedures for the layperson.) The original *Practitioner's Guide to RET* was the first text written for the therapist-in-training, and it evolved out of our own experience as trainees and trainers.

Over the last decade, the corpus of RET literature has grown to include other training manuals (e.g., the briefer *Primer* by DiGiuseppe and Dryden), new self-help books and software, and many special-topic books (e.g., on working with children, families, marital problems, etc.). During this time, we have continued to serve as RET supervisors and have learned more about the content areas as well as how to teach RET to new therapists or therapists new to this model. In this second edition, therefore, we offer changes in the theory and practice of RET as they have evolved, and changes in the art of learning to do RET as a therapist.

Explaining the basic principles of RET is not difficult. The format is simple and the concepts, as explained by Dr. Ellis, are catchy (e.g., *"Mus*turbation leads to self-abuse"). After reading *A New Guide to Rational Living* (Ellis and Harper, 1975), one can easily give an engaging lecture. In fact, many patients can give the lecture, although they may not yet be able to apply the principles consistently to their own problems. Leading a client successfully through the RET maze often sounds a lot easier than it actually is.

We recall our own initial confusions in discriminating rational beliefs from irrational ones, in pinning down specific emotions in the complaints of clients, in the ease with which we as beginning RET therapists became mired in slippery disputations. In other words, therapist–client interchanges are not always as clear-cut in therapy sessions as they are made to seem in texts. The fuzzy predicaments brought in by patients don't seem to follow the script!

Over the years, many therapists have come to the Institute for Rational-Emotive Therapy in New York for training in RET. Even in the brief but intensive 5-day practicum offered by the Institute, significant progress in therapist behavior can be seen as practice therapy tapes are made and supervised. In this supervision work, one hears a strong oral tradition of RET. Supervisors give their students (who, in turn, may become supervisors) a wealth of helpful hints in doing RET. As is common in oral traditions, the original source of a hint may be lost but the useful information continues to circulate. Some of the bits of clinical lore in the present manual, for example, are derived from a legacy left by supervisors such as Bill Knaus, Ed Garcia, Jon Geis, Janet Wolfe, Ginger Waters, Howard Kassinove, Bill Golden, Rose Oliver, Michael Bernard, and especially Albert Ellis, as well as a host of others.

The purpose of *A Practitioner's Guide to RET* is to codify some of the traditional oral teachings. We have tried to include many of the common stumbling blocks and basic confusions of the new therapist as reconstructed from our own experience or the experience of training others. These confusions seem to fall easily into the basic A-B-C model of RET. So, too, do the battery of hints, aphorisms, examples, and explanatory devices that form the bulk of the oral tradition.

We have organized the chapters in the book for easy referencing of therapist problems. For example, patients may present difficulties in focusing on A (an activating event); they may complain that "everything hurts" or that nothing is wrong but they merely want to become "self-actualized." What does the therapist do? Chapter 6 has some helpful suggestions. Perhaps the therapist has identified a "should" but is not sure how to dispute it; Chapters 10, 11, and 12 may be useful. Thus, at its core, this manual is meant to be practical—something to reach for when you, as a therapist, feel stuck.

The book is aimed at practitioners new to RET, but because RET is a broad cognitive-learning therapy, we assume the reader has some knowledge of psychological principles, behavior modification tools, and general counseling skills. Without these, RET, like any other system of psycho-

To our teacher,
Albert Ellis

Foreword

When *A Practitioner's Guide to Rational-Emotive Therapy* was first published in 1980, it was a pioneering training manual for RET practitioners, especially for neophytes. Since that time it has served beautifully to introduce thousands of trainees to RET and has been a core text for the Primary Certificate Program and the more advanced training programs of the Institute for Rational-Emotive Therapy in the United States, Canada, Mexico, and a number of other countries in Europe, the Middle East, Asia, and Australia. When I have been a speaker and a supervisor in a large number of these programs, I have been repeatedly startled to see that some of the participants conduct amazingly good therapy sessions right from the start because they have assiduously studied and followed the exceptionally clear formulations in the first edition of this excellent book.

This second edition includes all the virtues of the 1980 presentation and also brings the theory and practice of RET quite up-to-date. When I created this form of therapy in 1955, I heavily stressed its cognitive and philosophic elements, because the therapies of the 1950s, especially psychoanalysis and person-centered therapy, sadly neglected those aspects of helping clients to become less emotionally disturbed. But even early rational-emotive therapy was highly emotive and behavioral, because a good many years before I started my training as a clinical psychologist in 1942, I had used in vivo desensitization (which I borrowed from John B. Watson) and shame-attacking exercises (which I largely created myself) to overcome my own social shyness and enormous fear of public speaking. I was also an active-directive sex therapist from 1943 to 1947, when I unfortunately sidetracked myself (until 1953) by getting trained in and practicing psychoanalysis. So after I became disillusioned with analysis and created RET in 1955, I returned to active-directive methods and incorporated a number of emotive and behavioral techniques in my early use of RET. Why? Because a combination of thinking, feeling, and behavioral methods, I soon found, worked better than did a one-sided emphasis on cognitive restructuring.

Just as theory leads to practice, so is the reverse often true. The more I practiced RET in the 1950s in a fashion that Arnold Lazarus later nicely called "multimodal therapy," the more I developed its present emotive-evocative theory. I saw that my clients had what I called Irrational Beliefs (Ellis, 1958, 1962) and thereby disturbed themselves emotionally and behaviorally. I also discovered that their central schemas or core philosophies were Jehovian, absolutist musts and commands; that they often held these musts very *strongly* and *powerfully;* that they compellingly *felt* them and incorporated them into their psychosomatic responses; that they clearly habituated themselves to *acting* on their dysfunctional convictions; and that they holistically *integrated* their (conscious and unconscious) demands, commands, imperatives, and insistencies into almost everything they thought, felt, and did.

I also realized, by the early 1960s, that children, adolescents, and adults learn much of their goals, desires, and values from their parents and their culture, because they are born gullible, teachable, and impressionable. Therefore, their "normal" personality is—as Sampson (1989) and other social psychologists have noted—intrinsically enmeshed with their sociality. They are consequently both unique individuals *and* highly social creatures. But as Kelly (1955) saw a half-century ago, and as many social thinkers recently have seen again (Mahoney, 1991), humans actively *construct* and *reconstruct* their ideas and behaviors, and do not *merely* and blindly accept them from their families and their societies.

Although RET has been wrongly accused by Guidano (1988), Mahoney (1991), and others of being sensationalistic and rationalistic, it is actually more constructivist than most of the other cognitive and noncognitive therapies. Let me briefly mention some, though hardly all, of its constructivist theories and practices.

1. RET holds that almost all humans have a strong, largely innate predisposition to learn or adopt familial and cultural standards and preferences and then to *create* and *construct* rigid musts and demands *about* these preferences. Thus, they dogmatically often convince themselves, "Because I greatly *like* success and approval, I *absolutely must* have them almost all the time, under nearly all conditions" (Ellis and Harper, 1975).

2. People's basic self-disturbing musts and demands are not merely

superficially or consciously held, but are often tacit, implicit, and unconscious and are strongly clung to in the "deep" structures of their minds and bodies.

3. Children are usually born, as Bowlby (1980) showed, extremely attachable to their parents and significant others; but they often also *create* a dire "necessity" for being loved and seriously disturb themselves (not *get* disturbed) when their affectional preferences are not fully met.

4. RET holds that children (and adults) are largely *taught* to evaluate their behaviors as "good" and "bad," but that they mainly construct (rather than merely learn to rate) their *self* or *personhood* or *being*. If they act "well," they naturally tend to "deify" and if they act "badly" they easily tend to "devil-ify" or damn their entire *self,* and not merely their *behaviors*.

5. RET theorizes that virtually all humans, however reared, have two somewhat opposing creative tendencies: (a) to damn and deify themselves and others (as noted above), and thereby *make themselves* disturbed; and (b) to change and actualize themselves, and thereby *make themselves* healthy and less disturbed. RET tries to teach people how to use their self-actualizing capacity to reduce their self-disturbing tendencies, and thus to *construct* a more enjoyable life.

6. RET is opposed to rigidity, "musturbation," one-sidedness, and stasis, and strongly favors openness, alternative-seeking, nondogmatism, and flexibility. It upholds a scientific, nondogmatic outlook and theorizes that when people fairly consistently adopt that kind of philosophy, they are considerably less disturbed than when they are devoutly antiscientific.

7. RET tries to help people achieve what it calls "a profound philosophic or attitudinal change" and not merely to modify their unrealistic attributions and inferences, as some of the other cognitive-behavior therapies emphasize doing.

8. Mahoney (1991) states that cognitive constructivists hold that acting, feeling, and knowing are inseparable experiences of adaptation and development. RET agrees. However, as I noted in my first paper on RET that I presented to the American Psychological Association Convention in Chicago in 1956, and as I restated in *Reason and Emotion in Psychotherapy* (Ellis, 1962, p. 38), "The theoretical foundations of RET are based on the assumption that human thinking and emotion are *not* two disparate processes, but that they significantly overlap and are in some respects, for all practical purposes, essentially the same thing. Like the other two basic life processes, sensing and moving, they are integrally interrelated and never can be seen wholly apart from each other."

9. Guidano and Mahoney, along with Freud (1965) and Rogers

(1951), stress the importance of the therapeutic relationship for personality change. But, as the present book by Walen, DiGiuseppe, and Dryden clearly indicates, RET stresses collaboration between the therapist and the client; in particular, that therapists had better always give clients unconditional acceptance, and not merely *tell* but *show* their clients that they are accepted by the therapist, *whether or not* they perform adequately and *whether or not* they are nice and lovable. But in addition to *showing* and *modeling* unconditional acceptance, RET practitioners *teach* clients how to accept themselves philosophically, not because of but also independently of their therapist's acceptance (Ellis, 1973a, 1977a, 1988; Ellis & Harper, 1975). This double-barreled approach uniquely emphasizes people's ability to *choose* and *construct* their own self-acceptance and is therefore more constructivist than most other cognitive-behavioral and noncognitive approaches.

RET, then, is unusually constructivist and integrative (Ellis, 1987c). What I like immensely about this revised edition of *A Practitioner's Guide to Rational-Emotive Therapy* is that it goes beyond the first edition and emphasizes RET's integrative, constructivist, emotive, and behavioral aspects. Its discussion of RET's cognitive disputing of irrational beliefs is so good that it can easily be called superb. But it also shows that the "complete" rational-emotive practitioner disputes his and her clients' dysfunctional inferences, attributions, and core philosophies actively *and* collaboratively, precisely *and* emotively, intellectually *and* behaviorally. Specific or preferential RET, as this book shows, has its unique flavors and significantly differs from the therapies of Beck (1976), Maultsby (1975), Meichenbaum (1985), and other cognitive behaviorists. In general, however, RET decidedly overlaps with the other major cognitive therapies and adapts and uses many of their methods.

RET also has considerable humanistic and existential elements (Ellis, 1990b, 1991c) and is probably more emotive than any of the other popular cognitive-behavior schools. Its holistic, integrative, and emotive emphases are clearly presented in this book, and whoever wants to understand the flavor and context of rational-emotive therapy in the 1990s can find them beautifully presented herewith.

Institute for   Albert Ellis, Ph.D., President
Rational-Emotive Therapy
New York City

A Practitioner's Guide
to Rational-Emotive Therapy

therapy, runs the risk of being conducted mechanically—which, although not awful, is probably of less value to the patient.

If you were in training at the Institute for RET in New York, you would tape-record virtually all of your therapy sessions for supervision. You, the reader, will be asked to perform many self-checking exercises throughout this manual, so that in addition to obtaining outside supervision, you will be able to supervise yourself. Therefore, if you are not already in the habit of taping your therapy sessions, *begin now*.

Baltimore	S. R. W.
New York	R. D. G.
London	W. D.
January 1991	

Contents

Part I
The Infrastructure of RET

1 Rational-Emotive Philosophy

Perhaps more than any other system of psychotherapy, RET grows out of and actively utilizes strong philosophical underpinnings. In fact, Ellis has selected a quotation from Epictetus, a Stoic philosopher from the first century A.D., as one of the benchmarks of RET:

> Men are disturbed not by things, but by the views which they take of them.

Disturbance, in other words, is largely (but not completely) a function of our perceptions, our evaluations, and our value systems—components of our personal philosophies.

RET is, in part, a philosophical model and, as such, has embedded within it an epistemology, or a theory of knowledge; a dialectic, or a system of reasoning; a system of values; and ethical principles. Let us take each of these in turn.

Epistemology: The Art of Knowing

How do we know a thing to be true? What are the most reliable and valid ways of obtaining knowledge? These are questions of epistemology. Each of us (and each of our clients) operates under at least one implicit epistemology.

For example, a common stance is an *authoritarian epistemology*, that is, something is true because a credible authority says it is true. One variation on this theme is seen in religion. Many religious individuals consider revelation or divine inspiration to be a valid source of knowledge, whether the words are found in the Bible or come from the local minister, priest, or rabbi. A somewhat less divine but no less dogmatic source may be a parent or teacher, prior therapist, or the vague "everyone" (e.g., "everyone knows that . . .").

A particularly frustrating sort of thinking might be called *narcissistic epistemology* or, "It must be true because I thought of it," and "It seems right to me." A more demanding version of this philosophy rests on such rules as, "It's that way because I say so" or "It's got to be that way, because that's the way I want it."

In rational-emotive therapy, we search for more reliable and valid ways of obtaining knowledge and determining how we know a thing to be true. Rational-emotive philosophy suggests that it is through the methods of science that we can best obtain knowledge about the self, others, and the world. RET advocates scientific thinking and an empirical stance to knowledge. For every belief expressed by a client, an appropriate RET question would be, "Where is the evidence that what you believe is true?" In RET, we seek to make better scientists of our clients so that they can acquire correct information, use evidence logically, and construct sound, self-helping beliefs.

Science starts with questions about what is, and then proceeds to question the relationship between events. Hypotheses are formed to answer the questions, and observation and measurement are conducted to test the hypotheses. If the observations are consistent with these hypotheses, the hypotheses are strengthened and intellectual errors are reduced. The emphasis on the observable tends to eliminate mysticism and magic. In addition, acceptable observations are verified by more than one observer, to eliminate the use of "special powers" of intuition or inspiration.

How, then, do we know a thing to be true? We cannot know for certain. We determine the *probability* of its truth through repeated verification by observable data. Of course, we hope to do more than confirm isolated facts; we hope to build them into a coherent picture or theory of reality. From our theory we can predict new occurrences of similar events and deduce new hypotheses to fit different circumstances. The important point is that we *continue to question* and remain open to new evidence.

Dialectics: The Art of Thinking

The art of logical thinking is not easy to acquire; most people seem to be expert at illogic. A typical bit of self-deprecating illogical reasoning goes like this:

I must be perfect.

I just made a mistake. How horrible!

That proves I'm imperfect and therefore worthless.

Would this reasoning stand up to logical scrutiny? Not at all. Where is the evidence for the statement, "I must be perfect"? There is none, although there is ample evidence that I, like everyone else, am imperfect and thus, in a sense, "must" be imperfect, not perfect.

How about "I just made a mistake"? Perhaps it can be demonstrated that I made a mistake (although I'd better be careful not to make a rash judgment here, for it may be too soon to tell whether it was a mistake), but how is a mistake "horrible"?

That I am imperfect is surely proven by my mistake, but does it follow logically, therefore, that I am worthless? Obviously not, although people who are thinking dichotomously will say that it does. In dichotomous thinking there are only two categories, such as "perfect" and "worthless."

Consider another syllogism:

If Arthur loved me, he'd call me.

He hasn't called.

Therefore, he doesn't love me any more.

Can you spot the errors? Is the first premise correct? (Not necessarily.) The second statement? (Yes.) The conclusion? (Not unless the first premise is true.)

Clients are rarely aware of the major premises in their thinking or the syllogistic flow of their thoughts. More commonly, they focus only on the conclusion which, if it is distorted, is likely to produce emotional problems. Rational thinking, then, involves logical reasoning based upon empirically verified or verifiable statements. If we think rationally, we are not likely to reach conclusions that lead to extremely disturbed feelings.

Values

Two explicit values in the philosophy of RET are widely held by people but not often verbalized. These two major values are *survival* and *enjoyment*. The system of psychotherapy derived from these values is designed to help people live longer, minimize their emotional distress and self-defeating behaviors, and actualize themselves so as to live a more fulfilling and happier existence.

The underlying concept is that if people are enabled to *think* more rationally, more flexibly, and more scientifically, they may be better able to live longer and happier lives. Similarly, appropriate *behaviors* enhance survival and happiness, as opposed to those that are self-defeating or socially damaging. Helping people to feel appropriate *emotions*, whether positive or negative ones, will also tend to increase longevity and satisfaction.

Our commonly held goals, therefore, are to live the only life we are sure of having with as much enjoyment as possible, given the limitations of the human body and the physical and social world; to live peacefully within our chosen group; and to relate intimately with certain people of our choosing. These are the explicit values advocated by RET.

Ellis and Bernard (1986) have outlined several important subgoals that are consonant with the basic RET values and which may help individuals to achieve these values:

> *Self-interest*. Emotionally healthy people tend to put their own interests at least a little above the interests of others. They sacrifice themselves to some degree for those for whom they care, but not overwhelmingly or completely.
>
> *Social interest*. Most people choose to live in social groups, and to do so most comfortably and happily, they would be wise to act morally, protect the rights of others, and aid in the survival of the society in which they live.
>
> *Self-direction*. We would do well to cooperate with others, but it is better for us to assume primary responsibility for our own lives rather than to demand or need excessive support or nurturance from others.
>
> *Tolerance*. It is helpful to allow oneself and others the right to be wrong. It is not appropriate to enjoy obnoxious behavior, but it is not necessary to damn the person for doing it.
>
> *Flexibility*. Healthy individuals tend to be flexible thinkers. Rigid, biased, and invariant rules tend to minimize happiness.
>
> *Acceptance of uncertainty*. We live in a fascinating world of probability and chance; absolute certainties do not exist. The healthy individual strives for a degree of order, but does not demand complete predictability.
>
> *Commitment*. Most people, especially intelligent and educated ones,

tend to be happier when vitally absorbed in something outside themselves. At least one strong creative interest and some significant interpersonal involvement seem to provide structure for a happy daily existence.

Self-acceptance. Healthy people freely decide to accept themselves unconditionally, rather than measure, rate, or try to prove themselves.

Risk-taking. Emotionally healthy people are willing to take risks and have a spirit of adventurousness in trying to do what they want, without being foolhardy.

Realistic expectations. We are unlikely to get everything we want or be able to avoid everything we find painful. Healthy people do not waste time striving for the unattainable or for unrealistic perfection.

High frustration tolerance. Paraphrasing Reinhold Niebuhr and Alcoholics Anonymous, healthy people recognize that there are only two sorts of problems they are likely to encounter: those they can do something about and those they cannot. The goal is to modify the obnoxious conditions we can change, and learn to tolerate—or "lump"—those we cannot change.

Self-responsibility. Rather than blaming others, the world, or fate for their distress, healthy individuals accept responsibility for their own thoughts, feelings, and behaviors.

Thus, the goals of rational-emotive therapy are consistent with its values, which are to minimize distress, maximize the length of our life, and enhance our joy in the process of living. These values are sometimes referred to as "responsible hedonism."

Responsible Hedonism

The philosophic stance of RET is frankly hedonistic. Unlike the blindly compulsive hedonism of the Freudian id, however, the hedonism of RET is both guided and individualistic. Whereas according to the concept of the id we are all driven by the same impulses that originate in bodily processes, individuals in RET are recognized as enjoying and therefore seeking a wide variety of pursuits. Thus, RET does not prescribe *how* or *what* to enjoy, but it does hold that enjoyment, along with survival, are main goals in life.

Hedonism can be thought of as merely seeking pleasure and avoiding pain, but such a principle would not necessarily lead to *continued* enjoyment. If you derive pleasure from something that has harmful side effects, you clearly will not enjoy the pleasure very long. Thus, if you drink or use drugs to excess, you may experience considerable pleasure in the short term but more pain than pleasure in the long term. Because short-term pleasures may actually work against the other main goal of survival, RET teaches, and even advocates, moderation.

The term for moderation is *hedonic calculus,* a concept taken from the pragmatic philosophers of the nineteenth century. It is not a true calculus, of course, because no numeric values are assigned to our various pleasurable pursuits. Rather, hedonic calculus refers to the sensible habit of asking ourselves whether the pleasure we experience today is likely to backfire in some way tomorrow, next week, or even years from now. Conversely, if we live only for the future, we might pass up a good deal of current enjoyment, and that too would be irrational. So, as you can see, the pursuit of the simple hedonistic goals of survival and happiness can be quite complicated. Both immediate gratification and delay of gratification have advantages and disadvantages. RET advocates noncompulsively seeking an optimal solution that sacrifices neither the present nor the future.

A special form of hedonism that deserves careful consideration is when one avoids pain, discomfort, and inconvenience and in so doing cuts oneself off from a desirable outcome. A person may want to do something but be unwilling to work toward a long-range goal. In RET, this avoidance is considered to result from *Low Frustration Tolerance* (LFT). Clients demonstrate LFT when they refuse to do what they agree would be beneficial for them, citing reasons such as, "It's too hard," "I'd be too scared," or "I can't stand it." LFT is perhaps the main reason that clients do not improve after they have gained an understanding of their disturbance and how they create it.

LFT is a personal philosophy of life that states, in effect, "I absolutely shouldn't have to do anything that is unpleasant or uncomfortable, and I'd sooner maintain the status quo than risk discomfort." Although people clearly have a right to live by such a philosophy, it can create unhappiness by blocking them from goals they would like to attain.

Does the frank hedonism of RET lead to irresponsibility and anarchy in human relations? No, not if the person has thought through the consequences of his or her behavior, which includes getting cut off from future opportunities to pursue happiness. Exploitation of other people is hardly in our long-range best interests.

Ethics

Rational-emotive philosophy suggests that ethical guidelines for dealing fairly with other people can be based upon human reason, and on anticipating and understanding the consequences of our actions.

Rational-emotive theory proposes that generalized ethical principles of right or wrong are distorting and oversimplified for the reasoning adult. What is ethical is specific to each situation. There are no *absolute* rights and wrongs. In fact, the self-imposition of absolute rights and wrongs is precisely what leads to guilt, shame, anxiety, and depression, as well as to hostility and intolerance of other people.

Research in the psychology of moral philosophies, such as that by Kohlberg (1976), suggests the developmental nature of ethical ideas. In a typical research paradigm, moral dilemmas such as the following are presented to subjects of varying ages.

> Johnny, 6 years old, was told by his mom not to touch her expensive new vase. One day, feeling particularly loving toward his mom, little Johnny went into the backyard and picked a bouquet of flowers for her. He carefully put them in the new vase, but a few moments later, he remembered that flowers need to have water or they'll die. So, very carefully, he carried the vase to the sink for water; but on the way back, the vase slid from his slippery wet fingers, fell to the floor, and broke. Just then, mom came into the room.
> Dilemma:
> Did Johnny do a bad thing?
> Is Johnny a bad boy?
> Will mom be mad?
> Should Johnny be punished?

When puzzles such as these are presented to very young children, the moral judgments are clear: Johnny's bad and he should be spanked! The older the subject, however, the more complex the moral reasoning, and the less clear-cut the ethical solution. Factors such as Johnny's motivation, the role of intentionality, the purpose of punishment, the severity of punishment, the nature of the relationship of the parties, and other complications begin to come into play. With greater maturity comes greater flexibility; the act in question is seen in a larger context. This maturity—the ability to reason in terms of *situational ethics*—is consonant with the principles of rational-emotive philosophy.

It might be argued that with situational rather than absolute ethical rules, ethical behavior would break down. If there are no absolute rights and wrongs, goods or bads, what would prevent total moral chaos from occurring?

RET seeks to help the individual use *reason* in solving ethical dilemmas, to evolve an undogmatic, nonabsolutist philosophy of living that is socially responsible. The ethical principles are derived from answers to the question, "Will my actions harm other people?" not "Does this act violate some God-given rule?" Ethically responsible acts are both pro-social and pro-self; that is, they harm neither others nor ourselves.

Why is it desirable to behave ethically? Without resorting to abstract morality, we can outline a number of simple, pragmatic reasons. For example, experience shows that if we treat others unfairly (lie, cheat, steal, cruelly criticize, etc.), they will eventually retaliate. What happens is obvious when you examine the norm of fair play (more technically, the "norm of reciprocity"). The norm or unwritten rule is that people should deal fairly with each other. While it is often difficult to state the specific details that constitute "fairness," people usually have an implicit understanding of what is fair in a given situation. If you break this norm, the same social processes are likely to occur as when other norms are broken. First, other people try subtly or directly to influence the norm breaker to conform. This process may include attempts to teach, threats, and even punishment. If the norm breaker continues, he or she will be expelled from the group. Since most of us have as one of our goals of happiness to relate to many people compatibly and to a few people intimately, the threat of rejection is enough to keep us from breaking norms. It is not in our best interests to act unfairly, inconsiderately, or selfishly.

On a broader scope, if you behave unethically, you help create a world in which people behave unethically, and you, in turn, will suffer in such a culture. It is in your own best interests to promote an ethical society.

Thus, according to the ethical principles of rational-emotive philosophy, it is wrong to exploit and act harmfully toward other people. It is wrong for the individual because it may defeat his or her goals. RET does not specify what is right or wrong in an absolute sense, for that smacks of dogmatism. RET holds that rigidity, authoritarianism, dogmatism, and absolutism are among the worst features of any philosophic system and are styles of thinking that lead to neurosis and disturbance.

In essence, the ethics of RET are much like the golden rule—that is, act in ways that set good examples for other people (or, do as you would have others do).

Ethical Humanism

Virtually all Judeo-Christian religions are based on the golden rule, and the golden rule is the essence of rational–emotive philosophy. RET provides an ethical system for how we are to treat other people, and a nonjudgmental philosophy of accepting oneself and others, exactly as they are. Nonetheless, RET is more aligned with ethical humanism than with religion.

In ethical humanism, the reasoning individual is the source of wisdom, not almighty "God." The concept of "God" is not needed to explain

A clinical example: the client was a 38-year-old Catholic woman, whose tearful presentation was soon shown to be related to a severe case of guilt about an abortion she had had—twenty years before. For twenty years she alternately repressed her awareness of the abortion or acknowledged it with immense emotional suffering. Abortion, in her mind, was wrong; she had "killed her child," which therefore made her a murderer, a sin for which she could not forgive herself. Attempts to dispute the "wrongness" of the abortion were futile. No matter what her life circumstances had been, in her value system the choice to abort was a wrong and evil thing to have done. Attempts to dispute her devaluation of herself as a person were also futile; in her mind, the "murder" made her a "murderer." Our successful disputation asked whether it is conceivable to forgive people who acknowledge that they have made mistakes, especially when they have attempted to do penance for a bad deed. With the help of an enlightened clergyman, we reached an agreement that twenty years of self-inflicted guilt was sufficient punishment for the "crime," and that if Jesus were able to forgive the sinner it was only fitting that she follow suit. Her ability to do so was quite dramatic thereafter, and was followed soon by a long-desired pregnancy!

the creation of things (that is the job of science), or to generate an ethical code (for that can be done by clear thinking). Ellis himself is clearly an atheist, and in several articles has postulated that although religion (that is, a philosophy of life) may be rational, religiosity (that is, dogmatic and absolute faith unfounded on fact) is not merely the opiate of the masses but a major cause of psychopathology (Ellis, 1987b). He contends that it is the acceptance of absolute notions of right and wrong, and of damnation for doing wrong, that leads to guilt, shame, anxiety, and depression, as well as hostility and intolerance toward other people.

Even though Ellis is an unabashed hedonist, humanist, and atheist, one can retain religious beliefs and practice good RET, which is what many pastoral counselors, in fact, have done (e.g., DiGiuseppe, Robin, and Dryden, 1991; Hauck, 1985). Religious zeal may not be compatible with enjoyment of life, self-acceptance, and toleration of others, but it is not necessary to insist that clients give up all forms of religious belief. In fact, it is possible to utilize the client's religion or the Bible in the support of rational thinking and healthy behavioral change. The trick is to work with enlightened clergy and sensible Biblical selections.*

What RET Is Not

Many people assume that because Ellis frequently quotes the Stoic philosopher Epictetus, RET is a form of Stoicism. Not so! The true Stoic works to develop an immunity to feelings, whether physical (such as pain) or emotional (such as mourning). By contrast, the RET position is that rational thinking can lead to feelings, even *very strong* negative feelings, without resulting in disturbed feelings and unnecessary suffering.

RET also should not be confused with Rationalism, which posits that one attains knowledge by logic alone. RET is not an armchair philosophy, nor does it suggest that logic can conquer all. RET proposes that knowledge comes through logical and empirical challenges to our troubled thinking, and advocates also that we had better *act* on our new beliefs.

It is also important not to confuse rational thinking with rationaliza-

---

*A small pamphlet that may be helpful in this regard, written by Hank Robb, is entitled "How to Stop Driving Yourself Crazy with Help from the Bible." It can be ordered for $1 from the Pacific Institute for RET, 4550 S.W. Kruse Way, Lake Oswego, OR 97035, or from the Institute for RET, 45 E. 65th St., New York, NY 10021.

The old parable of the fox and the grapes is a good example of rationalization. No matter how high the fox jumped, he was unable to get at the luscious grapes, but he continued to try, becoming angrier and angrier. The only way he was able to stop his foolish persistence was to decide that the grapes were probably not ripe, and he stomped off muttering that he didn't want those "sour grapes" anyway.

What might be a rational response (as opposed to a rationalization) to this frustrating situation?

tion, a so-called defense mechanism, which is, in fact, a form of *distorted* thinking. When we rationalize, we invent an explanation for an action, thought, or emotion rather than face an undesirable reality—quite the opposite of rational thinking.

Rationality as a Personal Philosophy

When RET practitioners begin to explore a client's belief system, they will encounter some rules of living that the client has been trying to follow. These personal rules, or philosophies of living, may rest upon parental and religious teachings, widely held common wisdom, or highly idiosyncratic opinions about how life should be lived. These rules, because they are dogmatically held, rigidly self-enforced, conflicting, or otherwise maladaptive, are the basis of the client's disturbance. When personal rules of living hinder a client's attainment of the goals of happiness and survival, they are fair game for examination and change.

The RET therapist hopes to help the client evolve a new philosophy of life, one that will help to reduce emotional distress and lead to increased happiness. The therapist holds the view that people can choose to either add to their misery with illogical and unscientific thinking or promote their enjoyment with careful reasoning from evidence. The goals of a rational philosophy are to establish beliefs and habits that are congruent with:

- Survival
- Achieving satisfaction with living
- Affiliating with others in a positive way

Philosophy in the clinic: working at a philosophical level may be a very practical clinical strategy because it can result in deep change that affects many behaviors. If you are working behaviorally, you may have to hit each (behavioral) nail on the head separately; but if you can work philosophically, you may hit one board which will drive many nails at once.

- Achieving intimate involvement with a few others
- Developing or maintaining a vital absorption in some personally fulfilling endeavor(s)

RET therapists know and help patients remember that all persons are fallible, forever destined to often fail and err. They help clients to give up their demands for perfection and to strive to develop constructive self-acceptance as well as acceptance of others. In its best form, this change comes about by scientific and logical thinking, which results in deep philosophic and attitudinal change.

2 Rational-Emotive Theory

There are three main psychological aspects of human functioning: thoughts, feelings, and behavior. All three aspects are intertwined and interrelated, since changes in one will often produce changes in the others. Thus, if individuals change the manner in which they think about an event, they will most likely feel differently about it and may alter the way they behaviorally react to it. Changes in our behavior may likewise lead to changes in our thinking; once we've done something we had been afraid to do, we may no longer think of it as dangerous or difficult.

Behavioral psychologies focus on changing environmental contingencies to alter behavior, and cognitive psychologies focus on altering thought content, but few psychologies deal directly with emotions because they are difficult to influence directly. RET theory is perhaps unique in this regard since it takes as its focus the cognitive–emotive interface. Thus, rational-emotive theory deals with Ellis' conceptions of the causes of human emotions.

In this chapter, we review some of the fundamental principles in the theory of RET, discuss how it relates to cognitive theory in general, and illustrate how it applies to clinical treatment.

The Six Principles of RET Theory

1. The basic principle of rational-emotive theory is that *cognition is the most important proximal determinant of human emotion*. Simply stated, we feel what we think. Events and other people do not make us "feel good" or "feel bad"; we do it to ourselves, cognitively. It is as if we are writing the scripts

for our emotional reactions, although usually we are not conscious of doing so. Thus, past or present external events contribute to, but do not directly induce or "cause" emotions in us. Rather, our internal events— our perceptions and, especially, our evaluations of these perceptions—are the more direct and powerful sources of our emotional responses.

2. A second principle suggests that *dysfunctional thinking is a major determinant of emotional distress*. Dysfunctional emotional states and many aspects of psychopathology are the result of dysfunctional thought processes, which may be characterized by exaggeration, oversimplification, overgeneralization, illogic, unvalidated assumptions, faulty deductions, and absolutist notions.

3. Because the basic notion of rational-emotive theory is that we feel what we think, to break out of an emotional problem, we begin with an analysis of our thoughts. If distress is a product of irrational thinking, *the best way to conquer distress is to change this thinking*. Clinically, this approach is often the only (or at least the most practical) aspect of the emotional experience that we can encourage clients to change.

4. *Multiple factors,* including both genetic and environmental influences, are etiologic antecedents to irrational thinking and psychopathology. Ellis has repeatedly pointed out that we humans seem to have a natural predisposition to think irrationally (e.g., Ellis, 1976a, 1985). While we may have a tendency to easily learn irrational beliefs, as witnessed by the fact that they are so widespread, the culture in which we live seems to furnish the specific content of these beliefs.

5. Like many contemporary psychological theories, rational-emotive theory *emphasizes present* rather than historical influences on behavior. Another tenet of rational-emotive theory, therefore, is that although heredity and environmental conditions are important in the acquisition of psychopathology, they are not the primary focus in understanding its continuance. People maintain their disturbance by continued self-indoctrination. The adherence to irrational beliefs, rather than how they were acquired, is the cause of emotional distress. Thus, if individuals reevaluated their former thinking and abandoned it in the present, their current functioning would be quite different.

6. Yet another principle of rational-emotive theory is that beliefs can be changed, although such change will *not necessarily come about easily*. Irra-

tional beliefs are changed by active and persistent efforts to recognize, challenge, and revise one's thinking, thereby reducing emotional distress.

Cognitive Theory and Rational-Emotive Theory

Cognitive theory, broadly understood, states that dysfunctional cognition is associated with many aspects of dysfunctional affective states and behavioral tendencies. Cognitive theory is the underpinning of many different types of cognitive therapies and is embodied in the work of contemporary clinicians and researchers such as Aaron T. Beck, David Burns, Donald Meichenbaum, and others whose work will be cited throughout this book. RET is properly placed within the field of cognitive theory, but holds a unique position there, because Ellis has emphasized the relevance of a particular kind of cognition called evaluative beliefs.

Some thought processes are *inferential* in nature, and others are largely *evaluative*. Inferential cognitions represent our perceptions of reality and the inferences we draw from these perceptions. For example, suppose you are walking down the street and see a co-worker approaching, on the other side of the street. You wave your arm in greeting, but your gesture is not returned. You may infer from this event that your co-worker saw you and decided not to greet you. You may even go further and assume that the absence of a greeting has some interpersonal meaning; perhaps the co-worker is upset, or angry at you, or doesn't like you, and so on. Many of these cognitions may be incorrect inferences, which take the form of negative automatic thoughts, erroneous assumptions, global and fixed internal attributions, and thoughts of low self-regard. Many of these inferential cognitive constructs have been associated with emotional disturbance and psychopathology.

RET recognizes that these cognitions are associated with pathology but does not believe that they are central. What is considered central to emotional disturbance are the evaluative beliefs, which in RET parlance are known as the core Irrational Beliefs and fall into four categories: demands, awfulizing, low frustration tolerance, and global evaluations of human worth. (We will discuss these briefly here, and go into more detail in Chapter 8.)

> *Demands* reflect unrealistic and absolute expectations of events or individuals, and are often recognizable by cue words such as "must," "ought," "should," "have to," and "need."

Awfulizing is a way of exaggerating the negative consequences of a situation to an extreme degree, so that an unfortunate occurrence becomes "terrible."

Low Frustration Tolerance (LFT) stems from demands for ease and comfort, and reflects an intolerance of discomfort.

Global evaluations of human worth, either of the self or others, imply that human beings can be rated, and that some people are worthless, or at least less valuable than others.

Let's look at some examples. Suppose you get up to give a speech in front of a group of colleagues and you experience tremendous anxiety. You observe one person yawning and a few others looking around the room. You then draw inferences: "Maybe they don't like what I have to say. They think that I'm boring." Those beliefs may be true or false, but it is the *evaluation of their possible truth* that is the focus in RET. According to RET, the negative automatic thought ("They don't like what I have to say") or the belief in a lack of effectiveness ("I'm boring them") are not necessarily sufficient to directly produce emotional disturbance. Disturbance, in RET, arises when you evaluate these inferences as *horrors.* Your more central evaluative beliefs may be something like:

I must please them and earn their approval.

If I bore them, I'm a worthless, boring person.

That would be awful!

This discrimination between inferential cognitions and evaluative cognitions sets RET apart from other cognitive therapies. An RET therapist acknowledges the importance of inferential processes and uses a variety of strategies to modify those distorted cognitions, but the evaluative cognitions are considered the key to understanding psychological disturbance. Thus, even if you think your wife doesn't love you, even if you think you are never going to be able to accomplish certain feats, even though you think you lack efficacy in certain areas, you may be able to protect yourself from undue emotional pain about these unfortunate realities if you evaluate them rationally.

Ellis often leads clients through the following vignette, which illustrates this model of emotional disturbance:

T: Suppose, as you left the house this morning, you said to yourself, "I'd like to have $20 with me today. It doesn't have to be any more than

$20, and it's not that I must have it, but I'd prefer to have that much money in my pocket." Then later you check in your pocket and find that you have only $5. How do you think you'd feel?

C: Well, disappointed, I suppose.

T: Right! You'd feel disappointment or regret, but you wouldn't want to kill yourself over it. Now, suppose instead when you left the house you had said, "I must have $20 with me today. It doesn't have to be any more than $20, but I've *got* to have that much in my pocket at all times." Then later if you reached into your pocket and found $5, how do you think you'd feel?

C: I guess I'd be pretty upset.

T: Sure you would, if you didn't have what you thought you MUST have. Now, suppose you were still saying you must have $20 with you at all times, but you reached in your pocket and found $30! How do you think you'd feel?

C: Happy. Maybe ecstatic?

T: Yes, you probably would feel happy, but very shortly after, you'd feel anxious again. Do you know why?

C: No.

T: Well, suppose you lost the $20 bill, or spent $10, or got your pocket picked! So you see, you're miserable both ways when you think you must have something. You're anxious when you don't have it, and anxious even when you do!

Remember that attributions, self-efficacy statements, and automatic thoughts do not necessarily have to lead to emotional disturbance; it's the evaluative irrational beliefs that are the key. Here is another example of that same discrimination. Consider two different attributions for failure:

lack of effort

lack of ability

In the United States, if we think we failed because of lack of effort ("I didn't really try"), we may find this an acceptable excuse, but if we think we failed because of lack of ability, we may feel very threatened and uncomfortable. In Japan, on the other hand, one is embarrassed by lack of effort, but not by lack of ability. The principle is that it is not the attribution per se that causes us emotional distress but the personal significance and evaluative appraisal that we give it.

Global, stable, internal attributions for failure (e.g., "I'm dys-lexic," or "I'm too bad a writer to do this paper") only lead to depression because we put ourselves down for having these quali-ties. This assumption leads RET therapists to a strategy that is a little different from other cognitive therapists.

For example, if I were brain-damaged by a stroke and I could no longer do certain things, how would you help me to feel better?

Many therapists would try to show me what I *could* do. But what if I still was unable to do the things that used to be impor-tant to me? These therapists would probably try to show me that I could do *other* things. Although their strategies might be some-what helpful, they would also miss the core philosophical point of RET: "I'm an OK person even though I can't do [and probably will never be able to do] what I used to do and what others can do easily. It's too bad that I can't, but it isn't *awful.*"

When we hold an irrational belief, we are likely to misperceive reality and therefore reconfirm the irrational belief. If I believe that I need you to love and approve of me, when you leave and don't say goodbye, I may take your behavior as evidence that it's true: you really don't like me. In this way we construct and cement our views of reality via a cycle of distortions. Evaluative beliefs can exacerbate inferential beliefs.

An experimental model of this process was conducted by Dryden, Ferguson, and McTeague (1989), who asked their subjects to rehearse to themselves one of two attitudes:

"I absolutely must not see a spider, and it would be terrible if I did," *or*

"I really don't want to see a spider, but if I do, it won't be terrible."

Subjects were asked to imagine themselves about to enter a room and were instructed that in that room there was at least one spider. With that scene in mind, subjects answered questions such as:

"How many spiders are in there?"

"How big are they?"

"In what direction are they moving?"

The results indicated that those subjects who rehearsed the "must" (I must not see spiders because they're terrible) imagined more spiders, saw them as heading toward themselves rather than randomly moving about the room, and rated the spiders as bigger than did subjects in the other group. The "must" affected their (imaginary) perceptions.

Let's go back to the example of public-speaking anxiety: if I believe that I *must* be able to speak fluently and it would be *terrible* if I didn't, then when I am not fluent, I am much more likely to believe that everybody will be critical of me. As Ellis has repeatedly taught, "musts" make you more likely to have misperceptions and make misinterpretations. Then, when you *awfulize* about your misperceptions, a vicious cycle occurs.

RET often advocates locating the underlying beliefs that fuel misperceptions and misattributions as the primary focus of therapy. Although automatic thoughts and misperceptions are more accessible in the patient's communications, their accessibility may mislead the student therapist into focusing only on them rather than striving for more profound philosophical change.

A MAJOR MYTH AND MISCONCEPTION

At this point, we would like to dispel a common misconception of RET. "Rational" does not mean "unemotional." Rational–emotive theory does not say that all emotions are to be eliminated, but rather that it is not inevitable that one feel *terribly* upset or emotionally disturbed. Even when thinking rationally, the individual may experience uncomfortable negative emotions—even strong ones. The distinction between the consequences of rational and irrational thinking is reflected in the *frequency, intensity, and duration* of the negative affect rather than in its presence or absence. If emotional turmoil blocks constructive action, it is consequently self-defeating and nonadaptive for the individual.

Emotions are important motivators for behavior as well as for behavioral change. The classic Yerkes-Dodson law, described in most general psychology texts, attests to the relationship between levels of emotion and behavior. When people experience no emotion or, at the other extreme, excessive emotion, behavioral efficiency is lost. For example, an extremely anxious student may do poorly on a test; the student who has no concern at all may never be motivated to study and will also do poorly.

Thus, we are distinguishing between *emotional disturbance* and the presence of negative (even strongly negative) emotions, a distinction on which we will elaborate in Chapter 7.

One argument raised by critics of rational-emotive theory is that if people do not believe that events are "awful," they will not be motivated to change them. "Rational," however, does not mean passive acceptance of events. There are two general kinds of events: those we can possibly change and those we cannot. Accepting an unfortunate reality and not getting overly upset about it acknowledges that the reality exists, that it is unpleasant, that it would be irrational to demand or insist that it should not have happened, and that we will attempt to change it, if we can. One can certainly be vigilant in trying to prevent similar events from happening again. When we are feeling upset, however, we may not be adept at problem solving or working effectively at changing our environment.

In summary, the basic principles of rational-emotive theory are as follows:

1. Cognition is the most important, though hardly the only, determinant of emotion.
2. Irrational thinking often produces dysfunctional emotional states.
3. The most effective way to reduce emotional distress is to change our thinking.
4. We have a natural tendency to think irrationally and upset ourselves, which gets reinforced by the environment.
5. We perpetuate our emotional distress by repropagandizing ourselves with our irrational beliefs.
6. Changing irrational beliefs, therefore, will not necessarily be easy work, and is likely to require persistence and practice.

Remember, rational thinking leads to a reduction in the frequency, intensity, and duration of emotional disturbance, not to flat affect or the absence of feeling.

3 Rational-Emotive Therapy

The therapeutic system evolved by Ellis over the years is a pragmatic and efficient clinical discipline, useful with moderately dysfunctional neurotic adults, severely disturbed adults, psychotic individuals, and children as young as seven to eight years. The therapist takes a persuasive, active-directive role, yet patient and therapist share in working toward common goals. In addition, RET uses an educational approach, and as in school, encourages the patient to do reading and homework assignments to help the patient incorporate the therapy into living and enjoyment outside the therapy sessions.

RET does not claim to undo the mental and emotional effects of physiologically induced dysfunctions, such as those attributable to hormonal imbalances, seizure states, or affective illnesses or psychoses that are basically heritable neurochemical problems. It is important to note, however, that patients often have a neurotic overlay to their neurochemical problems that *is* amenable to rational-emotive therapy. For example, patients with bipolar illness, even when taking appropriate medications and not in a depressed state, often worry about when their depression will strike again. Although RET does not cure the underlying bipolar illness, it can be extremely helpful in dealing with emotional problems *about* being ill and may be helpful in managing the illness when it is active. When used in conjunction with psychotropic drugs, RET may be distinctly valuable in helping to ameliorate the course of such illnesses (Ellis and Abrahms, 1978).

Teaching tip: as you begin to practice the techniques of RET, you will find it easier if you begin with an individual adult client. RET is certainly useful with children, couples, and families, but each of these populations present specialized problems. Trainees have told us that RET requires their intense concentration at first, so that having young children or more than one client in the room may make your learning more difficult.

The A-B-C Model

Ellis has conceived a simple conceptual schema to illustrate the role of thinking processes in emotional disturbance. He calls this schema the ABC's of RET. In this system, the A stands for Activating event (or activating experience), which is usually our perception of some obnoxious or unfortunate environmental occurrence. C stands for the emotional and behavioral Consequences; it is this uncomfortable affective reaction which, in fact, propels the patient to the psychotherapist's office. The B is the patient's Belief system. The belief system consists of two parts: rational and irrational beliefs. It is the latter cognitions which will be the therapist's focus.

Belief systems, and irrational beliefs in particular, will be taken up in detail in Chapter 8, but for now we can summarize them briefly into what Ellis has called "the three Major Musts":

I must do well or get approval (and I'm a worm if I don't).

You must treat me nicely and kindly (and you're a louse if you don't).

The world must give me what I want quickly, easily, and with great certainty (and it's awful if it doesn't).

These three "Musts" almost invariably lead not only to the parenthetical evaluations above but to the following derivative cognitions:

It's awful that things are so bad.

I can't stand it.

I'm [or you're] a rotten person.

Small wonder that anyone uncritically believing these ideas would be upset. Because rational-emotive philosophy assumes that a major goal in life is to be reasonably happy, it also assumes that such disturbing cognitions and emotions are incompatible with this goal.

When patients believe that the A event is directly responsible for C (their emotional upsets), they are ignoring, or more likely are unaware of, the presence and impact of their cognitions, attitudes, philosophies, and beliefs. Patients in psychotherapy are experiencing debilitating and disturbing emotions. If they are disturbing themselves, presumably they can also refuse to disturb themselves. In other words, patients have a choice of feelings and unwittingly, because of the way they think, end up suffering—although they don't have to. It is a primary task of the therapist to teach clients that their psychological problems result from the cognitive processes of misperception and irrational thinking.

This basic principle, easy enough to state, is often difficult for patients to grasp. Our everyday language is filled with examples antagonistic to

---

Before you're adept at teaching the A–B–C notion to your client, you'll want to do a lot of practice at training your own ears. Eventually, when you listen to your clients, their words will sort rather automatically into the three categories.

One way to begin to train your ears is to divide your therapy notes in a three-column format. Begin now. Divide the page into three segments, and label one A, another C, and a third (perhaps larger in size) as B. You'll find that clients usually begin by telling you about their A or C. If you can fill in one of these columns, proceed to the next. Thus, if you know A (what happened), ask for C (how the client felt); if the client begins by expressing affect ("I was anxious"), ask for the trigger or context (the A). When you have A and C, proceed to ask for B.

If you can make a copy of your notes on the spot, you can hand one sheet to the client and go over the columns with him or her. For example, "You see, Mary, here is the A–B–C model. Let's look at what I've written down today. See, these are your thoughts—and these are your feelings—and this is what happened." You will be surprised at how often clients find this organizational strategy to be helpful.

this concept. How often do we say or hear phrases such as, *"He* made me so mad!" or *"It* has got me so upset!" More correctly, we could say, *"I* made myself mad" and *"I* got myself upset." How strange these revised statements sound to our ears! Yet they share an important concept: we are responsible for our own emotions. Thus, emotions are not foisted upon us or inserted magically into us, but result from something we actively do. Specifically, emotions result largely from what we tell ourselves. Clients come to therapy firmly believing that A causes C, and this belief is reinforced by virtually every significant person with whom they come in contact. You, the therapist, will be teaching the quite revolutionary idea that B largely determines C, and your first teaching responsibility is to help your client understand and believe this concept.

TEACHING THE CLIENT THAT EVENTS DO NOT CAUSE FEELINGS

How can the therapist illustrate to clients that internal rather than external factors are primarily affecting their feelings and actions? One way to explain the B-C connection is to ask clients how a hundred people similar to themselves would react to their problem. For example, a client has just discovered that his wife would like to get a divorce, and he is very depressed. The therapist might ask him how he thinks a hundred different men would react to the same event. Clients usually respond with, "Well, most of them would be depressed." (If the client says instead, "100 percent," the therapist can point out how unrealistic such an estimate is.) The therapist persists and asks, "But what percent would be depressed—40, 50, 60 percent?" After the client has answered, the therapist leads the client to examine other possible reactions that the remainder of the population would have. In this way, the client is faced with the fact, by his own admission, that while possibly 50 percent of the sample might be depressed, some of the remainder would only be sad, others would be a little displeased, some would be neutral, a few relieved, and a small percentage would be downright exuberant. At this point, when other emotional options have been set forth, the client is confronted with the crucial question, "If activating events (A) do, in fact, cause emotional consequences (C), then how do you explain that the same event can lead to so many different emotional reactions within this hypothetical sample?" Most clients respond at this point with something like, "Well, I guess A doesn't really cause C" or "They're all different, so they react differently." The about-to-be-divorced client has given the therapist an opening, for he has mildly and ever so slightly hinted that A did not cause C. The therapist can reinforce the client for reaching this insight and for doing so on his own, and then explain further, "That's correct; they're all different; they all reacted differently because they evaluated it differently." The therapist can now elaborate further on this point.

A story such as the following may help to make the A-B-C connections clear:

> Three vice-presidents were fired from their jobs at the same time, when their corporation was taken over by another. All three men equally loved their jobs, and all three were at the same salary level. The activating event was virtually identical for them. Do you think all three VP's reacted the same way? Actually, they didn't. One said to himself, "This is terrible. I'm going to kill myself." Another said, "Great, this will give me the opportunity and the push I needed to go into business for myself." And the third said, "Well, this is certainly undesirable and not what I wanted to happen but I'm going to use this experience in some way, I'm sure, and I'll just make the best of it for now." Can you see how these men would *feel* quite different emotions about the same event?

TEACHING THE CLIENT THAT OTHER PEOPLE DO NOT CAUSE FEELINGS

Commonly, patients object that other people in their environment do, in fact, cause them to be upset. This concept is embedded in the linguistic structure of our everyday experience. "I make myself so angry when you say that" is a phrase that sounds strange, while "You make me so mad" sounds "normal."

Again, a story may help the client to see the B-C connection: three kids have played hooky from school, gotten caught, and are now in trouble. They are sent to the principal's office: Do they all react the same way when the principal comes out of his office and glowers at them? As it turns out, one kid is frightened, the second is angry, and the third is concerned and decides not to get in trouble anymore.

The use of hypothetical situations and analogies can help to get the point across. As an experiment, the therapist might suggest:

> "OK, Marsha, if people can give you emotions, let's see if I can do it right now. (pause) Marsha, I really like you and I want you to feel good forever. Now—how do you feel?"

Analogies such as the following might be useful:

C: She makes me feel so guilty!
T: No, Marsha, they're your guilt buttons. She may be pushing on them, but you're in charge of the electronic wires. If you learn to disconnect them, she could push all she wanted and you wouldn't have to respond.

Another way of disputing the notion that other people give us feelings is to point out the incongruity between this notion and the belief that Americans, particularly religious ones, tend to have in free will. Most Judeo-Christian religions teach people to believe that human beings are different from the rest of the animal species because human beings have intellect and free will. Thus, these religions strongly profess independent action and self-determination. The therapist might ask: "If someone made you angry, you therefore had no say in it. Well, how much do you believe in free will and self-determination?" By phrasing the question in this way, the therapist is pointing out to the client that he or she has some choice. If something negative happens, you probably will feel negatively about it, but you have a choice in how bad you feel about it. You can decide to be self-defeatingly angry and miserable, or to feel constructively annoyed and motivated to do something about it.

There are a number of other ways of illustrating that the A–causes–C hypothesis is incorrect. As an example of an alternate strategy, the therapist might say:

"Well, John, if your father really is the cause of your anger, we'd better terminate therapy. You see, if the cause of the anger is outside you, how can I help you? You'd better send your father to me instead, and let me change him!"

The following example involves teaching this point to young children:

T: Jeremy, it sounds to me as if you believe everyone controls you. No matter what happens to you, it's someone else's fault. They make you angry, they make you sad, they make you unhappy. Well, I have a great idea! Why don't we create a Jeremy doll? We could probably get Mattel to market it. You know, we'll have this little doll with a set of remote controls and every time we press a button we can make it happy, we can make it sad, we can make it depressed, we can make it dance or sing. We'll control the doll just like a remote control. Or maybe we can make a puppet and call it a Jeremy puppet. Other people pull the strings and Jeremy does it. What do you think about these ideas?

C: (laughs) That's funny. But that's not how it is. I don't sound that way!

T: Oh, yes you do. You sound as if you believe you're a puppet and other people control you.

Ed Garcia, formerly co-director of training at the Institute for Rational-Emotive Therapy, uses dramatic procedures to point out to his clients their self-imposed powerlessness:

C: (Complaining about how other people controlled her, made her feel badly, etc.)

T: (Opens desk drawer, pulls out a large box or bag, and hands it to client.)

C: What's this?

T: This is your power. I'm giving it back to you. Obviously you've been walking around without it for a long time. You keep telling me how this person made you angry, and this person made you upset, and this person made you love him, and this person made you this and that. You go on and on telling me how other people are controlling your life. You must have left your power here one day when you ran out in a hurry. I really think you had better take it back now. Maybe you can get some more control over your life.

Once clients grasp the idea that their thoughts affect the way they feel, the next task for the therapist is to show them that changing their thinking can lead to changes in their emotions. Rene Diekstra, an RET therapist from the Netherlands, has pointed out that we often plan in advance how we will behave in a particular situation. We commonly script our verbal behaviors in everyday life in order to affect *other* people's reactions; we preplan in order to maximize the probability that we will get the reaction we want. This planning is customary and socially acceptable. We rarely spend any time, however, examining and preplanning how we talk to ourselves. It might be pointed out to clients that how we talk to ourselves will affect our own reactions as surely as how we speak to others affects their reactions. Similarly, we often ask ourselves, "How can I say this *to him* [or her] so that my message will be clear and I will have communicated correctly?" How often do we ask ourselves the same questions about our internal dialogues?

TEACHING THE CLIENT THAT THE PAST DOESN'T CAUSE FEELINGS

Not uncommonly, patients find it difficult to understand that the correction of current thinking patterns is a prime focus of therapy. The difficulty arises because many patients believe that their past history causes their present behavior, and thus, they are either helpless to change or must first discover the "roots" of their disturbance. If clients have spent many months or years in a therapy that emphasized this belief, it may take a lot of convincing to change their focus. Unfortunately, it is not only former therapy patients who suffer from the belief that the past fixedly determines the present. This basic misunderstanding of Freudian theory seems to have permeated Western culture. It is popularized on television and in the movies, and is heard from even very unsophisticated clients.

As part of this therapeutic logjam, clients may believe that change is impossible because of their past. A client might assert, for example, "But I can't change; I've always been that way!" The therapeutic challenge then involves correcting the client's language and thereby the concept. For example, the therapist could respond:

> "You mean you haven't changed *so far*. Even if that's been true up to now, does that mean you won't change tomorrow? That's my business, you know—showing you how to change."

The literature on developmental issues in personality suggests that some aspects of our style of behavior are relatively fixed; we refer to these fixed qualities as "temperament." It would be a fruitless endeavor to try and change one's basic temperament. These qualities, which may be comprised of biological predispositions in conjunction with prolonged early training experiences in our families of origin, may mean that change is *difficult* or take a great deal of *time* or require the use of *multiple strategies*. The fact that change may be difficult does not mean that change is impossible, however. Yet the client who firmly believes that he or she *cannot* change may be mired in a self-fulfilling prophecy, which ironically will be self-defeating. An instructive analogy might be the therapist saying:

> "If you go into a ball game believing 'I can't win, I can't win, I can't win', you'll find that attitude very self-defeating. If you go into therapy believing 'I can't change; my early experiences fixed me permanently', that's also self-defeating and you may not change."

A useful challenge to the notion that the past determines present distress is to point out that although past events may have had an important role in contributing to past distress, they continue to be a problem only because the client continues to think about them in the same way. It is present cognitions, not past events, that affect us. Thus, although your mother may have worked hard to convince you that you were a worthless no-goodnik, it is only because you continue to take her seriously *today* that you upset yourself with this notion. Merely leaving home will never solve the problem, because you'll figuratively take your mother with you wherever you go unless you dispute your irrational thinking. Thus, if clients believe they are no good, and believe they hold this opinion because it was taught to them, the therapist might respond with questions such as:

"And you believed it?"
"Why did you believe it?"
"If you were told so today, would you believe it?"

A brief review: when your client says something like, "My husband makes me irrational!" does a red flag go up for you? What kind of a treatment goal would you begin to formulate to help this woman? What do you already know that you will have to do to be helpful? Stop and answer these questions for yourself now.

_____

_____

Answer: You will need to address the core philosophical belief that sounds something like, "My distress can be externally caused."

If your client *is* thinking that her husband is the culprit responsible for her emotional turmoil, what emotion would she *have* to be feeling?

_____

Answer: anger.

The important point, therefore, is that past beliefs continue to be a problem because patients *currently reindoctrinate* themselves with these beliefs. An analogy such as the following might be useful to teach this point:

> Suppose you had learned to play basketball very well in high school, but did not play again for twenty years. If you then went out on the court to play, you wouldn't do very well at all. You would have lost a lot of the skills because you hadn't practiced them, right? It's the same with holding irrational beliefs. If you learned to think irrationally when you were young and didn't practice it for twenty years, then right now you wouldn't be all that disturbed. But you keep practicing it over and over again, reindoctrinating yourself, and that's what keeps you so good at being distressed!

DISTURBANCE ABOUT DISTURBANCE

A unique aspect of rational-emotive therapy is its focus not only on the A-B-C structure of emotional distress but on the client's ability to upset himself or herself about being upset. Emotions or behaviors that would be classified under C frequently themselves become new A's. Essentially, clients watch themselves behaving ineptly and then "put themselves down" for this ineptitude. To illustrate, consider the following cycle:

> *Activating event* (A)—Client's mother keeps bitterly complaining about the client's behavior.
>
> *Rational belief* (RB)—"I wish she wouldn't act that way."
>
> *Irrational belief* (IB)—"Since I don't like it, she *shouldn't* [*must not*] do it, and she's a bitch for acting that way."
>
> *Emotional and behavioral consequences* (C)—Feeling angry at mother and yelling at her.
>
> WHICH LEADS TO . . .
>
> *Secondary Activating event* (A_2)—The client's anger and yelling.
>
> *Secondary Rational belief* (RB_2)—"I wish I were better at 'keeping my cool'."
>
> *Secondary Irrational belief* (IB_2)—"I should [must] be able to 'keep my cool', and *I'm* a bitch for blowing up like that at my mother."
>
> *Secondary Consequence* (C_2)—Anger at self or feelings of shame.

Clients will often become anxious about their anxiety attacks, depressed about their depressions, and angry at their temper tantrums, and generally give themselves problems about their problems. We refer to these as *secondary emotional problems*. It is important for the therapist to deal with these second-level symptoms first, for the added layer of distress will prevent clients from working most efficiently on the basic A–B–C's. (Secondary emotional problems will be discussed more fully in subsequent chapters.)

EXPANDING THE A-B-C MODEL

The ABC model of RET helps to explain to clients the source of their emotional distress; in its expanded form, an *A-B-C-D-E* model, it illustrates how they can reduce this distress. D stands for *Disputation,* in which clients learn to challenge and debate with themselves, cognitively and behaviorally, about their irrational thinking. When successful, then at E they will experience a new *Effect*—a more rational philosophy and a level of affect which is compatible with effective problem solving. Thus, the RET therapist works not only at helping to change beliefs but also at helping to change activity, and often makes use of behavioral homework assignments to accomplish both ends.

Once clients have mastered disputation skills and developed a more rational coping philosophy, there may still be work to be done; unpleasant activating events may remain to be confronted. Even when clients are not disturbing themselves, they will probably be less happy if unpleasant activating events frequently impinge on their life. Since the therapist cannot insure that clients will always live in a stress-free environment, however, the preferred strategy is to teach them how to cope with the unpleasant aspects of their environment. As long as they remain upset, their problem-solving skills will tend to be adversely affected, and their ability to get what they want will be impaired. After the disturbance is reduced, interventions can focus on teaching clients how to choose or change their environment to minimize aversive conditions.

Ultimately, of course, a goal of therapy is to have patients learn to be their own therapists. After learning to identify and dispute their irrational beliefs, patients can decide and implement the decision to not upset themselves. We now move on to discuss how the therapist teaches the A-B-C's of RET.

New therapists often ask whether it is necessary to teach the A-B-C's directly to the patient or to include these phrases in the active therapeutic vocabulary. The answer is that it is not necessary to do so, but it may be highly desirable, as the patient can use this clear conceptual schema to do structured cognitive homework assignments and to aid him or her in generalizing beyond the course of therapy. The new practitioner is advised to actively teach the A-B-C model because it will also help the new practitioner to keep to the RET structure. Some experienced RET therapists, including Ellis, occasionally or often omit these descriptive devices. For the *new* practitioner, however, we strongly recommend the formal adoption of the A-B-C system for use in listening, speaking, and teaching work with clients.

A Demonstration

As an overview of the basic tenets of RET, we include a highly condensed version of a therapeutic demonstration given by Dr. Albert Ellis at one of the institute's five-day practicum courses. The client was a young professional who attended the course and wished to discuss the difficulties of beginning a new practice. In brief, the A was wanting to try new professional activities, such as giving workshops, and the C was inertia. The therapist asked the client what she was saying to block herself; the response was:

C: I might flub it.
T: And what would that do?
C: People might think I'm a crummy teacher.
T: And that would do what?
C: I wouldn't like it.
T: Just *that* evaluation wouldn't make you upset.
C: I can't stand it.
T: Why can't you stand their thinking you're a lousy teacher?
C: (long silence) . . . I think I have to be a good teacher in their eyes.
T: And why *must* you be a good teacher in their eyes? I'm a scientist—prove it (grinning).
C: (long silence)

T: As long as you believe that *must,* how will you feel?

C: Anxious.

T: *Must* they all like you?

C: No.

T: Then why must—

C: Because I want them to!

T: Whatever I want, I *must* get? Where will that command get you?

C: Scurrying around . . .

T: Right! Anxious, depressed. Now suppose you *get* it—they all adore you. You know you'll still be in trouble? (pause) How do you know you'll get it the next time? Aren't you asking for, *demanding* guaranteed adoration?

C: Hmmmm. Yes.

T: You'll be anxious as long as you believe that. How could you *not* believe that? How could you get so that you desire, but don't *need,* their approval?

C: Give some workshops?

T: Take some risks, right. What else? (pause) "If they don't approve, I could stand it. What would that make me as a human being if they don't like my teaching?" Suppose you're just lousy at giving workshops? Too bad! Can you be a happy person even if certain things you want you don't get?

C: Ye-s-s-s-s-s. (tentatively)

T: See how mildly you said that? How could you say that even stronger? (models) "Goddamn it! I'm determined not to put myself down even if I *never* do many things well!" Rating yourself as OK is also wrong. Why are you OK? Proving you're OK is just as impossible, empirically, as proving that you're a bad person. "I am I. Nancy. Now how the hell do I *enjoy myself* without trying to *prove myself?*" You see, you can choose not to label yourself at all. You don't need a grade for yourself, a continual report card. You can rate your behaviors in the workshop, because it will be pleasurable to do well.

Part II
General Therapeutic Strategies

4 Getting Therapy Off to a Good Start

In one sense, therapy begins at the first moment of contact between you and your client, and develops as you and the client attend to some important preliminary groundwork in the therapeutic process. Included in this groundwork are two primary tasks:

Interpersonal—developing a therapeutic alliance, establishing a therapeutic rapport, and building a collaborative set

Organizational—socializing the client for therapy, beginning the process of assessment, agreeing on the problem areas, and establishing treatment goals.

Each of these tasks works in the service of the other; for example, the active, collaborative setting of treatment goals begins to forge the therapeutic relationship. This chapter addresses the ways that an RET therapist might work at these tasks to set the stage for cognitive-behavioral work.

"Setting the Stage" Interpersonally

It might be useful to begin this discussion by asking you, the reader, to recall your own first session with a psychotherapist. If you have not had that experience, try to visualize yourself in the patient's shoes. Imagine coming into new surroundings, facing a complete stranger, and then trying to discuss your most difficult or embarrassing problems. What would you be feeling just then, and would that emotion be compatible with open discussion?

> Remember that the client comes to therapy because in some way he or she is *suffering*. It is our task to find out about this suffering and figure out how we can be helpful in reducing it. To start, we want to provide a sense of hope and to demystify the therapeutic process for the client. It is our contention that the active-directive approach of RET is ideally suited to accomplishing these aims.

A good way to start work with a new client is to ask if he or she has been in therapy before. One benefit of this question is that you can assess the client's expectations of therapy. A positive expectancy increases the chances of a positive therapeutic effect, while incongruency between the client's expectations and the therapist's view of therapy decreases therapeutic efficacy and increases the dropout rate (O'Leary and Borkovec, 1978). It is helpful, therefore, for the therapist to take time to outline the general nature of RET.

Patients often think of therapy as pouring out their hearts to the doctor and getting sympathy. Although this may provide some relief in the manner of a confession, it is merely palliative, for the patients will not

> Take a moment to practice outlining RET to a naive client. The encounter takes place on the phone, because the potential client has looked you up in the telephone directory and wants to ask a few questions before making a choice of therapists. She says, "I see, Dr. X, that you are listed as a rational-emotive therapist. I'm afraid I don't know what that is. Could you tell me something about this kind of therapy?" Compose a brief response; try to answer in three sentences or less.
>
> _____
>
> _____
>
> _____
>
> Now, get some feedback from your supervisor or a colleague about whether your mini-explanation is clear as well as concise.

have learned the important insight that they are responsible for their own disturbed emotions.

Especially for the new client, it is therefore quite important for the therapist to describe what therapy is like and the procedures involved. Take time to outline what you expect from the client (e.g., being on time for appointments, doing homework) as well as what the client can expect from you (e.g., introducing the client to a cognitive-behavioral model of therapy). This explanation is best given during the first session, usually after the client has presented some major problem(s).

> "I'll be showing you how you can control many disturbed feelings and emotions. I'll be doing that by pointing out some of your thinking styles, asking you to reevaluate some of your perceptions of the world, correcting some of your belief systems, giving you homework assignments to help you change your thinking or your problem behavior, and asking you to read books and listen to tapes. Your active role in therapy is what is most important for you to reap the most benefit. I'm a therapist, not a magician. I can help you and I can advise you, but you will do the work."

A second benefit to knowing about any previous therapy the client might have had is that it can help the therapist avoid unnecessary mistakes. As a rule of thumb, don't do something that a previous therapist has already tried unsuccessfully, or at least present it differently. If the therapist who used the technique was not skilled at it, it may be possible to try the technique again; to avoid an expectation of failure by the client, change its label. So, be sure to ask, "What did you do with your former therapist? What do you think helped you? and "What do you think wasn't helpful?" Occasionally, the client will report, "The other therapist never talked about what was really bothering me." This may give the therapist a good opportunity to ask, "What was that?" If the client replies, for example, "I was raped when I was fourteen," the therapist may respond: "Then let's talk about that. It seems like a good place to begin."

Like the behavioral therapies, RET is problem-oriented, and this focus may be communicated to the patient in the early therapeutic exchanges. The therapist may suggest, for example, "You say that you've been feeling depressed lately. Let's find out what's going on there." If the patient has listed a number of areas of difficulty, the therapist may simply ask, "Which problem would you like to begin to talk about in therapy?" In succeeding sessions, the therapist can begin by asking, "What problem would you like to work on today?" or "Last week, we were discussing

Many RET therapists attempt, even during the first session, to help patients learn to conceptualize their problems in RET terms, to uncover some of the irrational ideas that are causing their troublesome behaviors and emotions, and to help them begin to discover what they're doing to disturb themselves. Ellis himself is particularly active and directive in his initial sessions with patients. Perhaps because of his temperament, many years of clinical experience, eminence in the field, and diagnostic acumen, Ellis sets a fast pace that many new RET therapists assume they *must* follow. Such an assumption would be incorrect, however, since the novice may not be able to replicate Ellis' performance, nor is it always desirable. RET therapists have many different yet effective styles.

such-and-such problem; how have you been working on that this week?" Opening remarks that provide structure are preferable to more general questions (e.g., "How was your week?"), because they set a problem-oriented tone and help keep the session focused.

Many therapists find that another important opening question to ask the client is, "Why did you make this appointment *now?* What happened this past week that propelled you to this decision to act now?" The active-directive stance of the RET therapist is in evidence: we want to get to the immediate crisis and try to begin to be helpful. We are mindful that the patient is in pain in some way.

BUILDING RAPPORT

Self-disclosure is a prerequisite for psychotherapy, yet self-disclosure of the sort and extent necessary for psychotherapy is considered inappropriate behavior in most social situations. In many families there is little talk of emotions and cognitions, so that prior modeling may be lacking. Also, the self-disclosure which is required for therapy may be suppressed by fear. For children and adolescents, self-disclosure may be particularly difficult. It is often not until late adolescence, when close friendships or love bonds develop, that children begin sharing personal secrets. Clients may, therefore, not be accustomed to self-disclosure or may not know how to do it.

Psychotherapists frequently fail to recognize this discrepancy in expectations for self-disclosure. Some therapists expect their patients to freely discuss personal problems, while the patient may have quite a different agenda. Failure to self-disclose may be viewed by some therapists as resistance or as a symptom of deep psychological disturbance, but we suggest that the therapist avoid such preconceptions. Be willing to consider multiple hypotheses—specifically, that problems of self-disclosure may also be a result of a lack of prior modeling of this behavior, or suppression due to fear.

Discomfort with self-disclosure may be particularly evident if patients view their problem behaviors as socially unacceptable. Issues such as homosexuality, promiscuity, and even suicidal wishes may fall into this category. The therapist may have to spend a number of sessions establishing a climate of trust before such problems are brought up. Alternatively, clients may repeatedly work on "easy" problems for most of the therapy session and, just when the time is up, "casually mention" an emotionally charged issue. With patience and gentle confrontation, the client will usually become less hesitant across sessions about bringing up major issues.

If self-disclosure is initially absent, make use of encouragement and example. Encourage the client whenever he or she does self-disclose and show by your own (relevant) self-disclosure that it is safe and desirable behavior. In addition, we would suggest that you allow an adequate period of time for the client's fear to subside, which will be difficult if you are very active or appear to be impatient.

Sometimes you can begin to socialize patients to RET even before the first session, and even when they are in emotional distress. For example, in your first telephone contact, you might comment on the patient's affect in a general way (e.g., "You sound like you're having a tough time") and begin to provide some structure. For example,

> "What I'd like you to do in the time between now and when I see you is to think about how to tell me what kinds of problems you're having in your life, and what kind of help you may be looking for. In addition, I'd like you to keep a diary. If you're feeling distressed, that's a good time for you to sit down and just freely write about whatever is going on inside you. So, if you're feeling really upset, remember that those feelings can be very useful to our work, because you will have some good material to present in our first meeting."

Relax. It is not necessary to solve the patient's problems right away. In order to assess the problems, take some time to get to know the client and get a feel for his or her thinking. The patient is more likely to discuss personal problems if he or she believes that the therapist is truly interested in listening.

Many therapists believe that being *active and directive* is incompatible with the development of rapport; we disagree. Remember that the basis for the therapeutic relationship is not friendship but professional competence, credibility, respect, and commitment to help the client change. Thus, rational therapists are not friends to their clients, although they could be, but rather concerned professionals. Rapport, therefore, *can* be developed when the therapist behaves directively.

This point was particularly evident to us while co-leading psychotherapy groups with Dr. Ellis. As directive as he is, the group members frequently reported feelings of warmth and respect for "Al." When questioned by us, group members reported that he demonstrated his concern by his many questions, his complete attention to their problems, and his advocacy of an accepting and tolerant philosophy, and by teaching them something immediate that they could do to reduce their pain.

Special problems in the development of rapport can occur with various populations: court referrals, unwilling spouses with marital problems, and especially children and adolescents. Many of these difficult clients may not really understand the role of the psychologist, and why they

---

Some clients come to RET therapy with prior expectations—especially those who have previously experienced nondirective therapy. They may talk (seemingly endlessly) about their problems. For example, Jay came in week after week, describing in poignant detail all of the many hassles he'd experienced at work and yet how fruitless it was to think of leaving his job. He was stuck and wallowing.

RET is an active therapy. We need to communicate to the client that (a) we can offer something more than a good shoulder to cry on, and (b) the client can do more than merely complain. We try to convey these messages in a respectful way. Here's an example: "Jay, you've done a really super job of identifying the problem. Now that that stage is accomplished, are you ready to move into the next stage? What do you want to do about it?"

are being sent to see one. Children, for example, may believe that if you are a doctor, you will jab them with needles, drill their teeth, or do the kinds of painful things to them that other doctors have done. Some reluctant clients believe that only "crazy people" go to a "shrink" and refuse to cooperate because doing so would be an admission of such a diagnosis. Still others think that you are a righteous judge or harsh disciplinarian who will humiliate or punish them for their misdeeds. In all these cases, the same directive, honest approach is recommended.

Consider how the therapist in the following dialogue reeducates the client and challenges his misconceptions. The client is an 11-year-old boy:

T: Bobby, I'm a psychologist. Do you know what that is?
C: No—well, the kinda doctor for crazy people?
T: Well, that's not totally true. Psychologists are doctors who study how people learn things and who help people learn things they've been unable to learn themselves. For example, some children have trouble learning to read, and some psychologists help them learn to read better. Other children are anxious or depressed and don't know how to feel better. Psychologists help them learn not to be depressed. We help kids with other problems like fears, anger, bed-wetting, and making friends. Do you understand?
C: Yes.
T: Well, what problem can I help you with?

Note that, first, a problem-solving tone is established, and second, the participants' roles are defined clearly. We suggest that you try rewriting the dialogue above as if the client were:

An angry and therapy-reluctant spouse, *and*

A court-referred client with a DWI (driving while intoxicated) arrest record.

Many RET therapists believe that the best way to establish rapport is to *do therapy* with the bond developing through the conjoint activity.

Perhaps this sequence is more true of the experienced therapist. The new therapist who is awkward and unsure of his or her skills may need to begin to establish rapport not by doing therapy but by talking with the client about the *process* of doing therapy.

"Setting the Stage" Organizationally

SOCIALIZING THE CLIENT TO RET

As we said above, socialization can begin on the telephone, before the first appointment, by teaching clients the kind of therapy you do, informing them about what to expect in their first visit, and being open and collaborative in your style of communication.

RET is a problem-oriented approach to psychotherapy. When the therapist asks the client, "What problem would you like to discuss first?" or "What problem bothered you the most this past week?" a number of messsages are being delivered:

> You are both there to get a job done.
>
> RET is a focused and efficient approach to emotional problem solving.
>
> The process is going to be largely active and directive.

GENERAL ASSESSMENT

Clients at the Institute for RET in New York City are given a packet of questionnaires to fill out at the time of their first visit. The purpose of these forms is varied: to provide demographic data for Institute analyses, to reduce the amount of session time needed to get basic biographical data, to help the client to focus his or her needs, and to provide cues for the therapist's formulations of the clinical work to be done. In addition to helping the therapist to generate hypotheses about the client's problems, these data provide a baseline of disturbance against which to monitor progress.

The packet includes a biographical intake form, a Million Clinical Multi-axial Inventory II (Millon, 1987, 1988), the short form of the Beck Depression Inventory (Beck and Beck, 1972), the General Health Questionnaire (Goldberg, 1972), the General Psychological Well-being Scale (DePue, 1987), the Satisfaction with Life Scale (Diener, Emmons, Larsen, and Griffen, 1985), and the Attitudes and Beliefs Scale 2 (DiGiuseppe, Exner, Leaf, and Robin, 1989). All forms are computer-scored at the Institute and returned to the therapist shortly after the client's first visit. The biographical intake form is provided as an appendix to this chapter.

In many mental health clinics, patients may initially be subjected to

lengthy social histories and routine psychological testing. Often, the patient is not given any reason why this is necessary. These standardized
procedures may contribute to the well-known tendency of clinic patients
to drop out of treatment very quickly, not necessarily out of impatience,
but because they have lost confidence that their needs will be met. To
begin the work of rational–emotive therapy, much of the information
other therapists look for is initially unnecessary, or fails to give us the type
of information we need in order to start therapy. Background data are
useful, but following a rigid pattern of elaborate history-taking before
initiating therapy may reduce client rapport. Some patients may feel
threatened by an impersonal battery of standardized tests; others believe
that much of the testing is irrelevant and the therapist is wasting valuable
time that could be used to help them. If patients are ashamed or uneasy
about exposing their problems, they are as likely to conceal them during
an extensive assessment as in a shorter one.

Patients are best served by working with the therapist efficiently on
an issue that they want to discuss, while the therapist transmits nonjudgmental acceptance in the hope that they will come to view the therapist as a
competent and trustworthy person to whom they can divulge their "secrets." Thus, you do not need to wait for the "real" problem or a list of all
the problems before beginning the work of therapy. Take whatever activating event or emotional consequence the patient is willing to present and
use it to teach the A-B-C model. In this way, the patient will receive some
help while being educated about RET theory.

Because RET is a cognitive therapy, it is to the therapist's advantage
to briefly assess the cognitive functioning of the client. Psychological assessment by means of a formal battery of tests is recommended for most
children but is not considered essential for adults. There may be some
cases involving adults, however, in which standardized tests may be helpful in attaining information on cognitive functions. Cognitive deficits may
have a neurological basis that is responsible not only for the psychological
problems but for any accompanying deficits in social skills as well. This
neurological base can go unnoticed unless careful detective work and psychological testing are done. Keep in mind that George Gershwin spent
years in psychoanalysis for the treatment of headaches and then died of a
brain tumor.

Sometimes cognitive deficits are a result of chronic substance abuse,
which may be surprising news to the client who claims, for example, to
have "never missed a day of work." It is generally good practice to ask the
client directly (even if the written intake forms include this topic) about
the typical use of alcohol and other drugs in his or her life, and about times

when greater than normal use may occur. If the therapist suspects that the client is not giving an accurate picture, corroborative interviews with family members are recommended.

Good diagnosis is the first step in good treatment. In RET, the major diagnosis focuses on identifying the dysfunctional belief systems that produce emotional distress, but diagnoses of other problems are also important. From the first session onward, the therapist is building up a picture of the patient's current level of functioning by amassing pieces of information about the client's life. Some of this information has been gathered in the biographical data form or other pencil-and-paper measures, but much of it will emerge more informally in the therapeutic hour.

In addition to an A-B-C analysis of the patient's cognitive system (as described in the succeeding chapters), the therapist does a careful behavioral analysis of the major problems. Good detective work is often required to establish the *antecedents* and *consequences* of specific target behaviors. For example, if the patient is requesting help with obesity, the RET therapist may follow behavior therapy prescriptions and ask the patient to keep data on where and when the patient ate, what was eaten, the patient's mood and thoughts when eating, and the immediate consequences (internal and environmental) of eating. The role played by significant others in the patient's life may also be important: Does the obese patient's spouse encourage him or her to eat second helpings? What motivates the spouse's behavior? What would it mean to the spouse if the patient shed weight?

Because patients are each unique, they want different things; some jump right in and begin therapy, and others go more slowly and want to tell you more of their history. One client vigorously defended against the attempts of the therapist to "get to work," saying, "I want to tell you more about myself, my family, and my background. That way, I'll feel like you have a better chance of understanding me, and maybe I'll be better able to trust what you say."

If you're not sure what the patient wants, ask him or her. You might say: *"What type of information do you think I need in order to help you?"* This question also helps make explicit the client's implicit theory of therapy. *"What do you think will help you?"* This question makes explicit the client's conception of the tasks of therapy.

IDENTIFYING AND AGREEING ON PROBLEM AREAS

Patients typically state their problems in vague or behavioral terms or express them as external problems. For example:

> I have trouble with my daughter.
>
> I'm having trouble with my social life.
>
> We need help with our marriage; we don't communicate.

One of the first tasks in setting up therapy, therefore, is to reach an agreement on the definition of the problem(s). In RET, we try to focus the patient on how the problem affects him or her. In this way, we draw the patient's attention to the behavioral and affective aspects of the problem, and ultimately to the B-C connection. For example:

C: My problem is that my 18-year-old daughter just sits around the house and plays her music and drives me crazy!

T: It sounds like your problem is that you're angry and you walk around your house feeling resentful.

Sometimes the patient's conception of the problem can obscure the real diagnostic issues. Consider the client who says he has "trouble with his social life." One might assume that the affective problem is social anxiety, or the behavioral problem is a social skills deficit. A little digging, however, may reveal that in social situations, the client puts himself down unmercifully, makes bad jokes about himself, and, of course, is not pleasant company. What's the real problem? Likely, it's depression. The point is that the therapist had better ask the patient to be explicit and concrete in elaborating the nature of his or her problem. In this instance, for example, the therapist might ask: How do you know you have a problem with your social life? When was the last time you had a social problem in this area? What was it like? What kind of feedback did you get from others? And so on.

Suppose you and your client don't agree on the presenting problem, or you feel that the presenting problem is a kind of screen, concealing deeper problems. Do you work at the problems that are presented to you and show the client the RET process—or do you try to get at the "real" problem? We suggest that you do the former. Occasionally, screen problems may be a test by clients to see if you really can help them. Cases such as these may provide an argument for why a diagnostic assessment done in the first visit may not be very productive. In any case, it teaches us that assessment goes on *throughout* therapy, not just at the start.

Problems can be stated as tentative hypotheses which you are willing to modify. There is no such thing as a definitive assessment or diagnosis of the nature of a problem. Good clinicians are always willing to be wrong or to change their minds about their conceptualizations as they listen to new information. By sharing our conceptualizations with our clients, we're modeling self-disclosure, willingness to test out thinking and be wrong, and use of the scientific method. Sharing hypotheses builds collaboration and respect. When the therapist says, "Sharon, I have a hypothesis that your social problem may be due to depression, and I'd like to know what your thoughts are about that?" you're demonstrating respect by asking for the client's feedback.

One guideline you may want to follow is to share your hypotheses with the client. However, it is advisable not to do so in declarative sentences. Use suppositional language; phrase the item as a question that needs feedback.

What if the client cannot identify a specific problem? A question the therapist might ask is, "What would you like to achieve from therapy?" The client may then begin to formulate his or her goals for treatment, and perhaps be able to explore feelings or behaviors that are impeding him or her from achieving those goals.

If, at this stage, you have not yet reached an agreement with your client concerning the nature of his or her problem, you can suggest to the client that he or she keep a "problem diary." Encourage your client to monitor disturbed feelings during the week and suggest that he or she write down what these feelings were, and when and where they were experienced.

Generally, we suggest that you agree on the definition of the problem(s) with your client before proceeding to a problem–specific assessment phase. In doing a more specific assessment of the problem area, be as *concrete and detailed* as you can. Your patient experiences the emotional problem and holds related irrational beliefs in many contexts. Being specific will help you to obtain reliable and valid data about A, B, and C. One way to model specificity is to ask for a *recent* or *typical example* of the target problem, for example, "When was the last time X happened?"

IDENTIFYING TREATMENT GOALS

Within the first few sessions, the RET therapist will try to establish with the client the goals of therapy. Implicit or preferably explicit agreements will be made with the patient so that both parties will be able to determine when and if therapeutic progress is being made. In fact, frequent reassessment of these agreed upon goals encourages not only therapeutic responsibility but also the client's involvement and commitment to the process.

A stated commitment to goals also enables the therapist to refer back to them when the client is goofing off. For example:

> "By not doing X, aren't you hindering yourself from getting what you set out to achieve, Alice?" or
>
> "How can you accomplish your goal of marriage, Sam, if you don't go out and meet people?"

Most therapists follow a professional code of ethics, which implies that they are there to help the client change what he or she wants to change. The therapist's purpose is not to stamp out all irrational beliefs that clients may have, but to work on their problems as their consultant. The therapist may see major problems that clients haven't brought up and want to discuss them, for example, "John, I think you have some other problems that you haven't brought up, and here's the reason why I think we'd better work on these." The ultimate decision, however, rests with the client.

In addition to establishing long-range goals for therapy, we also recommend that you set weekly treatment-plan goals. At the end of each session, you can review each of the problem areas, determine the next step in working on the problems, remind yourself to check up on the progress of older problems, and outline the goals for the subsequent session(s). (The use of formal treatment plans is taken up in greater detail in Part V, "The Therapeutic Whole.")

AGREEING ON TREATMENT GOALS

By this point, collaboration on treatment goals is usually straightforward. In some instances, however, things get tricky. You may *not* find that you and your client share common goals, for example, in marriage counseling, sex therapy, anger issues, and guilt problems. Clients want the A's changed; they want practical or behavioral solutions. In RET, we approach the *emotional solution* before we attack the practical or behavioral solution. In other words, we encourage clients to begin by working on C. Why do we want to work on the emotional problem first? There are three main reasons:

> *Disturbed negative emotion can interfere with learning.* The Yerkes Dodson Law, which many of us may remember from introductory psychology classes, reminds us that there is generally a U-shaped inverse relationship between performance and intensity of affect. With too little affect, we function like "relaxed incompetents"; with too much affect, we struggle along as over-anxious nonlearners.
>
> *Disturbed negative emotion may interfere with the individual's problem-solving ability.* Coming up with sensible solutions to life problems may therefore be impeded.
>
> *Even when functional behaviors are learned, disturbed negative emotions may interfere with the production of these behaviors.* For example, Schwartz and Gottman (1976) found that problems in assertiveness are not usually a result of skill deficits but rather of performance inhibition.

Dealing with the emotional problem is necessary, but *not necessarily sufficient:* resolving emotional problems gets rid of emotional disturbance; dealing with *practical* problems leads to self-actualization and improvement in the patient's quality of life. Both are important.

PROBLEMS IN ACHIEVING COMMON GOALS

Be suspicious of clients who phrase their goals in terms of therapeutic *process* rather than outcome. For example, "I really want to *understand* why I'm so depressed." "I want to learn what my irrational beliefs really are." RET is a problem-oriented therapy, and we measure effectiveness by the degree of change; these client goals are so vague that both therapist and client are likely to end up frustrated when they look back to determine the utility of the therapy experience.

Be wary of clients whose goals do not seem either *realistic* or likely to be useful to them. For example, Paul's wife has just left him, and he has determined that his goal in therapy is to *be happy, not care* about his wife's abandonment, and acquire a belief that it's *perfectly OK* that she did so. It is unlikely, and perhaps undesirable, that Paul will be successful in this endeavor. When a lonely Saturday night rolls around, or when Paul has to visit old marital haunts, that cavalier attitude is likely not to hold up. The view that the separation "doesn't matter" will quickly fall apart. If the client selects an inappropriate emotional goal, he won't be able to maintain it because the a priori beliefs are irrational. In order to be happy about your spouse's abandonment, you'd have to believe something like, "It's wonderful that she left." That belief is likely to be inconsistent with reality, so that the goal is unattainable. The ending of Paul's marriage is an unfortunate event, and rather than colluding in denial or emotional dissociation, the therapist would do better to help Paul aim for more moderate beliefs that acknowledge the unfortunate reality and allow for appropriate sadness and even mourning, without resulting in despair and torment.

Sometimes people are in a bind; their emotion causes suffering, yet is seen as *appropriate* to hold onto. Those emotions are often guilt, almost always anger, and sometimes depressive moods. For example, an Italian woman, whose husband was quite ill, was discussing with her therapist the appropriateness of grieving. She was sure that when her husband died, her life would be over too. The therapist asked if it would be inappropriate for her *not* to be miserable, and the client responded that she couldn't imagine it. The therapist teased, "You know, you could do it like some old Italian women I know, and you could go on grieving forever!" The client seemed astonished at this comment and reflected for a moment. She then responded that some years ago, she and her husband had been touring Sicily, and the guide had pointed out a house draped in black, which was described as "the widow's house." The Sicilian woman's husband had died twenty-six years ago, and she was still grieving. This memory caused the client to muse, "I guess that *is* going on too long, and isn't appropri-ate." Once she decided that *prolonged* grieving was an emotional burden that she didn't have to have, she was able to work at giving up some of her dread about her husband's impending death.

Sometimes an emotional goal seems unattainable to clients because they cannot *conceptualize* the new emotion and may not agree that it is adaptive and more functional. Lila, for example, was very sexually active and also felt very guilty; she initially wouldn't contract to give up her guilt because she felt that to do so would lead her permanently to a life of sexual excess and promiscuity. She believed that she needed her guilt to maintain self-control. Eventually, Lila learned to differentiate feeling responsible from feeling guilty.

Here's another example: for five weeks the therapist had been work-ing with a father to help him learn not to get enraged at his kids. In the sixth session, the father looked up in amazement and said, "Wait a second. You want me to not be angry with my kids?" The therapist responded, "You finally got it!" The point is that the therapist hadn't gotten it! He had neglected to show this father that there were other ways to feel, beginning with disliking a child's behavior without becoming enraged by it.

Many times, clients have no *role models* for appropriate emotional reactions. What the therapist can do is ask them to pick out people they know in their life (or public media figures) who had the same activating event but reacted appropriately, even if negatively. In this way, the therapist helps the patient find a model: the patient cannot work toward a goal he or she can't conceptualize.

C: I could never be happy without a man.
T: Do you know anyone who is in that situation? Without a man, but reasonably happy?
C: No. Well . . . maybe.
T: Let's find that person and interview her. Maybe we can also find women who are occasionally sad without men, but not depressed. They're not always happy about it, but they function well in their lives.

Of course, the therapist had better be careful about the beliefs expressed by the model. We don't want to promote parallel irrationalities, such as "All men are vermin, so who needs them?" That role model may not be depressed because she's replaced despair with the equally debilitating emotion of anger.

Sometimes role models can be found in specific coping or support groups. For example, the distraught parents of a young child with Tourette's syndrome may find not only support but also models for negative albeit *nondisturbed* levels of affect in a Tourette's support group. One young mother, whose small son developed alopecia ariata and suddenly lost all the hair on his body, found what she needed by starting an alopecia support group, using RET as its underpinnings.

Appendix: Biographical Information Form

Date_____ Name_____

Instructions To assist us in helping you, please fill out this form as frankly as you can. You will save much time and effort by giving us full information. You can be sure that, like everything you say at the Institute, the facts on this form will *be held in the strictest confidence and that* no outsider will be permitted to see your case record without your written permission. *Please type or print your answers.*

1. Date of birth:_____ Age____ Sex: M____ F____

2. Address:

3. Home phone: Business phone:

4. Permanent address (*if different from above*)

5. Who referred you to the Institute (*check one*)

   _____(1) self _____(2) school or teacher _____(3) psychologist or psychiatrist _____(4) social agency _____(5) hospital or clinic _____(6) family doctor _____(7) friend _____(8) relative _____(9) other (explain) _____
   Has this party been here? _____Yes _____No

6. Present marital status:

   _____(1) never married _____(2) married now for first time
   _____(3) married now for second (or more) time
   _____(4) separated _____(5) divorced and not remarried
   _____(6) widowed and not remarried
   Number of years married to present spouse _____ Ages of male children _____ Ages of female children _____

7. Years of formal education completed (*circle number of years*):

   1 2 3 4 5 6 7 8 9 10 11 12 13 14 15 16 17 18 19 20 more than 20

8. How religious are you? (*circle number on scale that best approximates your degree of religiosity*):

   very   average   atheist
   1   2   3   4   5   6   7   8   9

9. Mother's age: _____ If deceased, how old were you when she died? _____

10. Father's age: _____ If deceased, how old were you when he died? _____

11. If your mother and father separated, how old were you at the time? _____

12. If your mother and father divorced, how old were you at the time? _____

13. Total number of times mother divorced _____ Number of times father divorced _____

14. Number of living brothers _____ Number of living sisters _____

15. Ages of living brothers _____ Ages of living sisters _____

16. I was child number _____ in a family of _____ children.

17. Were you adopted? _____ Yes _____ No

18. What kind of treatment have you previously had for emotional problems?

_____ hours of individual therapy, spread over _____ years, ending _____ years ago.

19. Hours of group therapy _____ Months of psychiatric hospitalization _____

20. Are you undergoing treatment anywhere else now? _____Yes _____No

21. Number of times during past year you have taken antidepressants _____

22. Type of psychotherapy you have mainly had. (*Briefly describe method of treatment—e.g. dream analysis, free association, drugs, hypnosis, etc.*)

23. Briefly list (*print*) your present main complaints, symptoms, and problems

24. Briefly list any additional *past* complaints, symptoms, and problems:

25. Under what conditions are your problems worse?

26. Under what conditions are they improved?

27. List the things you like to do most, the kinds of things and persons that give you pleasure:

28. List your main assets and good points:

29. List your main bad points:

30. List your main *social* difficulties:

31. List your main *love and sex* difficulties:

32. List your main *school or work* difficulties:

33. List your main life goals:

34. List the things about yourself you would most like to change:

35. List your chief physical ailments, diseases, complaints, or handicaps:

36. What occupation(s) have you mainly been trained for?

    Present occupation _____
    _____Full-time _____Part-time

37. Spouse's occupation _____
    _____Full-time _____Part-time

38. Mother's occupation _____
    Father's occupation _____

39. Mother's religion _____
    Father's religion _____

40. If your mother and father did not raise you when you were young, who did?

41. Briefly describe the type of person your mother (or stepmother or person who substituted for your mother) was when you were a child and how you got along with her:

42. Briefly describe the type of person your father (or stepfather or father substitute) was when you were a child and how you got along with him:

43. If there were unusually disturbing features in your relationship to any of your brothers, briefly describe:

44. If there were unusually disturbing features in your relationship to any of your sisters, briefly describe:

45. Number of close male relatives who have been seriously emotionally disturbed: _____ Number that have been hospitalized for psychiatric treatment, or have attempted suicide: _____ Number of close female relatives who have been seriously emotionally disturbed: _____ Number that have been hospitalized for psychiatric treatment, or have attempted suicide: _____

46. Additional information that you think might he helpful:

5 Basic Therapist Skills

In RET, as in other forms of psychotherapy, certain therapist qualities can help to build rapport and maximize therapeutic gains. Below we list some therapist characteristics described by Rogers (1951) and Carkhuff (1969), and follow each with a description of how these attitudes are communicated by an RET therapist.

Qualities of the RET Therapist

Empathy is the ability to perceive accurately what another person is experiencing, and to communicate your perception. The empathic therapist will be attuned not only to the words of the clients but to the nonverbal aspects of their behavior in order to perceive accurately their feeling state. By return communications, the empathic therapist lets the clients know that he or she is aware of the clients' positive feelings and emotional discomforts.

The empathic *RET therapist* lets clients know that he or she understands not only what the clients are feeling but also what they are *thinking*. For example:

> "It sounds like you're really unhappy. Could you also be thinking it would be awful if you *did* fail?"

When both the thought and the emotion are reflected, the client has an option to begin dealing with either; emotive reflecting alone, however, precludes this option. Often clients are startled by such dual reflections and appear amazed that the therapist has "read their mind."

Often you'll see rather dramatic improvements in a client's mood during the course of a session. Clinical research, using pre- and post-session measures, suggests that about 90 percent of the variance in this mood shift can be predicted by two factors:

The technical portion of the therapy hour, for example, the percentage of change in the patient's belief system, *and*

The perceived empathy of the therapist (the degree to which the therapist is seen by the patient as understanding, caring, and supportive)

These are independent but additive effects.

Respect is evident when the therapist indicates a deep and genuine acceptance for the worth of the clients, separate and apart from their behavior. The mere fact of the clients' existence justifies this respect. The therapist respects the right of clients to make their own decisions, even if they are in error, for much can be learned from failure. As a respectful therapist, you are neither rejecting nor overprotective. Instead, you foster client independence, self-confidence, and self-reliance.

The *RET therapist* shows clients that they can be respected despite their disagreement with the therapist over certain philosophical issues. Thus, the RET therapist clearly discriminates between the clients and their dysfunctional thoughts and behaviors.

Warmth is communicated to the client by appropriate use of touching, smiles, and other nonverbal gestures of appreciation, as well as by positive comments of concern and affection for the client.

The *RET therapist* also demonstrates concern and caring for the client in some of the following ways: by carefully attending to the client's behavior, by frequent questions for clarification or therapeutic intervention, by recall of personal details about the client and his or her problem, by the use of gentle humor, by unconditional acceptance, and by quick, active attempts to help the client solve difficult issues.

Genuineness is conveyed by not being phony or trying to play roles. Make your verbal and nonverbal behaviors congruent. Your behavior in the counseling relationship need not be dramatically different from that outside the relationship.

As an *RET therapist,* you are likely to go a step further. Active con

Be careful to monitor your level of warmth, caring, and concern. Too much of a good thing can also be problematic. Therapists as well as clients are often vulnerable to the "dire need for approval," and the RET therapist takes a cautious approach, being careful to note irrational beliefs that may arise in the context of the therapeutic relationship. Unchallenged, approval needs may block clients from really working hard to change themselves or even block therapists from being firm enough to help them change! Attentive self-monitoring is essential.

frontation requires genuineness, and genuineness, in turn, requires honesty. Thus, the RET therapist is likely to disagree openly with the client, to ask directly for clarification when confused, and to respond to client questions without hesitation.

Concreteness refers to specificity in the therapist's work on the patient's problems. Attention to detail is evident; the therapist will ask for concrete details (the what, why, when, where, and how) of the patient's experience. Concrete therapists often ask for specific examples and lead the client through a comprehensive analysis of these situations.

The *RET therapist* places importance on concrete details of the patient's perceptions, cognitions, and emotions. Do not encourage the client to supply details only about external circumstances (A), but focus primarily on the belief system.

Confrontation is used when the therapist detects discrepancies (a) between what the clients are saying and what they have said before, (b) between what the clients are communicating verbally and nonverbally, and (c) between the way the clients view their problem and the way the therapist views it. Confrontation in counseling is particularly encouraged when the therapist notes discrepancies in the client's thoughts, feelings, and actions. For example, the therapist may point out, "John, you just described how your father would come home drunk and once picked up your brother and threw him across the room—and you told me that with a smile on your face" or, "Mary, you began by telling me that you had a wonderful family life, but the facts don't seem consistent with that assessment."

Confrontations take courage, and are among the most powerful and valuable tools of the therapist. For example, the therapist might suggest,

Some areas of clinical inquiry require a gentle persistence of confrontation rather than a battering ram. A prototype of such an approach is seen in work with survivors of abusive or alcoholic homes who often seem to be "super-stoics" because they cope by "not knowing." Their conversation may suggest that they live in a fantasy ("my childhood was wonderful") or in denial ("I had fun in the hospital while I was a child"), or somewhere on the continuum between repression and dissociation ("I don't remember much of my childhood").

Remember that these are defense strategies and they exist for good reasons. Defenses are attempts to ward off what seems to be "unknowable" and, more important, "unbearable" memories and affective states. Our goal in confrontation is to help these survivors of abuse to know what happened to them, to feel strong negative feelings about it, and to not be overwhelmed by those feelings.

"You say you aren't angry, Mary, yet you're sitting there with your fists clenched!" or "You say you have no problems, Fred, but what are you doing here in jail?"

Carkhuff (1969) has outlined various levels of confrontation strategies, ranging from very mild to frontally assertive. The *RET therapist* typically operates at the top of this hierarchy, at the most direct levels. The approach is based on a number of theoretical assumptions: (a) there is no concept of "readiness" of the client for confrontations or insights, as in other therapies; (b) by confronting clients with aspects of their behavior that are not in their awareness, problems can be quickly brought into focus; and (c) clients are unlikely to be devastated by confrontations and do not need to be overprotected. Thus, by confrontations, the RET therapist actually expresses respect for the client. However, we advise that a good working relationship or therapeutic alliance be established before confrontations at the top of the hierarchy are used.

The key to facilitating collaboration is to follow such confrontations with requests for feedback: "What do you think or feel when I say that to you?" The therapist's comment is seen as a stimulus to elicit an emotional and cognitive response. The feedback can be used either diagnostically or collaboratively, depending on how the client reacts to the content of the

Windy Dryden has used himself as a coping model in illustrating to clients how he overcame his anxiety about stammering. The core strategy was to repeatedly force himself to go into situations in which he was likely to stammer, practicing "opening his mouth" and rehearsing the attitude, "If I stammer, I stammer. Big deal." The idea was to do this many, many times until he got used to the discomfort of doing so.

confrontation and/or the act of confrontation. Different elements of the client's response may thus be teased apart.

Three additional qualities that are important in building rapport are self-disclosure, the use of humor, and an active-directive style. *Self-disclosure* brings human sharing to the communication. Therapists can expose their own thoughts, ideas, feelings, and attitudes at special times for the benefit of the client. For example, the therapist might say, "I know what you're going through, Joe. As a matter of fact, some years ago I went through the same thing, and here's how I dealt with it." The therapist's model may provide hope in such instances, in that the therapist is suggesting that he or she has had a similar problem and successfully grappled with it. Thus, the therapist models rationality, demonstrating appropriate thinking and behavior for dealing with a specific problem. In addition, the therapist is modeling self-disclosure and thereby demonstrating trust in the client; this behavior reverses the typical one-way street of therapy. Self-disclosure can also be a good way of teaching the model of RET, in a coping rather than mastery style.

Self-disclosure is useful, however, only when it is relevant; the therapist may check on relevancy by asking himself or herself, "What is the payoff for the client from this self-disclosure?" Keep in mind that the rationale for self-disclosure is primarily to build rapport and to model cognitive and behavioral strategies.

In addition, RET therapists are encouraged to develop and utilize a healthy *sense of humor*. Obviously, the patient is never the butt of a joke, but by gently poking fun at the irrational beliefs or events that the patient views as catastrophies, the therapist may put problems into a more realistic perspective. For example, "You seem to have a healthy case of perfectionism. It doesn't do you much good, but it's nice to know it's well developed!" Or in attempting to point out a client's demandingness, the

> One therapist had a client who, after the therapist's relevant self-disclosure, said, "Doctor, I'm not paying good money to hear about your problems—let's get back to mine." What we suggest, since you cannot know your client's response beforehand, is:
>
> > Don't do too much self-disclosure at the onset of therapy.
> >
> > When you self-disclose, first ask yourself "Who will benefit from this story?"
> >
> > Use self-disclosure in small doses, and ask your client for feedback, for example, "What do you think about that? Is there anything in my story that is meaningful for you? How could you apply that?"

therapist may suggest, "You seem to be using the Reverse Golden Rule. Remember the Golden Rule? Do unto others as you would have them do unto you? The Reverse Golden Rule says others should do unto me as I do unto them!" As Ellis (1977c, p. 269) has pointed out, "A sense of humor, in itself, will not cure all emotional problems. But the refusal to take any of the grim facts of life *too* seriously largely will."

Conducting the Session

Within the cognitive-behavioral model, there is a session framework or format, the purpose of which is to set up goals for each treatment session. This section outlines a suggested format for a typical working session. We

> It is extremely important that therapists understand the powerful impact they can have on the patient. The therapist's words, deeds, and facial expressions—even breathing patterns—are usually exquisitely monitored by the patient. Don't underestimate the impact you may have, whether it is clearly expressed by the client to you or not. Support, caring, and reframing in a positive manner are crucial skills and, unfortunately, occasionally missing or neglected in skill-focused clinical training. Be sure to get some supervision on the interpersonal aspects of your work as you go along.

recommend for a number of reasons that you spend some time trying to follow this outline.

First, a session format is helpful to clients whom you are inaugurating into treatment. Many clients take comfort in knowing what to anticipate each week in the structure of the therapy hour. In addition, many new therapists (or "old hands" who are attempting to learn a new model) find this structure helpful because they have so much to think about that they often feel overwhelmed, and the structure simplifies the framework.

OUTLINE OF A WORKING SESSION

1. Old business from the previous session
2. Checkups: mood, symptoms, medication
3. New business: any major life changes
4. Check on homework
5. Setting the agenda

   DOING THE WORK . . .

6. Summary of work done
7. Assignment of homework
8. Closing questions

Note that "work time" is sandwiched between two sets of setting-up and wrapping-up tasks. In order to maximize work time, these other items should be brief. You might aim to set up the session in approximately 10 minutes and allow 10 minutes to close it. In a typical 50-minute therapy hour, therefore, you may really only have 30 minutes of work time. This realization may help you to keep your agenda for each session to realistic proportions.

RET is a structured as well as an active-directive therapy, and the outline above can help you to do more structured work. If the beginning and the end of your therapy sessions are tidy, the middle working part will go much more smoothly. The therapist skill that is required here is *agenda setting*.

The idea behind agenda setting is that the session must be blocked out in terms of tasks that need to be done. Agenda setting prevents the tendency to let the session meander wherever the client's opening comments happen to take it. Frequently, these opening remarks are more like social chitchat and avoid the emotionally charged material the client wants to

Some new therapists object to agenda setting because it seems to run counter to the helping skills they have been cultivating. Here, for example, is an extract of dialogue between a student of RET and his supervisor:

Student: I find it so hard to get the client to stop talking and just fix the agenda. It feels so rude. Therapy has had the kind of flavor that says: "This time is yours and you can use it any way you want, to talk about yourself, and so on."

Supervisor: It *is* hard. It's against your social skills training. It feels businesslike. But I find that once clients understand that this is a structured kind of therapy, they usually appreciate the structure. They socialize to it fairly quickly IF the therapist is consistent. They quickly learn that what will happen is the therapist will say, "Do we have any leftovers from last time? How did your homework assignment go? Any crucial events I should know about? What else goes on the agenda for today?" Pretty soon the client gets into the swing of this and will usually come prepared with agendas. Those clients with whom I've done the most focused work have walked in with notes or index cards containing their agendas.

discuss. If the therapist is following rather than leading the session, it becomes the client's task to break the social mold and redirect their attention, which the client may be reluctant to do in order not to appear rude or disinterested.

Our working model suggests items on which the therapist can check, in order to negotiate with the client what the focus of the day's work will be: "How much of the session shall we spend on 'this' or 'that'? Is there anything else we should talk about today?"

The skilled therapist will be able to lead the client quickly through these checks, using each point to decide whether an item needs to be addressed in the *working part* of the session. Setting up the session in this way gives you time to do some work, at the end of which you stop and roll the session back to the beginning and say, "OK, here's what we did; was it helpful or useful?" "What will we give you for homework? Where shall we start next time?"

Agenda setting is a skill that requires training, supervision, and lots and lots of practice. It is important to not let the client orally digress in the therapeutic hour before you agree on the items for the agenda. Once the agenda is set, it is then more productive to let the client talk and the therapist listen.

Let's take each of the items on the outline in turn.

1. *Old business.* The therapist may say something like, "Margo, did you have any negative thoughts or feelings left over from our last visit that came up after we parted company?" Note that the therapist is asking a more focused question than "Any old business?" Specifically, he or she is asking for problems because problems are what the pair is there to work on. At the end of the previous session, the therapist asked if there were any immediate reactions, so he or she doesn't need to ask that again. Now, the question is whether—after the session has "percolated" for some days— there were any *delayed* reactions that need to be put on the immediate agenda.

2. *Checkups.* The therapist checks on the patient's current mood in a variety of ways. For example, the patient may be asked to take the BDI or some other self-report measure while in the waiting room. Alternatively, the therapist may have asked the patient to do a mood log or to keep a record of anxiety attacks over the week and uses this checkup time to glance over the log. If a particular symptom has been troubling the patient (e.g., sleep disorder, medication side effect, etc.), the therapist may simply want to ask about the particular symptom. In any case, once the patient acknowledges a mood or symptom issue, the therapist's task is to ask, *"Would you like to put that on our agenda for discussion today?"* The patient's response may be surprising if this question is asked directly. Clients frequently will say, for example, "No, I don't want to work on that; I want to talk about what my boss said to me!" If the therapist disagrees (e.g., thinks the client is avoiding a discussion of (say) a panic attack because that, in itself, arouses anxiety), then he or she may question the client's decision. The point is that checking on the client's current mood is phrased as an inquiry because what the therapist and the client are working on at this point is to collaboratively set the agenda.

3. *New business.* The therapist will ask, "Are there any major life changes or events that I should know about before we go on?" This question serves many purposes. It can prevent "door-knobbing," that uncomfortable occurrence when the client says, while opening the office door to leave, "Oh, by the way, doctor, I got fired. . . ." or, "the biopsy was posi-

> *Student:* Suppose the client says, "I'm in crisis and I just want to talk to you right now and tell you what happened"?
>
> *Supervisor:* Then that's the agenda!

tive. . . ." or, "I'm pregnant." Knowing the social happenings of the week can also change the meaning of the client's symptom report by providing a context in which to understand it. Most important, when answered in the affirmative, this question allows the therapist to ask, *"OK, does this go on our agenda for today?"* Remember, at this point what we are doing is setting the agenda.

4. *Homework check.* This is a particularly important item, because unless the therapist makes an inquiry, the client is likely to decide that the homework is not a really important part of the therapy process, which in RET is certainly not the message we want to communicate (see Chapter 14). The therapist can check briefly by making a few inquiries, such as: "Did you have a chance to do your homework? How did it go? Was it a useful assignment?" The trick here is to avert a prolonged discussion of the homework by being businesslike and reminding the client, "If there's a lot about the homework to discuss, *shall we put that on our agenda for today?"*

5. *Setting the agenda.* At this point, the therapist may have some items on the agenda and can more broadly ask if there are any other items that belong on the list: "Is there one particular problem you want to talk about, or shall we pick up where we left at the last session?" The therapist may also have to prioritize and negotiate with the client if there are many items. The agenda may have too many items to discuss in the allotted time. In that case, the therapist may ask the client, "If we only have time for one item, which one shall we focus on?"

The work time left, after the setting-up questions, may be 20 to 40 minutes, depending on the total session length. That may seem like a very short therapy time, but the therapist will probably find that it is much more efficiently spent because of the preliminary structuring that has been done.

6. *Summary of work done.* The summary items at the end of the session are as important and informative as the setting-up questions. Good teachers

RET is quite different from traditional, more nondirective therapies. In nondirective work, the client often emerges from a session not really able to describe what is being accomplished in therapy. Even at the end of a course of therapy, patients often cannot clearly state the nature of the work. Our contention is that being able to summarize and articulate the work of a therapy session significantly assists clients in remembering and utilizing therapy in their everyday lives.

know that it is useful to review the lesson just taught while it is still fresh in the student's mind. This end-of-session summary can be done by either the therapist or the client and take just a sentence or two. It serves to wrap up and replay the major task or learning theme of the "work time" part of the session. It might sound like, "OK, Sean, let's wrap up. What we did today was to review how your need for approval caused you a problem in the work place, and you not only disputed those irrational demands, but practiced more assertive communication, right?" If the client is the one to do the summarizing, the therapist can get a good idea of how well the client understood the work.

If the client's summary is vague (e.g., "We just kind of talked through the problem again" or "It just felt good to be here"), the therapist will want to add some structure so that the client has something to hold onto as an outcome of the hour spent together. A few clarifying questions or simply a restatement by the therapist may help.

7. *Assignment of homework.* If it has not already flowed naturally from the working part of the session, at this point homework may be assigned by the therapist, the client, or the two working in collaboration. The homework is used to provide a review or rehearsal of the sessions's work, or to extend the client's understanding of some area under discussion. The various kinds of homework assignments used in RET are discussed more fully in Chapter 12, but for now be aware that homework is an integral aspect of RET. There is a strong positive relationship between progress in therapy and working on homework outside the therapist's office.

8. *Closing questions.* The therapist will ask for positive and negative reactions in turn. To assess the positive reactions, the therapist may say, for example:

> Here's another piece of a conversation between a supervisor and a student of RET that may answer some questions you have about the outline session.
>
> *Student:* Do you follow this structure with all of your patients?
>
> *Supervisor:* I try to do so with most clients, especially at the beginning of therapy. I have a tendency to loosen up after a while and get sloppier. I always regret it when I do. When I organize sessions, they come out better.
>
> *Student:* How do you know they come out better? It's not like research. When things work out better, how do you know it's because of the therapy? Do you just *think* it comes out better because you've followed the structure you laid out . . . or is it really true?
>
> *Supervisor:* I get the data from which to say "better" when I ask the closing questions. When I run very structured sessions, there's practically no latency; clients are bubbling over to tell me what was useful. They can toss it off 1-2-3 because it's organized in their minds, too. When I run looser sessions you can see them falter, and they may say something like, "Well . . . it was good to talk about the problem." I have to help them fish to take something home in an organized way at the end because I haven't structured it well during the session.

"What did you find useful today?" *or*

"What do you think was the most helpful thing we did today?" or

"Was there anything I did or said today that you found particularly helpful?"

This is important and potentially useful feedback for the therapist, so ask the question more than once, if necessary, in order to encourage the client to be clear and concrete.

To assess negative feedback, the therapist might say:

"Is there anything that happened today that leaves you feeling worse?" *or*

"Is there anything I did or said today that you feel bad about?" *or*

"Did anything rub you the wrong way today?"

If this is the first session or two, the therapist might encourage the client to share negatives: "John, if there *were* any negative moments, would you be *able* to share them with me? Would you give yourself permission to tell me, in the future, if I say or do anything that rubs you wrong? It's really important and helpful to this process if you'll do that, ok?"

Obviously, a number of messages are being communicated this way: feedback helps the collaboration, it's acceptable to feel negative responses in therapy and it's good to tell your therapist about them, negative feelings can be used in a helpful way, and the therapist can handle hearing negative feelings without becoming angry or hurt.

When the client expresses negative reactions, the therapist may have time to deal with them immediately (e.g., by clarifying, teaching, or apologizing) or simply put those reactions on the next session's agenda (e.g., "Thanks for telling me that, Linda. How about starting with that next time, since we're out of time today? Could we put that on next week's agenda?")

Note that not every session must follow this model. A model is just that: a *model,* not a "must." It is intended to be used as an example, not rigidly adhered to as a requirement. Some sessions are devoted to getting the patient's relevant history, listening sympathetically, giving counsel, or providing information. There are a range of good practices of RET. Some rational-emotive therapists work with very short agendas; Albert Ellis, for example, typically begins by asking about the homework. He also gives his clients the assignment of making brief notes during the week about anything that really bothers them (e.g., anxiety or depression) and about any time they defeat themselves behaviorally (e.g., procrastinate or behave phobically). In this way clients largely structure each session by bringing in these notes and spending much of the session discovering, first, what they told themselves (B of the A–B–Cs of RET) to make themselves disturbed; and, second, what they did (or now can do) to become more rational (e.g., disputing their IBs and acting against them).

Some therapists eschew the concept of a structured therapy hour altogether. However, we strongly urge you, as a *new RET therapist* to use this model faithfully, to see if it is useful for you and your clients. As in many fields of endeavor, such as art, music, or cooking, it's a good idea to begin by following the basics. Sketching from a still life, practicing scales, and following written recipes give students some fundamental skills upon which creativity can later embellish. As a creative therapist you may emerge with a model quite different than the one outlined above. If so, and it really works for you and your clients, fine!

Part III
The
A-B-C's of RET:
Assessment

6 The A

Identifying the A

When patients describe a troublesome event in their lives, the therapist can think of it as containing three elements: (1) what happened, (2) how the patient *perceived* what happened, and (3) how the patient *evaluated* what happened. The first two elements are aspects of the A, the Activating Event; the latter relates to the client's belief system. For example, if at A the patient reports, "She said a horribly critical thing to me," the patient is confusing all three elements. The issue of what actually happened involves an objective description of what was said and the tone and manner in which it was said. That the comment was a criticism may be a perceptual issue, and whether it need be viewed as horrible that she was criticized is an evaluative issue.

We are making a distinction, therefore, between objective reality and perceived reality. *Perceived reality* is reality as clients describe it and as they presumably believe it to be. *Confirmable reality* refers to a social consensus of what has happened. If it were possible for many observers to have witnessed the same event, and they all described it the same way, we would have obtained confirmable reality. In our example above, if a group of people had heard the exact words and the manner in which they were said to our client, and a high percentage of the onlookers perceived the event as an insult, we would conclude that in confirmable reality the woman had indeed intended to insult our client.

A further distinction we are making is between two types of cognitions. The perceived reality entails clients' *descriptive cognitions* about what they perceive in the world. Rational and irrational beliefs are *evaluative cognitions* about descriptions of reality. To avoid confusion, realize that the term "belief" or "believe" is commonly used in our language to refer to descriptive cognitions, inferential cognitions, and evaluative cognitions. For example, "I think Sue is avoiding eye contact with me" (descriptive belief). "I believe Sue isn't looking at me because she's upset with me" (inferential belief). "It's terrible that Sue is upset with me" (evaluative belief). **To maximize clarity, we shall use the term "belief" to refer only to evaluative cognitions, that is, rational and irrational beliefs.** It will become clear in the next several chapters that it is important to make a distinction between these types of cognitions when the word "belief" is used by the client.

In effect, therefore, the A-B-C model of RET can be expanded at this point as follows:

A (confirmable)—the activating event as it could be validated by a group of observers

A (perceived)—what clients perceive has happened; that is, their subjective description of it

B—the clients' evaluation of what they perceived

C—the emotional and behavioral consequence

For example, a male client may present a problem of "depression because nobody in his office likes him." Further questioning reveals that co-workers interact with him primarily about business matters, that they infrequently chat or invite him to lunch, and when they do, he refuses. Thus:

A (confirmable)—"Few people ask me to lunch or attempt to socialize with me."

A (perceived)—"I think that no one likes me."

B—"It's terrible and awful that no one likes me!"

C—Depression

A crucial distinction for the new RET practitioner to understand at this point is that the client's perception of the activating event does not in itself cause upsetting emotional reactions. In the example above, clients could conclude that no one in their office liked them, yet not upset themselves about that perception. How would they do so? By choosing not to *evaluate* A as something terrible. Thus, if at B they believed that not being liked was merely unfortunate or perhaps (less probably) that not being in the social circle had certain advantages, they could, at C, feel quite differently about the situation. Although the perception of A does not cause C, the client who misperceives A *and* holds irrational evaluative beliefs is more likely to be upset than the client who is merely irrational at B. Thus, the client who thinks that almost everyone dislikes him or her and who irrationally evaluates that as terrible will be upset more often than the client who does not make that interpretation of reality yet who also evaluates social disapproval as awful. The first client has more cues to set off his or her irrational thinking.

The client who thinks rationally at B, but who continues to distort reality at A, will not be terribly upset but, according to rational–emotive theory, can still experience negative affect. Let's return to the example above. If the client now believes that he doesn't *have to* be liked and that it's not awful but merely unfortunate that people at the office don't like him, he will still experience a negative emotional response, such as displeasure or disappointment. Thus, the cognitive element of the A does have an effect on the C, albeit a less significant one. Therapeutic work on these cognitive distortions is, therefore, an appropriate endeavor.

Before going on, we encourage you, the reader, to test your understanding of the crucial distinction between A and B. Examine the following client statements. For each, underline the activating event and circle the evaluative component (Answer key is on p. 368):

"I did poorly on that exam. Oh, I'm such a failure!"

"No one talks to me. I just can't stand being so alone!"

"My mother's always picking on me. I know she hates me!"

"Doctor, the most terrible thing happened last week. My wife told me she wanted a divorce."

"I ate like a pig! You see, I know now that I'm really no good."

"I only make $40,000. Do you call that success? What kind of person makes that little money?"

"I'm on top of the world when I'm with George because it makes me feel so important that he loves me."

What are the options available to the therapist if both types of cognitions (distorted descriptive cognitions and irrational evaluative cognitions) are presented by the client? Two strategies are frequently recommended. Some cognitive therapists, such as Aaron Beck (1976, 1979), would begin by challenging the accuracy of the patient's perception of A. So, if a male client stated that nobody liked him, Beck would challenge the accuracy of this statement, calling into question the word "nobody" and the criteria the patient uses to determine how others feel about him. As he has escalated his belief in this unexamined A, the patient has presumably escalated his evaluation of its terribleness.

As you can see, Beck's assumption is that the work of cognitive therapy is accomplished by first tackling the distortions of A. Ellis (1977a, 1979a), however, refers to these attempts to correct perceptions of A as the *empirical* or "inelegant solution." He considers it inelegant because this strategy does not provide the patient with a coping technique to deal with his or her distress should reality ever match or approach the patient's distorted version of it. For example, although unlikely, it is entirely possible that our client above may indeed find himself in a social environment in which no one likes him. He would be prepared to endure such a fate if in fact he believed it to be only unfortunate and not "horrible."

The rational-emotive school of thought suggests that the more elegant solution is to enable the client to *assume the worst* and not upset himself even if it were true. If the client insists that no one likes him, Ellis might say something like, "Well, we don't know if that's true, but let's just assume for the moment that it is. What do you tell yourself about that?" The assumption in this therapeutic approach is that if the client can deal with this distorted view of A, dealing with the reality will be even easier.

Which is the better way to proceed? There are no empirical answers since the crucial experiments have not been done. In addition, the question itself is perhaps misleading since both Ellis and Beck ultimately do lead the client through an assessment of the accuracy of A.

If the therapist elects to challenge the perception of A as an initial maneuver, we recommend that this be done thoughtfully. Some clients may react to an early challenge by feeling threatened, misunderstood, or unsupported by the therapist. Although these untoward reactions themselves reflect irrational beliefs and may be "grist for the RET mill," they may also weaken therapist-patient rapport.

In summary, the RET practitioner believes that assuming the worst and aiming for an elegant solution is valuable since, in real life, the A situation for the patient may worsen and new difficulties (new A's) arise.

Consequently, we recommend that the new practitioner follow Ellis' model, reserving the challenge to the patient's perception of A until some work on disputation has been done. Some helpful hints on how to challenge "at the A" are found in Chapter 13.

Clarifying the A

UNNECESSARY DETAIL ABOUT A

As we stated in Chapter 1, patients typically come to therapy because they are upset in some way (C) and believe that they are upset because of some event (A). Usually patients have little difficulty in describing A and often want to spend a great deal of time sharing the details of the event with the therapist. Elaborate detail about A is unnecessary, however, since the focus of therapy will be on B, the Belief System. Communicating this focus without appearing to be disinterested or unsympathetic may occasionally be difficult, particularly with clients who have an expectation that it is appropriate to present elaborate detail about their past or present troubles. Historical A's can never be changed, of course; only the client's evaluations of them are available for discussion, and evaluations can be presented succinctly.

The ability to speak succinctly is a problem for many patients; they tend to get lost in details of A, as in the following example:

T: Well, Joe, what were you upset about this week?
C: Well, Doctor, let me tell you exactly what happened. It all started Saturday morning. I went over to visit my wife and children. I got out of my car and my kids came over and greeted me with a big hug. I wasn't doing all those things that usually upset my wife. I went into the house. I didn't say anything about the newspapers being all over the floor or the house not being clean. I didn't say any of those things like I usually do. But then I said to my wife . . . (the client goes on for fifteen minutes describing all the details of what happened and what didn't. He finally concludes) and after I begged her to take me back, she didn't!

The therapist has allowed too much detail from the client. The patient's final point is really the most crucial one and is really the A about which he is upsetting himself. One strategy utilizing more appropriate therapist behaviors would have been to stop the patient's monologue earlier and direct the patient to the point, as in the following example.

T: Well, Joe, what were you upset about this week?
C: Well, Doctor, let me tell you exactly what happened. It all started Saturday morning. I went over to visit my wife and children. I got out of the car and my kids came over and greeted me with a big hug . . .
T: Is that what you were upset about?
C: No! Let me tell you some more.
T: Before you do that, Joe, let me point something out to you. You often give me a lot of extra details that confuse me rather than help me understand your problem. Try to tell me exactly what you are upset about in as few words as possible.
C: But if I don't tell you what happened, how will you understand?
T: We'll go back and get the details later, but for now, just try to stick to the question: Exactly what happened just before you got upset?

A second strategy to deal with verbose clients is to train them to monitor and condense their own stories by giving them feedback that their present mode of communication is inefficient. With the patient above, the therapist could allow the story to run its course, and then intervene in the following manner:

"Joe, you've just given me a great deal of information and detail. I'm confused about what's the most important part. Could you go back and tell me just what was the reason you got upset?"

Note the manner in which the therapist allows the client to review his own report and learn to succinctly extract the relevant information. If the client has mistaken the forest for the trees and is unable to summarize the relevant incident, the therapist may reflect the critical portion for the client and thereby model condensed speech. For example,

"Joe, it sounds to me that you're upset because even though you've tried to change, your wife won't take you back. Is that it?"

VAGUENESS IN REPORTING A

Occasionally the therapist will encounter patients who have difficulties in presenting A, being either vague or denying that a specific event triggered their disturbed emotions and behaviors. What are some possible reasons for this vagueness? The therapist may consider:

Defensiveness—The vagueness may be a way to avoid negative reactions from the therapist and significant others in the patient's life, which he or she fears.

Style—Perhaps the patient has learned to communicate in an ambiguous manner and does so habitually.

Cognitive functioning—The patient may really think in these vague terms and is not clear even to himself or herself.

Life functioning—The patient may lack a clear A because the problem is one of absence of meaningful relationships, constructive activity, or work enthusiasm. These voids may be difficult to verbalize.

Difficulty in locating A is not uncommon in patients who have psychophysiologic disorders, such as migraine or tension headaches. The patient may complain of headaches, for example, but insist that nothing is wrong in her life. Now, RET as a cognitive-change therapy depends on two antecedents: (1) the belief that it is acceptable to self-disclose, and (2) the ability to recognize that a psychological problem exists. The former goal may be approached by remaining patient and empathic; active listening over a number of sessions will be helpful. The second goal may be approached in two ways. The first is to ask the patient not for problems but for information on how the patient could make his or her life even better or could become more self-actualized. Second, the therapist may help the patient learn problem identification skills and help him or her to recognize areas of conflict in interests, desires, and so on. The most constructive approach to problem identification entails getting a behavioral analysis. For example, the headache patient may be asked to keep a ledger in which she records overt and covert antecedents (events, thoughts, and feelings) as well as consequences of each headache episode. As these data accumulate over a number of weeks, patterns will usually unfold.

Some patients sound as if they are experiencing a so-called identity crisis. When asked why he came to therapy, Ted might respond, "To find myself—who am I?" The RET therapist would respond by asking the client to change the question "Who am I?" to "What do I enjoy and what do I value?" Little progress will be made unless the therapist can determine what characteristics the client would like to have. RET therapists would do well to communicate to the client that they do not teach self-discovery but self-construction. The RET therapist's view is that the client is not an entity to be found but rather an evolving process.

The use of pinpointing questions is helpful. Joan, a depressed patient, for example, may claim that she is depressed "all the time." The following questions may help her achieve some focus on her affective state: "When did the depression begin?" "When are you most often depressed?" "What seems to make the depression worse?" If the patient responds that she doesn't know, the therapist may initially refuse to accept this answer and press by gently insisting, "Yes, you do." If this tactic fails, logbooks may again be useful.

Another difficult A statement occurs when Jim simply but repeatedly complains, "Life is meaningless." A therapeutic clarification might entail asking, "What would it take for life to be meaningful?" Such a patient may be harboring the irrational notion that he needs noble motives or prestigious goals in order to be happy. For most people, however, their often unverbalized goals are simple and desire-directed (e.g., having sufficient money, relationships with others, interesting work). Such goals can be justified as being rational because they bring pleasure or avoid discomfort. If the therapist can communicate the message that hedonism and self-pleasuring are acceptable, Jim may more readily identify his goals and his unfulfilling activating events.

The need to clearly identify A is particularly important in phobias; unless the therapist knows what the specific fears are, therapy may proceed along the wrong track. Marie may say she is afraid of subways, for example. Although this statement may initially seem specific, careful probing may reveal a core activating event. What is it about subways that is frightening? Perhaps the feeling of being closed in. What might happen then? Perhaps Marie fears she might faint. What might happen then? People on the train might look askance at or disapprove of her. Thus, in this example, the patient's basic fear is of disapproval, not of trains.

The most severe problem of identifying A is presented by the patient who does not do so at all. Robert might report, for example, that he has been depressed for weeks but has no idea why. Patients faced with this problem frequently choose to reduce their discomfort by creating an attribute for their depression. Understandably, the conclusion that they often arrive at is that they are simply "depressives," thus giving themselves a new A about which they further depress themselves. When Robert does not identify an A at all, the therapist may frequently be helpful by asking pinpointing questions, such as, "Has anything changed in your life in the past few months?" or "Do you anticipate any changes in your life in the next several months?"

In summary, when the patient's description of activating events is confused, vague, or absent, the therapist may keep in mind the following suggestions:

Talk in the patient's language in drawing the data from his or her experience.

Pin down the patient with detailed questions.

Ask for recent examples.

Avoid abstractions.

Request logbooks of experiences.

Keep on track, not only to reduce the problem of scattered focus but to serve as a model for the patient.

Ask about recent or impending life changes.

TOO MANY A's

Many patients come to therapy with multiple problems and a wide array of activating events to discuss. The initial therapeutic focus is on selecting a target problem on which to work. Therapist and client may list problem areas, and a starting choice may be offered to the patient. Alternatively, therapists may wish to make the choice. They may, for example, wish to select a small problem with minor affective consequences because (1) they think they can best teach the RET principles in a less complicated area, (2) they believe that progress can be made in a very few sessions so that their credibility and the patient's enthusiasm will bolster further success, or (3) they presume that one specific problem may be the cause of the others.

Take the case of a client, Sam, who is overweight and has low frustration tolerance problems in controlling his eating, is anxious about dating situations, and is guilty about not visiting his mother as frequently as she would like. It would be very difficult to work on his fear of dating situations, since he is unlikely to be successful in this realm if he is considerably overweight. Dealing with his low frustration tolerance may (1) help him to lose weight, (2) help him to go through the difficulties he may encounter in meeting women to date, and (3) help him to put up with his mother. Overcoming the LFT would, in effect, help overcome all three problems and would therefore be the target belief the therapist might choose to work on first.

Is it wise to allow the client to bring up new problem areas before some resolution of old ones has been achieved? Usually, yes, since the patients typically spend only one hour a week in therapy and 167 hours in their normal environment. New problems and crises are bound to arise, and therapists who rigidly insist on sticking to the previous week's agenda may not only fail to be helpful but may jeopardize their relationship to the client. As a caveat, however, the therapist may be watchful for diversionary tactics by the patient. Is the presentation of a new problem a way to ward off discussion of difficult or troublesome topics? For example, a compulsive overeater may bring up a number of other problem areas to avoid the work of dieting; the diversionary behavior may thus be another example of low frustration tolerance. If new topics are repeatedly brought up over a number of sessions, the therapist would do well to confront the patient directly by pointing out and discussing this aspect of his or her behavior.

In some cases, the therapist may note a common theme in the new problems or a correlation between them and the original or core problem, and can use the new material as a wedge to get to the core. Consider, for example, the case of a young woman who presented problem after problem with the common theme of failing. She reported not being able to do well at a job interview because she believed she didn't deserve the job. She described sabotaging love relationships because she believed she wasn't good enough for her partners. She told of alienating friends because "no one could like a person like me." She seemed to believe that it was good for her to be in pain. After several sessions of listening to these activating events, the therapist then asked her if she recognized the common theme in all of these examples that she had to suffer because she was not good enough to reap any of life's rewards. The patient replied that, in fact, she did recognize that theme and recalled how the other members of her immediate family had suffered greatly. Her sister died after a very painful car accident, her mother died after a bout with breast cancer, and her father after a sudden heart attack. Only she had remained alive and apparently believed that it was only right, proper, and moral for her to suffer as well.

A's BEYOND THE THERAPIST'S EXPERTISE

Clients' problems usually have two components: the practical problem, and the psychological problem. If the practical problem is clearly outside the therapist's area of expertise (e.g., a medical problem), then he or she would do well not to deal with it and perhaps to refer the client to a specialist in the problem area. If the therapist is able to deal with the practical problem, he or she may elect to give the client advice about it. Remember, however, that the patient will most likely have a psychological problem *about* the practical problem; if so, the therapist had better deal with the psychological issue *first*.

Since therapists' competence is in dealing with cognitions, emotions, and behaviors, they would do well to refocus the discussion back onto these areas. Here is one suggestion for how refocusing may be approached:

> "Look, Mary, you know that the information that you're giving me is outside my area of professional competency. I can't advise you about medical matters. You obviously have some pretty strong emotions about these issues, however. Why don't we talk about how you're *feeling* about the medical problems?"

C BECOMING AN A

One of the most important activating events that the RET therapist will quickly seek is *secondary disturbance*. In other words, the patient's symptom (e.g., depression) becomes a new A and itself requires an RET analysis. A hallmark of rational-emotive therapy is its focus on these higher-level problems as a *first* order of business. The cycle of events can be described:

> A—Original symptom (e.g., depression)
>
> B—"Isn't it awful that I have this symptom!" "I mustn't feel this way!" "I must be able to get over my problem quickly and easily."
>
> C—Further anxiety, guilt, or depression.

The patient can become upset about B's or C's in such a cycle. For example, patients may become angry or depressed about their irrational beliefs:

> "There I go thinking irrationally again. Damn it, I'll never stop. What's the matter with me? I should've learned by now. . . ."

Similarly, patients may become anxious over the physical signs of anxiety, a problem which is particularly prominent in agoraphobia (Goldstein and Chambless, 1978). These clients appear to focus on the physiological symptoms of anxiety and believe that they are signs of impending death, doom, or unbearable discomfort:

"I'm terrified of panic. When I get in the car and I feel the anxiety come, I know I won't be able to stand it!"

Ellis (1979a, 1979d) has called this form of anxiety *discomfort anxiety,* to distinguish it from *ego anxiety.* "Phrenophobia," fear of going crazy, is the most common example of such a problem. Some estimates of its occurrence are as high as 77 percent of the patients seen in an office practice (Raimy, 1975). Clients with this problem anticipate losing control of their minds, such that they will become raging homicidal maniacs. Raimy has identified symptoms that phrenophobics believe are signs of impending insanity or mental breakdown:

Constant feelings of anxiety

Any errors in reasoning or memory

Inability to concentrate

Irritability

Insomnia

Patients commonly upset themselves over their behavioral difficulties as well. Thus, the drug addict may suffer equally from guilt addiction, the overeater typically overindulges in self-blame, and the man with erectile difficulties not only "can't get it up" but can't get it off his mind!

Primary focus on this secondary problem may be particularly important when dealing with seriously disturbed or psychotic patients. Psychotherapy of any sort may be difficult or even ineffective in ameliorating primary symptoms such as thought disorders or endogenous depressions which may well be a function of biochemical imbalances (Davison and Neale, 1990). Often, however, there is a neurotic overlay or secondary symptom, for example, depression about manic–depressive episodes. A useful therapeutic goal may be to help patients learn to accept themselves with their handicaps instead of depressing themselves about such handicaps. The same principle is true, of course, with less seriously disturbed patients. Consider again Sam, the compulsive overeater. Whenever he breaks his diet and overeats, he immediately begins to cognitively castigate himself, which inevitably leads to uncomfortable feelings of guilt or shame. Once he is feeling bad enough, he is liable to "do something nice for himself" in an attempt to feel better, and that "something nice" may very well be another hot fudge sundae. Breaking the second-level shame

Secondary problems are particularly troublesome in clients who have begun to understand their RET. The more sophisticated they become, the more upset they get with themselves for over-reacting. The particular emotional problem these clients feel is *shame*.

It may seem like a paradox, but half the goal of therapy is to change disturbed negative feelings and the other half is to accept oneself with these negative feelings—and to do both at the same time!

and guilt cycle may be a prerequisite to helping Sam stay on task to achieve his long-range goal of weight loss.

The RET therapist will usually try to determine whether the client has a secondary emotional problem about the primary one by *asking directly*. For example, if the primary problem is anxiety, the therapist may ask, "How do you feel about being so anxious?" It is also important to determine if there are secondary emotional problems about *appropriate* negative emotions, such as sadness. If the secondary emotional problem interferes significantly with the client's ability to deal with the primary problem or if you can show the client why it makes more sense to deal with this second layer first, then that will be the initial contract.

Once a second-level disturbance has been identified as A, RET therapy proceeds in the usual fashion: C is clarified, irrational beliefs are identified, and the client is assisted in disputing them.

ON CHANGING A

Broadly speaking, activating events fall into two main classes: those that *can* be changed and those that *cannot*. To paraphrase the motto used in Alcoholics Anonymous, a job of therapy is to help the patient try to change those events that can be changed, to gracefully tolerate those that cannot, and to try to discriminate between the two.

Generally, it is not profitable to try to change the activating event first. Merely changing A may make the patient feel better, but perhaps for the wrong reasons. In other words, doing better is always nice, but a more useful accomplishment may be learning not to be self-downing or self-rating even when one is not doing well. As Ellis is fond of pointing out, "life" is really spelled H-A-S-S-L-E, and whether we like it or not, new and unpleasant activating events will always appear on our horizons.

In addition, RET therapists work under the basic assumption that when activating events can be changed, doing so will require patients to use their own problem-solving skills. They will be in the best position to solve problems when freed from debilitating emotional states by acknowledging and then challenging their core irrational philosophies. To understand how these preliminary steps can be accomplished, we turn in the next chapters to emotions and cognitions.

7 The C

Why do patients come to therapy? Usually because they are feeling bad: they are in emotional distress. The therapist will not want to lose sight of this focus. Patients usually don't just come in to talk or to rid themselves of irrationalities. It is C, the affective Consequence, that typically brings them to the therapist's door.

Many RET therapists have found that clients can clearly explain their emotions about certain Activating events. In fact, it is not unusual for clients to begin sessions by discussing their feelings. Thus, the client may reply to the question, "What problem would you like to discuss?" by saying, "I feel very depressed lately." If the client does not volunteer the emotion, the advised strategy, in accordance with RET's emphasis on active-directive intervention, is to ask. After the client has described the activating event, the therapist typically asks, "Well, how do you feel about that?"

More experienced therapists may be able to use a clinical hunch about the patient's emotional state and phrase the question in another way such as, "Are you feeling anxious about that?" This technique may also serve as a strong rapport builder, for clients may conclude that the therapist truly understands their problem. We advise against telling your clients how they feel, however. Phrase your comment as a question and be prepared to change your mind when you have sufficient data that your hunch is wrong.

The more experienced therapist will also learn to recognize that certain emotional states are frequently associated with specific clinical problems. For example, avoiding certain situations usually indicates anxiety, assaultive or verbally abusive behavior generally points to anger, lethargy

When his clients experience difficulty in identifying a specific emotion, Albert Ellis encourages them to "take a wild guess," a method that surprisingly yields quite useful information about C.

or inactivity probably means depression, self-injurious or self-deprecatory behaviors indicate guilt, and a recent loss is likely to lead to grief.

In other words, there are three ways that the experienced therapist can infer the presence of certain emotional states: (1) by using cues from the client's behavior, (2) by understanding typical emotional consequences to common life situations, and (3) by deduction from rational-emotive theory, so that from knowing a client's belief system one can infer a specific emotion.

A Key Concept: Disturbed versus Undisturbed Emotions

A warning to new therapists: not all emotions are inappropriate or are targets for change. RET theory does not say that emotions are undesirable; in fact, they are part of the spice of life. The distinction the RET therapist makes is between helpful and harmful emotions. A harmful emotion impedes clients' ability to reach their goals, to enjoy themselves, and may result in self-defeating behavior. Also, some emotions are physiologically harmful—such as anxiety, which can lead to psychosomatic disorders (e.g., colitis, duodenal ulcers, and hypertension), or intense and damning anger, which at least knots up the stomach. Thus, while it is quite appropriate for a client to feel sad—even very sad—about a loss (for example, when a parent dies, a spouse leaves, or a child becomes ill), when the sadness is extremely prolonged or very debilitating, it then becomes a potential target for therapeutic intervention. At some point, we would say that it is more than a negative emotion, that is, a *disturbed* negative emotion.

It is very difficult to discriminate between a negative but adaptive emotion and a disturbed emotion, but here are some suggestions to differentiate them, qualitatively and quantitatively:

> *Phenomenologically,* an adaptive emotion may not be sensed internally by the person as "suffering," although it may be quite intense and negative.

Physiologically, a disturbed affective response may be much stronger, accompanied by many signs of autonomic nervous system hyper-reactivity.

Behaviorally, the disturbed emotion may lead to self-destructive behaviors or block problem-solving behaviors so that the person remains "stuck."

Cognitively, disturbed emotions may be distinguished by the overvalued, irrational thoughts that go along with them.

As a social stimulus, the disturbed emotion has a higher probability of eliciting punishing or avoidance behaviors in others, rather than empathy or supportive nurturance.

The English language is notoriously impoverished in affective language. In addition, most of us are raised in homes in which emotions are not discussed. At the dinner table, mom or dad may ask what we did during the day, but it's the rare family in which they follow up by asking how we *felt* about what we did. Combined with our culture's virtual prohibition on affective display, particularly for men, it is small wonder that many Americans would be described as *alexythymic.* Alexythymia is a psychiatric term that derives from the prefix "a," meaning "without"; "lex," a stem from which we get the word "lexicon," indicating "language"; and the suffix, "thymia," meaning "mood." Thus, the term implies being without a language to describe mood.

Without a lexicon in a topic, it is difficult if not impossible to express ourselves, and certainly we have trouble indicating subtle shadings of meaning. Semanticists have taught us that the absence of a rich vocabulary also tells us about how the culture values the topic (for example, the storm of words Eskimos have to describe variations in snow, or the mounds of descriptors available to Arabs for varieties of sand). The science of General Semantics, has taught us that it is difficult if not impossible to make discriminations when we do not have words to describe what we are differentiating.

Even in our clinical arena, language is confusing. Consider the word "depression." We know what it means, don't we? Or do we?

William Styron, the Pulitzer prize-winning author, states: "I want to register a complaint about the word *depression.* [It is] . . . a term with such a bland tonality that it lacks any magisterial presence, used indifferently to describe an economic decline or a rut in the ground, a true wimp of a word for such a major illness" (Styron, 1990). Similarly, can we distinguish between a depressed mood, grieving, a depressive syndrome, and depressive illness?

> Sadness is a mood state, a normal reaction to negative life events, which usually remits without undue laboring. . . . Grieving [is] a more prolonged and intense mood typically precipitated by a major loss . . . [in which] the focus of the patient is on the loss rather than on the self and self-blame. . . . More than a blue mood, the syndrome of depression is a cluster of symptoms which may include an overreaction to a negative Activating Event, and other cognitive, emotive, behavioral, and physical symptoms. . . . [and then there is] depression, an illness. Actually, this title would more accurately be, "depressions: a spectrum of illnesses" [which seem to be largely heritable and almost always recurrent] (Walen and Rader, 1991, pp. 232–33.)

Clearly, we had better teach a vocabulary and a set of discriminating words to our clients so that we can be sure that we are understanding each other!

While the discrimination between disturbed and nondisturbed emotions is, in our view, one of the most helpful aspects of RET theory, it is also one of RET's most problematic aspects because of the difficulty in establishing an operational definition of these terms. Even so, the distinction between disturbed and nondisturbed C's can serve to give a clear focus to one of the main goals in therapy: transforming suffering into appropriate, adaptive, albeit negative emotions. In addition, the therapist can acknowledge the severity of a negative activating event, communicate empathy for the problem the client faces, and address the reality of dealing with difficult, prolonged A's without colluding with the client's "awfulizing."

We suggest that you adopt the typology and vocabulary of common emotional expressions presented in Table 7.1 in order that you and your clients may better discriminate between appropriate, helpful, adaptive, undisturbed emotions, and inappropriate, harmful, maladaptive, and dis-

Table 7.1. A vocabulary of appropriate and disturbed emotions

Appropriate	Disturbed
Concern	Anxiety
Sadness	Depression
Annoyance	Clinical anger
Remorse	Guilt
Regret	Shame
Disappointment	Hurt

turbed ones. The terms in Table 7.1 are not carved in stone, but provide a start toward facilitating clearer communication.

Trouble-shooting Problems with C

A common problem in the work of new therapists is the failure to accurately identify C. Sometimes this problem arises because therapists simply do not take the time to clearly label C or because therapists assume that they and/or the client intuitively understand what C is. Such an assumption is often wrong, of course. More often, problems in identifying C come not from the therapist's negligence but because emotions are a difficult and confusing problem for the patient. The following sections may help the therapist to trouble-shoot some of the reasons for the patient's difficulty with C and offer some ideas to break the emotional blockade.

GUILT ABOUT C

Trouble in identifying C may stem from guilt; patients may be unwilling to label their affect if they are experiencing a negative emotion for which

---

A general rule of thumb to remember is not to ask your client questions that reinforce the "A causes C" confusion. As supervisors, we frequently hear new RET therapists phrase questions such as, "How does *it* make you feel?" Try writing in the space below an alternative question that does not imply that A causes C:

they denigrate themselves (cf., "C becoming an A," p. 85). For example, in family therapy, children may be unwilling to acknowledge their anger in front of their parents. A somewhat more subtle example was seen in the case of the wife of a devoted rabbinical scholar. She often felt compelled to interrupt his studies to remind him of his responsibilities to his parishioners, such as visiting the sick or bereaved. He would do as she suggested and received the thanks and approval of his flock; while she, being quiet and shy, was regarded as aloof and, of course, received no credit for her contributions. She stated her problem as one of wanting more support, understanding, and appreciation, yet she could not define a specific C other than to say that she felt she was overlooked and taken for granted. Again, the underlying C was anger, but as the wife of a cleric, she felt she was not entitled to such an emotion.

What might the therapist do in such cases to encourage the client to face the emotion? One of the following suggestions might be useful:

> *Try a Gestalt or psychodrama exercise,* such as the empty chair technique. For example, the rabbi's wife might be asked to imagine her husband or one of the ungrateful parishioners sitting in an empty chair. She might then be engaged in a dialogue in which she plays one or both parts, perhaps moving between the two chairs as she exchanges roles. Loosening the usual stimulus constraints in this way may increase the likelihood that she will acknowledge her anger.

A very powerful way to tap into the emotions is through the use of visual imagery. Ask the patient if she would be willing to close her eyes. Tell her you will be giving her some very open-ended instructions and that you do *not* want her to report her thoughts or give you a lot of words, but rather to be very still and wait until a picture or image comes to her mind. Very mild direction for this image might be, "Let an image of you and your family come to mind" or "you in the best love relationship you've had" or "you in a very early part of your life."

Often, you will find that this is an extraordinarily evocative and emotive procedure, particularly when you probe the image by inquiring what is going on, what feelings are being expressed in the image, and what thoughts the characters in the image might be having.

Try modeling. The therapist might say, for example, "Jim, if I were in your situation, I think I would be annoyed or even downright angry!"

Try using humor. By deliberate exaggeration, gently poking fun at the situation, or humorous analogy, the therapist may set the climate for a less threatening acknowledgment of anger. Examples: "I guess you really are a saint; most people would be boiling mad!" or "It's great how you let them walk all over you; everybody loves that!"

SHAME ABOUT C

Patients may not be in touch with their emotions because of a tendency to intellectualize their predicaments. Such individuals will avoid labeling their feelings and instead describe their thoughts. They may even deny that they experience emotions at all. Underlying this affectional anesthesia may be the belief that the expression of emotion is weak, and avoidance prevents the patient from feeling foolish.

The key concept that the therapist will want to communicate in this case is that all emotion is justified in the sense that it exists. Emotion need not be validated as acceptable by pinning it to an external event, since emotions are internal and come from what a person is saying to himself or herself about the outside events.

A useful goal for such clients may be to appreciate the extent to which all people react emotionally. As a homework assignment, the therapist may request patients to write down all the different "I feel _____" or "I'm in a _____ mood" statements that they hear others make in the course of a week. They can also monitor their own statements of this sort. In addition, the therapist could make use of the three techniques described above.

LITTLE OR NO AFFECT IN THE SESSION

The therapist may observe the lack of affect in the session. Assuming that the absence of affect is not a psychotic symptom, the therapist may want to check out two possibilities for this occurrence.

1. Clients may believe that they are "supposed to be serious" in therapy, that it is a solemn occasion requiring hard work and a no-nonsense attitude. The therapist will want to disabuse clients of such notions by direct suggestion, modeling, and use of creative strategies to elicit more affect (e.g., encouraging disagreement with the therapist, or

asking patients to pantomime their problems or express them in song or poetry).

2. The therapist's behavior may be fostering little affect. For example, the therapist may be making long-winded speeches, asking closed-ended questions, moving too fast and confusing the client, and so forth. Listen to your tapes with such a client and evaluate your own remarks that precede instances of minimal affect. Try to encourage verbal expression by asking simple, open-ended questions (e.g., "And then what?").

FLAT AND INAPPROPRIATE AFFECT

The patient may describe experiencing flat affect—an emotionally anesthetized reaction ("feeling dead" is a common expression)—or show inappropriate affect. Disturbances of either type often reflect a psychotic process, or Major Depression, and RET alone may not be appropriate. You can help more by making referral for medication (Ellis and Abrahms, 1978).

PAINFUL EMOTION

Patients may not be aware of their feelings because they fear the emotion; the problem may thus be one of avoidance of affective states. For example, being depressed is, after all, an uncomfortable or even a painful experience. The patient may avoid discussing life situations that are evocative of this emotion.

The problem in this case seems to be one of LFT, low frustration tolerance, in which patients convince themselves that the emotional turmoil is more than they can stand. The therapist can encourage and support such clients—for example, by pointing out that it is normal to have bad feelings and that it would be helpful to discuss the painful emotions. As has been found useful in the research on helping patients through delayed grieving or mourning states, the therapist can figuratively hold the patient's hand through more extended therapy sessions in which desensitization to the discomfort is allowed.

Another aspect of painful emotions is the shame patients fear if others see them having feelings. The job of the RET therapist is to help clients accept themselves and their own emotions, for shame may prevent them from confronting the emotion and doing an A-B-C analysis of it. For example:

C: (crying)

T: You're obviously in distress about something, Jean. What's going through your head right now?

C: I'm so scared that I'll cry at work. I might lose control of myself in front of the other people in my office.

T: Well, what would be so terrible about that?

C: I couldn't stand it!

T: Well, what's the worst thing you could imagine happening? If you lost control, would you run amok through the halls? Would you not be able to function at all?

C: (smiling) No-o-o. I guess I just wouldn't want them to think I was upset.

T: And if they did—would that be so bad?

C: Ummmm. No, you're right. It wouldn't.

T: OK, so can we give you permission to be quite upset while you're still upset?

CONFUSION OF B AND C

People in our culture frequently confuse thoughts and feelings. Sometimes you may ask a client to describe a feeling and he or she will respond with a belief. For example, the client may say, "When she said that, I felt dumb." At other times, you may ask a client to identify a belief and get a feeling for a response. You may ask, "What were you thinking then?" and the client may respond, "Oh, I was thinking I was anxious."

A difficulty that new therapists and patients often share is discriminating B's from C's, and this problem may relate in part to the imprecision in our language. The word "feeling," for example, may have many different meanings in everyday speech:

> *Physical sensation*—"I feel cold."
>
> *Opinion*—"I feel that taxes should be lowered."
>
> *Emotional experience*—"I feel happy."
>
> *Evaluation*—"I feel that it's terrible."

The therapist can carefully listen for clients' meaning of "feel" and encourage them to use the term to describe emotional consequences rather than opinions and evaluations. This distinction will help clients detect the difference between their beliefs and emotional C's, which will be of greater value to them when they attempt to dispute their irrational beliefs. Thus, when patients mislabel B as a feeling, it is often useful to stop and correct them. For example, if the therapist asks Tom, "How were you feeling?" and the patient says, "I felt dumb," the therapist will recognize that Tom (1) has a strong feeling of depression or guilt, and (2) is making a self-deprecatory statement. After acknowledging these two issues, the therapist would attempt to point out to the client that "dumb" is not an emotion but really reflects a thought: "I think I am dumb." In fact, Tom's statement "I felt dumb" is usually shorthand for "I believe that I'm dumb and I feel depressed about that." It is important to make this distinction because the client may wrongly attempt to dispute his feeling of "dumb" or to justify his belief that he is dumb because of this so-called feeling. Feelings are not open to dispute; they are phenomenological experiences for which only the individual has data. You cannot argue with such subjective states, whereas thoughts, beliefs, and opinions are open to challenge. Thus, in the example above, the therapist would point out to Tom that he does not feel dumb; he feels depressed because he believes that he is dumb and that he must not be. The stage is now set for working on this irrational belief.

DESCRIPTIVE DEFICITS

When asked how she is feeling, Myra may state, or her behavior may imply, that she is confused. The confusion may result from the fact that she is experiencing a mixture of emotions or simply that she lacks an adequate emotional vocabulary. In general, the more the therapist can help her simplify and label her emotional problem, the more easily she will be able to grapple with it. Again, if Larry can only describe himself as feeling "down," the therapist may inquire what he understands by the word "depression." In other words, the therapist may want to take the opportunity to expand the client's vocabulary. A side benefit of this procedure will be to increase the patient's ability to profit from bibliotherapy, since most books are written using terms such as depression, "anxiety," and so on.

The therapist may help patients label their emotions by instruction and modeling. Initially, the difference between positive and negative emotions may be suggested (e.g., "Did you feel good or bad?"), after which more descriptive terms may be suggested and discussed. Some of the following exercises may be useful either in session or as homework assignments:

1. Here are the names of some emotions or feelings:

happy	sad
angry	disappointed
proud	hurt
embarrassed	curious
scared	frustrated
nervous	guilty
relaxed	anxious

   (a) Pronounce each word to yourself; say it out loud.
   (b) Do you know what each word means?
   (c) Pantomime (act without words) each of the words that you know. (Different people express the same feeling in different ways, so there is no right way to do it!)
   (d) Are there any other feelings you can think of? If so, write them down.

2. Orally or in writing, complete the sentence, "I feel _____" in as many ways as you can.

3. Start a diary of "I feel" or "I felt" statements. At first, just write the statements. Later, begin to add "When such and such happened, I felt _____." For example, "I felt anxious when I started writing this diary."

DICHOTOMOUS THINKING

Many patients tend to categorize emotional states dichotomously; for example, they believe that the only way they can respond is very negatively or as if nothing happened. In fact, however, emotions occur on a contin-

---

Your client may report feeling "frustrated" at C. Some RET therapists prefer to regard frustration as an activating event rather than a feeling (e.g., Trexler, 1976). You might say to your client, "'Frustration' often means a blockade—something that blocks or frustrates us from getting what we want. When you were frustrated by your secretary yesterday, Fred, what emotion did you feel in your gut?"

uum of intensity, and it is important to assure yourself that the client understands there is a range of emotions to feel and a range of behaviors to express them. For example, if John has trouble in his marriage and has only been able to feel *rage* and to express it by beating his wife, he may not know the concept of *annoyance* or have the skills to express it. Imagery experiences, modeling, and direct training may be needed to help him extend his conceptual schema of emotions in order to discriminate between feeling annoyed and feeling angry.

If the patient can envision and label various levels of emotion, he or she may also be able to envision ways (cognitions) to arrive at a more desirable or adaptive feeling state. The therapist might, for example, present a group of emotional labels to the client and help him or her to classify the words as *mild, moderate,* or *strong* emotions. It can then be pointed out that rational or helpful thinking usually leads to mild/moderate feelings or to strong feelings (such as intense regret or sorrow) which are appropriate, and irrational or hurtful thinking leads to strong and debilitating emotions.

Dichotomous thinking about emotions can also occur on dimensions other than intensity. John may believe, for example, that once he learns how to get over his anger at his wife, he must never be angry again. A useful distinction here would be between appropriate irritation and annoyance versus inappropriate anger, the difference being based on (1) his demand that his wife *must* not act irritatingly and annoyingly, (2) the length of time he was angry, (3) the effects of the anger on himself, and (4) the effects of his displays of anger on others in his life. In other words, it would be irrational for the patient to believe that he should *never* be angry, depressed, anxious, and so on. These are normal and overlearned reactions. Strong inappropriate emotions are problematic mainly when they persist for prolonged periods and thereby interrupt goal-directed behaviors.

MISLABELING EMOTIONS

Patients often mislabel their emotional states, so that it is a good rule of thumb to clarify the affective referent. The therapist would be wise to ask routinely for some explanation or expansion of the patient's emotional label (e.g., "What do you mean by guilty/anxious/bothered/etc.?") and, if the client seems to be in error, point it out (e.g., "Sam, it sounds more like you're angry than anxious"). Emotions that clients frequently seem to mislabel are guilt or anger, which are confused with anxiety.

Some clients, more often men, are likely to somatize their feelings rather than clearly label the affect. When asked how they are feeling, such clients might describe having "tension in my neck," thus describing the physiological sensation rather than the emotion.

UNCLEAR LABELING OF EMOTIONS

Clients may use a label which, although clear to them, may be unclear to the therapist. For example, May says, "I was so indignant!" Do you understand precisely what she means? Is this level of affect mild, moderate, or intense? Does it reflect a rational or irrational belief? The answers to these questions are best found by asking her clarifying questions: "What do you mean when you say 'indignant'?" or "That sounds like you're angry; on a ten-point scale, how angry are you?"

Common examples of unclear labels include:

I feel bad.
I feel upset.
I feel distressed.
I feel stressed out.
I feel uptight.

The therapist can help with clarification by asking directly, "Martha, when you say you feel upset, do you mean you feel angry?" or by asking a multiple-choice question, "Jan, by 'stressed out', do you mean you feel anxious? or sad? or angry? or guilty?" Writing this simple affective menu on a chalkboard or even an index card can help the client clarify his or her current mood and provide a teaching model for future communication.

Sometimes clients will assert that they can't exactly find the word that describes their emotion, and you may help by suggesting that they show you how they feel by using their facial movements or body postures, and modeling yourself just a bit to break the ice. This strategy of using exaggerated kinesthetic facial and body cues may give the therapist a clue as to what the emotion might be and help the client by evoking a keener awareness of the affective state.

LACK OF APPARENT DISTRESS

Occasionally, one will interview a client who rattles off a list of problems but is not obviously in distress about anything. The therapist may want to consider the following possible explanations for this behavior. Perhaps the patient (1) is truly not in distress, (2) has come to therapy for companionship rather than help, (3) is worried about not being "normal" and has come to therapy to find out and get reassurance, or (4) is engaging in avoidance maneuvers which prevent the appearance of negative affect. If despite the therapist's patience for allowing emergence of affect, no emotional distress is apparent, confrontation might be recommended. One or more of the above explanations may be discussed with the client so that appropriate goals for action may be set.

Avoidance maneuvers pose perhaps the trickiest problem, for if patients' behaviors effectively prevent them from experiencing negative affect, both they and the therapist will be in the dark about C. If an emotional consequence is not evident but patients describe troublesome behaviors, it is often helpful to apply a learning theory model to the behavior problems. Quite simply, behavior can be viewed as being maintained either by its pleasurable results or by the avoidance of negative stimuli, and often the negative stimuli are the patients' own hidden emotions. Sometimes direct confrontation may break the blockade, as in the following instance. The client was avoiding taking a major exam, yet claimed he felt no anxiety over it.

T: Jerry, if that were so, if you had no anxiety at all, why would you not take the test?

C: But I don't experience any anxiety now.

T: Right, because as long as you stay away from that test, you avoid experiencing much anxiety. Do you see that something is blocking you from getting too close, and that something is your anxiety? Now what do you think would happen if you took the test and *failed?*

C: Wow! That's it. That's so simple, but that must be what I'm worried about. . . .

Often, a more extensive use of projective fantasy is called for in order to discover what the client fears. One client, for example, reported that she was concerned about the fact that she was dating only married men; she denied any particular negative emotion and stated that she was simply more attracted to married men. The therapist guided her through a fantasy in which she imagined herself out on a date with an attractive man who suddenly announced that he was single and, in fact, found her to be the only desirable woman he'd ever met. In another case, an obese client fantasized being very slim and out on a date with an attractive man. In both instances, the imagery exercise allowed the clients to get in touch with a great deal of interpersonal anxiety which their avoidance behaviors (dating married men or being overweight) had successfully blocked. The anxiety then became the focus of therapy.

A similar problem was presented by a male client who experienced no specific emotional problems except exhaustion. He complained of feeling tired almost all of the time, and no matter how much sleep he got, he never felt truly rested. Medical evaluation revealed no physiological basis for his fatigue. Extensive questioning revealed that he had a demanding yet fulfilling job, enjoyed a full social life, and was active in athletic events. In all respects, he appeared to be "living the good life." On closer questioning, however, the client reported that he did not always enjoy all of his activities and occasionally did not want to do them. Thus, since the intrinsic pleasure of the activity was not always maintaining his behavior, we assumed that some of his busy schedule was actually avoidance behavior. The client was asked to fantasize a typical day in his life, omitting one of his activities, such as athletics. He continued in imagery, reducing his work activity and then diminishing his social life. After each imagery scene, the client reported, much to his own surprise, feelings of guilt. Further analysis revealed an irrational notion of self-worth based on accomplishing all that he thought he should do; thus, the underlying emotion of guilt was successfully avoided by maintaining an extremely active life.

A similar problem is often encountered with clients who report an inability to control addictive behaviors such as drug abuse, smoking, drinking, and overeating. They may not acknowledge any emotional problems that increase the frequency of their addictive behaviors, although they do sense guilt over having done them. With such clients, the therapist may ask them to imagine that they are sitting in front of the food or cigarettes and are denying themselves these pleasures. Clients usually report a very uncomfortable feeling akin to intense agitation, heightened arousal, muscle tension, or jitteriness. This emotional consequence, a result of their irrational belief that they *need* to have what they desire, may have remained out of their awareness since they were so successful at avoiding the unpleasant feeling by quickly devouring what they desired. Such an imagery exercise may help clients get in touch with their C's.

EMOTION IN THE SESSION

Whether or not patients are able to identify emotional reactions in relation to their life events, the therapist will want to attend to affective cues within the therapy session. Body position, tensed muscles, clenched teeth, breathing changes, perspiration, giggling, and so forth may be scanned so that emotional factors may be dealt with.

When you see these signs of affect, you may begin to do an A-B-C analysis. Don't make the mistake of avoiding working with emotions expressed in the session. Therapy does not always have to deal with problems of past or recent history. For example:

T: Sally, I notice that tears are starting to well up and you look as if you're ready to cry.
C: Oh, you're right! (sobs)
T: Sally, you obviously are feeling really upset right now. I wonder if you could tell me what emotion you're feeling.
C: Well, it's so hard. My whole life is ruined. I have nothing to live for.
T: I understand. It seems that you're feeling real depressed about that.
C: Yes.
T: Well, why don't we talk about that now rather than the other problems you brought up—for as long as you're believing that, you're going to feel depressed and cry.

Deciding to Change the C

Once clients have acknowledged and correctly identified the distressing emotion, they have a decision to make: Do they want to keep or change this emotion? For example, they have the right to keep or give up their anger, and the pros and cons of their choice may be an interesting topic for discussion. Anger, after all, has its advantages, since acting aggressively often moves people to give you what you want. On the other hand, intense rage may be socially detrimental and physiologically destructive to the individual.

Consider the example of anger presented by a young mother. In many ways her anger worked for her; for instance, when she yelled at her son about his messy room, he quickly tidied up. The display of anger also appeared to be intrinsically reinforcing; after she had a temper tantrum, she felt a pleasant state of fatigue and relaxation akin to the aftereffects of exercise. Quite simply, it felt good when she stopped. In addition, the woman was providing her own cognitive reinforcement for her abreactive display (e.g., "I did the right thing by getting angry!"). Thus, interpersonal, kinesthetic, and cognitive factors were operating to help maintain her angry feelings and behavior. To help overcome these factors, the

One strategy used by RET and CBT therapists to increase the client's motivation to change is the two-column format (e.g., Burns, 1980). The client is assisted in developing a list of advantages and disadvantages in changing a particular emotion. Here, for example, is one client's (partial) list of pros and cons in giving up her chronic anger at her husband:

Advantages of eliminating anger	*Disadvantages of losing anger*
I'd have more energy.	I'll become a doormat.
Long-term health consequences would be improved.	It works. I'd be giving up a useful tool.
It would be better for the kids.	I might be manipulated.
I'd be less jealous of other couples.	I don't have any other way of getting my needs met.
I'd feel proud of myself.	I won't be standing up for my principles.
I'd be more comfortable in my own home.	

Can you see some of the work that this client has to do before she can begin reducing her anger?

therapist could suggest that (1) the woman consider the long-range consequences of her behavior; certainly her displays of anger did not endear her to her son; (2) she was providing a poor model for her son; (3) there were more helpful ways of achieving a release of tension, such as relaxation exercises; (4) there were more effective ways of controlling her son's behavior, and (5) her cognitive statements were misplaced and stemmed from an exaggerated and unflattering sense of righteousness.

A more subtle source of gain may also sometimes be operating, in which a debilitating emotion is maintained in order to avoid a more distressing one. Consider, for example, the case of a mother who lost custody of her children to the father, an event that precipitated intense and prolonged depression, which the patient seemed unwilling to surrender. What would it mean to this woman to give up grieving? Apparently she believed that it would prove her to be an uncaring and uncommitted mother, a concept that induced an even more intense feeling of guilt. Once this irrational belief was successfully disputed, however, the patient was able to give herself permission to work at relieving her depression.

Patients may, at least on some days, decide to stay upset rather than do the hard RET work of disputing. In essence, they may be saying either "That's the way I am, and I can't change" or "It's more rewarding [or easier] for me to be upset." Once identified, either or these hypotheses may be challenged, perhaps by simply requesting that the patients do an experiment that will allow them to test their hunch: "Is it in fact true that you cannot change or that it's easier to be upset?"

The point to keep in mind is that there may be many reasons why the patient is reluctant to change C, some of which the therapist may be able to challenge. If the client does not want to change C, however, rational-emotive therapy usually cannot proceed.

Teaching Transcript

In the following therapy transcript, additional therapeutic problems are addressed. The therapist is confronted with a client who describes experiencing a number of unpleasant emotions, and the therapeutic task is to label them, rate their severity, and rank-order them for investigation.

Transcript Segment

T: Your wife, Mary, called and said you were feeling particularly depressed and suicidal, and she was very concerned about you. How are you feeling today?

C: I have very confused moments. The reason I originally felt suicidal—I don't even know how to express the feeling that I had, because I know if I really wanted to commit suicide I would have accomplished it.

Note that the client really hasn't answered the therapist's question.

T: You know how to do it?

C: It was very simple. I was just taking the privilege of indulging myself in self-pity obviously, by taking eight pills instead of twenty-five.

T: So you don't seriously think you were trying . . .

C: Well, I felt this way, if it happened, if the eight pills had done the job that would have been OK, and if they didn't, fine.

T: But you weren't going to insure that they did by taking twenty-five or thirty?

C: Exactly. That's how I felt.

T: Have you had any previous suicide attempts?

The therapist is assessing suicidal thoughts and behaviors before doing anything else.

C: No.

T: Have you had any previous plans to commit suicide?

C: Well, after my first divorce I was pretty uptight and I thought about it. Twice, as a matter of fact.

T: Did you have a plan to commit suicide those times?

C: No, no plan.

T: You never said, "I'm going to do it by slicing my throat, or jumping off a bridge, or leaping out of a cable car?"

C: No. It was just like, frankly, I would be driving my car, the self-pity would come on, and I'd say, "I'm going to crash into the wall." I'd head toward the wall and then pull away.

T: So you're not having that many suicidal thoughts today?

C: No.

T: How about your feelings? How are you feeling today?

Here the therapist returns to the client's feelings after making reasonably sure that suicide was not imminent.

C: Extremely anxious.

T: Anxious?

C: Yes.

T: Usually, most people who attempt suicide are depressed, but you're anxious?

Notice that the therapist is working from a conceptual schema and checking the patient's response against it.

C: Yeah, I'm pretty anxious.

T: How anxious do you feel?

C: Well, when I become nervous my back goes out.

T: You get muscle pains?

C: That's why I'm wearing my girdle now. It went out Sunday night, and I didn't do anything physical. I just bent over and it went. So I know that's an indication that something's not right.

T: Have you been to a physician about your back problems?

C: Yes. I slipped a disc about fifteen years ago. It's been a chronic thing. Many times I think it's due to muscular strain because I do work physically. And sometimes this has nothing to do with any . . .

T: Well, it could be just muscular tension. So, you do tend to get muscular tension and get real tight?

C: Well, I wasn't aware of it, but it's really become more of a chronic situation. My children live in Canada and that's when it really started to become chronic, when they moved to Canada. Mary brought it to my attention.

T: How long ago was that?

C: Four years ago.

T: So for the last four years your anxiety had been getting worse?

C: Only when I know they're coming in.

T: When they're coming you get more anxious. How frequently does that happen?

The therapist is acknowledging and accepting the client's feelings while gathering additional information about the client's life situation.

C: Well, they're supposed to come in twice a year. This year it's been only once and they'll be coming again in three weeks. It's starting to build—the anxiety's started.

T: So, as your children come closer you get anxious, or frightened, as if there's something you won't be able to cope with, and you feel immobilized? Or do you mean that as the kids get closer, you get concerned about it, become committed to action, and still feel in control? Or do you mean that you're just excited about it?

C: No, I'm really anxious, panicky.

The therapist has just modeled the key differential issue for this client: the discrimination between disturbed emotion (anxiety) and a nondisturbed version of it (concern or excitement).

T: Now, can I ask you something else? What is it about your children coming that frightens you?

C: Well, let me say, anytime anybody mentions my children to me I sort of swell up. (client gets tears in his eyes)

Note that the therapist will deal with this in-session emotion.

T: So, that sounds like you're feeling sad. So there is a little sadness along with your anxiety.

C: Maybe it's because what I do is I become afraid and I think about what I'm going to feel when I see them—also when they leave.

T: So, in other words, what you're doing right now is experiencing or imagining your feelings when they come off the plane or when they go on the plane and you feel sadness then—and you're feeling anxious about the sadness?

The therapist hypothesizes that a C has become an A, and he asks for feedback about this hypothesis.

C: Right.

T: Which one of the problems do you think is more important, then, the anxiety or the sadness?

C: That's a very interesting question.

T: Both emotions are there.

C: What I'm trying to find out myself is if it's a totally self-pity type of feeling I have. I don't know. I've been trying to analyze that for four years.

T: Let me ask you this: Do you have any anxiety about other issues besides your children?

C: Yes. What brought about the suicide—let's call it that for the moment . . .

T: The attempt.

C: . . . may have been due to many other things. That is, like anything I have to do I have to work very hard at; nothing comes easily for me.

T: Even killing yourself! You can't even do that easily, right?

Note the therapist's attempt at humor and how it is received by the client.

C: I could have if I really wanted to. That was maybe part of many of my problems. But I was married eighteen years the first time. And for literally seventeen of the eighteen years, I felt I had a very happy marriage. I was very content and we, my ex-wife and I, became very friendly with another couple and before I knew it, my best friend and my wife took off. I found out the hard way—detective, the whole thing. And I felt after I had overcome the initial shock that I would never trust another woman again. I was very secure and all of a sudden not only did I lose my wife, I lost a friend, I lost my children—it was a three-way disaster.

T: Can we stop?

C: Yes.

T: When you think about your children and you feel the sadness when they visit, does it also remind you of the sadness you felt at that particular time?

C: No.

T: Does it remind you of how vulnerable you are?

The therapist is working from a hypothesis that the client, in the face of serious problems, has an irrational belief that he cannot cope.

C: Oh yeah, because in a way I blame myself for the situation of losing my children. I'm not happy about losing my ex-wife because I loved Carol very much. There's no priority. It's just that I lost my children and there are no feelings going back to that point.

T: You agree with me that when you think about your children coming, you remember the vulnerability you had. Now is it vulnerability toward the children or the vulnerability of being deserted by your wife—that kind of feeling?

The therapist has just heard the word "blame" in the client's remark but is holding that concept for a later intervention.

C: No. Just the sadness that it's just a temporary thing I have with my kids and I feel myself becoming distant on both sides. Their distance and my distance. It's such a brief period that we see each other.

T: So what you're sad about is that you don't see your children a lot.

C: Right.

T: Let me stop and redefine your words. You said that you feel sad. I agree that you do, but are you feeling *just* sad? Or are you feeling sad and *depressed*? It's normal to feel sad about negative events, but you may be feeling a more disturbed emotion that we call depression. Which are you feeling? Just sadness, or sadness and depression?

C: Well, let's bring a little guilt in there . . .

The therapist is not letting the client deflect the conversation. He is finishing the work on sadness about the children and, while he has heard the comment about guilt, he is saving it for a later point in the session.

T: I guess technically, it may be important for us to discriminate—and maybe what you're feeling really isn't just sadness but is really, largely, depression. Because I think any man would feel sad about losing his children the way you did—and sadness now. But they would not be as debilitated as you are. So, the sad feelings you're probably never going to get rid of. You're going to feel sad about not having your children . . . at least I hope so. You're not going to be cold-hearted, and I don't think I could help you to be that way; even if

I could, I don't think I'd want to. But the point is, your problem isn't sadness—it's depression. You're really depressed about this. And I think it's important that maybe we use different words, rather than just sad. Now, what is the guilt factor?

The therapist has discriminated and helped the patient correctly label his emotions. Not only the high intensity, but the guilt and self-denigration and the suicide attempt, are clues that his problem is depression, not merely sadness.

C: In whatever my ex-wife needed—it was mostly the financial area—I overindulged her. Our life-style went far beyond my financial means because I felt it was what she needed. And I work hard, many hours, and I go home and go to sleep. Get up and go to work, go home and go to sleep. That was the vicious cycle. Except the weekend. I used to look forward to the weekend like it was a vacation of two months coming up instead of only a few days—just so I could spend time with our friends and enjoy my life. The guilt comes in where I wasn't smart enough to realize that there's more to life than just working.

T: And because you didn't realize that, what happened?

C: She found the fun part of her world with my friend.

T: Because you weren't there, she went somewhere else, and if you were smart enough to know better, you wouldn't have lost your children?

C: Exactly.

T: You're really stupid, aren't you?

This is an attempt at humor and was said with a grin.

C: No.

T: You're really beating yourself up about it.

C: Well, I'm beating myself up about it because I was almost falling into the same problem in my new marriage again. And I wasn't quite aware of it and I'm very confused about it. Because what I started to say before and I want to get that part out of me, what brought on this attempted suicide was my lack of confidence in living—and also friends. I don't have a true friend, even after this past weekend.

T: You don't trust them, like you don't trust women?

C: Exactly. Except maybe, after this weekend, I've found a new friend. It's about time. But Mary has always made me feel fidelity, honesty, on a conscious level, and that I'm Number 1 and no other man will ever come between us. And I was very comfortable. It took a lot of work for me to believe again. And unfortunately a very ridiculous situation came up. Mary has been very depressed about not being able to find a job. This has been going on for two years now. And last week, I don't know how the conversation came up, Mary said to me, she could even go to bed with a guy if he would get her a job—the right job.

T: It's not his penis she's after, or his mind—just his connections?

C: Yeah. But in the meantime, my mind has really had it. So I told Mary how I felt and that weekend became a disaster. I couldn't cope with the fact that my wife would go to bed with another man at any price.

T: It appears to me, at least in RET terms, there are several activating events, several emotions, going on at the same time. Some of them being depression, some of them anxiety, and some of them guilt. The activating events appear to be seeing your children, missing your children, and having left your children or causing that to happen; and another is a futuristic one that your wife would leave. From what you tell me, it appears that the thing that upsets you the most is something that is right now. That you are afraid your wife will leave. And any slight indication that that might come true really leads to an awful amount of anxiety. And it appears that when you think about your children, possibly you think about your wife having left you suddenly, and if it could happen *then,* well . . .

Even though this was a first session, the client had been introduced to RET through books he had read. Note that the therapist summarizes the complexity of the client's problems and is hypothesizing that the client believes that he caused his former problems and may do so again with his present wife.

8 The B

Beliefs and cognitive phenomena are at the center of RET and other cognitive-behavioral therapies. The scope of the material necessitates dividing the study of B into two chapters. This chapter describes various kinds of beliefs, and Chapter 9 discusses the details of assessing the client's belief system.

There are two kinds of belief systems, which Ellis (1962, 1971, 1973a, 1979b) calls Rational Beliefs (RB's) and Irrational Beliefs (IB's). Both rational and irrational beliefs are *evaluations* of reality, not descriptions or predictions of it. Thus, they are not merely statements such as, "Something might happen," but rather, if something does happen, they express an evaluation of it. For example, a rational statement might be, "How unfortunate!"; an irrational one, "What a catastrophe! How horrible!"

People are able to have both of these types of thoughts at the same time. A task of therapy is to help clients discriminate RB's from IB's, and then to ask them to challenge their IB's and replace them with more rational philosophies. How, then, does one discriminate rational from irrational thoughts?

Attempts to characterize RB's have resulted in the following suggested criteria. Examine the rational statement, "It would be bad if my wife left me," against each criterion.

The B-C connection is epitomized in the following definition: *anxiety equals a crisis of the imagination.*

1. *A rational belief is internally consistent;* it is logical and coherent. Note that a rational belief is not merely a logical belief; logic is necessary but may not be a sufficient ingredient in identifying a rational philosophy.

2. *A rational belief is empirically verifiable;* it can be supported by evidence. Consider our example above: we could prove that unpleasant effects would result from the client's wife leaving him. Presumably he would lose many pleasant things.

3. *A rational belief is not absolutist;* instead, it is conditional or relativistic. A rational belief is usually stated as a desire, hope, want, wish, or preference and thus reflects a desiring rather than a demanding philosophy. Can you see how the example above reflects a preference rather than a demand? The client simply implies, "It would be better if . . ." or "I'd prefer it if . . . [my wife stayed in our marriage.]"

4. *A rational belief results in adaptive emotions.* Thus, RB's can lead to negative feelings that may range from mild to strong but which are not upsetting or dysfunctional to the individual. This is an important distinction, since a common misconception about RET is that rational thinking leads to the absence of emotion. Quite the contrary; it would be quite a stretch of the imagination to assume that a zero level of emotional concern would be helpful or rational. Adaptive emotions serve as motivators to problem solving (e.g., looking at the activating event to see if it can be changed), whereas emotional disturbance usually hinders this skill. Returning to our example, when the client thinks about his wife leaving him, he probably feels sad but not clinically depressed.

5. *A rational belief helps us attain our goals.* Thus, RB's are congruent with satisfaction in living, minimizing intrapsychic conflict as well as conflict with the environment, enabling affiliation and involvement with others, and growing toward a vital absorption in some personally fulfilling endeavor. More simply, perhaps, rational beliefs provide us with the freedom to pursue goals in a less fearful, noncondemning fashion and allow us to take the risks that may be involved in attaining these goals. From our sample rational belief, we conclude that our client's goal is to live as happily as possible, and this cannot be done if he is clinically depressed. In addition, if the strong evaluative thoughts about his wife leaving were to result in a clinical depression, his behavior would perhaps drive his wife, friends, and other potential mates away.

Irrational beliefs, on the other hand, are characterized by different, often opposite, features.

1. *An irrational belief is logically inconsistent.* It may begin with an inaccurate premise and/or lead to inaccurate deductions, and it often represents an overgeneralization. IB's, therefore, tend to be extreme evaluative exaggerations of a situation and are often reflected in evaluative terms such as "awful, "terrible," or "horrible."

2. *An irrational belief is inconsistent with empirical reality.* It does not follow from actual events. A sample irrational belief might be, "I couldn't bear it if my wife left me." Such a statement probably does not accurately reflect the client's ability to cope with his situation.

3. *An irrational belief is absolutist and dogmatic.* As such, it represents an absolutist rather than probabilistic philosophy and is expressed as demands (versus wishes), absolute shoulds (versus preferences), and needs (versus wants). Irrational beliefs are often overlearned, rehearsed since childhood, and are frequently based on narcissistic or grandiose demands placed on the self, others, or the universe. Ellis (1979a, 1979b; Ellis and Harper, 1975) describes these constructs as the three Major Musts:

> *I must* (do well, get approval, etc.)
>
> *You must* (treat me well, love me, etc.)
>
> *The world must* (give me what I want quickly and easily, treat me fairly, etc.)

The derivatives of these thoughts generally take the form of (a) it's awful, (b) I can't bear it, and (c) I'm a louse for behaving lousily.

We occasionally even manage to disturb ourselves with completely contradictory musts, for example, demanding to make a great deal of money while simultaneously demanding to be universally loved. If you set out to make as much money as possible, you will probably step on some toes!

To return to our sample IB, the client is typically saying, "Since my wife *must* not leave me, I can't bear it if she does!" as well as "Since I can't bear it if my wife leaves me, she *must* not leave me." Can you hear the command in these statements?

4. *An irrational belief leads to disturbed emotions.* Anxiety may be debilitating at worst and nonproductive at best. If a client has not been functioning well in his or her recent life and thinks, "Isn't it awful that I'm functioning so poorly," he or she will most likely experience an unhelpful emotional extreme of anxiety. Appropriate concern, however, would be generated by a more rational thought, such as: "It matters, and I'm going

to work on functioning better, but in the meantime it's not awful or the end of the world that I'm functioning poorly."

5. *An irrational belief does not help us attain our goals.* When we are tied up in absolutes and shackled by upsetting emotions, we are hardly in an optimal position to work at the ongoing business in life of maximizing pleasure and minimizing discomfort. The client in the example above illustrates this problem. He will not be able to attain his goal of a happy life if he is continually worried about his wife leaving him.

Words and Meanings

Ellis (1979a, 1979b) has suggested that in discriminating irrational beliefs, we look for the *should* and the *must*. Although these key words may indeed be clues to an absolutist and demanding philosophy, they are often used innocuously. A common error made by new RET therapists is assuming that all utterances of words such as "should," "ought," must," or "have to" represent a demand. These words have many meanings in our language, one of which is *predictive*. The sentence "It should rain tonight" means "I expect it to rain tonight because of certain information I have." A second meaning is *advisory,* as in the sentence "You should see the movie I saw last night," which means "I liked the movie and I think you will too." Another meaning is *conditional,* which reflects an "if–then" proposition: "I should have the vacuum repaired" probably means "If I'm going to clean the rugs, I should have the vacuum repaired." The troublesome definition represents an *imperative*—as if it were moral dogma, like an 11th commandment—implying that an event must occur. Each of the examples above might or might not have an absolutist meaning, and the therapist can make this discrimination by attending to the context of the client's statement and his or her emotional state. As a caveat, it would be wise for the therapist who hears a client's "should" to rephrase the sentence and feed it back, to ensure that it represents demandingness. Otherwise, time may be lost in stamping out irrelevant shoulds (i.e., shoulds that are not at the core of the client's emotional disturbance), and the therapist may merely succeed in developing a new unexamined taboo ("I should not say 'should'").

If, as we have pointed out, it is self-defeating to hold irrational ideas, why do we do so? A number of factors come into play. First, this tendency is certainly reinforced by common cultural stereotypes that are reflected in our language, our stories, and our songs. A review of popular music, for

As an exercise, go through the following sentences and see how many you can correctly identify as rational or irrational. Answers are given on page 369.

I wish I had succeeded at X; it would have made things a lot easier.

What a shame that things didn't work out well.

Damn, I wish it weren't raining!

What a disappointment it was, not getting that job.

I wish we lived closer to school so I wouldn't have to walk so far.

I am so disappointed when my husband nags at me.

It certainly is annoying to listen to that music.

If you want to pass that test, you should study hard.

These exercises really are a bother.

example, found that 82 percent of country-western and rock songs expressed irrational philosophies (Protinsky and Popp, 1978). Second, there may be a kind of self-reinforcing thrill achieved when we are irrational. Think of the boy who has tearful hysterics because he didn't make the team or the girl who didn't get invited to the dance. Distortion and exaggeration can be exciting and, of course, may also elicit attention or sympathy from others in our environment. Perhaps the most basic reason why people are irrational, however, is stated by Ellis (1976a), who suggests that almost everyone thinks irrationally some of the time; it is the human condition. Strange as it may seem, this last explanation for irrationality may be clinically quite comforting. Such a suggestion appears to function well because it changes the attribution and allows clients to stop blaming themselves for their irrational beliefs.

THE MAJOR IB's

Originally, Ellis (e.g., 1977b) conceptualized the irrational beliefs he heard in therapy with thousands of his clients into several major categories. Keep in mind, however, that the following list is a typology of broad classes; they may not be expressed in pure form by any given client. A significant job of the therapist, therefore, is to locate the client's *idiosyncratic* irrational beliefs, which may or may not be subsumed into one of these categories. To aid in training your ear, we have included sample phrases or sentence fragments in which the pertinent irrational belief is embedded, and elaborated the fuller statement of the IB in parentheses. Following the discussion of each irrational belief we include an illustration of its rational counterpart. We encourage you to test your understanding by trying to anticipate, in writing, the RB's.

Here, then, is the list of Ellis' original major irrational beliefs.

I must be loved and approved of by every significant person in my life, and if I'm not, it's awful.

> I can't stand being called a castrating female.
>
> Nobody likes me (. . . and someone *has* to.)
>
> I'm afraid to ask her for a date (. . . because I couldn't stand the rejection).
>
> I couldn't stand it if he were mad at me!
>
> I'd be a fool if I did that.
>
> I couldn't do that in public (. . . because I couldn't bear it if people thought badly of me).
>
> I would do anything for this person (. . . in fact, I *have to* or he'll leave me and that would be terrible).

This irrational belief is among the most pervasive and troublesome in therapy. It represents a fear of rejection or disapproval by others. Ellis (1974b, 1977a) occasionally refers to the problem as "love slobbism," and it may be particularly evident in female patients as a result of our culture's sex-role socialization messages. A woman without a partner often views herself as an unfinished product, an incomplete entity. As Janet Wolfe (1975) has pointed out, women holding such a concept often engage in many self-defeating behaviors. They may not assertively ask for what they want or may passively go along with what they don't want in sex-love relationships for fear that if they speak up, their partner might think them inadequate and reject them.

RB: It would be desirable and productive to concentrate on self-respect, on winning approval for practical purposes, and on loving instead of being loved.

When other people behave badly or unfairly, they should be blamed, reprimanded, and punished; they are bad or rotten individuals.

It's all your fault (. . . and that makes you a total no-goodnik).

He shouldn't have done that to me.

My parents should have been fair. Then I wouldn't be in this trouble (. . . and it's awful that I am).

She's no good.

You male chauvinist pig!

He's totally stupid.

He deserved it.

I'd like to see him pay (. . . in fact, he's *got* to pay).

I'll get back at him (. . . I *must* have my revenge).

Of course, he should be punished (. . . he *deserves* it, the louse).

By listing this belief as irrational, we do not mean to imply that punishment is in some way irrational or ineffective. Although we believe that imposing penalties can be an important way to influence others' behaviors, we do not believe that any human being morally *deserves* punishment. The elements of irrationality in this belief are the concepts that (a) the *person* is to be comdemned, (b) the person *should* or must be punished, and (c) the person can be rated as totally bad. Behaviors, not people, are legitimately rated; similarly, punishment is effective in changing behaviors, not in condemning people.

RB: Certain acts are inappropriate or antisocial, and those who perform them are behaving stupidly or neurotically and would be better helped to change.

It's awful when things are not the way I'd like them to be.

I won't be treated unfairly (. . . because I can't stand it).

I can't go on without it.

I can't imagine not having it (. . . meaning, too awful to contemplate).

But if I don't get into graduate school . . . oh, my God!

She never has sex with me (. . . and I can't stand it).

I can't stand being fat.

He's always given me what I wanted in the past. (Damn it . . . how could he deny me now?)

All the other kids have . . . (and it's not fair . . . I should too!).

If he does that one more time, I'll scream (. . . thus illustrating how I cannot stand it!).

I spend all my time picking up after you (. . . you horrible, inconsiderate wretch!).

The patients' statements are a good illustration of unfinished speech. In some of the examples the client does not directly state an evaluation of the situation described; it is implied in the context of the speech or the tone of voice in which the comment is made. For example, in the statement "She never has sex with me," there may be an unspoken conclusion, which we have put in parentheses: ". . . and I can't stand it." It is useful to encourage the patient to finish the thought and realize that he or she has, in fact, made an exaggerated evaluation of the problem and its consequences.

RB: It's too bad that things are not often the way one would like, and it would be advisable to change or control conditions so that they can become more satisfactory. If change is impossible, one had better temporarily accept the status quo.

I should be very anxious about events that are uncertain or potentially dangerous.

It could happen (. . . and therefore I must be constantly vigilant because it would be terrible if it *did*).

Oh, my God! (Note that appeals to a deity almost always signal a superhuman problem, beyond the scope of mere mortals.)

I can't think of anything else but that. It's on my mind all the time. [The theme of these statements are (. . . it's so awful I just can't stop thinking about it.)]

Nobody seems to understand how serious this is (. . . and they should).

I can't just let it happen (because it would be terrible if I did).

If you're not upset, you probably don't understand the situation (anyone else—including me—would find it awful).

What do you mean, "relax"? (How *can* I when it's so horrible?)

But how can I be sure it won't happen? (I *have* to have a guarantee that it won't!)

Me, get on a horse? (. . . that could be a disaster!)

This irrational belief is based on the demand for certainty in our lives and results in anxiety when we do not receive guarantees. Patients who hold this irrational belief are giving themselves two troubles for the price of one. They will probably upset themselves not only when the unfortunate or undesirable event happens but also well before it occurs.

RB: One would do better to face the danger or fear and render it harmless or, when that is impossible, accept the inevitable.

I am not worthwhile unless I am thoroughly competent, adequate, and achieving at all times, or at least most of the time in at least one major area.

What an idiot I am.

I shouldn't have screamed at the children (. . . what a monster mother—and rotten person—I am!)

I'm not smart enough to apply to graduate school. (If I found out that that was the case I'd hate myself.)

I can't face myself.

What can I do with myself now that I'm retired? (. . . and worthless).

How could I get a C? (. . . that shows how dumb I am).

I shouldn't have come so fast (. . . I'm a lousy lover, and a lousy person).

My client didn't get better! (. . . I'm a rotten therapist and a less than worthy person).

This irrational belief is one of the two or three most commonly heard by therapists. It is perhaps most prevalent among males in our competitive, achievement-oriented society. It is usually connected with a strong fear of failure; the person believes that if he doesn't succeed, *he* is a failure—not simply that he failed at a task. This form of self-denigration is particularly anxiety-provoking when failing is anticipated, and particularly depressing when failure has been experienced.

RB: It is more advisable to accept oneself as an imperfect creature with human limitations and fallibilities. It is better to do, than to need to do well.

There's got to be a perfect solution to this problem; I must be certain and have perfect control over things.

> There's got to be a better way (. . . there *must* be!).
>
> If I keep searching, I'll find it (I *have to*).
>
> I just can't make a decision (. . . and I've *got* to).
>
> But how can I be sure? (I *must* be certain).
>
> Isn't that risky? (I can't tolerate any risk!)
>
> How will I know what's the best way to do it? (There's got to be one *best* way).
>
> I know what I want, but I still can't decide (. . . perfectly).
>
> If I stay, I'll be miserable, and if I go, I'll be miserable.
>
> I lack self-confidence (. . . totally).
>
> Doctor, do you mean you can't tell me what to do? (I can't possibly figure it out on my own).

There are basically two parts to this irrational notion. The first is that there is an ideal or *perfect solution* to the problem, one must be able to find it, and if one doesn't, the results would be terrible. The second element is that whether or not there is a perfect solution, the patient believes he or she must have *perfect control* over the problem as it is evolving. This IB can also be directed at other people. The patient may become angry at others who don't provide solutions to or control over difficult conditions. One of the people the patient is most likely to be angry at is the therapist when problems aren't resolved easily and quickly or the therapist can't point out the way to a perfect ending.

RB: Our world is one of probability and chance, and life can be enjoyed despite this.

The world absolutely should be fair and just.

> How could she do this to me? (She damn well shouldn't have!)
>
> Why does this always happen to me? (. . . it's nor fair and it shouldn't be this way!)

He shouldn't have done that.

I didn't deserve it (. . . and I should only get what I decide I deserve).

But I did everything I was supposed to do (. . . and I should have been rewarded).

They had no right to fire me.

How dare you?

He'll get it in the end (. . . as he must).

You can't tell me what to do.

I don't ask for much (. . . therefore, I should get what I ask for).

This belief is irrational primarily because of its elements of entitlement and demandingness. Clients who harbor this belief are unwilling to accept things as they are and feel that they can and must be better constructors of the world than whoever created it. This IB is often one of the key elements in the cognitive system of adolescent clients. Therapists would do well not to agree with clients that it's awful and terrible that the world isn't treating them fairly, but ask them, rather, where they ever got the idea that the world *should* and *must* be fair. Adolescents can be very idealistic and tend to have fixed notions of how the world should be (. . . their way!).

RB: The world is often unfair, and good guys sometimes do die young. It is better to accept this fact and concentrate on enjoying oneself despite it.

I should be comfortable and without pain at all times.

I needed this aggravation? (. . . I can't stand it).

It's just too hard (. . . and it shouldn't be).

But I don't like it (. . . therefore, it must cease).

I might get hurt (. . . how awful).

But I get so hungry (. . . and I shouldn't have to suffer hunger in order to lose weight).

I can't stand it.

What a hassle (. . . and why should I have to be hassled?).

I'd be happy if I could just get away from it all (. . . and unless I get away from it *all* I won't be able to be happy).

Can't we park closer? (I won't stand any discomfort!)

What, me go to the dentist? That hurts too much. (It should be painless, no matter what!)

We've been standing in line five minutes already (. . . how much can I stand?).

I'm afraid to get pregnant because it'll hurt to give birth (. . . and I can't stand any pain).

It may be surprising to see the word "pain" used in the description of this irrational belief; we refer to both psychological and physical discomfort. Physical discomfort often occurs in situations unconnected with physical illness, such as inconveniences of various kinds. Belief in one's inability to stand discomfort is a form of low frustration tolerance (LFT) and can lead to addictions and behavioral excesses, or at the very least to whining and complaining which is interpersonally offensive. Discomfort anxiety may also prevent patients from achieving long-range goals or pleasures because they define the present discomfort as unbearable. If you are going to walk up a mountain stream in order to bathe in a waterfall, you're probably going to have to step on stones and rocks. Many people believe that they must be comfortable in whatever they do; such a notion is obviously self-defeating.

RB: There's seldom gain without pain. I can tolerate this discomfort, although I may never like it.

I may be going crazy, but I must not; that would be unbearable.

I can't even think straight anymore (. . . oh my God, I'm going crazy).

I saw a TV show last night about a man with my problems, and he ended up in the nuthouse. (If I ended up there, that would be the end of the world!)

I'm so afraid I won't be able to control myself (. . . and if I lose control, that would be terrible!).

What'll happen to me? (whatever it is, I don't think I can take it!)

I'm scared I might crack up! (That would be awful!)

What if I lose control? (How horrible!)

I think I'm losing my mind. (I'm not coping as well as I should.)

Anyone with my problems must be very disturbed (. . . and that would be unbearable).

I could end up like my mother . . . she killed herself (. . . and it would be terrible if I did the same).

What does this symptom mean, Doctor? (I'm already assuming the worst, and beyond. It'll be awful if it isn't benign.)

Is that normal? (. . . because if it isn't, I'm going to go to pieces!)

"Phrenophobia," the fear of going crazy, is a common concern among patients and often underlies what we have called secondary disturbance (Walen, 1983). Victor Raimy (1975) has referred to this problem as "psychological hypochondria." Why are people deathly afraid? Typically, as nonprofessionals, they are grossly misinformed about psychopathology and imagine themselves becoming raving maniacs who must be locked away for prolonged stays in a "snake pit." The underlying cognitive themes usually involve both self-rating ("I'm no good") and discomfort anxiety ("I couldn't stand the hassles").

RB: Emotional distress is certainly not pleasant, but it is hardly unbearable.

The remaining four irrational beliefs take a somewhat different form. They are less clearly evaluative but they do reflect irrationality, since they are neither empirically verifiable nor conducive to achieving one's goals.

It's easier to avoid life's difficulties than to face them.

Well, nothing's going to help anyway, so I might as well give up. (It's terrible that I have to work persistently to change.)

Why bother trying? (It should be effortless.)

I'll do anything to avoid that (. . . because I can't stand hassles).

It's no use. (It's too hard to change.)

Oh, it's not such a big problem anyway . . . so I don't really need to do anything about it, do I? (. . . because if I recognize that it is a big problem it would be too hard to tackle it).

The booze helps me forget, Doc (. . . and I can't stand remembering).

I'd just rather get high. (I need that buzz.)

I don't like where my life is now, but . . . it's easier than changing it. (Change should be easier than it is!)

If I don't think about it, it doesn't bother me. (When I think about it, it's terrible!)

It won't help anyway. (If I did it, it has to work quickly!)

I'll think about that tomorrow. (It's too hard to think about it today.)

I've been meaning to do something about that but just haven't gotten around to it. (It's too hard.)

This notion is similar to the belief "I should be comfortable and without pain at all times" and implies an evaluative component: "life's difficulties are so horrible that they must be avoided at all costs." This avoidance can be a significant impediment to progress in therapy, and the therapist would be wise to confront the procrastination directly and to encourage clients to vigorously challenge this IB.

RB: The so-called easy way is invariably the harder way in the long run.

I need someone stronger than myself on whom to depend or rely.

A woman needs a man

I can't cope without her.

When things get hard, I just rely on the Lord. (It's too hard to rely on myself.)

I can't do it alone (. . . because life would be too hard).

But he always knows what to do (. . . unlike helpless me).

Behind every good man, there's a woman (. . . and without one, I couldn't cope).

You can always rely on the Man Upstairs (. . . rather than yourself).

What'll I do if you leave? (Answer: I have no idea! I couldn't cope without you!)

Doc, I've been waiting all week just to tell you this (. . . and meanwhile, I've avoided taking any constructive action on my own because I shouldn't have to do it on my own!).

Doctor, you *can't* go on vacation! (I need you!)

In this irrational belief we find people stating that they cannot cope or solve their own problems. Many of us find it helpful to turn to others for advice and counsel, including counsel in prayer, but exclusive reliance upon someone else or on a higher power simply defeats our own efforts to solve problems and work toward our goals in life. The key element in this IB is the word "need." As it is said, "God helps those who help themselves."

RB: It is better to take the risks of acting and thinking independently.

Emotional misery comes from external pressure, and I have little ability to control or change my feelings.

> He made me feel like two cents.
> I'll be devastated if she leaves me.
> He made me so mad.
> When he comes in the room, I see red.
> He'll ruin my evening.
> Well, society's trained us to be that way.
> You made me love you.
> If you'd stop picking on me, I could change.
> If only I had that job I'd be happy.
> You make me sick.

Changing this belief is a cornerstone of the work of the rational-emotive therapist. Unless clients assume responsibility for their own feelings and understand that they have produced them and can therefore change them, they will be continually blaming their misery on a variety of outside factors. This IB is actually a hypothesis about the effects of environmental stimuli on human behavior. Thus, according to our strict definition that beliefs are evaluative cognitions, it is not an irrational belief per se. It is, however, an idea that prevents people from helping themselves and discourages them from correcting their IB's unless it is changed.

RB: Emotional disturbance is caused largely by the view we take of conditions. We have enormous control over our destructive emotions if we choose to work at changing the bigoted and unscientific hypotheses that created them.

My past is the cause of my present problems; because these events were such strong influences, they will continue to affect me.

> That's the way I am! (. . . so don't expect me to change).
> Well, I was brought up that way.
> My whole family's like that (. . . so I have to be too).
> I must have been conditioned to do that (. . . and can't change).
> Well, I was adopted.
> I never did well in school (. . . so why try now?).

When I was a kid . . . (and so I'm locked into the same pattern now).

I had a rotten childhood (. . . so I'm doomed to failure).

All of us Italians are emotional.

Doctor, you couldn't understand it unless you were Jewish.

It really is my mother's fault; she made me this way.

This idea, again not clearly evaluative in form, is one of the most insidious and pernicious impediments to successful psychotherapy. It implies that therapy cannot work and that clients are unchangeable. Clients may cite their personal history, their genetic or ethnic background, or some significant life event as a reason that they cannot change. Of course, when they believe they cannot change, they are unlikely to try to change. If this belief is irrational, it is so because it is an impediment to the person's happiness as well as because of its absolutist nature. It is a prediction about influences on human behavior but, we believe, an incorrect one.

RB: One can learn from past experiences while not being overly attached to or unrelentingly influenced by them.

It may be helpful for the new RET therapist to remember that all of the IB's may be reduced to one of three core irrationalities:

- A philosophy of self-denigration
- An intolerance of frustration
- A blaming and condemning of others

It is suggested that the therapist keep questioning clients until they admit one or more of these core notions. Core irrational beliefs can also be identified by patients' evaluative definitions. An event is irrationally labeled as horrible by *definition* rather than because of an objective calculation of its negative consequences.

A MORE CONTEMPORARY MODEL

More recent theorizing (e.g., Bernard and DiGiuseppe, 1989; Ellis and Dryden, 1987) has condensed the description of irrational thinking into the grid shown in Figure 8.1. On the horizontal dimension are four core types of *irrational processes:*

Irrational Processes

	Demandingness	Low frustration tolerance	Human worth ratings	Awfulizing
Affiliation	Demanding about affiliation	LFT about affiliation	Condemning about affiliation	Awfulizing about affiliation
Achievement	Demanding about achievement	LFT about achievement	Condemning about achievement	Awfulizing about achievement
Comfort	Demanding about comfort	LFT about comfort	Condemning about comfort	Awfulizing about comfort
Fairness	Demanding about fairness	LFT about fairness	Condemning about fairness	Awfulizing about fairness

(left margin, rotated: Belief Content)

Figure 8.1   Model of irrational beliefs.

Demandingness—the tendency to substitute demands for wishes or preferences, as reflected in word choices such as "should," "ought," "must," and "have to" (e.g., "My mother has to love me").

Awfulizing—extreme and exaggerated negative evaluations of events (e.g., "It's terrible and awful if my mother doesn't love me!").

Human worth ratings—generalized evaluations or denigrations of people including the self as well as others (e.g., "I am a worthless person if my own mother doesn't love me!").

Low frustration tolerance—the person's perceived inability to withstand the discomfort of an activating event (e.g., "I can't stand it if my mother doesn't love me!").

Ellis' most recent writings (e.g., 1989; Ellis and Dryden, 1987) propose that all emotional disturbance shares a single root: demandingness. Ellis believes that rigid and dogmatic thinking is at the core of all psychopathology, so that IB's concerning demandingness are always present in emotional disturbance. The remaining three IB processes (rating, awfulizing, and LFT) are thought to be logical derivatives of demandingness.

Along the vertical dimension are the four possible content or contex-

> Take a minute to bring to mind several clients with whom you
> are now working. Jot down the name of each client and his or her
> presenting problem. Then try to figure out where on the grid
> each client's thinking falls, for example, the IB may be demand-
> ingness about comfort, demandingness about fairness, LFT
> about comfort, and so on.

tual areas (the A's) to which the cognitive processes apply: *affiliation,*
achievement, comfort, and *fairness.* Proponents of this model argue that it
makes the concept of irrational beliefs easier to understand and, thus,
easier to assess. The grid has also led to some hypotheses about irrational
beliefs involved in specific disorders. For example, human rating IB's
about the self may play the major role in depression, IB's about comfort
are thought to be prominent in agoraphobia (Burgess, 1990), and low
frustration tolerance IB's are often considered crucial in addictive behaviors (DiGiuseppe and McInerney, 1991).

Clinical experience suggests that the content dimension could be expanded to also include the factor of *control* (thereby expanding the model).
Thus, "demandingness" in interaction with "control" might result in a
belief structure such as, "I must be in total control of my marriage in order
to feel safe"; LFT × control, "I can't stand it when things happen that I
can't control"; rating × control, "I think I'm worthless as a person when I
can't control things"; and awfulizing × control, "It's awful when things
are beyond my control."

Levels of Cognition

In summary, three basic levels of cognitive awareness, are important in
understanding the client's distress, but some are more difficult to retrieve
and change than others. Closest to awareness are the thoughts or thought
fragments that Beck (1976) has referred to as *automatic thoughts.* They are in
the stream of consciousness, and clients can usually easily report these
thoughts after a moment of reflection. The type of questions that most
directly lead the client's attention to these thoughts are "What are you
telling yourself?" or "What did you tell yourself when X happened?"

Inferences and *attributions* that we make about our observations and
automatic thoughts are in the same stream of consciousness and, again,

Rational-emotive therapy, in its most complete or "elegant" form, strives for what we may call "profound philosophic change" or "basic attitudinal change." Ellis has argued for the concept of "personality change." The notion is that a cognitive therapy that only disputes disturbed inferences or attributions is superficial, because these attributions are seen as stemming from deeper philosophic assumptions.

For example, consider the statements, "My parents scolded me. I infer that they don't love me." The therapist could obviously challenge this thinking, but to do only that would miss the deeper issue, which may be approximated as, "I must always do well and be completely loved by my parents."

may be easily discovered by a direct question. The therapist might ask, for example, "What did you think it meant?" or "What did you infer from that?"

Evaluative cognitions, especially dysfunctional ones associated with emotional distress, are usually somewhat less obvious to the client, since the evaluation is often parenthetical or silently assumed. Focused therapeutic questioning, as outlined in the next chapter, may be required to help the client hear his or her silent assumptions.

Core irrational beliefs are more difficult to tap; they are rules of living (Wessler and Wessler, 1980) or basic philosophies that we may not be aware are operating until they are activated by a change such as a major life stress, significant emotional upheaval, or even the process of entering therapy. (In the various terminologies of cognitive-behavioral therapy, these core beliefs are sometimes referred to as "underlying belief structures" or "schemas.") The next chapter suggests techniques for helping clients to unearth their core beliefs.

9 More about B

Finding the B's

Belief systems are not always easy to identify, because most of our thinking processes consist of greatly overlearned cognitive habits that have become automatic. We rarely stop in our busy lives to think about how we think. Many years ago, John Watson, the founder of behaviorism, suggested why our self-talk is covert: quite simply, talking aloud to ourselves is socially punished. The Soviet developmental psychologists Vygotsky (1962) and Luria (1969) traced in children the process of suppressing self-talk. At the earliest stages of verbal development, children's behavior is controlled by the overt vocalizations of others. Somewhat later, children can be heard giving themselves similar behavioral directives aloud. Ultimately, their self-talk is completely internalized. With repeated practice, not only is the need to focus on the internal commands reduced, but a kind of short-circuiting apparently takes place so that individual elements of the self-talk get subsumed under larger headings. This last point will perhaps be clearer if you recall learning to drive a car or watching your child learn to tie his or her shoes. In both cases, a complex task is initially broken down into smaller units of instruction and communicated by someone other than the learner, then usually verbalized aloud by the learner, repeated subvocally, and finally integrated into a continuous whole that can proceed without conscious attention. The thought processes that precede emotive reactions presumably follow similar, although perhaps more subtle, developmental patterns. Thus, a clinical task may be to help patients identify and verbalize their thoughts, beliefs, attitudes, and philosophies.

Sometimes the therapist may encounter clients who are in touch with their self-talk and volunteer it easily. More common, perhaps, are patients who, when asked what they are thinking, respond with feelings ("I think I'm sad/anxious/apprehensive/etc."). The therapist's task is then to teach the client to recognize, for example, that "apprehension" is not a thought but a feeling.

How do you help clients to verbalize their B's? The simplest procedure is to ask. Here are some questions you might use to elicit cognitions:

What was going through your mind? Or, if a client is emoting in a session, "What is going through your mind right now?"

What were you telling yourself?

Were you aware of any thoughts in your head?

There goes that old tape in your head again: What is it playing this time?

What was on your mind then?

What were you worrying about?

Are you aware of what you were thinking at that moment?

If clients claim that no cognitions were present, the therapist may want to keep in mind that not only the presence of irrational beliefs but also the absence of structured thought may be an indicator of psychopathology. Therapeutic work may begin by teaching clients how to tune into and monitor their thinking by the use of therapeutic *suggestion*. By piecing together information about clients' situations, behaviors, and emotional reactions, therapists may infer the presence of specific IB's, which they can then *model* for their clients as follows:

"Well, I don't know exactly what's going through your mind, but when people feel anxious, they're often saying something like this to themselves. . . ." *or*

"In my experience, when people have a great deal of difficulty making decisions, they're often saying to themselves something like. . . ."

Of course, it will be important to validate these hunches by conferring with the patient, for example, "Does that sound familiar?" or "Could you be thinking something like that?" In subsequent sessions, when the patient brings up another anxiety statement, the therapist can refer back to this teaching: "Do you remember that explanation of anxiety we were talking about last week? Well, what do you think you were saying to yourself this time?" In this manner, the therapist is helping the client to recognize the thought–emotion connection.

In a similar manner, the therapist may wish to actually state the irrational belief, rather than merely allude to it, with clients who are particularly halting or ruminative. The irrational belief may be stated as a generality and followed up by a question. For example: "Many people might say to themselves, 'If she thinks I'm stupid, that would be terrible!' Are you thinking anything like that?" If the answer is yes, the hunch is validated and the point has been made. If the answer is no, the therapist may then inquire, "Well, what were you thinking?"

Frequently clients talk to themselves in what, syntactically, are half-sentences. In essence, they have punctuated their verbalization with a period, although the thought is not completed. For example:

C: For a long time I wasn't thinking about what I wanted to do with my life.
T: And now that you are thinking about it?
C: I've decided that I want to go back to school, but I don't think I can make it now.

In this illustration, the therapist has fed the thought back to the client as a *sentence-completion* task. Similarly, clients may verbalize only the rational part of their thinking, so that the therapist may want to append the unstated irrational philosophy as an hypothesis. For example:

C: I want to do well in school.
T: And therefore you *must*, right?

This sentence-completion assessment strategy is one of the most frequently used by RET therapists.

Missing thoughts can also form the end of a *syllogism*, as in, "If he loved me, he'd marry me . . . but he hasn't found a way to marry me." The patient may stop her verbalization at this point, but then why would she be depressed? The therapeutic query at this juncture might be to ask the patient what she concludes about the situation. Most likely, she has finished this illogical syllogism covertly: "Therefore, he doesn't love me and that's *awful!*" A moment's reflection on the logic of this statement will reveal that "if–then" statements do not follow this pattern, for example, there could be many other reasons for his failure to appear at the altar—and even if her partner doesn't love her, is it really so awful?

A related technique to get at the core irrational belief is to lead the client through a chain of thoughts by *repeating a simple question*. Consider the client who reports difficulty in making a decision:

T: Why would that pose a problem for you?
C: Well, I might make a mistake.
T: And why would making a mistake be a problem for you?
C: But if I made a mistake, I'd feel stupid [or guilty].
T: Well, that's how you'd feel, but what would making a mistake mean about you?
C: It would prove I was inadequate.

Similarly, a chain of *time-projection* questions may be useful: "OK, suppose you lost your job, then what happens? . . . OK, you lose your home, and then what happens? . . . OK, and then what happens?" etcetera. Note that the therapist does not challenge the client's projection but works with the assumption that the worst might happen.

T: What's the worst that could happen if you stood up to your wife?
C: She might leave me.
T: What's the worst thing that could happen if your wife *did* leave you?
C: I might not find another woman. My God!
T: But let's suppose you never did find another woman. What's the worst that could happen then?
C: I could get sick and no one would care for me.
T: Well, what would be the worst thing about that?
C: That would be the worst thing! That's so terrible I hate to even think about it.

Don't be surprised if, when you get to the bottom line, you find you are far away from the original problem; patients can be quite unaware of their core irrational philosophies.

As in the example above, the therapist continues to probe for the client's core irrational beliefs by asking questions and, along the way, may uncover additional irrational thoughts. Patients may begin by complaining that they want their mother, their spouse, their children, their boss, and so on to do what they want ("It's awful when things are not the way I'd like them to be.) The therapist's next question might be, "Why is it important to you to have them do that?" The answer might reveal that patients view themselves as "special," perhaps as weak and dependent, as people who need others to take care of them ("I need someone stronger than myself on whom to rely"). If the therapist continues to ask why being taken care of is important, still more irrational beliefs may be revealed. In this example, the client may state that he believes that it would be awful if his wife didn't care for him, because it would prove that he was worthless. His belief in his worthlessness would be the core IB.

How does one intervene therapeutically with such a chain of IB's? Essentially, there are two ways of proceeding: the therapist can stop at each irrational belief and dispute it, or continue questioning and begin the disputation at the bottom line. We have no empirical evidence about which procedure is better, but clinical experience suggests that the therapist may profitably go right to the core notions. In either case, unless the core IB's are tackled, the client may well develop new problems. For example, clients who never successfully understand why self-rating is irrational may selectively give up rating themselves on *one* issue (i.e., their "need" for the adoration of their love partner) but later decide their self-worth depends on their job performance. It is, therefore, important to keep the patient's core IB at the forefront of the therapeutic plan. Thus, after beginning a session by asking, "What problem would you like to work on this week?" try to bring new presenting complaints back to the core IB: "How does this relate to what we've identified as your main problem?" This factor may make the difference between Band-Aid therapy and a more elegant solution.

A key point to note here is that behavior usually has *multiple determinants*. Too often, the new RET therapist will obtain the C (affect), find one IB to dispute, and consider the case closed. By allowing the patient to talk freely or by persistent questioning, the therapist may find that C is a result of several IB's, often with spiraling, lateral, or hierarchical connections.

The therapist needn't be dismayed to find a group of B's, or a "regular B-hive." The therapist can simply jot down the irrational notions as they emerge and then present the list to the client for discussion and evaluation. Perhaps the therapist can point out any common themes; if there are none, patient and therapist may work together to hierarchically arrange the beliefs for disputational attack.

New therapists sometimes have trouble maintaining a broad perspective, so that while uncovering IB's on one aspect of the client's problems, they may be ignoring IB's the client may hold if he or she took a different course of action. Suppose that Bert, for example, presents the problem of guilt over adultery or adulterous thoughts and asks the therapist to alleviate this guilt. Should the therapist advocate sexual libertarianism or stress the virtues of monogamy? Neither; it would be better to decipher all the core IB's that may be operating in this instance. Thus, the patient has two alternative paths, adultery versus monogamy, and it is not the therapist's job to pick one for him but rather to help the client identify IB's that prevent him from selecting one or the other path. For instance, one set of IB's may revolve around self-denigration and result in the client's guilt about his adulterous thoughts or actions. Alternatively, Bert has the choice of remaining monogamous. What IB's and emotions have prevented him from doing so comfortably? It is possible that he suffers from low frustration tolerance, believing that he must act on his desires for an outside partner and cannot tolerate the perceived discomfort of monogamous living. The goal is to uncover such irrational notions so that the patient can engage in problem solving, that is, weighing the alternatives, making a decision for himself, and learning to live with it.

GUIDES TO FINDING THE B FOR SPECIFIC
EMOTIONS

At this point, you may find yourself overwhelmed with what seems like an infinite number of connections among B's and C's. You may be reassured to find, however, that specific common thoughts generally lead to specific common emotions. The work of the rational-emotive therapist derives from this theoretical assumption. By way of illustration, we will present the irrational philosophies that underlie four major emotional dysfunctions: anxiety, depression, guilt, and anger.

When clients have trouble identifying cognitions, the therapist can suggest a variety of thoughts, urging clients to signal or stop when one feels "right." You can explain to clients that you're not clairvoyant, but that because they have helped you to identify the correct feeling, there are only a limited number of thoughts that could be going on in her head. Your job is to help clients to listen to their own cognitions, or to let you suggest a few and then tell you if any of the suggestions seem to fit.

Anxiety is the result of future-oriented cognitions; people are rarely afraid, for prolonged periods of time, of events in the here-and-now. The therapist would do well, therefore, to ask future-oriented questions: "What do you think *might* happen?" or "What kind of trouble are you anticipating?" What is usually heard in response is some form of catastrophizing or awfulizing. Fears may range from specific and isolated to pervasive and vague (so-called free-floating anxiety). The two most common fears, according to Hauck (1974), are the fear of rejection and the fear of failure, followed closely by the super-fear—the fear of being afraid.

There are three cognitive steps to anxiety:

1. Something bad might happen.
2. It *must* not happen.
3. It would be *awful* if it did.

The first statement might be a good prediction based on valid evidence, although the therapist would do well to check this out. The bad "something" that clients are anticipating might be an external event or their own self-condemnation because of some potential failure. Thus, they may be fearful of the future event because they believe it will prove their lack of self-worth. If we assume that the patient is correct about the event occurring, however, the patient's first logical error may appear at statement 2, the clearly irrational "should" or "must," as if the individual had command of the universe and could prevent bad events from happening. At statement 3 we see the irrational evaluation of A, which tends to keep the individual stewing and thinking about the future, as if doing so will magically ward off disaster.

Depression. Beck (1976) outlined a cognitive triad that *descriptively* identifies depression: a negative view of the self, a negative view of the world, and a negative view of the future. These views are similar to and overlap the dynamic irrational beliefs that RET theory (e.g., Ellis, 1987) suggests are the main *causative* agents in depression:

1. A devout belief in one's personal inadequacy
2. The "horror" of not having what one "needs"
3. The "awfulness" of the way things are

Hauck (1974), in his excellent book on depression, divides the problem of depression into three types, each with its underlying irrational structures. Depression can be caused, first, by *self-blame*. The thinking pattern that leads to self-blame is generally as follows:

1. I failed, sinned, or accidentally hurt someone.
2. I should be perfect and not do bad things.
3. I am, therefore, a bad person and deserve punishment.

The second cause of depression is *self-pity* whose irrational core is:

1. I have been thwarted in getting my way.
2. I must have what I want.
3. It's awful if I don't get it. Poor me!

Finally, one can become depressed by *other-pity* if one believes:

1. Bad things must not happen to other people when they don't deserve it.
2. The world is a terrible place for allowing such things to happen.

Guilt cognitions have two components. First, patients believe that they are doing (or have done) something wrong. These could be sins of commission or sins of omission. Second, they condemn themselves for doing the wrong thing. Again, the first statement may be an accurate assessment of reality according to the patient's value system. Considered alone, it is a statement of self-responsibility and can be useful in changing the patient's behavior. This type of statement, therefore, might not be the target of dispute in RET. Statement 2 adds an extra, unnecessary idea, however. Consider the difference if instead of statement 2, the patient said, "Yes, I did the wrong thing. I really regret that, but people make mistakes from time to time, and I'll try my best not to do it again." Thus, true guilt always includes the second component of self-denigration, which sabotages emotional or behavioral improvement.

Anger. The word "anger" is used to describe a broad range of emotional reactions, some of which are appropriate and helpful. *Clinical anger*, on the other hand (i.e., hostility, rage, or contempt), is an emotion that interferes with goal-directed behavior. Ellis (1977b) describes anger cognitions as a series of Jehovian demands. The first step consists of defining rights and wrongs, reflecting an absolutist kind of moral indignation. The second step is the absolutist should: "You should treat me differently" or "You shouldn't act that way." The third step is awfulizing: "It's horrible; I can't stand it!" And finally, we arrive at blaming and condemnation: "You're a bastard!" and "You deserve to be punished and damned!" What is the core irrationality in these notions? Angry feelings usually lead to inefficient behavior; damning and demanding amount to playing God; and criticizing others doesn't right a wrong or teach better behavior.

In addition, we can recognize "ego-defensive anger." We have found that some clients become enraged over other people's criticism because that criticism, when they focus on it, reminds them of their own inadequacy, for which they condemn themselves. As a defense, some clients frequently become angry toward the person who has made the criticism rather than condemn themselves for the fault.

Identifying Core Beliefs

The eliciting question that seems to be used most frequently by students of RET is, "What are you telling yourself?" However, this question tends to elicit the client's automatic thoughts which are in the stream of consciousness. These responses are not likely to be the core irrational beliefs. For example:

T: What are you telling yourself?
C: I'm going to fail this test.

The client has responded with a prediction, but has not clearly stated an evaluative belief and is quite removed from verbalizing an underlying belief structure, which is generally more difficult to tap. What can you do at this point? We suggest several strategies.

Inductive awareness. You can continue to collect automatic thoughts and inferences (e.g., ". . . and what else were you thinking?"), and then challenge and dispute them. The client who has done this process a number of times, with a number of emotional issues, may eventually become aware of a pattern, that may (by inductive inference) suggest the underlying irrational belief. The client comes to this realization on his or her own. For example:

C: You know, I think I'm *usually* afraid that I'm going to fail tests.
T: I agree; that's an accurate observation. Why do you think you predict failure so frequently?
C: Maybe I predict it so I won't be so devastated if it happens. The flip

side of that may be what I really believe—that I *have to* be successful each time!

The use of this technique, which allows clients to discover core irrationalities on their own, can work but also may be less efficient than other strategies. While we tend to value self-discovery over guided discovery in our society, the process may be more useful for the bright, articulate client. When we are working with a less intelligent, emotionally distracted, or unpsychologically oriented client, as is frequently the case, the fumbling of the client for self-discovery may entail a more protracted period of suffering than is necessary.

Inductive interpretation. A somewhat more active procedure utilizes interpretation by the therapist. After collecting and challenging a large number of automatic thoughts and inferences, the therapist may point out common themes and, by interpretation, suggest possible core underlying beliefs. This strategy, however, is relatively time-consuming.

Inference chaining. In this technique, the therapist works on the hypothesis that the automatic thought could be true, and helps the client discover the succeeding inference(s). "What if that were true? What would that mean?" Each question yields new inferences until an irrational belief is uncovered:

C: I know I'm going to fail that test.
T: OK, let's suppose you do fail the test. What would that mean?
C: I might not be as smart as the other students.
T: Well, I'm not sure it would mean that, but let's assume you're correct and you aren't as intelligent as your peers. What would that mean?
C: Well, it would mean I'm not as good as they are . . . like less worthwhile or important.

Related to inference chaining is the use of *conjunctive phrasing,* for example, ". . . and that would mean . . ." or ". . . and then . . ." or ". . . and therefore . . ." The therapist erases the "period" at the end of the client's sentence and inserts a conjunction. This strategy is often employed by Dr. Ellis. One reason it may be efficient is that it can be less distracting than a full reflection, which the client would then have to process for its accuracy before continuing the phrase.

C: I'm going to fail that test.
T: . . . and therefore . . .

C: I might not be as smart as the other students.
T: . . . and that would mean . . .

Another simple alternative for the therapist is to use as a *sentence-completion* phrasing:

C: I'm going to fail that test.
T: And you're nervous about that possibility because . . .

Patients are often surprised at how much information can be elicited by these inference-chaining strategies. Clinically, we have found that the more verbal and intelligent client may respond better to the use of conjunctive phrasing, and the more concrete and literal-minded client does better with sentence-completion phrasing.

Another alternative to asking open-ended questions is to ask *theory-driven questions*. For example, if the client is reporting anxiety about potential criticism from others, rather than asking, "What are you telling yourself about this criticism?", you might ask, "What demand could you be making about criticism from others?" or "What kind of person would you think you are if others criticize you?"

The danger in constructing your questions on the basis of RET theory is that you may wonder if you're putting words into the client's mouth or reinforcing the client for irrational beliefs that he or she may not really hold. You can do several things to avoid this problem: first, give up the notion that your hypotheses must be correct (be on guard against narcissistic epistemology). Second, don't communicate your hypotheses in declarative sentences; they are not facts, but hunches. Try instead to use suppositional questions. Third, always ask the client for feedback, and if he or she disagrees, use this information to try to formulate new hypotheses.

The advantage of such questions is that they effectively orient clients toward looking specifically for irrational beliefs. If it is clear that clients' emotional responses are inappropriate and self-defeating, what you will likely find is that clients experience a clear recognition when the therapist directs them to search for shoulds, musts, or related demands.

A variation in style. Cognitive therapy, as distinguished from more traditional RET, tends to stress the *idiosyncratic* nature of the patient's cognitions. In addition, cognitive therapists try to describe the patient's cognitive world without any editorializing, by using the patient's language exactly as stated. The patient is also urged to speak from the *direct experience* of his or her thoughts, rather than talking *about* those thoughts. For example:

> *Not:*   I was thinking about how stupidly I acted.
> *But:*   *What a jerk I am!*

Similarly, the more broadly stated silent assumptions are gathered in the patient's own language, rather than formed into categorical musts or shoulds. For example:

> "I need other people's approval to feel good about myself."
>
> "I may not be a very adequate human being."
>
> "Others will be very critical of me and won't accept me or respect me unless my work is of a very high standard."

There are advantages to both the use of RET jargon and use of the client's own words. In our clinical teaching experience, the structure of irrational beliefs laid out in RET theory helps therapists-in-training to look for and recognize their patients' core irrational processes. As RET therapists become more experienced, they may move from the language of RET theory toward the idiosyncratic language of the client without losing sight of RET constructs. For example, the experienced therapist can detect a client's demandingness even if a "should" or "must" has never been spoken. The use of the client's own language also frequently seems to make the disputation process more meaningful to the client.

Our recommendation is to experiment with both.

OTHER GUIDELINES

In the previous sections, we described how the RET therapist uses the client's specific C as a clue in identifying the relevant irrational beliefs, and uses automatic thoughts as guideposts to underlying belief structures. In addition, as you gather experience as a therapist, you will find that particular clinical problems are commonly associated with specific belief systems. Clues to irrational beliefs may be found in the A that the client describes or in characteristics of the client that you note. In other words, in searching for the irrational cognitions with which patients upset themselves you may begin with cognitive schemas derived from cumulative experience with similar cases. These schemas can serve as initial hypotheses. While it is beyond the scope of this book to suggest all of the common schemas, a few examples may be helpful to illustrate their form.

If the client is a mother who is experiencing a great deal of anxiety or anger at her children for their misbehavior, we have frequently found that the key irrational belief underlying the problem is one of self-worth. The mother may have not only identified the children's behavior as bad but may also have overgeneralized, concluding that she is a bad mother and, therefore, a worthless person. Thus, she may have rated and devalued herself based on the behavior of her children. In working with mothers, whether their children are infants or independent adults, the therapist may keep such a schema in mind as an hypothesis and focus on issues of the client's self-worth.

Another example of a schema derives from work with female clients in the age range from forty-five to sixty, for whom depression is a major symptom. During this time of life, women begin to experience the effects of menopause and often view their role as vital sexual creatures as coming to an end. The mid-life woman client may not initiate a discussion of menopause or sexuality, but then the therapist's schema may guide an opening of these topics for discussion so that any core issues and irrational beliefs surrounding them can be evaluated.

The development and use of such schemas will evolve as you accumulate professional experience. You may find, in fact, that you have many such decision-making schemas already. The point we wish to stress, however, is that schemas suggest hypotheses, not facts. Not all maternal anger is based on issues of self-worth, just as not all depression experienced by women in their middle years is related to beliefs about sexual decline. In other words, we advise you to present your schemas in suppositional language to your clients, and to empirically validate your hypotheses by data from the patient before you proceed further with therapy.

TWO FINAL CAVEATS

The therapist would be wise to listen for an irrational idea that commonly occurs to clients in rational-emotive therapy and prevents them from honestly bringing problems to the session or telling the therapist about their self-talk. This irrational notion is that they *should* have gotten over that particular problem or that they're not *supposed* to feel anxiety or think irrationally. Some clients may plainly reveal such an idea (e.g., "I'm ashamed to tell you what happened last week, Doctor"). In other cases, shame or guilt may prevent clients from getting any help. The therapist may find it helpful to think of this problem as a generalized schema and periodically investigate whether or not it is operating with clients.

Conversely, we can identify the salient *metacognition,* "I think I can." A patient's belief in *self-efficacy* may be one of the most important prerequisites for success in therapy, and the therapist would do well to focus on eliciting and reinforcing it. All humans have experienced intrusive negative thoughts; some end up in therapy. What is the difference between "normal" and "neurotic" negative thinking?

Some research suggests that in the nonclinical population, negative thoughts are:

less disturbing
less frequent
more acceptable to the person having them
easier to dismiss

Moreover, clinical and nonclinical populations differ in their self-efficacy metacognitions, namely,

"I have some control over my behavior."
"I have the ability to tolerate this discomfort."
"I have some ability to control my thinking."

Teaching Transcript

The following transcript* provides an illustration of an RET therapist assisting the client to identify his cognitions, and teaching the client to

*This transcript is adapted from a session by Dr. Norma Campbell, Baltimore, Md.

discriminate between rational and irrational beliefs and the corresponding emotions—in this case, functional and dysfunctional anger. The rational belief that the activating event *was* bad allows the therapist to empathize with the client and acknowledge the negativity in the situation, without colluding with the client's irrational belief that the event was "terrible."

The patient, Sam, is a 38-year-old married man whose 5-year-old daughter has a habit of waking in the middle of the night and calling for her mother. On a recent night, Sam got really angry. He flew into the child's room, picked her up by the shoulders, shook her and yelled at her, "Shut up, you little brat! This is ridiculous! And I won't stand for it!"

T: You must have been really angry to go in and shake her.
C: Yeah. And I yelled at her.
T: Yes, and how'd you feel about that afterward?
C: Pretty rotten.
T: What do you mean, rotten?
C: I felt guilty.

The therapist is thinking to herself that she'll want to go back later and deal with that guilt because she wants the client to let go of it. But she knows that they can work on only one thing at a time, and she makes an agenda decision at this juncture to focus on the frustration.

T: OK, Sam. Let's go back, if we can. There you are, resting in bed, and you hear that whiney voice, "Mommy, mommy. . . ." What thoughts go through your head? What are you saying to yourself?
C: I've had it with that kid. I'm just going to walk right out on her if she gives me any flak.

The therapist's initial query about self-talk results in behavioral not cognitive information. The therapist persists and again asks for thoughts.

T: Well, that's a conclusion you drew about how you *would* act. But before you came to that you must have had some other thoughts. If we could read your head, like some printed script, what were some of the words . . . what were you saying?
C: Dammit. I don't want to have to go through it again.
T: (repeats) OK, good. What else were you saying?
C: I don't need this aggravation. I get up early in the morning. I'm going to go in there and she's going to tell me to get out. Then my wife's

going to go in and she's going to get upset and be a grouch the next morning.

Note that the client continues to provide predictions but has not yet identified any evaluative beliefs.

T: You're anticipating all kinds of things. Is that what rolled through your head? Now, suppose for a minute that the situation had been a little different: your kid was throwing up, and she almost never throws up. Would you have had the same kind of automatic thoughts?

C: No, I don't think so.

T: OK, so was there something else going on here? In terms of anticipating that this could go on forever?

C: Yeah.

T: Well, what did you say about that?

C: Here we go again. It's never going to end. I don't know what we can do to make this kid sleep through the night. She keeps us up all the time.

T: So you were pretty helpless. You really didn't know what to do. You know, Sam, in addition to that, I think some other things must have gone through your head . . . because if that's all that went through your head, you would have only felt annoyance. That would've been very normal. You'd have said, "Oh no, I have to get out of this warm bed and calm her down now. Aw, shoot." You wouldn't have been very happy, but you would've done it, or at least have tried to, and if it didn't work, called your wife. Anybody would've done that. But that isn't exactly what you did, is it? What happened then?

C: I went in there and started shaking her, and yelled, "Stop it, stop it, stop it . . . I can't stand it!"

T: Ah. So you had some more powerful thoughts passing through your head. *I can't stand it. You shouldn't have done this to me. What's the matter with you? You're not playing fair.*

C: Uh hum (nodding assent).

T: Those are the kind of things that were going through your head?

Note that the therapist asks for feedback to corroborate her hypothesis.

C: Uh hum.

T: OK, Sam. Now I'm going to say something to you that may surprise you. And that is, it isn't so much that your daughter was crying in the night and interrupting your sleep that enraged you. It's what you said to yourself about that irritating event. Now, if you lined up a thousand judges, everybody would agree that this is an irritating event. Nobody wants to get up in the middle of the night, night after night. So for you to feel irritated, that's reasonable. But in order for you to get so upset that you actually wanted to go in there and throttle the kid or choke her or hit her with something. . . . See, you didn't just say, "Oh, gosh, here we go again." Which one of those things I said before . . . which one do you think really triggered you off?

C: I think, "I can't stand it anymore."

T: (repeats, twice, with emphasis) OK, now I'm going to say something pretty strange to you. (pause) *Did* you stand it?

C: I got through it. I didn't like it.

T: That's right; you didn't like it. But you didn't die, though, right?

C: (inaudible murmur)

T: Alright. See, you made an irrational statement to yourself. *I Can't stand it*. In other words, *she must not do this to me*. That's what gave you your irrational anger. By "irrational," I mean too strong, too powerful. Causing you to go in and commit an act that you were really sorry about later. You told me that the next day you felt guilty and wished you hadn't done it . . . it was overkill. Here was a kid howling in the middle of the night, and your overreaction certainly didn't help that problem any, and may even have made the situation worse. So now we've got two problems instead of the one problem, so that wasn't a reasonable thing for you to do. But do you understand what I'm saying to you?

C: Yeah. I'm telling myself that I can't stand something. I guess what you're saying is that when I say that, I make myself more angry?

T: Absolutely. You got it! You're the one . . . you're the author of your own feelings. Now that's a kind of a profound statement. I'm going to say it to you again . . . because it permeates a lot of your life and how you deal with yourself and other people. You are the author of your own anger. Do you believe that?

C: You're saying that *she* gets me irritated, and *I* get myself . . .

T: (cuts in) You actually—technically—irritate yourself about it, but I think most people would think it natural, because you are, after all, human. It's perfectly normal and reasonable for a man who's trying to get some sleep and has to go to work the next day, if he's awakened by a daughter who's not a baby and who has a bad habit of doing this. . . . For you to feel irritated is pretty normal. OK. But the fact that you lost control over yourself and actually went in and tried to throttle her in the night . . . *that* you did because of yourself. She really didn't have anything to do with that. And it's what you said in your head about the crying in the night that really got you so upset that you—well, frankly—lost control of yourself. See, that's what we're labeling disordered. You lost control of yourself. That's not a good feeling to go through life with—letting other people have control of pulling your strings. And I would like to help you understand that, so that you don't feel helpless about controlling your anger.

Teaching comment. See if you can identify which of the thirteen irrational beliefs listed in the previous chapter may be operating in Sam's example.

What do you see the therapist doing in this transcript? What steps did she take?

Part IV
Therapy:
Getting Down to D,
Disputation

10 Cognitive, Emotive, and Behavioral Strategies

In the preceding chapters we discussed the A, B, and C—the diagnostic groundwork—of rational-emotive therapy. Thus far, we might conceptualize the therapist's role as one of a diagnostician, looking for and amplifying clues that set up the problem. Clarifying the A, B, and C is an assessment procedure, useful for both therapist and client. Until the therapist understands the important connections between B and C, these cannot be clearly pointed out to the client. Unless clients understand the importance of these same relationships, they will not see the relevance of changing their beliefs. *Changing the beliefs* is the real work of therapy and occurs at D, the *Disputation*.

What is a disputation? It is a debate or a challenge to the patient's irrational belief system and can be of a *cognitive, imaginal,* and/or *behavioral* nature. Each of these disputational strategies will be discussed in the following chapters. Once the RB's have been discriminated from the IB's, the essence of D is to challenge the IB's. For example, the therapist may ask, "Why must you succeed?" The client may respond, "Because I want to." This is a rational belief, but the continuation, ". . . and it's awful when I don't get what I want," is an irrational belief. Only the IB's, not the RB's, are disputed.

Levels of Abstraction

In disputation, patients are confronted with their irrational philosophies and asked to examine them, bit by bit, to see if they make sense and are helpful. Disputation is, then, a logical and empirical process in which the

We want to emphasize the point that it is only irrational beliefs that are the targets for disputation, not rational beliefs, descriptions of reality, or—especially—emotions. In fact, one of the key differences between cognition and emotion is that emotions are not debatable.

Consider a parallel example: if I say I'm cold, and the other two people in the room say they are hot and sweaty and point out that the temperature in the room is 100 degrees, I still feel cold. The others' feedback is functionally irrelevant. "I'm cold" is not disputable, any more than emotions are. When others argue with my experience of being cold, they are really saying "There's something *wrong* with you for feeling cold," and "You really *shouldn't* feel cold." Now substitute some emotion for the experience of "cold," and you can see how invalidating it would seem to patients to have their experience and sense of reality challenged.

Emotions are to be respected. They are the patient's experience and are not to be disputed.

patient is helped to stop and think. Its basic goal is to help the patient internalize a new philosophy, epitomized in statements such as, "It would be too bad if I don't succeed, but I can bear it. I'm merely fallible, and that's not awful." This basic goal is known in RET as the *elegant solution*.

D, therefore, consists of two basic stages. The patient is helped to

1. Examine and challenge his or her present mode of thinking.
2. Develop new, more functional modes of thinking.

The result of disputation is to modulate clients' negative dysfunctional thinking in such a way that they can be relieved of the emotional disturbance from which they are suffering. The level of abstraction at which such modulation takes place will vary from patient to patient. For example, I may not be able to really "get" the most elegant and comprehensive idea that *I don't need anyone's love and approval*, but I may be able to "get" the idea that I don't need the love and approval of a particular person (e.g., to win the heart of a mate or spouse). While the latter idea is less inclusive, it is nonetheless rational and elegant; it would be consistent with happy living if I did not have that particular kind of relationship in my life. Usually, we do not need to go to the most abstract level of the irrational belief, since it is unlikely that the individual will ever have to cope with it in reality. For example, it is unlikely that an individual will achieve *no success* or receive *no love* within the space of a lifetime.

Let's take another example. If Ralph is angry at his spouse for not having dinner on the table when he thought she should, we could identify many levels of irrational thinking that lead to his anger:

1. My wife must make dinner when I want her to.
2. My wife must do chores the way I want her to.
3. My wife must do things the way I want her to.
4. Family members must do things the way I want them to.
5. People in my life must do things the way I want them to.
6. All people must behave the way I want them to behave.
7. The world must be the way I want it to be.

These thoughts illustrate a continuum of abstraction and, more important, they illustrate why the level of abstraction is clinically significant. If our client only believed the first irrational idea, there would be few activating events to which he would react, but the more abstract irrational beliefs he subscribes to, the more potential distress he may suffer. As a parallel, the less abstract the *rational* belief, the less generalizable it will be.

In therapy, clients are more likely to report beliefs at the lower end of the abstraction continuum. These lower-level beliefs are more readily experienced and admitted by the client, and thus may be more accessible to change. The client's ability to generalize from a specific example to new situations will be enhanced if the therapist also works at the more abstract levels. Our suggestion, therefore, is that the therapist be prepared to conceptualize the irrational ideas and dispute these irrational ideas *up and down* the ladder of abstraction as the work progresses.

Let's return to Ralph's situation. If Ralph's therapist begins disputation at a concrete level ("My wife must make dinner when I want her to"), Ralph is likely to gain some control over his emotions in a frequently occurring problematic situation and thus be reinforced for making progress in therapy. Later, the therapist may want to teach Ralph that he tends to be demanding about other things as well, and that the world does not have to be the way he wants it to be. Thus, by moving up and down the

Disputation has always been the heart of RET, or perhaps more accurately, the *art* of RET. As such, it is difficult to teach and can be perplexing to new students. More experienced practitioners spend much of therapy actively doing disputation; the beginner is likely to debate briefly and move on. A common pattern for the new therapist is one in which the client reveals an irrational belief and the therapist asks, "Where's the evidence?" The client looks confused, and says, "I guess there is none," at which point the therapist assumes the client "got it" and moves to another topic or asks the client what other problem he or she would like to work on.

As you study the next several chapters, we recommend that you focus on the *process* of disputation rather than on learning a particular technique. Techniques can be drawn from a variety of sources, such as other schools of therapy. It is hoped that the therapist's own creativity will also generate techniques, as long as they are consistent with the goals of disputation.

ladder of abstraction, the therapist will insure that Ralph learns to deal with specific activating events and can apply the RET solution to other similar aversive events; and that he understands the rule behind the reasoning and can apply it to future aversive events.

What to Dispute

To review, let's recall that when clients give us dysfunctional cognitions they will be of one of three broad types: automatic thoughts, including inferences, attributions, and predictions; irrational evaluative beliefs; and core irrational beliefs or schemas. RET therapists will aim disputations at any of these three targets, but prefer to work at the level of evaluative IB's and core IB's, and will certainly target them *first,* the assumption being that the automatic thoughts arise out of the core cognitive schemas.

When disputations are targeting the inferences and automatic thoughts that the client reports, we term the disputation an *inferential dispute.* The cognitive errors will likely involve errors of induction, in

Inferential disputations are seen in the early treatment manuals by Beck, whose methods stem from his study of patients with depression. Beck's empirical challenge (e.g., "Where's the evidence?") is useful for past events that may be tormenting the depressed patient. When the patient's attributional set is dysfunctional—that is, problems are seen as internal, global, and stable—it may be helpful to get the patient to reinterpret the problem as temporary, external, or limited in scope. Assume, for example, that I observe that a number of people in my audience do not seem to be paying attention to my lecture, and my mood plummets after I make the attribution that the audience is inattentive because I am boring. An inferential disputation might be to reassure myself that it is very early in the morning and people probably haven't had their coffee yet.

A limitation to inferential or attributional disputes is that they are temporary in nature. For example, what if my next lecture is given in the evening, and people still don't pay attention? The feared bad event could always happen. Arguing that it has a low probability of occurring will not give the patient a way to cope with it if it does happen and may lead to a disruption in the therapeutic relationship. More important, these temporary solutions fail to challenge the patient's underlying core evaluative beliefs and schemas.

which clients make overgeneralized conclusions based on insufficent data (e.g., "Since he didn't call me, he doesn't love me.")

Disputations targeted at the irrational beliefs or underlying schema of the client are referred to as *philosophic disputes.* As we outline the various processes and styles of disputation in subsequent chapters, be aware that these can be applied as either inferential or philosophic disputes, depending on the targeted belief structures.

Cognitive Therapy versus Cognitive Techniques

There is an important distinction between the cognitive therapy process and using a cognitive technique. The cognitive process refers to the therapist's conceptualization of the client's problem as emotional and behav-

When we teach new students of RET, we often observe them getting stuck at the opening of the disputation. They may have quickly and efficiently outlined a simple A-B-C, but instead of moving into D, they often return to assessment (e.g., ". . . and what else were you feeling?"). Perhaps one of the reasons for this error is simply not knowing how to get started.

A strategy that may help is to use a *setting phrase*. For example, you can simply repeat an irrational belief of the client's and then say: "OK. Now, that's your belief and we can see that it is causing you trouble, so let's go after that belief."

If you still feel unsure of how to begin, you might follow the setting phrase by putting the problem in the hands of the client, "Do *you* see any ways we could begin to attack that belief?"

ioral distress emanating from dysfunctional or irrational thinking. A cognitive technique is *any* strategy you can use to try to change these beliefs. These techniques can be rational-emotive, such as those outlined in this and subsequent chapters, or they can just as well be reflective, client-centered, gestalt, or other strategies drawn from the case studies of skilled therapists. The key is how the therapist *uses* the selected strategy to change dysfunctional cognitions. Creativity of technique within the context of a cognitive change process will develop with experience.

The modality you select can be based, in part, on an evaluation of the client's strengths and weaknesses. It is therefore helpful to determine the patient's current methods for solving problems. If their methods tend to be behavioral, and they seem to be relatively deficient in introspection, you might make better headway with behavioral techniques in the service of cognitive change. Likewise, if the individual deals with problems affectively, you may feel like you're talking to a Martian if you try to engage this client in detailed cognitive analysis. With the "hysterical" client, you might involve him or her in therapy and induce cognitive shifts by making creative use of the dynamics of the patient–therapist relationship or by using gestalt techniques.

For the moment, however, we will turn our attention to the major rational-emotive approach: cognitive, imaginal, and behavioral disputation.

Cognitive Disputation

Cognitive disputations are attempts to change the client's erroneous beliefs through philosophical persuasion, didactic presentations, Socratic dialogue, vicarious experiences, and other modes of verbal expression. One of the most important tools in cognitive disputation is the use of *questions*. We pointed out previously that as a rule, it is generally good to avoid asking "why" questions when assessing A's, B's, and C's; in disputation, however, "why" questions may be particularly fruitful. The answer to a "why" question requires proof or justification of a belief, and since there is no proof for irrational beliefs, the patient may see the logic for giving them up.

The following group of questions is culled from disputations by Ellis (1962, 1971, 1974b, 1979b) and other therapists at the Institute for Rational Emotive Therapy in New York City. We present them as examples to get you started. Note that by relying on such questions, the therapist is making the client do the work, and essentially asking the client to prove his or her irrational ideas to the therapist.

LOGICAL DISPUTATION QUESTIONS

The first group of questions asks for logical consistency or semantic clarity in the client's thinking, and can be used to challenge any IB.

> Is that good logic?
> Is that true?
> Why not?
> Why is that so?
> How do you know?
> Could you be overgeneralizing?
> What do you mean by that term?
> If a friend held that (self-downing) idea, would you accept it?
> Why is that an untrue statement?
> In what way?
> Is that very good proof?
> Explain to me why (e.g., ". . . you're so stupid you don't belong in college").

What behaviors can you marshal as proof?

Why does it have to be so?

Where is that written?

Can you see the inconsistency in your beliefs?

What would that mean about you as a person?

Does that logically follow?

What's wrong with the notion that you're "special"?

How would you be destroyed if you don't . . . ?

Why must you?

Let's assume the worst. You're doing very bad things. Now why must you not do them?

These questions are selected from logical arguments that focus on whether the client's irrational belief follows from the reasoning that the client uses to defend it. For example, when most clients are asked, "Why must the world be the way you say it must be?" they proceed to explain how it would be more *desirable* for them. Ellis' classic dispute points out that because something is more desirable, it does not logically follow that the world *must* provide what is desirable. Desirability and the client's given reality have no logical relation to each other; to proceed from desiring to demanding is to use a logical non sequitur.

Other disputes focus on the logical inconsistency among different aspects of the client's belief system. For example, Stanley condemns himself for not accomplishing a specific goal or reaching a specific aspiration. He could be asked (a) if he would condemn others for failing to reach that same goal, or (b) if he would condemn others for failing to reach their own goals. Clients often respond "no" to such questions. How is it logical, the therapist then asks, to condemn one person for failing, but not another? The logical inconsistency can be repeatedly illustrated with such questions and comparisons.

REALITY-TESTING DISPUTATION QUESTIONS

The second group of questions requires clients to evaluate whether their beliefs are consistent with empirical reality. For example, most "demanding" beliefs can be shown to be inconsistent with reality. No matter how strongly clients believe that the world "must" be the way they want it to be, the universe usually does not change to match the "must." Content analyses of Ellis' therapy tapes indicate that he often uses this argument. He asks clients what reality is, and then points out that it is not consistent with their "must."

Clients who endorse LFT beliefs can be shown that even though they think they *cannot stand* the occurrence of A, they have, in fact, "stood it" over and over again. Catastrophizing beliefs can be challenged with questions that point out that a negative A did not result in a totally, 100 percent bad outcome. Questions can require the client to evaluate whether future events will occur and if so, whether they will be as unpleasant as the client believes. Self-downing beliefs, in which the person condemns himself or herself as totally worthless, can be shown through questioning to be incorrect, because all people do some things well and are important to someone else in the world.

What is the proof?

Where's the evidence?

What would happen if . . . ?

Can you stand it?

Let's be scientists. What do the data show?

Why must she do that? Does she have to?

If that's true, realistically, what's the worst that can happen?

So what if that happens?

How would that be so terrible?

How is a disadvantage awful?

Ask yourself, is it possible to still find happiness?

What good things can happen if . . . occurs?

Can you be happy even if you don't get what you want?

Explain to me why you'd have to be done in by that?

What is the probability of a bad consequence?

How will your world be destroyed if . . . ?

PRAGMATIC DISPUTATION QUESTIONS

The third group of questions does not challenge the logic of the clients' thinking but rather persuades clients to assess the hedonic value of their belief systems. Remember, rational beliefs help one attain one's goals, so that beliefs can be evaluated on this *functional* criterion. Does a particular idea help the client to solve a personal problem? Attain a desired goal? Provide other positive consequences? Mitigate emotional turmoil?

> As long as you believe that, how will you feel?
>
> "Whatever I want, I must get." Where will that command get you?
>
> Is it worth the risk?
>
> Is it worth it?
>
> When you think that way, how do you feel?
>
> Does that thought motivate you to get to work?
>
> And where does that get you?
>
> What happens when you think that way?
>
> Why do you hold onto a belief that causes you so much trouble?

In using the questioning strategy, allow the client time to mull over your questions fully. (This suggestion implies that you will be careful to ask only one question at a time; no barrages, please.) Do not provide answers to your own questions until you give the client a chance to reach for his or her own answers. Be prepared for silences after your questions. New therapists seem to find these silences aversive, especially if they mistakenly believe that they *must* be directive at all times. Silence, in this instance, can indeed be golden.

Be aware, however, that these unusual questions can lead to discomfort on the part of your clients, primarily because many of the questions have no "legitimate" answer (e.g., "Where is the evidence for that belief?" There isn't any.). Therefore, while you are waiting for the clients' responses, observe any nonverbal signs of discomfort that may be exhibited during this period. If your clients are exceptionally distressed, ask them what emotional reactions or feelings they are having and find out what irrational beliefs they are telling themselves. Perhaps they are awfulizing about not knowing the answers to your questions or because they realize that they are thinking crookedly; if so, they will not be attending to the points you are making during disputation. Uproot these irrational beliefs before you continue with the original disputation.

Clients frequently respond to disputational questions by giving you evidence in favor of the *rational belief*. For example, when the therapist attempts to dispute the concept of awfulness (e.g., "Where's the evidence that this is so terrible?"), the response of the client will almost always be to justify why the situation is undesirable (e.g., "Because I don't like it!"). In this example, the patient is failing to discriminate between *undesirable* and *awful.* The most common error made by a new RET therapist is to be stumped by the client's reasoning. Instead, the therapist can point out to the client that his or her retort provides evidence for the rational statement but is not an answer to the original question. The therapist repeats the question until the client comes to the appropriate conclusion that no evidence exists for the IB.

C: But it's awful if I don't get this promotion!
T: Well, just how is that so awful?
C: Because . . . then I'll be stuck in the same job and I won't get the extra money or the prestige that goes with it.
T: Look, Jack, that's evidence for why it's unfortunate or bad that you don't get the promotion. Because it's bad, it doesn't follow that it's *terrible.* Now, try again. Can you show me how it's terrible?
C: But I've worked hard for this for a long time. I deserve it!
T: Jack, it may be true that you've worked hard. But that's only further evidence that it's unfortunate you didn't get it. How is it *terrible?*
C: You mean all those reasons for it being bad don't make it terrible?
T: That's right, Jack! Terrible means you can't live with this or possibly be happy. It means 101 percent bad. Now, how is failing to get the promotion that bad?

Clients will often persist in giving similar answers far longer than the client in the above example. The therapist had better be at least as persistent as the client.

OTHER COGNITIVE DISPUTATION STRATEGIES

A second set of cognitive disputation strategies are *didactic,* including the use of mini-lectures, analogies, and parables. Lectures, as we suggested earlier, are best kept brief and may be useful when new ideas are being presented to the client. As the patient becomes familiar with rational-emotive theory, the amount of time spent on lecturing can be gradually decreased. When you do lecture, try to assess if the client understands the concept you are trying to teach. A good way to do this is to follow up didactic discourse with some Socratic dialogue. Lectures can be illustrated with stories, analogies, and parables. There is great scope for creativity in devising stories to show how the client's reasoning is faulty. Some examples will be given in the following sections, in which suggested disputations for core irrational concepts are outlined.

Another widely used form of cognitive disputation and a primary tool of the RET therapist is exaggeration or *humor,* a variation of the paradoxical intention technique. Ellis (1977c) is particularly noted for his use of this strategy, not only in front of audiences but also in individual sessions. Thus, if the client says, "It's really awful that I failed the test!" the therapist might respond, "You're right! It's not only awful, but I don't see how you're going to survive. That's the worst news I've ever heard! This is so horrendous that I can't bear to talk about it. Let's talk about something else, quick!" Such paradoxical statements frequently point out the senselessness of the IB to the client, and very little further debate may be necessary to make the point. There is no rule that therapy must be stodgy, dull, or super-serious. Once you get used to using humor judiciously, you as well as your client may enjoy the hour together more. The use of humor does entail one caveat: the target of the humor is always the client's irrational belief and *not* the client.

A fourth cognitive strategy is the use of *vicarious modeling.* Therapists can frequently point out to clients that many people in their environment have similar activating events and yet do not suffer from exaggerated emotional reactions, because they do not adhere to the same IB's. Much can be learned by vicarious modeling: clients can be made aware that others are not devastated by similar problems and can be reminded that life goes on despite unfortunate happenings. This knowledge can then be applied to themselves. The process can also sensitize clients to look for data in their environment that may have been selectively screened out. Vicarious modeling is a particularly good strategy to use, therefore, when clients' A's are virtually universal, such as the common problems presented by children and adolescents. Almost all children have to cope with going to bed "too early" and, even worse, having to brush their teeth beforehand! The therapist can point out that most youngsters go through these same "tortures" and manage to do so unscathed and with significantly less horror.

New therapists are reluctant to use vicarious modeling when dealing with clients who have unusual or highly aversive activating events (e.g., rape, terminal illness, the death of one's child, etc.). Such clients are likely to believe that no one can appreciate how traumatic their experience was; yet coping models are available. The client may not personally have encountered such individuals, but referral to appropriate self-help groups will provide such exposure. One of the authors recently treated the mother of a child with Giles de la Tourette's syndrome.* She was unfamil-

---

*Tourette's syndrome involves multiple motor tics in conjunction with a verbal tic which may take the form of a barking sound or long chains of obscenities.

iar with the disorder and horrified by the child's bizarre behavior, convinced that her child was the only case in the world. Through some investigation, the therapist found an association for parents of children with Tourette's syndrome and advised the mother to attend a meeting of this group. This experience provided the woman with coping models, and at her next therapy session she concluded, "I guess it isn't so awful . . . people *can* learn to adjust to it."

Imaginal Disputation Strategies

A variation on cognitive disputational strategies involves the use of *imagery*. In one such procedure, after a verbal disputation, the therapist may ask clients to imagine themselves again in the troublesome situation; this may allow the therapist to see if the emotion has changed. If it has, the therapist may ask clients what they are *now* telling themselves as a way to rehearse more rational beliefs. If the emotion has not changed, there may be more IB's present, and the imagery exercise may allow them to emerge. If necessary, a new A-B-C-D analysis may be conducted and the results reexamined by a repeat of the imagery exercise. As an alternative, the therapist may wish to shift to one of the following imagery techniques, known as REI, rational-emotive imagery (Maultsby, 1975; Maultsby and Ellis, 1974).

In *negative rational-emotive imagery,* clients close their eyes and imagine themselves in the problem situation (A) and try to experience their usual emotional turmoil (C). Wait until clients report experiencing C and then ask them to focus on the internal sentences that seem to be related to these emotional consequences. Then instruct patients to *change the feeling* from a disturbed emotion to a more constructive negative emotion (e.g., from anxiety to concern). Assure clients that this can be done, even if it's only for a fraction of a second. Instruct clients that as soon as they have accomplished this task, they are to open their eyes. At this signal from the patients, you may simply ask, "How were you able to do that?" Almost invariably the answer will reveal a cognitive shift; usually patients respond that they have stopped catastrophizing: for example, "So I couldn't get an erection with my new girlfriend. She'll probably understand. And even if she doesn't, it won't be the end of the world." Here is another example:

T: Now, I want you to close your eyes and imagine yourself back in the situation in which you felt so anxious yesterday. Can you do that?

Wait until clients indicate they have the image.

C: Yes.
T: Now, I want you to make yourself feel anxious right now, as you did yesterday. Signal me when you're feeling anxious.

Wait for the client's signal.

C: (nods)
T: OK, now tell me what thoughts are going through your head to make you feel anxious.

Wait for the client's response, which will be some form of IB.

C: I'm saying, "My God, suppose I goof up? He'll think I'm a jerk!"
T: Now, I want you to change that feeling of anxiety to one of *concern*. Signal me when you are less anxious and now feel merely concerned—perhaps motivated to do something about the situation.

Pause until the client's signal.

T: Now, what are you telling yourself so that you feel only concerned and not anxious?
C: Well, if I goof, it's not the end of the world, and if he thinks I'm a jerk, that's too bad. I *do* make mistakes—everybody does—and I'm working at improving my performance all the time. I guess I'll be doing that as long as I live!

In *positive rational-emotive imagery* (Maultsby, 1975; Maultsby and Ellis, 1974), clients imagine themselves in a problematic situation but picture themselves behaving and feeling differently. For example, clients anxious about speaking in public imagine themselves speaking up in class or at a meeting and feeling relatively relaxed while doing so. As soon as clients report that they have had that image, the therapist asks, "And what were you saying to yourself in order to do that?" This technique is useful because it allows clients to practice a positive plan and develop a set of coping skills. For example:

T: OK, Mary, now I know you've been having trouble when you think about giving that speech to the PTA this week. I know you've been feeling very anxious about that.
C: Yes, I'm really scared.
T: What I'd like you to do now is to close your eyes and picture yourself up there at the podium addressing the parents in the audience. But I want you to picture yourself doing that and feeling relatively *calm* while you're doing it. You're speaking slowly and clearly, and feeling

not too anxious. You read your speech in a nice loud voice, glancing up frequently to look at members of the group. Tell me when you get that picture clear in your head.

Pause and wait for feedback from the client.

C: (nods)
T: Now, what would you have to say to yourself in order to do what you pictured?
C: Well, I have my ideas down on paper. I know what I want to say. The parents are there to hear my ideas, not to judge *me*. I can't really expect them all to like all of my ideas, and if some of them disagree with me, that's OK. It'll make for a lively discussion. Anyway, they'd probably be nervous up at the podium too, so I'm sure they won't mind if my hands shake a little. I won't think about that; I'll just concentrate on getting my point across.

Tosi and Reardon (1976) recommend inducing deep relaxation or hypnosis and then guiding the patient through an A-B-C; for example, the patient imagines approaching a feared A, making rational statements, and then experiencing an appropriate C, or emotional consequence. Such a procedure employs a "mastery" image which may be appropriate for children but less helpful to adults than a "coping" image (Meichenbaum, 1985). In a coping procedure, for example, patients imagine approaching A and saying to themselves the irrational messages they usually employ; they then imagine themselves disputing and replacing the IB statements

---

An advantage of positive and negative rational–emotive imagery techniques is that they encourage clients to be active in the session and allow the therapist to check whether clients are changing their dysfunctional affects by rehearsing appropriate rational cognitions. But be careful. Sometimes clients will surprise you, and you'll discover that they feel better, but for the wrong reasons. For example, Fred was very anxious about approaching women for a dance at a singles bar for fear he'd get rejected. When he rehearsed this experience in imagery, he was indeed able to lower his anxiety, but this is how he did it: "Who cares? She's a mean bitch and who the hell does she think she is?" The therapist pointed out that this kind of thinking was not rational imagery, but *hostile imagery!*

with more rational statements, such as, "This really isn't true . . . be calm . . . I can cope with this anxiety . . . things are not as terrible as I think they are"; and finally they imagine a reduction in emotion. This approach may be more helpful than one employing a mastery image because patients are often anxious the first few times they actually approach a feared A, and they want a tool to cope with this very concrete anxiety. Even highly skilled practitioners of RET occasionally experience debilitating emotions, such as anxiety or anger, and use their skills to *remove* this distress once it occurs. Thus, RET can be employed not only as a preventive device but a restorative one as well.

A related imagery technique employed by cognitive therapists is the "blow-up" procedure, in which the patient imagines future unwanted events and then blows them out of proportion, beyond what might realistically happen. For example, a client with a compulsive ritual of checking whether the gas jets were turned off imagined not only that the kitchen and his house were set afire but that his neighborhood, the city, the country, and finally the whole globe went up in flames! By the use of exaggeration the patient may learn to see the humor in his or her fears, so that the humor diffuses the fear.

Some therapists prefer to use imagery techniques after initially doing relaxation training or hypnosis to induce a state of greater suggestibility, particularly if the client is unusually anxious. The therapist who wishes to learn such techniques is referred to *Clinical Behavior Therapy* (1976) by Goldfried and Davison, or to *The New Hypnosis* (1985) by Araoz.

Imagery can be used in disputation in creative ways that utilize a client's special talents. For example, Herb, an artist, brought in a picture he'd sketched of himself with his father, the latter drawn in enlarged scale and looking quite menacing. After exploring some of the thoughts and feelings that were expressed in the picture, he was asked to draw, in session, a picture of himself and his father, both of the same size. When completed, the therapist asked Herb, "What is the 'you' in this picture believing that is different from the 'you' in the first picture?"

Notice that the therapist is using a unique modality—one that fits the client's needs but also clearly follows the RET model.

Behavioral Disputation Strategies

The third basic form of dispute is *behavioral,* in which the patient challenges his or her IB's by behaving in a way that opposes them. In fact, the RET practitioner will not be confident that the patient has internalized a new philosophy until it is reflected in behavioral change. Patients in therapy are engaging in verbal learning, and it is important to assure that their behavior in the real world matches their verbal behavior in session.

Behavioral disputes provide clients with experiences that run counter to their present irrational belief system; clients act against their IB's. For example, if clients believe that they cannot stand waiting for events, they are asked to practice postponing gratifications. If they believe that they cannot stand rejection, they are encouraged to seek it out. If they believe that they need something, they are exhorted to do without. If they believe their worth is based on doing well, they are asked to purposely do poorly. Since behavioral disputes are typically performed outside of the therapist's office, they are usually given as homework assignments. This topic will, therefore, be discussed in greater detail in Chapter 14.

However, some behavioral disputes are best done *in session,* a good example of which are many of the anxiety challenges. An experience of anxiety or, worse, panic, seems overwhelming to the client, and usually results in a secondary fear of the onset of the panic experience. In session, the therapist and client can plan and engage in behaviors that elicit some of the very sensations the client ordinarily tries to avoid. For example, the client may be urged to hyperventilate or do some vigorous movements that stimulate rapid, shallow breathing, sweating, lightheadedness, or tingling of the extremities, and can then work with the therapist to challenge cognitions such as "I can't tolerate these sensations," or "Something terrible is going to happen" (Beck and Emery, 1985).

Another in-session strategy is the use of role playing and rational role reversal. In *role playing,* under the tutelage of the therapist, the client rehearses a new behavior that is more consistent with a rational philosophy. *Rational role reversal* consists of asking the client to play the "voice of reason" when the therapist models the client's irrational beliefs, and is similar to what Burns (1980) has called "externalization of voices." This strategy may be a way of strengthening the client's conviction in a rational philosophy. Here, for example, is how a therapist may lead a client into this strategy:

A "cognitive" therapist may use a "behavioral" strategy but will examine its impact by inquiring of the patient, "Now, how do you *think* differently about that situation?" For example, "You've now been on the elevator six times; has your thinking about elevators changed?" or "Has your thinking about your anxiety changed?"

Cognitions, emotions, and behaviors are all dependent variables in measuring change. Whether change comes about by taking a pill, riding an elevator, or sitting in the therapist's office debating whether it would be horrible to feel anxious—or even sitting in an armchair practicing some of the symptoms of anxiety and adapting to them—the therapist always comes back to examining the patient's thinking. Until that thinking changes, the fact that the patient has been on an elevator six times may not have any relevance to future behavior. Because the B–C interface is the heart of RET, the patient's cognitions are ultimately our primary focus.

"In order to consolidate our disputing work today, how about if I play your irrational voice and see if you can play the voice of reason. Let's see if you can handle some of the criticisms that I've heard you say about yourself in these sessions. Anytime you get stuck and can't answer back the criticism, let's trade places and see if I can handle it. Then I'll give it back to you and we'll see what you can do with it. This will be a way of practicing more rational thinking."

Important Things to Know about Disputing

An important prerequisite for successful disputation is the *therapist's* ability to think rationally about the client's problem. How can therapists dispute something they believe really is terrible? First, we advise therapists to ask themselves, "How terrible is it, really?" If they are not convinced, how will they ever convince the client? One female therapist, for example, found herself overwhelmed by a client's fears of sexual rejection after a mastectomy. Only after the therapist had philosophically de-escalated the loss of a breast (as she said, "My sexuality is not located in my nipple!") was she able to calmly help her client to the same conclusion.

When you are ready to dispute, make sure you are disputing the appropriate philosophical concept, not the metaphor in which it is expressed. For example, if a client says, "I failed—what a horse's ass I am!" it is easy to point out that he is mistaken since he clearly does not possess the characteristics of equine buttocks. The philosophical point will have been missed, however, because the client's misconception about human worth being dependent on accomplishment is still intact.

Once you have uncovered a core IB, realize that it will take a significant amount of *time to dispute it*. Inasmuch as the essence of RET is to change irrational beliefs, D is obviously the most critical part. Don't be afraid to repeat a disputation over the course of many sessions if necessary. There are several ways to assure plentiful time for disputation. One way to increase disputing time is to avoid taking on a new problem in a session if you have not finished disputing an older problem from a previous session. You can begin your next session by asking the client if he or she recalls the problem, outlining the A's, B's, and C's quickly, and launching immediately into disputation. Another strategy is to take the new problems brought in by the client and show how they relate to his or her core IB's, and then proceed with the disputation.

Before beginning a disputation, remember to clarify whether the patient has a problem about the problem, or what we referred to earlier as a *secondary disturbance*. For example, is the patient depressed or anxious about being depressed? If so, what is the better level on which to work, the symptom or the disturbance about the symptom? In almost all cases, we recommend the latter, for as long as clients remain distraught about their emotional reactions, they will be in a poor position to work on them. This meta-problem may be particularly prominent in patients with perfectionist tendencies (e.g., "I shouldn't have these kinds of problems!) or low frustration tolerance (e.g., "I can't stand this anxiety!"). However, if after providing a rationale for dealing with the secondary problem first, the client still wishes to work on the primary problem, it is best to accede. Otherwise, you may threaten the good therapeutic alliance you have developed with the client.

Whenever possible, work first with the patient's *motivation* before beginning a disputational strategy. Point out to the client the benefits of changing his or her beliefs—especially the benefit of feeling less emotional distress. This strategy depends, of course, on assuring that the client does want to change C. If the patient has an anger problem, for example, the therapist may first inquire, "Can you see any advantages to being less angry?" After these are listed, the therapist may ask, "Can you think of any ways to feel less angry?" When motivation is established, the client may be more receptive to a cognitive or behavioral intervention.

Thus, among the disputational techniques to help the patient challenge distress-producing B's are those that first point out the lack of value of the distress. Again taking anger as an example, the therapist might state something like the following:

> "Let's first take a look at whether your anger is working for you or against you. What does rage do? It sets the stage for a fight! Also, it isn't good for you; it gets your juices flowing, makes you feel more irritated, and so forth. Now concern or annoyance, on the other hand, serves as a sensible cue for you to say, 'How can I change this? What can I do to help the situation? Perhaps if I explain to him . . . ?' See, now we're talking about *strategies*. And if a strategy doesn't work, what would you do? You'd go back to the drawing board and try another. You see, you can do that kind of problem solving once you're not in a rage."

If your clients are unsure about whether they want to change their behaviors or emotions, try to determine other motivations that may be serving to *maintain the pathology*. A good technique to help patients become aware of the reinforcers operating to perpetuate a problem is the following sentence-completion item from Lazarus (1972): "The *good* thing about . . . [e.g., procrastination] is . . ." Repeat this phrase until the patient has exhausted all suggestions. If clients can't think of anything to say, urge them to say something anyway, the first thing that comes to mind. Stress that they need not believe what they say, nor does it have to be true of them. The therapist may even suggest a sentence-completion line as a model to get the client started. The therapist would do well to listen for a pattern in the client's responses, for not only may the client's statements indicate reasons to keep the distress, but new irrational beliefs may be revealed as well.

Disputation is hard work, for what you are trying to do is shift the patient's position on major philosophic issues. To accomplish this task requires many trials and a great deal of *persistence* on the part of the therapist. Like any good persuader, therapists had better believe in what they are saying, and demonstrate this belief by their persistence and enthusiasm for their position—rationality.

Persistence, however, doesn't mean a continual hard sell; some dis-

Remind your clients that it is important not merely to be aware that one's thoughts are irrational, but to *actively dispute these thoughts outside of the therapy sessions*. In addition, it is important to *actively construct new rational beliefs* to replace the old irrational ones.

putations are subtle and can take place even when the therapist is being supportive or reflective. If you are in the early stages of therapy and attempting to build rapport, you may wish to be supportive but at the same time not reinforce irrational beliefs. For example, if your client says, "I need . . . ," you can reflect by saying, "I know that . . . is something you want very badly." The therapist is thus modeling a more rational statement while conveying understanding of the client's plight.

New therapists frequently assume that generalization of behavior change will automatically take place. Although we believe that generalization is one of the advantages of cognitive psychotherapy, we do not assume that it occurs without effort. As with behavior therapies, generalization often has to be built into the RET program. Thus, it may be desirable to dispute the same irrational notion across many situations, even though the irrational beliefs, the disputation, and the resulting rational beliefs may be the same in each example.

A prototype of the generalization problem is the male client with sexual difficulties, for whom a hierarchy of anxiety-arousing situations has been constructed. The client may have progressed through several exercises, such as sensate focus or masturbation training, during which he successfully counteracted his irrational beliefs about failure and performance. At the top of the hierarchy, when he is instructed to resume having intercourse with his partner, he may completely reinterpret the situation and resume his irrational catastrophizing. He then might be saying to himself, "This is the Real Thing; now if I fail, it will indeed be terrible!" Thus, although you may have helped him counteract his irrational beliefs at lower points in the hierarchy, you cannot assume that his rational beliefs will generalize to the next step. In this example, the therapist specifically questions the patient about his cognitions during the various performance stages.

In addition, do not assume that if clients are thinking rationally in one problem area, they are doing so in other problem areas as well. For example, Margaret may present several problems at once: anxiety in social situations, guilt about sexual performance, anger at her boss, and so on. Generally, it is wise to work on one problem at a time. If the therapist chooses to work on the anxiety in social situations and helps the client to successfully rid herself of all of her irrational beliefs in this area, there is no guarantee that she will automatically begin thinking rationally about sexual guilt or about her anger at her boss. These other problem areas will probably require separate work.

One strategy to maximize generalization benefits is to help clients believe that they are responsible for their own success. A number of studies in the behavioral literature have indicated that internal rather than external attribution for success at an endeavor is an important cognitive factor in generalization (Meichenbaum, 1977). If clients believe that their success was attributable to internal factors, they are more likely to believe that they have control over future problems and to apply what they have learned in therapy to new problems.

A final suggestion, before we turn to more examples of disputation, is to use as many disputational strategies with each client as possible. The more modalities you utilize (cognitive, experiential, imaginal), the more effective the disputation will be and the longer-lasting its effects (Lazarus, 1972).

Is Your Disputation Effective?

If your disputation strategies have "hit the nail on the head" for the client, you will know it, because he or she will likely report a shift in affect. The new rational beliefs will, ideally, put the lie to the old irrational thinking in such a way that the client experiences some relief of emotional distress. Such a transformation does not typically occur quickly, however. More than likely, your client will say something like this:

C: I understand what you're saying, but I don't *feel* it yet.
T: I don't expect you to feel it yet. In fact, it would be very unusual if you did. The reason I say that is because really integrating this new way of thinking into your feelings and behavior is what the next stage of therapy is about . . . putting this work into practice, deepening your conviction. But even now, if you were to raise your children in one of these two beliefs, which would you choose?

Dispute with respect. We are not making fun of client's erroneous or self-defeating thinking, but working to repair or modulate it. First, however, we accept and study it. IB's are there, presumably, for a good reason.

For example, one client had lost her parents at a very young age and been sent to live with her grandparents, who soon died, so that she ended up with distant relatives. Her silent conclusion, based on the data of her life, was that love, trust, or closeness was the "kiss of death." Small wonder that she had difficulty establishing intimate adult relationships, including a therapeutic rapport. The work in therapy consisted of respectfully understanding her early experience, as interpreted by a frightened young child, which had led to her *not illogical* core belief. Gradually she learned to reinterpret her experience, reassure herself, and trust in her ability to love and, as an adult, to tolerate the potential for loss of a love object.

An Outline for Disputation

To the new therapist, disputation is bewildering, and learning this complex set of skills can seem like a monumental undertaking. If you listen to the work of experienced rational-emotive therapists, however, an outline of typical disputation maneuvers emerges. We will present the common steps in a disputation, but it should be noted that neither the steps nor their sequence are fixed. These are, therefore, suggested proceedings rather than dogma to be rigidly followed.

Once you have identified the A, B, and C:

1. Point out to clients that as long as they hold onto their irrational beliefs, they will be upset. This step is one device for establishing motivation for the client to change.

2. Provide a rational belief and ask how clients imagine they would feel if they believed it. In this stage, you not only model more helpful ideas but your prospective examination again sets a motivational tone.

3. Once clients acknowledge that they would feel better, use this feedback to encourage them to give up the irrational belief.

4. Then proceed to ask for evidence for the IB. In this stage, all of the various cognitive disputational strategies described earlier can be employed, although often you simply repeat your request for evidence or proof until the point is made.

5. When clients admit that there is no evidence, ask them how they feel. This is done to point out the change in affect as a reinforcer for cognitive change.

6. If the clients are feeling better, check their understanding by questioning whether they can identify what caused the change in C. This is an important step; clients will sometimes surprise you by saying that they feel better because they "got it off their chests" or because they "know you understand them." Don't leave such misattributions unattended.

7. Finally, acknowledge that the clients have changed their thinking, but like a good scientist who entertains multiple hypotheses, point out that cognitive change factors could include changing from an IB to an RB, using distraction, or changing the perception of A.

Perhaps a transcript of portions of a sample session conducted by Ellis will clarify these stages. Before the relevant therapist comment, we will either list the number that identifies the stage at which the therapist is working or briefly describe the therapeutic intervention. This transcript is adapted from a public demonstration in which a member of the group was asked to work with Ellis; not surprisingly, the first problem dealt with was the individual's nervousness at being on display.

Getting at the B

T: What do you think you're telling yourself to make yourself nervous?
C: I'm an idiot for being up here!
T: You're an idiot *because* . . .
C: I might reveal sensitive areas of myself and I would feel uncomfortable.

Clarifying which IB is more prominent

T: And you should feel comfortable? Is that what you're saying? Or you should not reveal yourself at all?
C: Not at all.

T: Because if you reveal yourself, what? What are you predicting would happen if you reveal yourself?

C: An outburst of emotion . . . I would feel embarrassed.

T: So you might act foolishly in front of these people, right?

C: Yes.

T: Well, if you did, why would that be upsetting? Anxiety-provoking, if you did?

C: Can you restate the question?

Client's confusion is probably an index of his anxiety level.

T: Yes. You're saying, "I may act foolishly in front of this audience." But you'd never get anxious just from that statement. That's just an observation or prediction. But how are you evaluating yourself if you do act foolishly?

C: I don't understand.

Steps 2 and 3

T: Well, just that statement alone doesn't cause an emotion. Something follows. You might be saying, "I might act foolishly, and isn't that great! I might act foolishly, and that would be good practice at acting foolishly!" And then you wouldn't be anxious, right?

C: Right.

T: But you're saying, "I might act foolishly, and isn't that WHAT?" You're not saying, "It's great!"

C: I need to not act out of character.

T: "And if I act out of character—WHAT?"

C: I might act fearful.

The evaluative component of B is still missing.

T: "And if I act fearful, WHAT?" You see, you're still not giving me the evaluation. "I would like it? Dislike it? Be enthusiastic?" What's your evaluation of acting foolishly?

C: It would make me feel unstable.

Therapist clarifies that "unstable" is not an emotion but a self-evaluative belief.

T: So, "I would be an unstable person if I act foolishly up here"? Or, "They would think me an unstable person"?

C: Yes.

Assuming the worst

T: Well, let's suppose they do! Let's suppose they say, "Oh, shit, he's unstable." Now, you don't know that they'd say that! They may say, "Oh boy, he's got the guts to go up there and I'm scared shitless. But let's suppose they do say you're unstable. What's the horror of that?

C: That would support what I already think.

T: "That I *am* unstable." Well, how are you evaluating your so-called instability?

C: As a negative.

T: "I don't like this characteristic"? But then you'd only feel concerned. You wouldn't feel embarrassed or ashamed. You'd just say, "Well, I have a negative trait called instability." Do you see that you're saying something *stronger* than that to make yourself anxious?

C: Could it be rejection possibly?

T: Yes. "Because if I'm *rejected* . . ."

C: Then I'm different from them.

T: "And if I'm different from them . . ." What are you concluding from that?

C: I'd be lonely.

Rephrasing C as an A to show the A-C connection

T: "I would be quite alone." And how do you feel about being quite alone?

C: Depressed.

Therapist summarizes the A-B complex.

T: Yes. So if I hear you right, you're saying, "If I act foolishly up here, it would prove I'm different. Other people would know I'm different. They would probably boycott me to some degree, and I couldn't bear that—that would be awful." Is that right?

C: Yes.

Step 4

T: All right. But even if that occurred . . . and we don't know if it would occur . . . why would it be horrible? That they thought you were boycottable and you were alone? Why would that be awful?

C: The evidence is my past experience. By being different, I was alienated.

T: But why was that *horrible?* Let's assume that that occurred. You were
alienated and left alone. Why was that horrible?

C: I feel like I need someone to share things with.

T: Prove it! Prove that you need someone.

C: (pause) There is no evidence.

Step 1

T: But if you *believe* it, how will you feel?

C: Terrible.

Step 5

T: That's right! You've defined these things as terrible, and if you gave
up those definitions, you'd feel all right. How do you feel right now
about being up here?

C: A little looser.

Step 6

T: Do you realize why you're feeling a little looser? Do you know why
that is so?

C: I have more of an I-don't-give-a-shit attitude.

Step 7

T: All right. That's good. And also, you've gotten distracted somewhat.
Instead of focusing on the audience, you're focusing on what we're
talking about. Now, what other problem would you like to discuss?

You could think of a troublesome cognition as a balloon pinned on a corkboard. Imagine picking up a handful of darts, which represent disputational strategies, to puncture and deflate the IB. Each dart has a name:

Identification of the distortion

Examination of the evidence

Cost–benefit analysis

Rational-emotive role reversal

Downward arrow to elicit silent assumptions

Double-standard technique (e.g., "would you say that to a friend?")

Humor

Imagery

11 Specific Suggestions

Disputing the Core Elements of Irrational Beliefs

In Chapter 8, a number of ways of categorizing irrational beliefs were discussed, including Ellis' original list of thirteen IB's. In searching for a systematic way to present disputational strategies to new students of RET, we decided to teach how to challenge the core elements of irrational thought rather than each of the specific IB's. If you recall, the four basic irrational processes are

Demandingness—the belief in universal musts

Awfulizing—the belief that the world is full of terrible, awful, catastrophic things

Human worth ratings—the belief that people can be rated

Low frustration tolerance—the belief that one cannot bear what one does not like

We can see these four themes in Ellis' list of thirteen irrational beliefs. For example, consider the first irrational belief, that is, the dire need for love; notice how this IB may contain any of the four key elements:

Other people should love me.

It's awful when they don't.

I need love and affection to survive or be happy.

I'm a worthless person if I'm not loved.

Now, look at the core elements in the second irrational belief, which involves casting blame on or reprimanding others:

X shouldn't act that way; he has no right.

It's awful that X acts that way.

I can't stand it when people don't do what I want.

X is a bastard for not doing what I want.

Finally, here are the same elements in the fifth irrational belief, which deals with achievement in life:

I shouldn't have done so poorly.

It's awful that I failed.

I need to do well.

I'm no good—a worm—if I fail.

Let's examine each core element in turn and some ways to combat them.

Demandingness

Listen for the following words in the client's speech:

must	got to	should
have to	ought to	necessary

These can be heard in "I" statements ("I have to . . ."), "you" statements ("you've got to . . ." or "he should . . ."), or "the world" statements ("it's got to . . ."). Shoulds are often stated about past events in problems of depression, anger, and guilt (e.g., "He shouldn't have done that") but refer to present or future events as well in cases of anxiety (e.g., "I mustn't make a mistake").

Should statements are internally illogical and reveal a philosophy of demand rather than preference. The irrational component, therefore, is the client's insistence that events or people's behavior be different. Clients upset themselves by the logical fallacy that "because I want . . . , it must be so," or as Ellis has put it, "My will be done!" It is as if clients believe that they can control the universe, which is perversely thwarting their efforts. These demands produce what Karen Horney (1945) called "the tyranny of the shoulds."

Disputing the client's "shoulds" or "musts" involves three steps.

First, explain to the client the distinction between *wants* and *musts*. Second, affirm that the want or preference is accepted and not open to debate. Third, challenge the must.

T: Why *must* your husband behave romantically?
C: That's easy for you to say. You're a man, and you probably don't think that romance is important in a marriage!
T: Well, even if you were right about that, it doesn't matter what I want; what matters is what you want. And it's perfectly OK for you to *want* your husband to be romantic. But wanting it and *demanding* it are two different things, aren't they?
C: How's that?
T: Wanting has to do with your preferences; demanding something has to do with insisting that the world not be the way it actually is. Now, I accept that you want your husband to be romantic, and that you highly value romance in marriage. I have no debate with that. But what I would like you to focus on is why he *has to* comply with your desire just because you *want* it.

Many people, perhaps including yourself, believe that there *are* indeed musts about human conduct. After all, what about the Ten Commandments, not to mention the code of Hammurabi, right? Rational-emotive philosophy does not necessarily question the advisability of following such codes of conduct, but it does acknowledge that these are laws devised by humans. Even though moral codes are desirable, it does not logically follow that people must abide by them. Obviously all of us break these codes at times ("Let him who is without sin cast the first stone"). If these rules were part of human nature, they would not have been set down by moral philosophers but rather by ethologists. Thus, people would automatically exhibit moral behavior because they must do so by their very nature, and to do so would not be considered "noble." Most religious systems, while advocating a code of ethics, recognize an individual's choice in living up to it. Rational-emotive theory distinguishes between the advisability of a particular behavior and the individual's potential to choose; he or she can decide not to do what is desirable and advisable. The rational individual appreciates that even the Ten Commandments can be interpreted as conditional shoulds, not absolutes. Depending on your frame of reference—if you want to be happy in heaven or have an easier time of it here on earth—then you probably *should* honor your father and mother.

Recall our discrimination between absolutist musts and innocuous musts (p. 116). Clients confuse the two in their everyday problems, for example, "I have to go to work," "I have to take my medicine," or "I have to call my mother." It can be pointed out to clients that human beings rarely act without first deciding to do so. Words such as "must," "have to," and "got to" imply that we are being forced to behave in a certain way which, in fact, we choose to do. By using these terms, we place ourselves in a victim role and allow ourselves to indulge in self-pity. Instead, we could substitute more correct phrases, such as "I want to" or "I choose to." For example, if the client says "I have to go to work," the therapist can retort:

> "Oh, no, you don't. You could go fishing or to the ball game, or stay in bed if you really wanted to. If you do go to work, you're going because you *choose* to, regardless of what you tell yourself. It's just that you're not willing to accept the consequences of not going to your job. You see, you almost always have a choice. Even if someone holds a gun to your head, you can always choose to die!"

When the rational-emotive therapist hears an irrational must, he or she is quick to confront the client by asking questions such as:

Why is that "must" a nutty thing to say to youself?

What law is there that says it *should* be?

Explain that to me—why *does he have to?*

How does your wanting it prove it *must* be?

I MUST

Must or should statements about oneself usually imply a demand for personal perfection; clients with this belief are remarkably intolerant of their human fallibility. The primary dispute in this case is to teach the client that fallibility is characteristic of the human species. Technically, we do not make mistakes, merely choices. It is only with the information available in hindsight that we can characterize a choice as a mistake if the consequences do not work out well. While improvement is something for which we all can strive, perfection has yet to be achieved by anyone. After all, pencils have erasers for good reason!

When clients are distraught about having exposed their humanness by failing at some endeavor, the therapist may intervene with statements such as the following:

> "You shouldn't have acted that way and messed up? Well, why *should* you have succeeded? True, it would have been nice or advantageous; that we could prove. But there is no reason why you *must* succeed. True, it would have been preferable; but why must you *always* act well? There's no law of the universe that says you should."

It is highly advisable for the therapist to act as a contrast model in this disputation, as in the following dialogue:

T: It isn't OK to make mistakes or bad choices? Hell, I've made hundreds of bad decisions! Now, when you do that, don't you call yourself a shit?
C: Yes.
T: If *I* did that, would I be a shit?
C: No!
T: So there's two sets of rules in the world? Who made these rules?
C: I guess I did.
T: If you made the first one, can you legislate another set of rules to be fair to yourself, so that you can get to live under the same set of rules as the rest of the world?

The key ingredient in this disputation is to point out to patients that they are being what Ellis calls "profound musturbators." We are, to be sure, given certain standards, of behavior by our culture; "musturbation," however, escalates these standards into a must. Consider the following therapy excerpt:

T: That's a self-demand. Why *must* you be a loving person? Why *must* you be successful at intimacy?
C: Because I want to!
T: "And I must be everything I want to?" You see, you're taking a good value and turning it into a crazy demand. "Because it might prove better, I must do it." Wouldn't it be nicer to feel good and not suffer from such crazy ideas?

Similarly, in another case of a young woman who was enmeshed in value conflict about having an extramarital affair:

T: What did you tell yourself to make yourself feel guilty?

C: I'm doing something immoral.

C: Granted. You've been doing wrong by your standards—but you also feel guilty. Why should you feel guilty about doing wrong? Many people do wrong and don't feel guilty about it.

C: Because my husband and I have such a good relationship. I shouldn't do it.

T: No, I'd *better* not do it. There are no shoulds in the universe. You have three choices here: you can change your values, change your behavior, or change your evaluation of your behavior. And they're not mutually exclusive. In other words, you don't have to walk around feeling so guilty.

It is also important to point out to clients that there are good reasons to give up musturbation; it not only promotes emotional turmoil but also makes us behaviorally less efficient. Let's look at three different therapists commenting on this issue:

> There are no musts in the universe. Suppose you were saying, "I have to be rational! I have to be rational! I have to be rational!" That would be *irrational,* and how do you think you'd be feeling?

> You're saying that you've done something wrong and should be condemned for it. Well, we'll go back to the first part later, but for the moment, let's assume that it's true. Why would you have to condemn yourself, put yourself down, for that reason? What does guilt do to change the situation? All it does is make you entrench and fight, rather than analyze and see how you can fix the situation.

> If you're driving poorly and you say to yourself, "What a shit I am for driving so poorly!" how does that help you to drive better?

Another aspect of the search for perfection is when patients demand the Perfect solution to their problems. Patients often come to therapy in the midst of a dilemma, or to put it more psychologically, caught in approach–approach or avoidance–avoidance conflicts. They expect a perfect, problem-free decision from themselves, and when they fail to come up with one, turn to the therapist. It may be unwise for the therapist to suggest a possible course of action, for that may perpetuate the notion that another human being can provide the perfect solution. In addition, the patient will not have learned some important skills: decision making, for example, weighing pros and cons and constructing a "hedonic calculus"; understanding the reasons for being stuck at the decision point (e.g., "I might make the wrong decision and that would be awful''); and learning to cope with imperfect solutions.

The last problem often comes up with clients who report being unhappy about a love relationship in which they feel trapped. For example, a wife reported that she was desperately unhappy in her marriage and wanted to leave her husband, but was blocked by a number of factors:

She might later discover she regretted her action.

She might hurt his feelings.

She might not make it on her own emotionally.

She might never find another partner.

In addition, she believed that it was wrong to leave a marriage ("Didn't the vows say until death do you part?"), so that there was a value conflict as well.

Obviously, there are many irrational ideas to challenge in this woman's situation. The therapist could teach her, first, that she was not totally responsible for the feelings of others; for if she hung onto that belief, then the only way out of her dilemma would be to devote her life to keeping her husband happy. In considering the moral connotations of her behavior, the therapist might point out that right and wrong are not useful indices of behavior; what *are* useful are the consequences. Ellis' parable of the two Zen Buddhists might be helpful here:

Two Zen Buddhists were out walking. One was an old master about ninety years of age and the other was a young novice. They came to a swollen stream that had flooded its banks. Beside the stream stood a beautiful, luscious young woman who said, "Look, Masters, the stream is flooded. Would you help me across?" The young monk shrank away in horror because he would have to pick her up to carry her across, but the old one calmly picked her up and carried her over the stream. When they were over, he set her down and the two monks went on. The young man couldn't get over this incident, however, and finally said to the older, "Master! You know we're sworn to abstinence. We're not allowed to touch a beautiful young woman like that. How could you take that luscious young woman in your arms and let her put her hands around your neck, her breasts next to your breast, and carry her across the stream like that?" And the old man said, "My son, *you're* still carrying her!"

Thus, as with the old monk, one can choose to do something "wrong" and not feel guilty; or not do something wrong, as with the young monk, and even so plague oneself by it. Does the client want to stick to her values and be miserable, or does she want to be happy even if it means changing her values? Another technique that the therapist may employ is distancing. The client may be asked, "How would you advise your best friend if she had the same problem? Would you suggest that she remain in the marriage and make herself miserable?"

Ultimately, however, the client would be wise to confront the fact that she seems to be demanding that her decision be perfect—absolutely correct and without any negative consequences. Obviously, few of life's decisions fall in this category. What she does have are three options:

Remain in the marriage and be miserable.

Remain in the marriage and work at not being miserable.

Leave the marriage.

What clients often want in making such decisions are *new* options. For example, the client above might say, "I could stay in the marriage if only my husband were different." It would be easy to make decisions if one could construct realities and produce the best possible alternatives, but there are times when one can only choose from limited options. The therapist might point out to this client that, as in a TV game show, she has a choice of door 1, door 2, or door 3. There is no door 4.

Options do not come with guarantees; even if the therapist had some gilt-edged Happiness Guarantees printed, they would not help. Whatever clients decide will imply some risk, and clients can choose to either avoid risks or accept them as creative challenges. So, there are no perfect solutions.

OTHER PEOPLE MUST

The second direction "must" or "should" statements take is in demands for perfection in other people's behavior. There are three aspects to this dispute: other people have free will, and we do not have perfect control over them; negative consequences are often attached to attempts to control other people's behavior; and there are negative emotional consequences for insisting that others behave as we would like.

The client usually adds two additional points as well, such as, "How *could* they act that way?" and *why* do they act that way?" The answer to the client's first question, although it might sound glib, is quite simple. How could they act that way? Easily! Why do they act that way? This question can lead to an interesting discussion of why others act wrongly. Among the possible answers are that they are ignorant, misguided, crazy, suffering from an incapacity; or simply that "wrong" behavior pays off in some way (perhaps it serves to upset the client, which may be reinforcing to someone else). We might summarize these reasons as stupidity, ignorance, disturbance, or utility. Understanding the reasons for other people's behavior may be an important step in helping the client to tolerate that behavior. Understanding another person's behavior, however, may not produce change. Regardless of why the other person behaves as he does, he or she still behaves that way.

When the client is demanding that another person act differently, the therapist might respond:

> "Where is the evidence that X *shouldn't* act that way? There is none. In fact, he did act that way. To demand that people must not act in a certain way is silly, because once they have done something, they must do what they have done."

It makes much more sense for the client to search for evidence that X should, in fact, have acted as he or she did:

> "What's the point of being angry when someone acts the way they act? When a dog acts like a dog, we're not surprised. When a cat acts like a cat, we're not surprised. Why are you surprised when your husband acts like your husband? He has a track record. That doesn't mean he can't change. But why should we be surprised when he shows us his usual behavior, especially when he doesn't seem interested or motivated to change? We can ask for change in another's behavior, but it's silly to demand it."

Here is an example of Ellis disputing the same should:

C: He shouldn't do that!
T: Why is that a nutty thing to say to yourself?
C: But he was *wrong!*
T: Let's assume that he's wrong. Why is it still incorrect for you to say that?
C: I don't know.
T: Because you don't run the fucking universe. He has a *right* to be wrong; every human does!

As pointed out earlier, there seem to be no absolute rights and wrongs, merely situationally determined choices. In addition, RET holds that whether a decision is right or wrong is independent of the client's right to choose; one can even choose to do a wrong act.

The therapist can also point out to the client that attempting to control the behavior of others may produce further difficulties:

> "What does it mean to control other people? Usually we use negative means, such as punitive responses, whining, passive resistance, tantrums, and so forth. But no matter how it's done, we know one thing about human behavior: anyone who is at the mercy of another person will tend to hate that other person. So the more you try to force your husband into loving you, the less likely you are to get what you want from him."

In fact, the only certain control the client has is over himself:

C: But he's so unfair!
T: OK, it's not fair. That's correct. Where is it written that it should be? You're saying, "She must, she must, she must." Now, let me ask you, what control do you have over her? And what good does it do you to sit here and eat yourself up over it? Let's agree. It isn't fair. Now, you only have control over one person. What do *you* want to do about it?

Finally, the therapist will point out that as long as the client holds onto a demanding philosophy, the emotional upset will probably remain:

> "You have a right to ask for change. But you might not get what you want. Your job is to stop evaluating yourself based upon your ability to control others' behavior."

THE WORLD MUST

Clients also demand that they control inanimate objects, social institutions, and the fates themselves. How often have you heard clients wailing, "It shouldn't happen to me—it's not fair!" The primary dispute is that the world doesn't have to be the way the client wants it, and in fact, the world is the way it is for complex, often unknowable reasons, and it need not be any different. The following analogy is frequently used to make this point:

"Let's suppose that I am sitting in my office on a hot, sunny summer day, and I start fantasizing about how much I'd rather be skiing than working today. If I walked to the window and started shaking my fists and demanding that it be cold and snowy outside, you would look at me as if I were a little crazy. You might tell me that it's foolish to demand that it be snowing and cold outside. Well, you'd be right; it *is* silly to demand that the universe be the way I want. Obviously, the physical, astronomical, and meteorological factors that cause it to be sunny and warm outside have occurred, and my demandingness and temper tantrums obviously can't change these things. Is this similar to what you're doing about your problem? Aren't you also making such demands?"

This analogy can obviously be used to dispute all types of should statements; for example:

"If it's silly to demand perfect control of the weather, it's equally silly to demand perfect control of other people and even yourself."

If the client is demanding to control something about the self, he or she may object:

C: I see what you mean about external events, but I should be able to control myself.
T: Well, but you do have some control. Your mistake is insisting on total control, when, in fact, you are a fallible human being. So, it really is like trying to control the weather, do you see?

Needs

Need statements may be viewed as a special subclass of musts, for clients are failing to discriminate between what they would *prefer* to have and what they *must* have in order to live and be happy. The primary disputation in dealing with need statements is to show clients how to take their own language seriously and literally. There are relatively few things that we absolutely need in this world; a little food, liquid, air, and shelter are biologically necessary for survival. No one knows what factors are necessary for psychological adjustment, although patients who are having relationship difficulties are quick to claim that "all you need is love." The psychology literature indicates that children and young animals require some love and affection in order to thrive, but we have no evidence that a single adult has ever died without it. Love is highly desirable, both to give and to get, but we do not *literally* need it. As long as clients believe that they need it and talk as if they need it, they will behave as if they need it, and that's where the trouble begins. A first step, therefore, is to help clean up the client's language.

The ability to discriminate wants from needs is not taught by our society, but it can be learned even by young children. In the following therapy excerpt, the client is a seven-year-old girl who is having trouble making friends at school:

T: Do you *need* to play with them?
C: What does "need" mean?
T: A need means this: What are some of the things that you need? You need water. What happens if you don't have water?
C: You die.
T: That's right. You need air. What happens if you don't have air? Same thing.
C: You can die.
T: That's right. What happens if you don't have food?
C: Die.
T: That's right. Can we say that you need food?
C: Yeah.
T: And water?
C: Yeah.
T: And air?
C: Yeah.
T: That's right. Do you need television?
C: No.
T: But sometimes you say you need to watch TV, don't you?
C: Yeah, 'cause I like to.
T: Yeah, you like to and you want to, but that's not a need, is it?
C: No.
T: No, it's not. Do you need candy canes and ice cream?
C: No.
T: You don't need them, but you want them, don't you?
C: Yeah.
T: But you don't need them, do you?
C: No.
T: OK, do you need a new bike?
C: No, I got one already.
T: But what if your bike got broken, then would you need a new bike?
C: Yeah.

T: No, you would want a new bike, but you wouldn't need it. I mean, you wouldn't die without it, would you?

C: No.

T: You could keep on living without a new bike?

C: Yeah.

T: It may not be as much fun as having a new bike, but you could live, right? Do you need a new pair of sneakers if your old ones have a hole in them?

C: No.

T: So do you see the difference between a want and a need? What's the difference? You try to explain it to me.

C: A need is what you need to help you to live.

T: A need is something you've got to have to live.

C: And a want is that you want to have it.

T: That's right. You'd like it, it's enjoyable. Now, how about, "Lisa wants the kids in school to like her." Is that a want or a need?

C: Want.

T: It's a want, right?

C: Right.

T: So we talked a little bit about wants and needs. Now, what happens if you tell yourself "Oh, I need to have so-and-so play with me in school—I need to have her like me." How do you think you're going to feel if she doesn't like you?

C: Sad.

T: Sad. Like sad a whole lot or sad a little bit?

C: A lot.

T: A lot. How about if you said, "I need to have Kate like me. I need to be her friend."

C: I want to be her friend.

T: "I want to be her friend." Oh, but isn't there a difference? If you said, "I need to be her friend" and she wasn't, how would you feel?

C: And she wouldn't?

T: And she wouldn't. And you said, "I gotta have her friendship—I need it to live—and she won't be my friend."

C: Sad.

T: You'd be very upset. So what if you said to yourself instead, "I would like to have Kate like me. I want to be her friend, but if she's not gonna be my friend, I can live without it." Would you be sad a little bit or sad a lot?

C: Sad a little.

Awfulizing

Disputing this core element of irrational beliefs essentially entails attacking the notion of "awfulness." Because people tend to loosely use words such as "awful," "terrible," and "horrible," Ellis first gets his clients to agree with this definition: "awful" means many things—totally bad, the worst thing that could ever happen, the equivalent of being tortured to death *slowly*. In essence, it implies 101 percent bad, an exaggerated badness. In RET terms, therefore, no event is awful, although it might very well be a royal pain in the neck.

When therapists question whether an event described by a client is truly awful, many clients defend their evaluation as follows:

T: OK, let's suppose that you got rejected and you were alone. Why would that be awful?

C: Because of the depressed feelings in my gut; I'd feel terrible.

T: But you have that backward! The bad feeling comes from defining it as awful. Suppose you just defined it as a pain in the ass: "Isn't it too bad that she doesn't like me?" Do you think you'd still have that depressed feeling in your gut?

C: No.

T: See, if you gave up the awfulizing, you'd give up the depressed feeling. You'd still feel sorry and regretful, but not depressed. Now, where's the evidence that it would be awful, horrible, and terrible if you were rejected and left alone?

One way to convince a client that "X" isn't awful is by comparison: "Can you imagine anything worse?" or "If this is so unbearable, would you commit suicide over it?" A more concrete anti-awfulizing exercise would be to help the client construct an "awfulness scale" from 1 to 100. Thus, if 100 is the worst possible event imaginable (e.g., dying of cancer after having one's arms and legs amputated), where would the client place

---

Some therapists begin disputation by asking the client whether the event under discussion is more correctly placed in the category of "pain-in-the-neck bad" or "end-of-the-world horrible." Turning it into a forced choice may help the client get started on the work of de-horribilizing.

a particular problem? It may become clear, for example, that having a spouse in a bad temper is more accurately placed at about 20 to 30.

A variant of this strategy is to ask clients if they can imagine "X" being worse. For example, "Merv, now that Joyce has left you, it sounds like you feel this is one of the worst things that could happen in your life. I wonder if we could look at how bad it really is. For instance, losing Joyce might be coupled with losing your house, or having one of your children become seriously ill, or losing your job. Do you think it would help you to keep this loss in perspective if you reminded yourself that troubles can—and often do—add up?"

In working with children, Ray DiGiuseppe and Ginger Waters often use a similar device, the "horribles" list. On a blackboard or large sheet of paper, have the children list all the "horribles" or "catastrophes" they can think of. (Given the recent spate of catastrophe films and TV shows, this is easily accomplished.) After listing towering infernos, tidal waves, invasions from outer space, earthquakes, and atomic blasts, the therapist "remembers" one more, the child's complaint (e.g., "Tommy sat in my seat"). It will probably not be necessary to point out that this item does not belong on the list. This exercise is used quite successfully with adults as well.

Clients may also do their own anti-awfulizing if the therapist guides them through the following questions: "What are the real and probable consequences of the bad situation?" "How long will they last?" "How will you be able to bear them?" "Let's work out the details of your plan." Inviting clients into the system in this way is much more preferable than an anti-awfulizing speech. Such a device not only serves to de-escalate catastrophes but enables clients to show themselves the reality of the situation and to work out coping strategies to deal with it.

In a recent woman's group, one of the members asked, "What does RET tell you to do about really bad events? Are you supposed to feel good about bad things?" This is a common question asked not only by lay people but by professionals as well. Clearly, the answer is "No!" Unlike "positive thinking," RET does not take the position that every cloud has a silver lining; some are storm clouds through and through. We may not have a choice between a good and a bad event, but merely between two bad alternatives. How, then, can RET be of help? By helping the patient to not make a bad event worse by catastrophizing.

Suppose that A is truly bad (e.g., a spinal cord injury, loss of a limb, death of a child): What can the rational-emotive therapist do? First, acknowledge that the A really is painful and that most people would indeed feel bad about it, and then allow for a normal grieving process. After a few weeks or months, however, it will be time to get on with the business of developing attitudes or philosophies that can help the patient cope with bad but unchangeable A's.

The therapist will try to convince clients that holding onto misery is not in their best interests. Again, clients may not have the choice of something bad versus something good, but only between two bad things. By adding needless misery, both of these alternatives can seem worse. Here is a concrete example. The patient was a young man, paralyzed with a spinal cord injury, who in addition developed decubitous ulcers and muscle spasms. Nothing could be done to repair the spinal cord injury, but by becoming overly upset about his condition, the boy significantly increased the problem of spasms. In such a case, giving up his depression about his injury could directly affect the patient's well-being. He had enough bad things to deal with and certainly did not need to add depression.

Perhaps there is a relationship between helping the client to accept a problem, such as a physical disability, and the acceptance of death. As Kübler-Ross (1969) has suggested, acceptance is not a simple process but rather a series of stages. There are many feelings to be dealt with (e.g., anger and fear), and denial may be very strong. Acceptance of death as a series of stages is a conceptual schema; not all patients go through all of the stages, or follow them in any fixed order. However, RET may be useful in facilitating the process of moving from one stage to the next.

Many therapists tend to awfulize about clients who have a serious disability or terminal illness. These conditions are not, in themselves, reasons for emotional turbulence, however. In fact, research indicates that most people with terminal illnesses are not chronically upset but instead are quite adept at mobilizing coping mechanisms (Sobel, 1978). The therapist, therefore, needn't assume that distress is a normal reaction.

In addition to acknowledging the reality and painfulness of an activating event, the therapist can focus on patients' *abilities* as well as their disabilities. Although this dual focus may not be wise as an initial maneuver, as therapy progresses it is important to discuss with clients, "What can you do with what you *do* have?" Patients, after all, may be irrationally concluding that because they have problems, their life is over and no possibility of enjoyment remains. The useful principle here is *containment* of the disability to specific areas rather than overgeneralizing its effects.

In this regard, the RET therapist would do something that other therapists might not consider: acknowledge a situation as being very bad, but point out that it could always be worse. If patients are terminally ill, they might be reminded that they could always die *more slowly* and in *more pain*. If they've lost a loved one, they could have lost their lover *and* best friend. There are always worse catastrophes that could happen. Although this fact may not be very consoling, it can help patients get a better grasp on reality.

There are also pragmatic reasons to give up awfulizing. First, the high anxiety levels associated with catastrophizing impede problem solving. By decreasing anxiety, clients increase their ability to deal with difficult events. If clients awfulize about an impending problem, the therapist might point out that worrying only makes it worse, since they are living through the problem twice—both in anticipation, and when it actually occurs. If the discomfort is inevitable, patients might as well enjoy themselves as long as they can.

Awfulizing philosophies are usually associated with states of high anxiety, a common result of which is avoidance behavior. The problem with avoidance is that although it is temporarily effective in reducing anxiety, this very effect reinforces more avoidance behavior. As one behavior therapy text suggests, fears can easily generalize.

> If, for example, one had an irrational fear of stepping on dandelions, one might easily avoid the problem by walking around a single dandelion, with little cost to one's freedom. However, one small, neglected dandelion rapidly multiplies into many problems, and soon a fearful person will find himself severely constricted, every pathway in the field blocked with multiple dandelions. (Walen, Hauserman, and Lavin, 1977)

Don't be fooled by avoidance behaviors; sometimes patients will avoid *positive* events in order to ward off imagined future distress. A common example is seen with patients who avoid intimacy even though they highly desire it. They refuse to get into love relationships for fear that, at some future time, the relationship might end. Because they've defined the ending as awful, they have chosen to deprive themselves of present possible pleasures. Awfulizing, in this case, results in considerable cost to the patient.

An important behavioral dispute used by rational-emotive therapists to combat awfulizing is to have patients face their problems head-on, thereby disproving their hypothesis that the consequences are unbearably bad. Ellis has referred to such behavioral disputes as "risk-taking" experiences.

Ellis anticipated a research-based trend in behavior therapy by his insistence on the desirability of encouraging patients to take risks. By forcing themselves to do the very things that seem "too hard" or "too scary," patients will be able to abandon their notions of awfulness. In fact, Ellis has gone so far as to suggest that more traditional and gentle techniques, such as systematic desensitization or relaxation training, are sometimes iatrogenic in that they reinforce patients' avoidance of discomfort and strengthen LFT cognitions. In essence, he asserts, we continue to coddle patients and thereby help them to remain emotional babies. The most efficient way to overcome fears and avoidance habits is often to "close your eyes and force yourself to jump in with both feet." In other words, RET recommends a flooding or implosive model of treatment, starting at the top rather than at the bottom of a fear hierarchy. Research (e.g., Marks et al., 1971; Rachman et al., 1973) supports this contention, and the shift from imaginal to in vivo desensitization and from progressive to flooding techniques illustrates that the Zeitgeist is moving in the direction taken by RET. See Chapter 14, in which risk-taking homework exercises are described.

Human Worth

In his original writings on this topic, Ellis dealt with patients' denigrating statements of themselves and others ("I'm a worthless slob" or "He's no good") by analyzing human worth in the following way. Logically or scientifically there is no way to prove conclusively that one human being has more worth to the universe than any other. Because there is no way to evaluate differences in human worth, one is left with the null hypothesis that all people are of equal worth. A problem still remains with this formulation, however, since the assumption of a quality called "worth" implies the possibility of its opposite, "worthlessness." Ellis later refined his theory to eliminate the entire notion of worth, replacing it with unconditional *self-acceptance*.

Beliefs about *self*-worth appear to be among the most difficult to change. Self-acceptance may be difficult to communicate to children, who are surrounded by adults who persist in global ratings of the child (e.g., "good girl" rather than "good behavior"). It is often still more difficult to convince adolescents that they do not need the adulation of their peers. An important concept to teach in this regard is that people's opinions about one's worth are not facts. This discrimination may be more easily pointed out by referring to nonpersonal issues. For example, the therapist may point to his or her wristwatch and suggest that it is the most beautiful watch in the world. Does this make it so? What the therapist is teaching is the difference between an opinion and a fact. The therapist's statement, more correctly, means, "I judge this watch to be the most beautiful." If the client understands this concept, it may then be possible to move to personal opinions, as in this example:

> "Let's say that your friend thinks you're a turkey. Does that make it so? If all your friends said you were a turkey, would you be?"

In other words, self-worth need not depend on getting the support or admiration of others, even of deities ("Jesus loves me, I'm OK"). We can skip these intervening variables and simply choose to accept ourselves.

All self-worth statements are, in fact, overgeneralizations; this logical fallacy is corrected in the following dialogue:

C: I'm such a worm!
T: You're a worm? You seem to have trouble with your terminology. The label you just gave yourself suggests that some essence of you is rotten, not just your act. You've defined yourself as a rotten person. If that's true, you *have* to do rottenly, and do so exclusively and forever. That would be your fate. Don't you think you are over-generalizing?

Let's elaborate on that last point. It is important to teach patients the difference between being a louse and acting lousily. In other words, *patients are not their behavior.* One way to teach this concept is to help patients monitor their language so that they change their labels for themselves (i.e., nouns) into verbs. Thus, instead of saying, "I'm a bad mother," it is more correct to say, "I've been doing some bad mothering." The first statement is clearly an overgeneralization because it would be virtually impossible to find a person who committed only negative mothering acts. Even Harlow's "monster mother" monkeys were observed to fondle their infants occasionally (1958). The reason we urge clients to change their self-labels into verbs is that self-labeling statements use a linguistic structure that always overgeneralizes. The verb "to be" in the English language implies unity between the subject and the object of a sentence. "I am a psychologist" implies unity between "I" and "psychologist"; most of us, however, do many other things besides function in a therapeutic capacity. The basic argument is that people are far too complex to be judged within a single category. Their very complexity renders them unratable. Thus, Ellis suggests that clients "give up their egos," not in the sense of their executive selves but of rating themselves.

The following analogy is often employed by rational–emotive therapists to illustrate human complexity.

"Imagine that you have just received a large basket of fruit. You reach into the basket and pull out a beautiful red apple, and then a ripe juicy pear, and then a rotten orange, and then a perfect banana, and then a bunch of grapes, some of which are mushy and rotten. How would you describe the fruit? Clearly, some pieces are good and some are not good; you'd want to throw away some of it. And how would you label the basket? You see, the basket represents you, and the variety of fruits which vary in ripeness or rottenness are like your traits. Rating yourself by a single trait is like saying that the basket is bad because it contains one piece of bad fruit."

Rich Wessler has devised a schematic diagram that illustrates the absurdity of self-rating. Note the two intersecting continua in Figure 11–1. Many people's self-esteem ratings are contingent on the state of the horizontal axis. When things go well, they rate themselves highly (Point 1); when things go poorly, they give themselves a low rating (Point 2). What is wrong with this concept is the very act of globally rating oneself; "wonderfulizing" is as irrational as self-deprecation. Rating is a foolish venture, for as soon as external conditions deteriorate, you'll slide down the "irrational diagonal." The more rational perspective is to stay at the center point on the vertical axis, regardless of your position on the horizontal one. Thus, since rating oneself up implies the possibility of rating oneself down, the more elegant solution is to give up rating oneself altogether.

A general strategy, consistent with the concept that patients them-

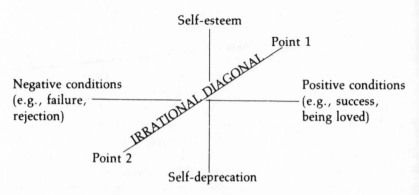

Figure 11.1. The self-rating fallacy.

selves do most of the hard work in therapy, is that instead of trying to prove to patients that they are not failures or worms, have them try to prove to you that they are. Not only is this strategy easier on the therapist, but it often provides the meaningful insight that "self does not equal one's behavior" to the patient. Again, the issue is to avoid self-rating and to substitute self-acceptance or self-tolerance.

T: All right, Jack, prove to me that you're a failure.
C: But I've just told you all the things I failed at.
T: That's true, Jack, but how does that make you a failure?
C: But I've messed up so many things!
T: I know that, Jack, but don't you see what you're doing when you call yourself a failure? You're making a prediction. To be a failure means that you'll always have that characteristic, and you're only doomed to fail at whatever you try.
C: That's what's upsetting me, that I'll always fail.
T: But you can't be a failure because we don't know that you'll always fail, and we have evidence that you haven't always failed in the past. You see, if you were an apple, you would always have had and will continue to have the characteristics of an apple. You couldn't change, and that's not true of failure. So you prove to me that you always have and always will fail!
C: (laughs) I guess I can't.
T: OK, so you see, failing is something you do some of the time; it's not what you *are*.

A difficult issue for many clients is accepting their physical attributes, and perhaps surprisingly, this problem seems to be as prevalent among men as among women. Trying to convince clients that their perception of physical reality may be distorted seems to be an exercise in futility. After all, when clients look into the mirror and don't like what they see, they are making an esthetic judgment. Matters of personal taste are difficult to challenge. The problem, however, is that in addition to acknowledging that the mirror image is not what they'd prefer, clients awfulize and refuse to accept themselves. Here is a sample therapeutic challenge to this refusal; note the therapist's acceptance of the client's perception.

T: OK, you have sunken eyes. What are you doing with that piece of information? Are you telling yourself that you must be miserable with yourself and your sunken eyes?
C: Well, I could always find someone who likes sunken eyes. (laughs)
T: And what are you saying now? Again, you're looking for *external* validation of yourself. Can *you* accept yourself with sunken eyes?

The client initially suggested that sunken eyes would be acceptable if she found someone who liked them; however, this would be a poor solution because it implies conditional acceptance. The therapist encourages her to continue to work at self-acceptance regardless of the approval of others.

Thus, physical appearance may be one area in which reexamining A may sometimes be unprofitable. Acceptance of qualities that cannot be changed is important, although if some physical attributes can be corrected (e.g., with plastic surgery or contact lenses) the therapist may certainly encourage clients to change what can be changed.

Many clients upset themselves about their appearance and condemn themselves when they are rejected by potential romantic partners. These clients believe that if they are not considered physically attractive to a particular partner, they are totally unattractive and worthless. A food metaphor may be useful in disputation:

T: So, Audrey wasn't interested in you. What does that mean about you?
C: Well, I guess I'm telling myself that no one will have me. I'm worthless.
T: What makes you worthless?
C: Well, she doesn't want me.
T: Well, that may relate to her taste in mates. It's sort of like food. Do you like chicken?
C: Yeah.
T: How about fish?
C: Yuck. I never touch the stuff.
T: Well, what does that say about fish? Or chicken?
C: Well, nothing, I guess.
T: That's right. Even though you don't like fish, lots of other people do. And just because you like chicken, that doesn't mean it's great food, or that other people should like it. People's views of you are just like food preferences. What they like says more about their taste or preference than it does about you. So, what does it mean that Audrey doesn't want you?
C: I guess (smile) I'm not her kettle of fish!

A special subclass of irrational beliefs concerning self-worth is the problem of competition; some clients believe that they must not only be competent but that they must be *more* competent than others. Their ability to feel comfortable depends on doing better than others and therefore involves both self-rating and other-rating. If they evaluate themselves against others and fall short, they feel depressed and also jealous. Comparing oneself with others is a normal part of life and may even be desirable for improving one's performance. It becomes problematic, however, when the patient overgeneralizes and uses the comparison in a self-derogatory way.

One suggestion to such clients is that they hardly change in any way each time they engage in comparisons; for example, "If you're 5' 2" and you meet someone 6' tall, does that make you shorter than you were?" or "If someone else gets a higher grade than you, does that make you stupid?" A more elegant solution, however, is again to work at giving up the concept of rating altogether. The therapist might point out that, after all, the basic goal in life is to *enjoy* oneself, not to prove oneself to the self, others, or the heavenly hosts.

We include at this point two sample disputations, one didactic and the other more evocative, on the general issue of self-worth.

A Didactic Disputation

I'm going to suggest something rather surprising to you. Know what it is? That you're *neither* a wonderful, bright, marvelous, intelligent person, nor the opposite—a terrible, awful, stupid, irresponsible *dumbkopf.*

You're neither of those things. You're a human being. And you belong to the human race. And to be human means that you have some strengths and some weaknesses. That in some ways you're probably quite intelligent, and coupled with that is a tendency to make human errors. Because that's also what it means to be alive and to be human.

And if we're going to get you better, we'd better go after your belief system. You're holding onto one now that insists on categorizing you as OK–not OK, stupid–smart. You think that you are a simple little commodity and you belong in either this box or that box.

And I'm suggesting to you that there's no box that could describe you. You're a complicated person; all humans are. That you could do an "A" paper, and from it you don't need to leap to the conclusion that therefore you're a wonderful, bright, intelligent, perfect person. 'Cause you're no such thing.

If you handed in a paper and it was not such a hot paper, you could do at least two things. You could say, "Oh my God, I'm stupid, I knew it, I knew it, I never should've handed it in. Now I see the evidence, just what I've always thought, I'm no good. Donna belongs in the Stupid Box." Or you could say, "Well, I'm only learning how to write stories. That's what I'm here for. I'm not already perfect or I'd be the professor. And she's not perfect either or she would be a famous writer! That doesn't mean she doesn't have something to tell me, so that the next one I write I do better at."

"So what" could be two favorite words to tuck in your pocket to say 100 times to yourself in the next week. "Well *so what* if it isn't an A+? What does that mean if it isn't a perfect paper? It just means that it isn't a perfect paper, and it doesn't mean another darn thing beyond that." "So what," however, doesn't mean "It's not important at all," but simply "It's not all-important."

An Evocative Disputation

T: You really believe that you're an utterly worthless person. By definition, that means that you're always doing things poorly. Can you prove to me that that's correct?

C: But I've failed at so many things.

T: Just how many?

C: I've lost my job, my wife is threatening to leave me, I don't get along with my kids—my whole life's a mess!

T: Well, let me make two points. First of all, that's not every aspect of your life. Second, you seem to take total responsibility for all of those events, rather than only partial responsibility.

C: But even if I'm not totally responsible, I'm still a failure.

T: No. You've failed at those things. There are other things you haven't failed at.

C: Like what?

T: You still manage to get up every morning, you keep up appearances, you manage your finances well considering your economic plight—there's lots of things that you do well.

C: But they don't count!

T: They don't count to you right now because you're overly concerned with negative issues, but they certainly *do* count. There are lots of people who don't do those things well. Are *they* failures?

C: No, but . . .

T: You know, Jack, you're one of the most conceited people I've ever met!

C: What do you mean? I've just been telling you how lousy I am!

T: The fact that you hold two different standards tells me how conceited you are. You hold much higher standards for yourself than for anyone else, which implies that you think you're much better than others. It's OK for those lowly slobs to have problems, but not a terrific person like you. Isn't that contradictory to your notion that you're worthless?

C: Hmmmmm.

T: How about instead of rating yourself as worthless, you just accept the failings that you do have and try your best to improve them?

C: That sounds sensible.

T: Let's take one of those problem areas now and see how we can improve things. . . .

Low Frustration Tolerance

Ellis has conceptualized the need for comfort as a core element of irrational beliefs. These common phrases may indicate *discomfort anxiety* (Ellis, 1978):

> I can't bear it.
>
> I can't live with (or without) it.
>
> I can't stand it.
>
> I can't tolerate it.

People seem to believe that they cannot tolerate pain, discomfort, or adversity; their willingness to bear discomfort is not necessarily directly correlated with the nastiness of the aversive event. Usually, in fact, they report that they "cannot stand" what they do not like. We referred to this problem earlier as low frustration tolerance, or simply LFT.

There are two ways to combat LFT: cognitively and experientially. In cognitive disputation, the therapist challenges patients to prove that they cannot bear something. Obviously such proof does not exist. Saying that they can't stand it is silly, because they can stand it (although they may not like it) and even be happy despite it. LFT demands are similar to Ellis' discomfort anxiety statements above. Clients insist that they must not be inconvenienced, made uncomfortable, or denied, and if they are it is awful. The following dialogue illustrates a challenge to these notions:

C: I can't stand it when my mother acts neurotically.

T: (with exaggerated intonation) "I should have had a happy adulthood. I'm so richly deserving, I should have had a happy time." But she may *never* change. What are you going to do about that?

C: Nothing.

T: Could you say to yourself, "Isn't it interesting that she's doing her number?" You could readjust your thinking so you're not making nutty demands. You see, it's akin to standing at the window *demand-*

ing that it not be raining. If environmental events are impossible to control, the same goes for people's behavior. Getting angry isn't going to make it different. It might be better just to accept the reality.

Dryden and DiGiuseppe (1990) suggest using "the terrorist dispute" to help clients understand that they can tolerate what they think of as unbearable, and that the situation may even be worth tolerating:

T: OK, Morris. So we're clear now that what's frightening about going to the party is the prospect of spilling your drink and drawing people's critical attention to you.

C: If that happened, I couldn't stand it. I'm getting anxious now even thinking about it.

T: So, in your mind it would be unbearable.

C: Right.

T: Well, let's see if you're right. Do you love your children?

C: Of course I do. What kind of question is that?

T: Well, bear with me for a moment since I want to help you really think about whether your explanation of the scene we've just identified as "unbearable" is correct, OK?

C: OK.

T: Right. Now, let's imagine that a group of terrorists capture your children and their ransom demand is this: "If Morris goes to 20 parties, spills a drink at each one, thereby attracting the critical attention of others, we'll release his children. But if he doesn't do this we'll keep them forever." Now would you do as they say?

C: Of course I would.

T: But you've just told me that even if you spill a drink once and are criticized once, that would be terrible. How can you do something that is so unbearable?

C: I'm beginning to see what you mean.

T: What would you tell yourself about doing this task twenty times that would enable you to do it?

C: That it's bearable.

T: That's right, that it *is* tolerable and presumably that it's worth tolerating in order to save your kids.

C: Right.

T: Now if you would do it twenty times to save your kids, would you risk it happening a couple of times for your mental health?

C: Yes.

T: And don't forget to practice convincing yourself that if the worst happens and you do spill the drink and attract criticism from others, that it's *bearable* and not unbearable.

Experiential disputes of LFT provide clients with homework assignments in which they actually practice the events they previously defined as unbearable. This practice can take the form of a generalized exercise such as one used by Bill Knaus:

> "Focus on an itch you are experiencing somewhere on your body right now and refrain from scratching it for thirty seconds—and now another thirty seconds . . ."

Or use one specifically tailored to the client's presenting problem. For example, if clients become angry in certain situations, they may be asked to behaviorally dispute their anger by staying in the very situation that provoked it and practicing "standing it," such as purposefully exposing themselves to an obnoxious individual at whom they were angry. Rational-emotive imagery may also be useful:

T: Let's go through the scene. OK, imagine yourself at your mother's front door. At the first sign of emotion, ask yourself what's going through your mind.
C: I'd better just pretend not to be angry.
T: Well, instead of just sitting on your feelings and denying them, ask yourself, "What would it take to get myself annoyed but not angry?"

Thus, the patient can accomplish both a rehearsal desensitization (behavioral) and a repertoire of rational coping statements (cognitive).

LFT may prevent clients from reaching many life goals, primarily because they refrain from putting in the hard work necessary to achieve those goals. The therapist can point out that there's seldom "gain without pain." Learning that they can stand discomfort helps such clients to face adversities more easily, take greater risks, and work harder to maximize their productivity. Thus, reducing LFT and attacking the need for comfort may help one write that new book, leave a spouse, start a new business, or accomplish whatever one's personal goals may be.

12 Problems and Solutions

Trouble-shooting Disputational Problems

Having outlined some disputational strategies, we realize that you may run into some snags in getting your points across. This section anticipates some common problems that new therapists encounter in disputation and offers suggestions to deal with them. Most of these problems have to do with clients who either don't understand or don't believe disputational arguments. Thus, after you have disputed an irrational belief, check to see whether your client understood the process.

Ask yourself, "Is the patient just saying the right words but not really believing them? Is the client placating me to get my approval?" How can you determine whether the patient is merely parroting? We suggest four strategies.

1. If patients come to the session in obvious emotional distress, or if you can create some emotional reaction by reenacting troublesome situations with rational barbs (see p. 279) or imagery exercises, you can validate their understanding by looking for signs of tension reduction. Examine whether or not the clients can calm themselves down in the session.

2. Sometimes you will not be able to determine the client's understanding in a particular session; instead, the proof will emerge over time. What you are looking for is *consistency* in the client's thoughts, feelings, and behavior across sessions. For example, if a male client claims that he "knows" that being rejected for a date isn't terrible but continues to avoid approaching women, the therapist will want to eventually confront this discrepancy directly by pointing out the difference between "knowing"

and "believing." One may know about the theory of Marxism or Catholic dogma and yet not believe in or choose to live by either.

3. Another strategy is to invite significant others from the patient's life into the session; obviously this is done only after securing the client's agreement and making sure that he or she understands the reason for this strategy. At such a meeting, the therapist may ask questions such as, "Do you see any changes in X's behavior?" or "How is X really acting?" Inconsistencies between reports from others and the patient's self-report may enable the therapist to confront the client: "You see, Jack, it looks like you don't *really* believe it. We'd better work harder at it!"

4. Some patients remain relatively passive in therapy (often because their therapists are too active), and the therapist will want to look for indicators that they can approximate a disputation by themselves. One good technique to check on patients' understanding is to have them fill out self-help forms (see p. 260) as homework between sessions. If they cannot accurately work through a self-help form, they probably haven't understood. Time can profitably be spent in the next session going over and correcting any errors on the form. A second technique to validate the understanding of this type of patient is rational role reversal (see p. 359), in which clients are asked to change roles with the therapist and thus demonstrate how they would help someone with a problem like their own. In this way, the therapist can estimate how much of the disputation the clients understand and their commitment to giving up their irrational, disturbing ideas.

Clients' misunderstandings may not always be obvious. One way to check this out is to listen very carefully to their choice of words and their intonation. For example, listen for "I am . . ." sentences, such as "I am incompetent." Clients may not be aware of it, but when they say "I am . . ." they imply unity and identity between the subject and predicate of their sentence. Help clients to rephrase these statements more accurately (e.g., "I acted incompetently"). The feedback that clients get from the way they use language may continue to propagate their irrational thinking unless the therapist corrects their statements.

Listen also to the client's tone of voice, specifically for the level of affect. The client may say something like, "I don't have much to offer men." Said in a flat tone of voice, such a statement can be easily missed by client and therapist, and the important irrational concept behind it left undisputed. If the client is interrupted, however, and asked to repeat the statement with more emotion, the therapist may help the client confront and deal with the IB behind his or her words.

You may miss the subtle residuals of the client's irrational beliefs if your active *listening skills* are not developed. One of the impediments to new therapists' listening skills is the tendency to monitor their own performance too closely: "Was the last intervention I made good?" or "Now, what clever thing am I going to say next?" and so forth.

Here is a training exercise to check on your active listening skills. Take a recent therapy tape and stop it approximately every two minutes, asking yourself, "What did the client just say?" Check to see if you have accurately recorded all the fine points in the client's conversation. Remember, don't focus primarily on your behavior in the session but on accurately hearing the client's statements.

Frequently clients do not *fully* express entire thoughts; they use syntactic shorthand which can hide irrational beliefs. For example, a male client was asked to stand up in front of a large group at work and spontaneously discuss a topic. When the therapist asked what he was thinking while he was being introduced, the client replied, "I thought, 'Oh my God, what will I say?'" Do you hear the beginnings of an IB here? People don't usually beseech deities unless some kind of awfulizing is going on in their thinking. The very question, "What will I say?" implies that the client is worried and *doesn't* know what to say. The "Oh my God" is an additional indicator of his anxiety and the belief that he must do what has been asked of him; that he's trapped in and victimized by the situation. Thus, a great deal of hidden information is contained in a very simple sentence.

How do you get the client to state these unspoken concepts? Help the client in the translation step by step, for example, guide the client into rephrasing the question, "What will I say?" to "I don't know what to say." At this point, you are in a better position to ask, "How do you feel about that?" Thus, until the premise is stated, the patient can't really explore how he or she is reacting to it. Once the client identifies that "I feel anxious," you have an A and a C. To get at the missing belief, the one-word interjection "because" can be very helpful:

T: You're anxious about not knowing what to say *because* . . . ?
C: I might make a fool of myself.

> Even if you are not using a formal A-B-C format in speaking with your client, we strongly advise you to use it in your *listening* style. Go over a recent therapy tape and, as you hear the client's story unfold, write down the A, B, and C as they emerge, also noting unusual key words in the margin. After you think you have uncovered the hidden B's, plan your next disputational strategy.

T: And if you act foolishly. . . .
C: That would be awful!

When we first began doing RET, we were surprised and chagrined when, following what we viewed as an exemplary dispute, clients returned the following week reiterating their irrational concepts. It took us a while to learn that RET is not a magic therapy; although one-trial learning may occasionally occur, it is not the rule. Most clients have a long reinforcement history for their IB's, and they are not going to give them up or change them easily. Success may come only after repeating the same disputes, filling out numerous homework sheets, and engaging in many challenges to the IB. A mistake that the new therapist makes is trying an RET strategy for two or three sessions, becoming discouraged when success isn't immediate, and turning to another theoretical orientation for the "Magic answer." We acknowledge that RET may not be the necessary and sufficient therapy for each and every case, but it is recommended that the therapist give it a fair chance. If several years of psychoanalysis are required before change is to be expected, more than a few sessions of disputation are not unreasonable. The therapist may have to spend months on the same concept before the patient "sees the light." Don't be afraid of repetition, therefore; repetition may be important in all communication but is essential in psychotherapy.

As you progress through sessions with your clients, it is important to stress not only rational beliefs but also the *process* of disputing. After you've spent one or two sessions challenging clients' irrational beliefs, it is easy to get into the habit of just providing them with rational alternatives. Disputing, however, is a process of *asking questions* about their irrational beliefs, not merely replacing IB's mechanically with rational statements.

When the clients are dealing with core, often tacit assumptions about themselves, they will likely not be able to disprove such material easily. Core issues about self-image, for example, are difficult and may rarely be dealt with consciously. Be respectful of the task. The patient deserves a lot of credit for broaching these issues and you, the therapist, deserve credit if you can create an atmosphere in which the patient feels comfortable doing it.

One helpful strategy is to put off disputation until a good deal of the self-deprecatory material is brought out into the open so that it can be examined in detail. For example, one client referred to herself as "manipulative"; another avowed that she "couldn't trust herself." These concepts were central to their self-image, and the clients had been amassing data to support their negative beliefs for most of a lifetime.

Collect the stories, examples, and images that the client believes support these core IB's. Then be prepared to slowly and methodically refute, reframe, and de-awfulize this mass of material. Remember, these are subtle, painful perceptions the client is facing. Your patience and persistence, as well as your enthusiasm for alternative points of view, will pay off in the long run!

The key element here is teaching scientific thinking, the search for evidence to support a hypothesis; merely substituting a rational belief omits this important step. Until clients have learned the skill of questioning themselves, they may not be able to generalize beyond their immediate problem.

Another inappropriate style that develops among new RET therapists is what we'll call the "knee-jerk disputer." Every time they hear a "need," "should," "must," or "terrible," these therapists are quick to ask, "Where's the evidence?" This reaction frequently misses the target. Remember that these words are harmful because of the concepts that they stand for, not their face value. Such words are used frequently in everyday language as figures of speech. For example, "That was a *terrible* steak!" or "You *have* to see the new ballet" or "I *need* a cup of coffee." Thus, the knee-jerk disputer may be shooting down pseudo-problems; although people may, in fact, be irrational about their need for coffee or the awfulness of their steak, these may not be clinically significant beliefs related to their pathology. So, make sure that you have identified the relevant irra-

What to do when you're stuck in a disputation: as with any problem, first do an assessment so that you can reach a differential diagnosis. Perhaps you aren't working skillfully. Perhaps the client doesn't want to give up the emotion, which often happens in anger. Perhaps the client wants you to do all the work. Perhaps the client wants the activating event to change. Perhaps the client doesn't really understand what disputation means. Perhaps the client has some personal, idiosyncratic, intrapsychic reason for not changing. And so on.

If you feel like you're arguing with or lecturing a reluctant client, then you're not collaborating. *Collaboration is the hallmark of therapy.*

---

tional beliefs before moving on to D, lest you merely establish silly new taboo words. Does it make sense for the word "shit" to be OK, but "should" to be taboo?

Client Behaviors that Block Change

Some clients pose special problems for the new therapist. Let's go over a few such types;

The argumentative client. Are you picking up antagonism in your clients? Do their voices have an edge? Do you feel you're fighting rather than disputing? Are you fatigued by your interaction? How can you handle such clients? First of all, stop fighting. If you sense that the two of you are tugging at opposite ends of a rope, let go of your end. Try to go through an entire session without trying to convince the client of anything, and see what happens. Or, play devil's advocate and agree with such clients (e.g., "You're right, Bill, you really are incompetent"). Imposing your ideas on such clients may only serve to intensify their resistance to you. Focus instead on the strength of the client by intervening primarily with questions (e.g., "What do you think you could do to get over your problem, Bill?").

The "yes-but" client. Clients who counter your suggestions with a yes-but response are demonstrating another form of argumentative resistance. A yes-but is really equivalent to a no. Such clients are playing helpless and often render the therapist helpless. Consider whether their resistance is attributable to your behavior; have you, in fact, focused the discussion on an irrelevant issue? If not, perhaps these clients are simply unwilling to listen to you because they attribute qualities to you that they have generalized from other troublesome people in their lives. For example, they may have difficulty accepting suggestions from anyone whom they view as an authority figure. In this case, you may consider bringing in a credible significant other from their lives to whom they may be more willing to listen—such as a spouse, sibling, or close friend—and using them as disputational models. If the message comes from them, or at least gets reinforced by them outside the session, you may increase the chance that these clients will accept the message.

Another possible explanation for clients' yes-but behavior is that they simply do not want to change. In this situation, a useful question to ask yourself is, "What's the payoff for the client?" In other words, what positive or negative consequences may be operating to maintain the dysfunctional beliefs or behaviors? One client of ours, for example, continually ranted and raged, and blamed her friends for not calling her as often as she liked; every disputation was met with a yes-but reply. It occurred to us that she was stuck on blaming others because it functionally served to avoid self-blame and self-examination. One technique to uncover such motivations is to repeatedly ask patients to fill in the following sentence: "The good thing about (blaming others, in this case) is. . . ."

The intellectualizing client. RET may be difficult to accomplish with intelligent clients whose defense against self-examination is to intellectualize. They combat the therapist with reasonable arguments, can beat the therapist at deductive logic, and even sound quite rational. Why, then, do they continue to come to therapy? Because although they do not clearly recognize or verbalize it, they have emotional problems. The therapist would be wise to keep the focus on emotions and, instead of relying on didactic approaches, bring in other procedures such as experiential exercises or imagery techniques. Such clients are very likely to object to these methods, however, and may refuse to do something they define as "silly." Proceed slowly.

The intellectually limited client. Disputation toward the elegant solution may not be appropriate for all clients. Among the exceptions are very young children, clients with limited intellectual ability, clients with severe brain damage, clients with severe psychosis whose pathological thought processes interfere with logical thought, and highly anxious clients, whose level of arousal is too intense to enable them to think clearly. The therapist will be more effective with such clients by simply *drilling* them in rational coping statements such as those recommended by Meichenbaum (1985), which are discussed in the next chapter, and by using operant principles to encourage the patient to exercise these rational replacements between therapy sessions.

The "it's-not-working" client. The statement that "It's not working" is common among clients who are beginning to learn RET and are impatient to experience change. Here are four sample therapist–client interactions that illustrate this problem and provide some suggestions for dealing with it:

C: I say to myself, "I don't *have* to, I want to," but it doesn't make me any calmer.
T: Well, Jim, that just indicates that you haven't really given up the *must*.
C: How do I do that?
T: By looking for your irrational beliefs and disputing them. Ask yourself, "Where's the evidence?" Be a scientist. We don't merely accept the fact that the world is round because it sounds good but because of the data. Where is the evidence that you *must* do well in school?

C: I know it *intellectually,* but I don't feel any different.
T: When you say you know it "intellectually," what you really mean is that you know it *some* of the time *weakly*. But most of the time you believe your irrational belief *strongly*. Do you dispute with yourself *convincingly?*
C: I guess I could work harder at it.
T: Right, and you won't believe it strongly until you begin to *live* it, to *act* on it. Now, what could you *do* this week to prove to yourself that you don't need Mary's love?

C: I know that the rational beliefs make sense, but I can't feel it when I'm actually in the situation.
T: Well, you can't feel more relaxed unless you rehearse a lot *before* you get into the situation. Let's practice how you'll handle your anxiety right now, to set a model for you.

C: I understand this disputation stuff, but I don't know how to do it when I'm not with you. I still get anxious and then I start obsessing.
T: Well, Mary, the trick is to use your symptoms as a cue to start the

chain: use your anxiety as a cue to think things through! "I'm obsess-ing. Why am I obsessing? To avoid anxiety. What am I anxious about? Some beliefs I'm holding. What are my irrational beliefs? Now I'll start to dispute them." So, you see how your symptoms are tied together? Your obsessions are partly an avoidance behavior to distract you from your anxiety. Instead of distracting yourself, use them as a signal to face your anxiety and uproot it, OK? Now you repeat that to me so I can see if you've got it.

The point of the examples above is that clients frequently hold to a false dichotomy, that there are intellectual versus emotional insights. The idea of an emotional insight runs counter to the most basic principle of RET, which is that thinking largely *causes* emotion. In addition, an "emo-tional insight" is a non sequitur; people do not achieve insight viscerally. When the client claims he or she has intellectual but not emotional insight, the therapist reinterprets this claim as either a problem of "knowing" but not "believing" the rational ideas, or of inconsistency of beliefs across time. The solution in either case is clarification and harder work for the therapeutic dyad.

Now that we have covered the basics of the disputational process, you have a blueprint that will help you to build a more elaborate structure. The work of the RET therapist does not end with disputation, however. The end product in disputation is not necessarily to get rid of the distress-ing Activating event, but to help the client to accept it if it cannot be changed or to calmly and methodically try to change it if this is possible. Thus, continued work may be needed both in and out of session. In the next chapter, we will focus on some of this in-session work.

Cautions

If your clients have achieved some control over their emotional distress, be sure to warn them to avoid holding perfectionistic standards in this new skill. Thus, if one client says that she thinks she can now control her anger, ask, "How long do you think it will be before you get angry again?" This question not only poses a gentle warning but can help the client prepare for this probability. If you omit this step, the client may become discouraged the next time she does become angry, and consequently devalue the gains made in therapy and no longer dispute when she is in troublesome situa-tions. You will recall that a major tenet in rational–emotive theory is that all people think both rationally *and* irrationally. With hard work, we can increase the proportion of time spent in rational thinking, but we can never expect to think completely rationally at all times.

In addition, there are often advantages to be attained by displays of strong affect, and even if clients can think rationally they need not give up these benefits. When clients discover the insights of RET, they sometimes make absolutist demands of their new rational beliefs and decide, for example, that they must never behave angrily again. A tenet of assertiveness training, however, is to escalate assertive behaviors until one gets what one wants. Ellis describes a personal incident as an example in which assertive behaviors were not effective, whereas threatening, acerbic remarks were instrumental in getting others to comply with his requests. When he changed offices, new slipcovers were ordered and were scheduled to be delivered six weeks later. This date came and went, but no slipcovers appeared. One assertive phone call later, he was promised delivery. The next week the scene was repeated, but another assertive phone call failed to change the laxity of the firm's service. Weeks later, when the man on the phone insisted that Ellis had to pick up the slipcovers himself now that they were, at long last, ready, he forcefully and deliberately suggested that he would be happy to remove the gentleman's "fornicating gonads" if the slipcovers did not arrive within the hour. The slipcovers arrived. The point of the story is that Ellis was *acting angrily* but was not actually feeling angry.* He knew that a *show* of anger would probably promptly get him what he wanted; so he feigned it. Clients who fail to discriminate between feelings and actions may frequently not get what they want, since strong language can be an important tool when dealing with "difficult customers" such as credit agencies, the phone company, government bureaucracies, and the like.

Another distortion occasionally encountered occurs when a client uses the concept of personal responsibility for one's emotional reactions as a justification for obnoxious social behavior. In one case of marital counseling, for example, the husband refused to deal with relationship issues, would not compromise on requests for behavior change, and continued to annoy his wife. He rationalized his behavior by claiming that she was responsible for her reactions and her problems; if she was upset, she was doing it to herself. The wife, on the other hand, was evaluating his behavior quite rationally and (in the opinion of the therapist) was appropriately annoyed. Although the husband correctly understood the basic principle

---

*Note that "acting angrily" can sometimes trigger the experience of anger, so caution is advised.

of RET, he did not understand that rational thinkers can have negative feelings and want to change the A. Although the husband was not causing his wife's C, he was nevertheless a component of A and had responsibility for the marriage. RET distinguishes between not *causing* but still *contributing* to a C by being obnoxious to someone at A. In reality, this man was demanding that his wife have no objections to his behavior and was misusing rational–emotive theory to justify his position. The therapeutic response to this misinterpretation of RET involved teaching him that marriage is a social contract, and although it is not necessary to behave ethically and responsibly, it is clearly *advantageous* to do so. The advisability of living within social contracts is a key element in rational-emotive philosophy.

Although the client in the above example was misusing RET principles, rational–emotive theory holds that we are not *totally* responsible for other people's emotions. The client may clearly have the responsibility for being an activating event for another person but does not bear full responsibility for the other's emotional distress. Our behavior may not please others, but it is their own evaluative self-statements that *directly* cause their misery. If the client already understands that others don't cause his or her personal misery, this understanding may provide the most direct route to challenging any subsequent statements that indicate the converse supposition that the client directly produced misery in others. For example:

C: I feel guilty because he's so upset.
T: Now, wait a minute, Gail. You can't have it both ways. If you're responsible for your bad feelings, then so is he for his. He may not like what you did, but if he's very upset, how are you totally responsible for that?

The notion of *total responsibility* is crucial and may be more elaborately pointed out to the patient, as in this therapeutic segment:

"Are you making yourself totally responsible for someone else's problems? If it's a young child, you are somewhat responsible; but, for example, when your nineteen-year-old gets into drugs, your attitude had better be, "Well, I don't like that he's into drugs and I'll do what I can to influence him, but in the final analysis I can't control his behavior, and he will have to take the consequences." When the situation involves two adults, the nutty idea may take the form, "If I do this, then he'll be happy; if I don't, he'll be miserable. I therefore have to act the way he wants to prevent his misery." What's wrong with such a notion?"

Again, mini-experiments may help to get the point across. The following example from Norma Campbell, an RET therapist from Baltimore, deals with a young widow who wanted to take her small daughter to Europe for the Christmas holidays to visit a sailor she had met when an Italian ship docked in Baltimore. Her idea met with great displeasure from her mother-in-law, who carried on in the following way: "What a bad person you are! Your husband isn't cold in his grave yet. How dare you take the child to strangers at a holiday time?" The daughter-in-law was suffused with guilt, concluding that her idea of the trip had led directly to the older woman's upset and that she was therefore a rotten person. The challenge went as follows:

T: Let's do the experiment. Tell *me* you're going on a trip and see how I respond.
C: (complies)
T: That's great! (pause) So, your going on a trip can't produce upset in others. It's your mother-in-law's *perception* via her irrational beliefs that makes her upset. You can't be totally responsible for the fact that she's upset.

Notice that the young woman's dilemma can be construed in terms of the ethical principles discussed earlier in rational-emotive philosophy. The optimal choice is both pro-self and pro-social, and would mean pleasing both herself and her mother-in-law. There are times, however, when such choices are simply not available, as in this case. What is the client to do? She can either stay at home and please the mother-in-law or go to Italy and please herself. If she takes total responsibility for the mother-in-law's feelings, she will probably stay home, but if she realizes that her mother-in-law is creating her own unhappiness, this understanding may put a different light on the client's decision and help her to make a choice that is both ethical and rational.

We are *not* advocating that clients act in callous disregard of the feelings of other people. However, to make life decisions only on the basis of how others feel and to take total responsibility for their feelings is both unrealistic and personally unsatisfying. The goal in RET is to live compatibly with others and yet not be subservient to them.

Analogies may also be useful. The therapist could ask the patient to

As an exercise, list the cognitions that might lead to these three emotional consequences. Then see if you can expand the list further. (See answer key, p. 369.)

Depression

Pity

Mirth

contemplate going up to 100 different people and telling each one, "My, you're ugly!" Does the patient imagine that each of the 100 people would feel miserable? Probably not. A variety of reactions, in fact, is more likely to ensue, including depression, pity, even mirth.

Conclusion

We conclude our three-chapter discussion of disputation by providing a detailed transcript of a complete therapy session. In this meeting, therapist and client establish the A-B-C's of a problem emotion, and the therapist helps the client to dispute her irrational demands.

T: Let's check up on things. We were talking last time about your mother. What's the progress report?

C: Well, the exact day after I sat here and talked to you about not letting my mom bully me—in the sense of just trying to ignore it and not reacting—the next morning was like a major explosion. You know, I don't even know if it pays to go into all this, the details of it, but it ended up with my mother physically attacking me, my brother coming between us, and my mother pretending to faint right on the floor, kicking her feet and banging her hands on her head and pulling out her hair!

T: A temper tantrum?

C: Right. For two days she ignored me and then pretended that it didn't happen and—OK, so that's a given—I'm living with my mother, who is really neurotic, who is going to be picking on me until I leave and there's no way out of that, really. I mean, that's given. I've tried to channel, you know, my upsets about that and many other things into my studying. I mean, just in the sense of the harder I work the faster I'll get out, the quicker I'll have money. I see it as just alleviating so many difficulties, though not all, but many of them, so if I just sit here and study and study and study I'll work my way out of this situation.

T: Let me ask you a question. Are you saying that in a helpful or non-helpful way? You see, if you're still allowing yourself to get overly upset about your mother's behavior and are still viewing your situation as horrible, then you may be working frantically. You may be saying, "I have to work faster, I have to work faster—the horror is still too close!" Is that true for you? Are you doing good work when you sit down to study?

C: Well . . .

T: Or are you working frantically?

C: I'm doing that. I go, "I've got to hurry up and get out of here." I really am. The nit-picking is what gets to me. It's like she can't come out and say, "Gee, I really don't like you and I wish that you weren't here." Although she says that too when she gets mad, at the times she's not saying it, she's showing it in other ways.

T: It's not pleasant to be living with somebody who doesn't want you around. Remember, we talked about this last time—about the three different categories of things that she does. Sometimes she says "I don't like you, I wish you would get out of the house." Some comments are innuendos, and others perhaps no one else would react to, but you do because you're sensitized to react to them.

C: I try to sort them out. I mean, I've been hanging around you long enough to know at least to try to be rational about my problems, but it doesn't really stop the initial flow of rage and hurt. The feeling comes, and I start saying, "Well, even if she doesn't like me, even if she's showing obvious preference to my brother," things like that . . .

T: Then what? Finish the end of the sentence.

C: That it doesn't mean that I'm not a good person.

T: Her opinion is just her opinion.

C: But at the same time, the anger is still there, and when I'm alone and when I'm riding the train and thoughts are just flowing through my mind, the anger comes over me to the point where I . . . I really have very vicious fantasies about her.

T: OK, let me stop you for a minute. It sounds as if you're doing one very good thing. It sounds like when she starts her routine and you find yourself reacting to it, you do a good thing—which is using your emotional reaction as a signal. You say, "Oops, I'm overreacting."

C: I do that. I did that after the fight. But the next morning (proceeds to tell another story of an encounter with her mother)—and then she came flying at me. "Get out of my house. I hate you!" And then it escalated into a big fight. So I lost my temper and in that case I was human. Because I was angry. It was building up for a week.

T: OK, so you're not perfect.

C: No.

T: But let me get back to what I think one of the problems is. As I listen to you, it seems that sometimes you are quite good at this rationl self-talk and other times it's not working. Let's problem solve and see when it's not working and *why*. Now, you said that at the time your mother was acting crazy with you, you were able to say to yourself, "Well, her opinion is her opinion. If she thinks I'm a shit, that doesn't make me a shit." Those kinds of self-statements are very useful for counteracting a specific kind of emotion. Can you figure out what emotion that would be?

The therapist is helping the client to discriminate the B's and C's for two separate emotional problems.

C: Well, I guess feeling hurt—or putting myself down because someone else is criticizing me.

T: Exactly. Self put-down is depression. But those cognitions, those very helpful thoughts are not going to help in *anger* because there is a different set of irrational thoughts that are going on—different from depression. So, it's like taking the wrong medicine.

C: Do you think that it fits into this kind of therapy—the idea that suppressed anger becomes depression? Because I've heard that said.

T: I've heard it said too. Let's put it this way: I don't think that anger *expressed* is any more useful than anger *repressed*. The key to success is not whether you say it or don't say it, have your temper tantrum or don't have your temper tantrum, but to uproot the anger itself from its antecedents. You uproot it from its causes, just like you did with your depression. You get to the head talk. You've got some really good coping techniques for depression; now let's develop some coping techniques for the anger, OK?

C: OK.

T: First of all, let's do a little A-B-C on the situation. A, mother does something, and C, you feel anger, not depression. What are some of the B's you can imagine?

C: When I feel angry?

T: Anger. Not depression.

C: OK.

T: Look for a "must" again.

C: Well, I must not be in this situation where someone is being so unjust to me.

T: OK, that's a good thought to be in touch with. Now, is that an anger-provoking thought? It sounds like a poor-me thought.

C: Yeah.

T: Poor-me's don't get you angry.

C: Well, my mother should be understanding.

T: That's usually where it falls. Anger is directed outward, not at yourself, but outward. It's mother "should." "Mother shouldn't yell at me, she shouldn't say nasty things." Any others you can think of?

C: (tells another brief story of an incident at home)

T: OK, stop there. What's the irrational belief?

C: All right. Even though they're treating me that way—they *are* treating me that way. The reality is that my brother is definitely preferred.

T: And what's the irrational belief?

C: That it doesn't mean that I am the way they see me.

T: No, what's the irrational idea that you're saying? Do you know?

C: Somehow, because I allow myself to be treated that way, it really turns me into that kind of a person. And if I really had pride or self-respect or common sense or whatever, I could turn it around so that it wouldn't be that way.

T: That's your depression, your poor-me and bad-me thoughts. Let's leave those aside for the moment. What's the anger belief? Not only shouldn't she yell at you and say nasty things to you, but how "must" she treat you?

C: Well, she should treat me as an equal member of the family.

T: She *should* treat you fairly and squarely. These are some of your shoulds. We know from rational-emotive theory that shoulds and musts are where the trouble is; your belief is that your mother shouldn't do those things, that she should treat you fairly.

C: I also have those shoulds for myself. I should not yell at my mother. I should not, you know, express any kind of temper or dissatisfaction in ways that are going to make people uncomfortable. When inwardly, I really want to go in there and let her have it and say, "What is this crap, I mean, here he's been lying in bed all year and you've been telling me the reason is that he's paying you money, and then you're telling him that you're giving it all back to him."

T: That would be good to say if you weren't in a rage but were merely determined to try to change what could be changed. If you did those things assertively, you could do them better, more efficiently. But let's go back—we've got an A, a B, and a C.

C: OK.

T: We've got the anger and the anger cognitions, which are all those *musts*. Now let's do a D. What are some questions you want to ask yourself about this?

C: Why can't I tell her what to think? This is a big question to me. The fact that I have so much anger and that I just absolutely cannot find words to even begin to say "this is a raw deal." I don't know how to go about it, whether I approach my brother or my mother.

T: Wait. That's another issue. That's the "you" issue. We want the "them" issue. Those people out there who are treating you unfairly and your anger about that. First of all, do you agree that you would like to give up your anger? Not your determination, but your anger.

C: OK. At this point, I feel that it would really be sick not to resent it or to feel anger. It is justified at this point.

T: If you're asking, "Are you trying to get me to feel nothing or to just joyfully accept this horse shit?" I'd say "No, that's crazy." You'd be crazy to be happy about it. But I don't see that getting *angry* about it is doing you any good. For that reason, I think it would be best to get rid of the rage and bring it down to where you can say, "I don't like this and I'm going to do what I can about it. I'm going to try to change the situation." After all, what does anger do for you? It gets your stomach churning and it's not very good for your system, physiologically.

C: No; for a week I've been walking around definitely feeling all those physical things. And I try to hold it in so I just get really quiet and I don't want to talk to anybody, and then they get on my case that I'm depressed.

T: OK, so let's work on the anger. It's been a while since we've done an A-B-C-D formally, so let's sort of review. When you do D, you go back to the nutty ideas one by one, and you ask yourself questions.

C: Why *should* my mother be fair to me?

T: Right! Where's the evidence that your mother should act nicely to you?

C: I don't know. Going to school, I see so many people at home living well. They're running around with the family charge card and they're doing whatever the heck they want to do, and everybody's kissing their ass and they think it's the greatest thing.

T: I absolutely agree that that would be nice. But why *should* your mother do that?

C: Why *should* she? (pause) I think she *should*! She *should* be fair.

T: Why?

C: Just because I want her to. (laughs)

The therapist has allowed the client to repeatedly struggle with the question rather than answering it for her.

T: That's right. "She *must* do what I want her to do." Where's that going to get you?

C: Hmmmmm.

T: Now I'm agreeing 100 percent that it would be really nice if your mother treated you fairly. It would be pleasant, it would make your life simpler, it would be advantageous to you. Your life would be much easier if you had rich, loving parents who treated you fairly. We could prove that. We could do the experiment and prove that advantage. Could we do an experiment to prove why your mother *should* do that? Why does she *have to* do that?

The therapist never disputes the client's claim that it would be advantageous to have what she wants, merely the demand that it be so.

C: It's possible at some level—she's not that stupid—that if she realizes it, it can't make *her* feel good. I mean, how can a mother feel good about being unfair?

T: Right. So maybe it would even be nicer for *her* if she treated you fairly.

C: Right, it might be.

T: But why *must* she? Even though it would be good for you and maybe good for her. Why does she *have* to do what would be nice for you?

The therapist repeats the same disputation.

C: OK, so she doesn't have to.

T: I don't think you believe that.

C: One thing that helps me is to think, "Well, it's not my fault, the fact is that she's doing that." And the fact is that she doesn't have to be fair, and it's not really my job to make her fair, and I don't exist in this time and place to straighten my mother out and make her realize how important it is to be fair.

T: That's right. But if you don't really work hard at giving up the belief that "she's *got* to," you're going to be, first of all, continually disappointed in her, trying to control her. . . .

C: But in terms of everyday behavior, once in despair I was talking about this with my father, and she's been very domineering toward him all his life and picked on him unfairly, and he told me frankly, "I've found that the best way to deal with her is to submit. That's how I cope." And it's true. An observer in my home for three days would look at this man and say he's slavish and servile, and demeans himself rather than confront her.

T: OK, let me ask you a question. Does he upset himself? Is he quiet but seething inside, or is he really kind of philosophic about it?

C: For years I think he walked around exactly like I did, nursing a lot of inner hurts but not expressing them.

T: Now?

C: Now he seems to have accepted her behavior and decided that this is the easiest way to behave back. My way of dealing is . . . I find obsequiousness very bad. If she acts in a very domineering way, it's not given that I must act in a very obsequious way. That's unpleasant.

T: I hear you saying, "It's good that my father isn't upsetting himself about her nuttiness any longer. He lays back and it rolls off him." He's not trying to train her or shape her up by confronting her.

C: Right.

T: First of all, that tells me there's a good reason for her not to change at all. She's had years of training and reinforcement.

C: Right! Having everyone in the family submit to her.

T: So, if you decide to challenge the system it's going to be a tough job at best. You're going to try to retrain this woman who's had sixty-some years of reinforcement for her behavior. You're going to have a tough job. That knowledge may help you make your decision about whether or not to stand up to her—is it worth it?

C: Right.

T: Another thing I hear, however, is your choice of words to describe your father's behavior—obsequious, slavish. That he's a schlemeil; people walk all over him. That's *your* perception you're talking about.

C: Right. This has played a very big part in the kind of men I've been attracted to. I could never stand a guy who would do whatever I said. I watched my father do that for so many years and I did get that impression of him.

T: Right. But that's a perception. Now what I'm suggesting is, if you were to try to *objectively* describe your father's behavior, without using words like obsequious which are rather negative or pejorative, how would you very objectively describe what he does?

C: Hmmmm. Objectively. When my mother attacks my father without any just cause, he doesn't defend himself and he doesn't attack back.

T: What *does* he do?

C: He either remains quiet or says a very gentle "now-now, dear," but then proceeds to do what she tells him to do.

T: And then the issue blows over?

C: It blows over but it's a constant thing. Not just once a day, but from the second you enter to the second you leave her presence. It's a barrage. Nothing but orders.

T: So your father lets her do that, he goes along with her requests, but he also doesn't *upset* himself. He's not stewing. So he's made his own kind of adaptation.

C: Right.

T: There are two components to adaptation. First, what he does inter-
     nally, his emotional turmoil; and second, what he does on the out-
     side, how he responds behaviorally.

The therapist is helping the client to empathically understand her father's behavior.

C: OK.
T: What I hear you saying is, maybe the emotional reaction is OK. His
     apparent ability to not upset himself about his crazy wife is something
     you'd like to acquire. Be philosophical and let her be her nutty self.
C: Right. But not follow the same behavior patterns.
T: Right.
C: Because I find that that image of myself is unpleasant. I've found that
     very often what I do is just give tit for tat. When she starts digging at
     me, I dig back.
T: Let me suggest that maybe we could look at the behaviors as a sepa-
     rate issue—as a series of *strategies*. Step one, however, is still the same.
     You want to get over the rage. Once you accomplish that, you can
     probably problem solve the situation better. "Let's see, I can try
     experiments. I can try retorting and see how that works. I can try
     reinforcing better behavior and see how that works. I can try doing
     what my father does and shutting up and doing whatever she asks,
     and see what that does. I can try being very assertive and confronting
     her. I could try giving her lectures. I could try giving her books to
     read." You might try strategies. If a strategy doesn't work after a
     reasonable effort, you end the experiment and say, "Well, that didn't
     affect her behavior, I'll try something else." All of these are
     strategies—they're just behaviors.
C: They're good, though, because they make me feel empowered. I
     could try this or that.
T: Yes, like a scientist. But a scientist is never going to be a good scien-
     tist if she's demanding that the data come out the way she wants!

The therapist is pointing out why an inelegant solution would not be appropriate.

C: Yeah.
T: As long as you're *demanding* that your mother change her behavior,
     you're going to be angry at her.
C: Yeah.
T: Step one is to give up the demand, give up the anger and then try
     strategies and do experiments. So the best thing to do is to give up the
     shoulds. If you can really believe what you said, that she doesn't have
     to change . . . that she may never change. . . .

C: You're right. She's definitely not going to change!

T: She may or she may not. You can try strategies. But if you can give up the shoulds, the *demand* that she change, and absorb some of your father's philosophical ideas—"That's the way she is for now, she doesn't seem to want to change and she's not motivated to change, and me sitting back demanding that she change . . ."

The therapist is using the father as a rational model.

C: When you say it, I really see it! I feel what you're saying.

T: So you can imagine that if you can just remember this stuff and say it to yourself between sessions, you'll be OK. There's a great book, *Overcoming Frustration and Anger,* by Paul Hauck. Another useful book is *How to Live With—and Without—Anger,* by Albert Ellis. If you could read either of these it would reinforce what we did today.

C: I really feel better. I really do. I mean, it just went from this huge horrible thing to—well, she's just her and that's the way she is—tough noodles!

T: Bravo! That's fantastic! That's emotional proof that you can make disputing work.

C: Yeah.

T: What you'd better do is work hard at remembering to do it between our meetings.

C: OK.

T: That's why a good book is a handy thing to have.

13 Therapist Strategies: Advanced Variations on a Theme

Active-Directive Style

Rational-emotive therapists vary quite a lot in their style of interacting with patients, but as a group they can be distinguished from therapists of other schools by their active, directive style. Because rational-emotive therapists work with a model of identifying and challenging self-defeating thought patterns, they are alert for specific cues to these thoughts. Key words, phrases, and intonations as well as nonverbal aspects of the client's behavior are the cues, and the therapist will try to not let these slip by unattended. Thus, rational-emotive therapists avoid asking very general, open-ended questions and allowing a prolonged rambling response by the client, followed by another general question from the therapist, and so on. Instead, they tend to ask direct, specific questions so that the end result is more a dialogue than a client monologue, with the therapist carefully following up on words and concepts revealed in the client's responses. We envision the therapist as a kind of herd dog who guides the patient through an open field full of distractions, keeping the patient on course.

It is easy for active therapists to fall into the "advice trap," in which they either give patients solutions to their problems or appear to be recommending a particular solution. It is important to help clients see that they have choices, and to teach them that brainstorming and problem solving are skills that they can learn, particularly when they understand how not to upset themselves. This concept of problem-solving as a skill is consistent with the goal of ultimately encouraging independence from the therapist and will be discussed more fully in Chapter 16.

Similarly, therapists will want to be careful not to "plant" irrational statements in the client's conversation that RET theory suggests will be present. If they do make such suggestions to the client, they will want to speak tentatively and validate these ideas with the client. Thus, the therapist might say, "It sounds like you're saying you *must* do X; have I heard you correctly?"

It is preferable to draw out the irrational beliefs by phrasing questions in a guided manner. For example:

NOT: Why did you get angry?
BUT: What did you tell yourself to make yourself angry?
OR: Did you get angry because you were telling yourself something about the way you were treated?

NOT: What is related to your problems with power struggles?
BUT: What do you tell yourself to upset yourself when you find you are in a power struggle?
OR: Are you upsetting yourself because you're telling yourself something about the importance of winning when you're in a power struggle?

NOT: So you believe that he must love you?
BUT: What do you think about his not loving you?
OR: How do you evaluate him not loving you? Could you be awfulizing?

Thus, instead of suggesting ideas to clients (e.g., "You are demanding"), try to lead them to discover the ideas by themselves by questions such as, "What were you telling yourself?" Questions, rather than answers, put the responsibility for therapy properly on the patient.

NOT: That's not true!
BUT: How do you know that's true?
OR: What evidence do you have that that's true?
OR: What could possibly convince you that it's *not* true?

Lecture versus Socratic Dialogue

There are two different ways of presenting RET principles: a lecture format, and Socratic dialogue. The lecturer directly imparts information to clients about what they are doing to cause their own disturbances and uses explanatory devices such as parables, analogies, and metaphors to make the point. The therapist using Socratic dialogue relies on evocative questions to guide the client to an insight or an appropriate conclusion. Socratic dialogue, therefore, is a slower and more methodical procedure. Both techniques have value as educational devices, but the knowledgeable practitioner is also aware of their limitations.

It is advisable that a certain amount of lecturing take place in therapy, since it is the most efficient way to transmit information. Mini-lectures may be particularly appropriate in early sessions to familiarize clients with some of the basic principles of RET. You may also find lecturing useful for clients of low socioeconomic status, who expect a great deal of active direction from the therapist, or for clients with lower intellectual ability or brain injury, who tend to require more structure. Lecturing is, of course, appropriate when the client's problem results from ignorance about a particular topic (e.g., the female client who labels herself frigid because she does not come to orgasm in intercourse).

The use of mini-lectures, however, requires caution. If you give a lecture, even an excellent one, what is your client doing with the information? Probably what most students do: putting it in a (mental) notebook and filing it away for the next test—in this case, the next therapy session. Be aware of this tendency and, without labeling it as such, program little tests within the session to make sure that the client is really "with you." Do not go on to the next point until you're certain that the client has understood the previous one. Also, give behavioral homework assignments to assure that the client actively utilizes the lecture material (see Chapter 14).

Socratic dialogue has its own advantages, most particularly as an aid to learning and recall. Years of psychological research on the relative effectiveness of recall versus recognition memory suggests that getting the client to *generate* appropriate cognitions via Socratic dialogue will produce superior retention in comparison to lecturing, which merely allows the client to *recognize* appropriate cognitions. Whereas the lecture format consists of unequally weighted sequential monologues, in Socratic dialogue, the client expresses the therapeutic material in his or her own words and will recall it in this same modality, thus encouraging retention.

Contrast the following two presentations:

Lecture

> "Well, Sheila, you seem to be very upset and anxious about your mother not approving of you. Let me spend a little time explaining to you what causes people to be anxious. Most people believe that

Examine your own behavior when you attend a lecture. What are you doing? Not much, right? You're sitting silently, perhaps nodding your head in agreement and occasionally taking notes. These are quite passive behaviors and illustrate the advisability of not limiting your therapeutic interventions only to lecturing.

Listen to a session in which you have done some lecturing. Try to ascertain if the client understood your major points. What could you have done to test that understanding?

they're made anxious by the things that happen to them. You're believing that your anxiety is caused by your mother's disapproval. Actually, we don't think that's true. People usually get upset about things because of what they think about them. For example, 100 people experiencing the same disapproval from your mother wouldn't all feel the same way. Some would feel happy or relieved that their mother didn't care for them and left them alone, others would feel terribly upset and suicidal, and still others would feel kind of indifferent. There could be a whole range of reactions. So that the activating event, as we call what your mother's doing to you, doesn't cause all these different reactions. It's really what you think—your belief system. Now, different kinds of beliefs cause different kinds of emotions. Illogical or irrational beliefs which exaggerate things cause very disturbed emotions, and rational, logical beliefs cause more appropriate, less disturbed emotions.''

Socratic Dialogue

T: OK, Sheila, I understand you feel anxious when your mother picks on you or when you think about your mother picking on you. Now, where do you think that anxiety comes from?

C: Well, from my mother, of course. If she would stop picking on me then I wouldn't feel anxious!

T: Well, it sure might seem that way, but if your mother picked on me, I wouldn't feel anxious. Now, why wouldn't I feel anxious when you would?

C: Because you don't have to live with her!

T: Well, let's assume I did. I still wouldn't feel anxious. Now, what would be the difference?

C: Well, maybe she just doesn't mean as much to you as she does to me.

T: That could be. The word "meaning" is very important, isn't it? Be-

> Listen to some of your recent therapy tapes, paying attention to who was doing most of the talking—you or the client. Are you lecturing too much? Are you talking too little? What is your purpose in doing so?
>
> Now, pick a particular client and decide on a specific therapeutic style, either Socratic dialogue or a lecture, to get a point across; then tape the session. Later, review it to see if you met your objectives.

cause it's the *meaning* we put on situations, in this case your mother's behavior, that leads to our emotions. What meaning do you think you're putting on your mother's behavior?

C: (pause) That's a hard question.

T: But you're obviously not saying, "Oh, it's fine that she acts that way. I'm really pleased." Are you?

C: Oh, no!

T: What are you saying?

C: It's not nice at all! It's terrible that she's acting that way!

T: That's right! You're saying it's awful or horrible that she's acting that way. Now we call that "awfulizing" and it's an example of an irrational idea. And irrational ideas are the kind that lead to upsetting, dysfunctional emotions.

If you speak primarily in declarative sentences (as in a lecture format) rather than ask questions (as in Socratic dialogue), you run two major risks. First, you may slip into the role of "expert," who, for example, may be viewed as responsible for holding the patient's marriage together. Thus, the declarative style may oversell to clients so that they unthinkingly accept the therapist's judgment or rely on the therapist to solve their problems. Another disadvantage is that you may set up ideas that clients will perversely deny or debate, even if they are quite correct. Questions are usually the better way to elicit material from clients and to help them learn to help themselves. In order to do Socratic dialogue, however, it is necessary to learn how to ask good questions.

FORM OF THE QUESTIONS

The form in which questions are posed is important, and a common error made by new rational-emotive therapists is to begin too many questions with the word "why." "Why" questions are difficult to answer; the responses are often redundant, simply reiterating why the patient came to therapy. Examples:

NOT: Why are you anxious?
BUT: What do you think makes you anxious?
OR: Are you aware of the fact that you are in control of your anxiety?

As a handy substitute for "why," the therapist may sometimes reach for a "how."

Proposing hypothetical scenarios may also be a useful device. For a patient who fears certain life events, the therapist might say, for example, "What would you do if tomorrow morning you woke up and were married (or lost your job, etc.)?" These examinations of hypothetical events may aid not only in obtaining cognitive samples but also in directly reducing the patient's avoidance of the feared situation. Another example, from a depressed patient who suffered from headaches:

"Suppose you went to a neurologist today and he gave you a new miracle drug which took away your headaches. Tomorrow you'd wake up and have no headaches. How would that change your life? How would you cope?"

Such questions may also serve as mini-extinction procedures, resembling low items on a desensitization hierarchy. That is, patients may be avoiding a specific issue or undertaking in their lives, and confronting it on a verbal level is less fear-provoking than engaging in more direct behaviors.

PACING OF QUESTIONS

To stop the client's tangential monologues or to hold back an avalanche of unnecessary information, a useful strategy is to pace questions carefully. Ask the next question as soon as the client answers the last, even if this means interrupting the client's speech. It is difficult to guide the dialogue unless the therapist is willing to be assertive.

Try an exercise that Ed Garcia has used with many new therapists: attempt to conduct an *entire* therapy session using only
questions and avoiding all declarative sentences. Tape the session
and see how close you come to this goal. Note that we are not
recommending that all therapy be in the form of evocative questions. Too many questions may prove irritating to clients if they
believe that you have something to say and are "beating around
the bush" instead of saying it directly. This exercise is merely
designed to give you practice in the art of Socratic dialogue.

See that your client answers your questions. If he or she responds
with a non sequitur, this may provide valuable diagnostic information.
Some of the reasons clients do not answer questions are:

They have not paid attention.

They have not understood the question or have misunderstood it.

If they have not understood a question, they may be too nonassertive
to request clarification.

They may be avoiding a painful topic.

They may be unskilled at social conversation.

They may have poor thinking habits and think illogically or tangen-
tially.

Repeating a question is therapeutic; it models assertiveness skills and
helps clients to learn to focus their attention or to confront anxiety-
provoking situations. To ignore a non sequitur encourages the pathology.
If patients repeatedly fail to answer questions, a useful strategy is to stop
their tangential thoughts and ask if they remember the question; then ask
how the thoughts they have just expressed relate to it. This will give you
some information about whether the problem is an attentional deficit, an
avoidance issue, or a lack of social skills.

Many new therapists are uncomfortable with stopping the patient's
digressions and repeating unanswered questions. They may object that it
is rude to redirect the client and worry that the client will be offended or
even harmed. In fact, most clients do not object to redirection, but for
those who are offended, the rationale for the procedure can be explained in

detail. The point is that therapy is not a social engagement; with approximately forty-five minutes to work on problems, it is appropriate to stay on target.

Another instance in which rephrasing or repeating your questions is helpful is when you do not understand the client's response, for example, "I'm not sure I follow you there; could you explain that again?" In directive therapy, it is important that client and therapist understand one another. If you do not understand the client, your silence may communicate that you do. The client could become annoyed later, when it becomes apparent that you did not understand. You also waste valuable and expensive time by allowing the client to go on when you are unclear about the message. Once again, our experience suggests that most clients are not offended by the repetition of questions for clarification, but instead perceive the therapist more positively for behaving honestly. Both parties benefit from effective communication.

Maintaining the Focus on the Problem

A primary and often difficult task for the therapist is to keep the patient focused on the problem. Many therapists assume that digressions are a sign of pathological resistance. While this may sometimes be the case, it is more likely that your clients are simply displaying normal social behavior. To illustrate this point to yourself, monitor some social conversations and note how many different topics are discussed within a twenty-minute period. In therapy, however, digressions are innappropriate.

You can increase the patient's ability to focus by not dealing with too many A–B–C's in one session. It is better to take one problem area and focus on it until disputation is complete or some closure has been reached before moving on.

Keeping the client focused on the problem has additional benefits. If the client has a tendency to engage in tangential thinking, the therapist can provide important feedback and help the client avoid this behavior. Confront the client genuinely and empathically; for example:

> "Jane, I'm confused. You started out talking about topic X and now you've moved to Y. What's the relationship between them [or which do you want to talk about]?"

Being able to contribute to a conversation and being able to stay with the same topic for a period of time are, after all, prerequisite skills for effective psychotherapy. If these skills are weak or missing, the therapist may have to begin by doing attention training, which is similar to working with a hyperkinetic child; nothing will get accomplished until you train the child to attend to a task. The following techniques may prove helpful in this preliminary training:

> Listen to tape recordings of therapy sessions with the client in order to sharpen your skills in detecting conversational slippage.

> Clients may be encouraged to do the same, so that they learn to identify the problem behavior.

> Structure the conversation tightly, limiting the discussion to just a few topics.

> Use retraining procedures, including rewards for staying on the topic and penalties for digressions. For example, you may say to the client, "My, you've outlined your problem well! That's very good, the way you stayed on the topic; it's helpful to us." On the other hand, you might point out, "You know, you got off the track, and I really don't understand how that follows. Explain it to me again!" As in behavioral training, we recommend putting the emphasis on the positive reinforcers.

Implementing the above procedures is not easy and will require strict self-monitoring by the therapist.

Suppose, however, that the patient comes in obviously intending to take over the session with a topic that you believe is a deflection from a more important unresolved issue. What should you do? First, you can give yourself permission to redirect the session by assuming that you know best about therapy. How can you redirect the session? One technique is to remind the client of the goals for the session and to make use of the Premack principle,* for example:

> "Jim, I'm going to let you talk about your root canal work at the end of the session; we'll save time for that. But first, I have some very important issues that I want to discuss about your marriage."

---

*The Premack principle states that a high-probability behavior can be used to reinforce a low-probability behavior.

Another approach which at least sets some limits to the client's diversions is:

> "Jim, your root canal seems to be important to you. Let's give the first five minutes to discussing your problems with your teeth and then spend the last forty minutes on the issue of your marriage."

You may also, at this point, ask clients how they feel about the redirection. If they're angry, it may be useful to ask if they experience anger in similar situations—an issue that may be relevant to the main therapeutic problem.

If you sense that the client's new issue is a distraction maneuver, you may confront the client as follows:

> "I get the sense that you're afraid of something."

More directly, you may ask the client how this topic fits in with the avoided one:

> "Jim, what does your root canal have to do with the problems in your marriage?"

Ultimately, you may want to share an interpretation of the client's behavior:

> "Jim, it seems week after week you come in with an agenda that seems to get us off the track of the original problem—your marriage! It appears to me you may be trying to avoid that problem. What do you think you could be frightened of?"

If the patient has a persistent tendency to be wordy or flighty, or to go off the topic in response to the therapist's intervention, strong measures may be needed. You may bring the problem to the patient's attention by saying something like, "May I have your agreement to interrupt you if you're giving me far too much information?" Thus, with the client's collaboration, you can confront the problem forcefully each time by simply saying, "Wait a minute!" to the client. A "halt" hand gesture may also be useful communication. With particularly difficult patients, the therapist may temporarily have to resort to questions that allow only yes or no answers. If you become aware that the focus has already been lost and the conversation has drifted, stop and ask yourself two basic questions:

In a few sentences, what is the patient's main problem?
What are the most prominent irrational beliefs?

Another useful tactic for keeping patients focused is to keep asking for specific examples of their main problem.

Repetition

Therapy, like teaching, often demands a certain amount of repetition. It will be important for you to repeat rational-emotive concepts with the patient, even though you may feel that you sound like a broken record. RET philosophy contains subtle points that many patients find difficult; rehearsal is therefore very important.

Keep in mind that you are modeling RET skills for the patient, such as learning to attend to key phrases and to examine one's internal dialogue, and these skills require repetition with most clients. Particularly in the disputation phase, you may find yourself not wanting to say the same things again and again. It is interesting to contemplate how Dr. Ellis himself has managed to teach the same message to so many patients over his long career of practicing RET. Listening to Ellis provides a clue; rather dramatic variation in emphasis and vocal tone may serve to keep up the excitement and interest of the therapist as well as the patient. In disputation (as was seen in Chapters 11 and 12) you can vary your style of phrasing greatly, although you are basically training the client to ask the same questions, for example, "Where is the evidence?" or "Why is it awful?" or "Who says you must . . . ?"

Language Style

Adjustments in language style are often made, of course, since clients vary in their level of sophistication. Take the hypothetical case of a young woman, a high school sophomore, who is concerned about getting into a sorority. She complains of her shyness, for example, explaining that she is afraid to go up to the older or more stylishly dressed girls and initiate a conversation. It sounds to you as if she has catalogued and ranked people, and declared herself to fall below some arbitrary cutoff point. Her philosophy seems to be "some people are better than others," which is expressed in her beliefs as, "I have to be as good as they are! If they don't accept me, it proves that I'm not, and that would be awful!" With this client, it might not be profitable to begin by discussing "irrational beliefs" or "philosophical tenets." You might be more direct and helpful if you took a more casual approach. The first query, therefore, might be something like, "What do you think the others would *do* if you went over to them?"

USE OF OBSCENITY

Another aspect of style which rational–emotive therapists are flexible about is the "sprightly use of obscenity," to use Ellis' phrase. Many therapists model their style closely after Ellis in this regard. We have observed that beginning therapists can be distinguished from more advanced students by their liberal use of four-letter words. In RET terms, it is common to refer to the patient's self-denigration or his or her "shithood"; the therapist may ask, for example, how the patient's bad behavior makes him a "shit." Obviously, other terms will work as well, such as "worm," "no-goodnik," and "louse." You will want to use your own judgment as to which term best suits the client's manner of speaking.

Ellis has been criticized for using obscenity but often has commented publicly on his positive reasons for doing so. He hypothesizes that people typically awfulize in four-letter expletives, even if they rarely use these terms in their conversations. Sometimes even very subdued and conservative clients find that when they are describing serious life problems, four-letter words are the most appropriate and evocative descriptors. These words can help loosen people up and have a strong emotive, as well as motivating, quality.

A second reason for using obscene language is that it builds rapport. It might sound strange that clients would like a therapist who curses, but remember that most people use obscene language only within their closest circle of peers. One uses more informal language with those with whom one can be relaxed and off guard. Thus, a common observation of therapists is that if they provide a model and thereby give permission to the patient to use obscenity, the patient feels at ease.

Reflect on your own subvocal monologue the next time you are late for work and rush from the house, only to discover that you have a flat tire.

To prove that obscene language can build rapport, monitor your own four-letter words and note in whose presence they are comfortably used.

We do not recommend using obscenities indiscriminately. Their "sprightly use" is optimally directed at clients' irrational beliefs ("Why the fuck *should* you?") and self-denigration ("You sound like you think you're really a shit!"). A third use is to underscore significant points ("Isn't the goal of life to get out there and have a fucking ball?"). Realize, however, that obscenity is never directed at the clients themselves and that it is not necessary to curse at all, since the same points can be made using other words.

Intonation

A significant aspect of the therapist's verbal behavior to which the RET novice will want to attend is vocal intonation. A great deal of information about attitudes can be unwittingly communicated in this modality. The therapist will particularly want to avoid expressing horror or other value judgments. For example, suppose the patient is a young man who is discussing his feelings of guilt about not visiting his parents as often as they would like. The incautious therapist might say, "You only go once a *week?*" or "You hardly go *at all?*" Inflections of the therapist's voice may make a big difference in how the patient responds to such questions.

Inflection can also be used in helping clients discriminate between rational and irrational beliefs. When you listen to one of Ellis' public demonstrations of RET in person or on tape, notice that he uses his voice as an instrument for clarification. Whenever he pronounces one of the words that signify irrational concepts (e.g., "awful," "terrible," "should," or "need"), he drops his voice several notes, stretches out the word, and increases his volume, producing a dreary, dramatic sound. For example, ". . . and it's AWWWWWFULL that he doesn't like me!" Later, when he changes the "awful" to "unfortunate," or a "need" to a "want," Ellis again pronounces the words, now reflecting rational concepts, in a distinct way. He speaks the key word slowly, enunciates very clearly, and raises the pitch of his voice as well as the volume. Thus, different auditory stimuli are associated with different concepts, making them more salient and easier to remember. Howard Kassinove of Hofstra University makes a point of encouraging his trainees in RET to model Ellis' vocal style. He points out that variety in style is important in every therapeutic encounter; a significant shift in tone and volume increases the probability that the client will attend to and learn from the therapist.

Getting the client's attention is crucial when the therapist is about to make an important point. Monitor your typical style. If you are speaking rapidly and loudly and you want to make an important point, dramatically lower your voice and slow down. If your style is typically soft-spoken, on the other hand, you will attract the client's attention by raising your volume and speed. In other words, know yourself and be prepared to adjust your inflection when it is appropriate.

A second strategy is to signal an important concept by the content of your speech and the use of gestures. As in assertiveness training, leaning forward, touching the client on the arm, and making good eye contact are effective nonverbal cues. You can also prepare the client for a confrontation with a verbal introduction, such as:

> "I'm going to do something risky right now and tell you something that most people wouldn't dare to say . . ." *or*
>
> "This is a really important point. Stop and listen carefully to what I'm going to say . . ."

If clients habitually interrupt, ask them to agree not to talk for five minutes, and hold them to this.

Silences

Silence communicates. Your silent behavior may be construed as agreement with the patient. As an analogy, in Old English law if a separated wife or husband signed the spouse's name to bills, and this went on for a period of time without the spouse's objection, the wife or husband could be entitled to continue to do so, because the spouse's silence was considered consent. A similar phenomenon often occurs in conversations. For example, if the client loses focus on the problem and verbally meanders, your silence may inaccurately convey to the client that he or she is making sense or doing constructive work.

Similarly, *inconsistent* silences by the therapist may provide intermittent reinforcement for irrational beliefs, thereby prolonging their existence in the cognitive system. For example, consider a patient who is depressed and frequently makes statements such as, "I'm never going to get better." A better plan of action would be to vigorously confront and dispute such remarks, or to reflectively paraphrase them with rational statements, such as, "It sounds like you're saying that it would be hard for you to change."

The point we wish to stress is that silence is a form of communication, however, we don't always know *what* we have communicated. Patients may interpret our silences as disapproval, indifference, or agreement. It is wise, therefore, to check on your patient's understanding of your silences and correct any misperceptions that you uncover.

Flexibility

The previous sections have discussed a variety of stylistic variations in doing RET, and it is preferable that you become comfortable with all of them. Utilize specific variations when your clinical judgment suggests their effectiveness. Try not to behave rigidly—always talking fast or slowly, always using the same intonation, always being funny or glib, or never allowing any silent periods. Rigidly adhering to one mode of behavior is not productive for your client and can be boring for you.

The injunction to be flexible is consistent with RET philosophy that there seem to be no absolutes and thus no absolute prescriptions in psychotherapy. (Even the belief that there can be no absolutes, which is *not* an RET dictum, is dogmatically absolutist.) Consider some of the following absolutes from other areas of clinical practice:

There can *never* be secrets in marital therapy.

In family therapy, *all* family members *must* be present at *every* session.

In sexual counseling, a complete sexual history is *always* taken, and sensate focus is useful in *every* case.

Transference *must always* be analyzed.

Although certain therapeutic strategies may frequently foster the client's progress, we would echo Ellis' contention (1962) that there appear to be no absolute prerequisites for personality change—even rational thinking.

RIGIDITY IN OTHER THERAPIST BEHAVIORS

The practice of psychotherapy usually assumes a forty-five- to fifty-minute hour, but there is nothing sacred about the length of the session. It may be advantageous for you to alter the session length and use an individualistic approach. Some clients, for example, may require a double session. Perhaps they have many pressing issues to discuss, or they find it very disruptive to leave the session before they completely understand a disputation. On the other hand, some clients may be unable to sit through a fifty-minute discussion. Therapy may be the first time in their lives that they have undertaken such an endeavor. For these clients, it may be desirable to gradually increase the length of the session to fifty minutes. If you do schedule fixed-length sessions, you may wish to spend only part of the time in intellectual endeavors, and the remainder in relaxation training or nontaxing exercise, such as walking outside together.

Our experience with shorter sessions indicates that the amount of time spent discussing the crucial issues remains the same, and the amount of time spent avoiding topics or discussing unimportant issues is reduced. Not only is the client more keenly aware of time limitations and therefore the importance of getting to the point, but so is the therapist. With the shorter session, we have found that we are more directive, active, and confrontative, and a lot less distracted.

Similarly, there is no reason to adhere unthinkingly to restrictions of physical space in the session. For example, it is not necessary for you to always sit on the same chair or the client to always sit across from you on the sofa. In fact, there appears to be no therapeutic reason why every session must take place in the same office.* Sessions away from the therapist's office may be very effective at times. For example, in treating clients

---

Experiment with sessions of varying lengths to determine what is most beneficial for you and for your clients. Some therapists may well have been attention-deficit-disordered (ADD) as children and even now be unable to keep their attention span on one topic for more than thirty minutes. Recognizing the limitations of yourself and your client can only benefit both of you.

---

*Check your malpractice coverage on this point, however, particularly if you operate under an institutional policy.

with social anxiety or agoraphobia, it may be beneficial to go with them into situations where they experience the anxiety and dispute their irrational ideas as they occur. An example of effective therapy involved the treatment of a client with the presenting problem of an elevator phobia. During the first session in our six-story building in Manhattan, the therapist suggested, "Why don't we have this therapy session standing out in front of the elevator?" As the session progressed in the hallway, the client experienced a gradual reduction in anxiety. Halfway through the session, the therapist had talked the client into the elevator, and they eventually rode up and down while conducting the remainder of the session. This therapeutic format led to the reduction of the situation-specific phobia in three sessions.

Roles of the Rational-Emotive Therapist

RET practitioners may think of themselves in part as teachers, and of RET theory as an educational model. What do you teach? First and foremost, you teach mental health. Second, since the goal of therapy is to enable patients to do an A-B-C-D-E analysis themselves, you are a teacher of the logico-empirical method of reasoning. Good teachers not only ask many questions of their students but also question their own performance. Here are some questions you may want to periodically ask yourself:

Is the patient understanding what I have said?
Am I expressing myself clearly?
Am I doing too much of the work?
Does the patient really believe what I (or the patient) just said?
How can I get the patient to express rational beliefs more strongly?
Am I giving enough homework assignments and are they working?

You may also serve as a behavioral model. Suppose a couple is coming for marriage counseling and the husband expresses a desire to be more emotionally expressive, which his wife wholeheartedly endorses. In addition to suggesting outside models (e.g., encouraging the husband to study the romantic behaviors portrayed in movies), you may role-play appropriate responses (e.g., "If I were in your situation, I might say . . ."). Similarly, in teaching clients the fine art of self-acceptance, you will want to display clear acceptance of their disturbing behaviors. You may thereby demonstrate how they can refuse to rate their personal essence but merely rate their dysfunctional behaviors. Of course, serving as a model entails judging whether you can do what you are asking the client to do. In the case of the inhibited husband, you would have to ask yourself honestly if you thought you were a good model for emotional expressiveness.

ISSUES OF TRANSFERENCE AND COUNTERTRANSFERENCE

By transference, we mean that patients react (and more important, over-react) to the therapist as they do to other significant people in their lives. It may be very useful to point out this transferential data to the patient. The first task is to identify the emotional tone of the interaction and the beliefs behind the emotion. Once these are specified, you can ask clients whether they relate to others in their lives in the same way as they relate to you. For example, "You know, Bernie, every time we talk about sex, I notice changes in your voice, and you become very . . . well, loose with me. I wonder if that's how you relate to other women?" Such a confrontation can provide you with a way to pinpoint and discuss problem areas.

Attitudes toward the therapist also may be good indicators of attitudes in other interpersonal encounters. For example, suppose you had given your female patient a homework assignment. She comes back having successfully done it but also exclaiming, "Oh, Doctor, I thought of you, and I knew how you'd react if I *didn't* do it!" The patient is really telling you one of her irrational beliefs: if she failed to do her homework, you might think she was a shit, and then she *would* be a shit. Thus, you have excellent evidence to point out that the patient was doing good things but for all the wrong reasons. Essentially, the patient is saying that she herself is not worth doing things for, but that you are. Such a patient's task in therapy is to learn that she doesn't have to please the therapist.

Your attitudes and emotional responses toward the client are called countertransference, and it enables you to use yourself as a measuring device. Ask yourself how you feel when you know the client is coming to see you. Do you look forward to the visit or dread it? For what reasons? What are your feelings about the client during the session? What are his or her major interaction styles? Since the client is probably behaving toward you as to other people, you are in a good position to give feedback that others may not be willing to disclose; that is, how his or her behavior influences you. Try to be as concrete as possible and to describe to the client specific behaviors that can be later monitored (e.g., a whining tone of voice, unhappy facial expression, poor eye contact, delayed response time).

A shy, inhibited male patient has been discussing his problems in dating when he suddenly looks up at the therapist and asks, "Would *you* go out with me?" How would a rational–emotive therapist handle such a question? Directly! The therapist would either say "No, because . . ." or "Yes, if I weren't your psychotherapist." In addition, she could discuss with the patient why someone like herself might or might not date him. Subsequently, the therapist would also raise the issue of what the question meant and if it were asked with some serious intent.

It is certainly permissible for you to show your feelings. In response to a question about dating such as the one above, you might say, for example, "Yes, if I had met you in other circumstances or before we started therapy, I probably would have wanted to date you. That would have been nice, but the reality is that we are involved in a therapeutic relationship and I *will not* have personal relations with any of my clients. Those are the facts, and we'd better accept them."

Achieving this agreement on the subject of dating may help patients to freely and fully self–disclose. If the issue is left unresolved, they may withhold information in order to appear more desirable and keep alive the possibility of a personal relationship with you. In addition, by reaching closure in this way, you are also modeling a discrimination between thoughts and actions, for example, "I may have a nice sexual fantasy, but I choose not to act on it." This may be a very educational message about how to deal with desires; just because they exist does not mean you have to act on them.

Suppose the patient asks the therapist if she is attracted to him, and the therapist is not; what might she say in this case? Quite simply and gently, she would say, "No, I'm not." If the patient reacts to this information by becoming depressed, the therapist has a perfect inroad to a major irrational belief, for surely she is not the only female to have ever rejected him. His reaction may allow her to challenge him with such statements as, "Are you believing that because I don't find you attractive, no one else will?"

Perhaps you are surprised that we recommend the therapist respond immediately to patients' questions. One rationale is that with such a reply, the therapist is modeling good communication in an open, spontaneous relationship. This position, of course, is quite different from that of more psychodynamic therapies. Yet to first inquire, as an analyst might, "Why do you want to know if I'm attracted to you?" may seem like a phony

> Let's put some interchanges into different environments and examine them.
>
> Suppose you are sitting with a good friend over a cup of coffee and your friend asks, "Do you find me attractive?" An answer that dodges the issue would probably make the other person think, "Hey, she's not really my friend. She won't even answer my question!"
>
> Or suppose that you, as a therapist, go to your supervisor and ask, "How am I doing?" What might you suspect if your supervisor says, "Why do you want to know?" Wouldn't it cross your mind that the answer is not positive?

dodge to the patient. The question may be a good one, but it would be better to ask it at a later time. A solid, trusting relationship is not developed with "clinical" questions such as, "Why is that important? Why do you want to know?" Rather, the RET relationship is built on sincerity. It is usually preferable, therefore, to answer clients' questions fairly and honestly, and then to deal with the individual's subsequent thoughts and feelings.

Patients may also ask many personal questions of the therapist. Are there any limits to the therapist's self-disclosure? Probably not; the RET therapist knows that nothing is inherently shameful, so what could the patient ask that would be nontherapeutic? On the other hand, a barrage of questions may be distracting. After answering them directly, you might ask patients how they feel about this new information, how they feel about you, and what their reasons were for asking. For example, perhaps the patient looks on you as a mystical deity and then rejects you after learning that you are merely mortal. This pattern may very well reflect what the patient does in everyday relationships, so that you would then be able to dispute the irrational beliefs associated with this problem.

Patients may have a dependency on authoritarian figures in such a way that they cannot take orders except from "perfect people." This type of dependency often also results in self-depreciation. It might be profitable to ask such clients if they think they are as good a person as you are. If they respond, "Oh no, why you're a doctor and I'm just a lowly slob," you can guess that they are doing the same thing with other people in their lives, such as their boss, the president of their company, or the provost of their university. It will benefit these patients if you can demystify the rest of their gods in addition to yourself.

If patients do not bring up transference issues, you may choose to do so. Suppose, for example, that each time you give a male client a homework assignment, he appears to sulk and accepts the assignment with resignation in his voice. At this point, you might inquire, "You know, John, each time I give you a homework assignment, I hear some resentment in your voice. How are you feeling toward me right now?" Once these feelings have been acknowledged, you can proceed to identify the irrational beliefs that cause his feelings, inquire whether he has similar beliefs and feelings about other people, and identify the beliefs that led to the inhibition of direct expression of these feelings. Thus, transference issues are not explored for directly curative reasons but to help the therapist and patient recognize relevant A's, C's, and, most important, B's.

Concluding a Therapy Session

We offer two suggestions to keep in mind as the therapy session is coming to an end.

First, try to end each session, whether group or individual, by negotiating a *homework* assignment with clients or having them design one for themselves. Assignments may be in the form of thinking, reading, and writing, or trying new activities (see Chapter 14). Whatever their form, the purpose is to strengthen or extend the skills learned in the session and to bridge the gap between sessions.

As *feedback,* you may ask, "Was there anything I did or said in the session that bothered you in any way?" also "Was there anything I did or said today that seemed particularly useful to you?" and most important, "What did you learn from today's session?" Questions such as these enable you to adapt your style to your patient, provide information to be taken up in the next session, give an opportunity for a brief rehearsal by the patient, and help identify other B's to be taken up later.

Summary: Ten Common Errors to Avoid

Failure to listen. Among other problems, you may misdiagnose if you fail to listen critically. Patients may say they are "angry," for example; be sure to inquire carefully what they mean, because they may be mislabeling their state and therapy will take off in the wrong direction. Similarly, carefully attune yourself to key words, such as clients' idiosyncratic phrases, which indicate their irrational beliefs.

Failure to develop goals. Ask, rather than assume, what the client's goals are. You will also want to determine the client's expectations of therapy. It is important to know these ideas so that you can clarify and correct them, or if agreement cannot be reached, refer the patient elsewhere.

Errors in information gathering. As a new therapist, you may find yourself spending too many sessions gathering data before planning an intervention, or failing to obtain sufficient information and jumping too quickly into disputation. In either case, you run a risk of alienating or losing the client, or at least of doing inefficient therapy.

Errors in assertiveness. Again, errors may be made in either direction, by allowing clients to ramble or cutting them off too abruptly. What is happening when you are not sufficiently directive and too often allow the client to lead? Perhaps you have forgotten your game plan and are caught up in a patient's stories. Perhaps you are afraid of offending clients if you interrupt and do not want to appear rude. Clients will often let you know your error, by criticizing your behavior, asking what you think at a subsequent session, or complaining that you interrupt too much. You might keep in mind, however, that each therapy session is not a win-or-lose game; there's always a next time.

Errors in questioning. Avoid the following mistakes:

> Asking irrelevant or overgeneralized questions (e.g., "How've you been?") instead of directly relevant ones.
>
> Overusing rhetorical questions (e.g., "Where does your getting upset get you?").
>
> Using too many "why" questions, which generally lead only to "because" excuses. Instead, use "how," "where," or "what's the evidence" questions, or ask, "What are you telling yourself?" or "When

you do this, what are you thinking?" Overusing questions with a "yes" or "no" answer; queries that require a fuller response are preferred.

Bombarding clients with numerous questions and not allowing them to answer any of them.

Answering questions for the clients instead of letting them deal with them on their own or helping them to break the questions down into simpler components.

Failing to note whether the client has, in fact, answered your question or simply digressed. If the question is unanswered, refocus the client on the task.

Tendency to lecture. Avoid lengthy lectures, particularly when you have failed to check and see if the client is following you. Educators tell us that the best way to learn something is to teach it; the best way for the patient to acquire RET principles, therefore, is not to listen to a long didactic lecture, but to practice interactively, in session.

Failure to check understanding. Request frequent feedback from clients to assure that they are understanding you. Listen to tapes of what you think are your good sessions; make sure that clients weren't "Um-hmmm-ing" you into thinking they understood. It is useful periodically to ask clients to restate what you have just said or to ask, "What's your understanding of what I've just said?" or "What is your feeling about what we've been discussing?"

Having all the answers. Avoid trying to be a "Wise Person." If you have a wise thing to say, it might be wiser not to say it. It is generally preferable to lead clients, by Socratic questioning, to their own insights.

Attitudinal errors. You will want to avoid the following:

Blaming and condemning remarks (e.g., "You know how to challenge those ideas").

Scare tactics (e.g., "You have a big problem; it's going to take a long time to work this out").

Being unrealistic and offering false hopes (e.g., "Oh, we can fix you up in no time").

Judgmental remarks (e.g., "Why do you need the approval of a *creep* like him?").

Listen to a recent therapy tape and check your performance in each of the categories in the text. You won't be able to listen for all of these errors at one time; monitor each one separately.

Overgeneralizations (e.g., "You *are* smart").

Argumentative power struggles in which you try to force the client to accept your views (e.g., "I'm the therapist here; I'll tell you what's wrong with you").

Errors in the use of humor. Use humor frequently, but don't direct it at your client. Try not to be giggly. See that your humor is therapeutic and not used for entertainment purposes.

Part V
The Therapeutic Whole

14 Homework Assignments

Rational-emotive therapy is a cognitive-learning system. A major tenet in RET, therefore, is that unless clients practice their philosophical restructuring, the effects will not be meaningful or durable. If a client says, "it wouldn't really be awful to be turned down for a date" yet continues to avoid calling prospective dating partners, the therapist would first check whether the correct IB had been disputed. If it had, the therapist would then doubt the conviction of the client's new beliefs. Thus, RET is not merely a "talk therapy"; rather, it stresses that meaningful cognitive change is unlikely unless the client behaves differently. In fact, following a cognitive-dissonance model, behaving differently will often lead to thinking and feeling differently. One of the principal means of helping the client to behave differently is through the use of homework assignments, thus giving the client a means of generalizing the work of therapy beyond the confines of the therapist's office. Homework assignments are a routine element of RET. Some therapists prefer to use a more neutral term, such as *self-help work*.

The specific goals of the homework assignment may be to change a dysfunctional behavior or establish an adaptive behavior, reduce irrational cognitions and replace them with more helpful ones, or determine how well the client has understood the basic principles of rational-emotive therapy. Accordingly, homework may be assigned from any of the following categories:

Reading
Listening
Writing

Imagining

Thinking

Relaxation and distraction

Activity

As we suggested above, major emphasis is placed on the last category If that is so, you may ask, why do rational-emotive therapists use the other types? Different categories of assignments may accomplish different goals, but the therapist may also use various types of homework aimed at the same goal. RET is based, in part, on an educational model, which includes the use of multiple modalities and learning trials to maximize learning. After all, how much can the client learn in one forty-five minute session per week? In college courses, students are given lectures, field or laboratory exercises, and reading assignments; the RET practitioner will want to do the same. The question the therapist asks himself or herself in each meeting with the client is, "What can my client *do* this week to put into practice what we have discussed during this session?"

Before we move on to specific homework suggestions, let us point out that useful homework assignments share four important characteristics.

Consistency. The assignment is consistent with the work done in the session and is not irrelevant or arbitrarily assigned. Try to devise an assignment that follows naturally from the main theme of the session.

Specificity. The assignment has been given in sufficient detail and with clear instructions. For example, if you ask the client to generate possible solutions to a dilemma, do not vaguely say, "Think of as many as you can" but rather, "Think of at least five possible solutions." In this way, the client has specific instructions and is more likely to stretch his or her creative faculties. Specify the assignments as fully as possible, including when, where, and how the client will do them.

Systematic follow-through. Each week, try to be systematic about giving a homework assignment and checking on the last assignment. Also, do not assume that the completion of one homework assignment in a problem area will be sufficient. It may be wise to systematically repeat the assignment (or variations of it) for a number of weeks.

Efficiency. Rational-emotive homework assignments tend to follow a flooding model rather than one of gradual shaping. The rational-emotive therapist is likely to encourage the client to take large steps rather than small ones, for example, to "ask four women out on a date this week" rather than "try to speak to one woman this week." The rationale for this maneuver is that it is usually more efficient in producing change. Feedback from the client's weekly homework assignments will help the therapist to determine the size of the next step.

When helping the client to design homework assignments, try not to do so in an off-the-cuff or apologetic manner. Explain the assignment carefully, including the rationale for selecting it; understanding will help increase your client's compliance. It is also helpful to ask the client, "Do you think you can do that?" If the answer is "No," you have more work to do. Perhaps you can help the client rehearse the assignment in imagery (with the client narrating the scene aloud) or by role playing. Perhaps the client will agree to do *part* of the assignment or can suggest a variation of it that is acceptable. Once agreed upon, a useful question to ask is, "How will you remember to do that?" One technique to help the client remember the assignment is for the therapist to write it out in the manner of a medical prescription. Some therapists have pads of paper printed with the inscription, "Behavioral Prescription from the Desk of [John Jones, Ph.D.]" for this purpose. Formalizing the assignment procedure in this way not only aids the patient's memory but also underscores the significance of the homework.

Since homework is so integral to the therapy, you may want to prepare a statement for your clients about the importance of doing self-help work between sessions. In addition, Dryden (1990) suggests that the therapist:

Improvement across sessions has been shown to be directly related to the client's *willingness to do self-help* exercises. Not only are the types of tasks and the frequency of practicing self-help exercises relevant, but so also are the *cognitions* held about them. Assess these cognitions directly by asking the client, "How helpful do you think this assignment will be?" and "How willing are you to try this assignment?"

Negotiate assignments with the client rather than unilaterally choosing the assignments.

Negotiate assignments that are relevant to the client's stated goals.

Select assignments that are not too time-consuming for the client.

Choose assignments that are challenging but not overwhelming to the client.

Elicit a firm commitment from the client that the assignment will be completed.

Identify and prepare to overcome potential obstacles that may block the client from doing the assignment.

When the client brings in the results of the self-help work, be sure to determine what he or she learned or did not learn from carrying out the assignment. Identify and correct any errors that the client made in carrying out the assignment. Most important, reinforce success at doing the assignment, or if necessary, the attempt to do the assignment. In other words, don't forget the importance of reinforcement contingencies!

The following dialogue illustrates how the therapist can elicit from the client commitment to doing the homework.

T: Marvin, we've discussed the importance of the homework, and now I want to find out when you will do the assignment this week. Can you make a commitment to a particular day?

C: Well, I'm going to try to do it on Wednesday.

T: Ah, my trained clinical ears hear something important. I asked you when you would *do it,* and you told me when you would *try* to do it. Can you see the difference between these two things: doing and trying to do?

C: I think so.

T: Well, let's do a little experiment: I want you to *try* to lift your right arm, but don't do it. Try, but don't do. What happens?

C: I don't lift my arm. Nothing happens.

T: Exactly. Can you see how that's relevant to the homework assignment?

C: Sure. Let me try that again: I'm going to *do* the assignment on Wednesday. I'll make that commitment.

Examples of Homework Assignments

READING

Patients may strengthen their comprehension of the basic principles of RET and its application to specific problem areas with reading assignments. At the Institute for Rational-Emotive Therapy, for example, new clients are given a free packet of materials to read at the end of their first therapy session. Additionally, clients are encouraged to purchase a copy of *The New Guide to Rational Living* by Ellis and Harper (1975). Thus, before their second therapy session, it is hoped that they will have had some opportunity to become familiar with the A-B-C's of RET.

Suggestions for books and articles that clients may find helpful at various points in therapy are given in Chapter 17. However, it may be difficult or time-consuming for your clients to locate some of these materials. Purchase a few copies of the books that you are most likely to recommend. These can then be given, sold (at your cost), or loaned to the client.

LISTENING

You may recall our earlier suggestion to tape-record therapy sessions after getting the client's permission. Clients are also encouraged to bring in recorders and tape their sessions. In either case, it is useful to encourage clients to listen to their therapy tapes between sessions. Multiple trials of the same lesson are beneficial to learning.

Listening to prerecorded tapes can also be used as a homework assignment, either to supplement or replace reading assignments. Tapes of RET lectures (and even "rational songs" sung by Dr. Ellis himself) are available from the Institute for Rational-Emotive Therapy. An annotated listing of some of these tapes is given in Chapter 17.

Listening to tapes is particularly valuable when the therapist is teaching the client relaxation techniques. Professionally recorded relaxation tapes may be recommended. Alternatively, the therapist may also record his or her own relaxation instructions, or simply a session of teaching relaxation techniques to the client. This last procedure may increase the effectiveness of the training for some clients, since the therapist's voice is associated with the procedure and can thereby aid in generalizing the effects of relaxation from the therapist's office to the patient's home. The patient may be instructed to play the relaxation tape each night, perhaps just before bedtime. At the next therapy session, the patient can bring in the tape and practice using it in the therapist's presence. In this way, the therapist can periodically stop the tape and assess the client's degree of relaxation. Teaching relaxation techniques can become a tedious chore for the therapist and use up valuable session time, but both of these problems can be minimized by having the patient do much of the work as a homework assignment.

WRITING

Writing assignments are often used by rational-emotive therapists and generally take one of three forms: self-help homework sheets, written essays, and log books.

Self-help homework is done on a sheet of notebook paper, which the client labels "A-B-C-D-E" or "What happened-What I felt-What I was thinking- What was wrong with those thoughts-What thoughts would be more accurate and helpful." Self-help homework exercises allow the therapist to determine if the client really understands the A-B-C's of RET. Clients may, for example, have trouble identifying their relevant rational and irrational beliefs. They may write "I feel" when they really mean "I believe." Linguistic confusions and misunderstandings of the theory become clear in such an assignment and offer the therapist a chance to do some invaluable teaching when the assignment is reviewed during the next therapy session.

A client has filled out a homework form and given it to you, the counselor. A portion of the form is reproduced below. What would your response be? What corrections, if any, would you make?

> *Activating event*—I went for a job interview.
>
> *Rational belief*—I was turned down.
>
> *Irrational belief*—It is horrible that I didn't get the job.
>
> *Emotional consequence*—I felt depressed.
>
> *Disputing*—I don't care that I didn't get the job.

Answers are given on page 369.

A second type of writing assignment is the *essay*, which can also take a number of forms. For example, clients may be asked to write a debate to one or more of their irrational ideas. They can be told to pretend that they are on a debating team and their job is to argue the opposite side, *whether they believe it or not*. The therapist is thus employing principles of cognitive dissonance with clients who claim that they can write the debate but won't believe it. Attitude-change research suggests, and clinical experience verifies, that performing such a debate often convinces debators of their own arguments. Thus, at the end of a therapy session, the therapist can write out the statement to be challenged at the top of a sheet of blank paper (using a separate sheet for each debate); the client fills in the debate below. In this way, disputations that are unfinished in the session can be continued at home, or the work of a completed disputation can be consolidated. Here is a debate written by a female client.

Statement: If my children make mistakes in their lives, it proves that I am a bad mother.

Challenge:

1. Everyone makes mistakes, whether they had good or bad parents. It is a human characteristic.

2. My children need to learn by trial and error. Mistakes that I have experienced had a positive growth aspect. I learned to try not to repeat the mistake. Pain helps develop aversion to the pain. Also, having experienced mistakes has made me able to be more compassionate and insightful with others. I feel more sharing with people and enjoy more maturity. The same may be so for my children.

3. I am not the only influence on my kids. They have had input from many formative sources besides me. The difference between my two children shows that I couldn't have fully created their personalities or they'd have to be more alike. They continue to have even greater input from other people and experiences, and from themselves. As they meet each new life situation, they respond and make subtle adjustments called for by the moment. So I am not totally responsible for their problems. My *kids* have even indicated to me that I'm not a bad mother because they make mistakes—"that's silly!" they said.

4. I might as well take some credit for their good qualities too, if I were to insist on responsibility for their negative qualities. I know I've done much good for my kids.

5. If I concentrated on my finished mistakes as a mother, I would trap/freeze myself in the past. I would deny recognition of time elapsed, growth, and change taken place. That would be living the life of another (albeit someone I know most intimately). And continued guilt amounts to self-pity. That's bor-ring!

In a related assignment, the client can be asked to reverse a "should" and defend it. For example, if a male client has been complaining that his mother shouldn't be irascible and nag at him, the therapist may prescribe an essay in which the client describes why his mother should be exactly the way she is. If he explores what he knows of her upbringing and the history of his interactions with her, he will most likely find that her behavior is quite understandable. Such an exercise can be an important empathy-building experience to illustrate to the client that the behavior of others is not mysterious or arranged for his personal inconvenience, but is a logical outgrowth of past events and of people's ways of reacting to those events.

Written homework assignments are often useful when the therapist is teaching problem-solving skills. The client can be given the assignment of generating five alternative solutions to a problem. For example, an agoraphobic client who refused to drive her car for fear that it might break down while she was away from home alone, generated these solutions:

I could walk to the nearest phone booth and call a family member.

I could walk to a nearby house and ask to use the phone.

I could walk to where I was going.

I could flag down a passing motorist and ask for help.

I could walk to the nearest garage and get them to fix the car.

Similarly, the mother of a young sleepyhead who wouldn't get out of bed in the morning generated these alternatives:

I could drag him out of bed (that's what I do).

I could reason with him.

I could ignore him and let him take the consequences of being late.

I could do what he wants (wake him again in twenty minutes and meanwhile fix his lunch for him).

I could pour cold water on him if he doesn't get up.

I could promise him a treat if he's up within three minutes.

I could buy him an alarm clock and make him responsible for waking himself up.

A written essay assignment can also be given for the next stage of problem solving, consequential thinking. Clients are asked to predict the consequences of the alternative solutions they previously generated, and to seek out validation by discussion with other people.

The third form of written assignment used by rational-emotive therapists is the *log book*. The client keeps track of specific events and evaluates whether his or her prediction of events was accurate. The client may complain, "Every time I call up a woman to ask for a date I get turned down!" What are the data? How many women did he actually call, who were they, and how many refusals did he get? Similarly, the depressed patient who claims to be depressed "all the time" may discover useful information by keeping track of happy moments or times in the day when the despairing mood lifts (cf. Beck et al., 1978). The obese client can keep a log of the amount and kind of foods eaten, time and place of eating, and so forth. Accurate data records may serve to correct the client's distorted perception of A and attributions for why things occur, and to identify the appropriate antecedents and consequences of a troublesome behavior.

IMAGINING

Homework assignments employing imagery or fantasy are used by rational-emotive therapists as a form of imaginal disputation or imaginal desensitization. After the therapist has led the client through rational-emotive imagery (see page 165), an assignment can be given to practice this skill for ten minutes every day. The client thus uses imagery to produce the troublesome emotion, change it, and rehearse the cognitions that effect the change.

Clients can be asked to mentally rehearse new behaviors before attempting them, or to repeatedly confront their worst fears in imagination, for desensitization purposes. Techniques of covert conditioning may also be used. In covert conditioning, the stimuli, responses, reinforcers, or punishers may be imaginal. Here are some examples. The therapist is hoping to help change the valence of a stimulus for a client; perhaps a woman with vaginismus who fears the insertion of any object into her vagina, yet who is orgasmic with manual stimulation. The client can be instructed to imagine that her partner is inserting his finger (and later, his penis) into her vagina, and to do so just at the point of her orgasm. By pairing the aversive image with the positive experience of orgasm, her fear of penetration may be reduced. Similary, if a male client has a fear of penetrating the vagina, he can rehearse this act in imagination just at the point of a manually induced orgasm, thus changing the valence of his response. Conversely, clients can also be instructed to pair stimuli with aversive images, as in the technique of covert sensitization (Goldfried and Davison, 1976). The alcoholic can imagine himself drinking a mug of beer and discovering dog feces in the bottom of the glass. More detailed instruction on the implementation of covert conditioning can be found in some of the behavior therapy reference sources listed in Chapter 17.

THINKING

Clients can be asked to remember their irrational or disturbing thoughts between sessions. These recollections can then become the starting point for the next therapy session. Alternatively, clients can record what they have found to be helpful thoughts, either their own or those recalled from discussions with the therapist or others. The therapist may even prescribe a list of helpful ideas to think about.

Thinking assignments are often easy for clients to forget to do, since no concrete activity is involved. What is the best way to remember something? Write it down. As an aid to memory, therefore, encourage clients to make a checklist of "Things to Remember to Think." After all, pilots use a checklist of things to do before takeoff; why not a list of thoughts to ponder?

RELAXATION AND DISTRACTION

As mentioned earlier, relaxation is often taught by having patients listen to a prepared tape of instructions. Soon, however, patients can do the exercises without external cues. In fact, as their skill at relaxation increases, they may find that they can best practice it at their own pace. They may not need to work at isolated muscle groups (e.g., the right hand) but can combine them into larger units (e.g., both arms).

One aspect of giving a relaxation homework assignment is assuring that clients have structured both their time and their environment to maximize the probability of doing exercises successfully. Ideally, they will want to find a quiet room, away from distractions, where they can recline. Family members can cooperate by not disturbing clients and by taking phone messages while they do their homework.

Distraction assignments are particularly useful for very anxious and for socially phobic patients. Often, these clients can approach a difficult situation more effectively if they distract themselves from their anxious thoughts rather than try to dispute their anxious thoughts. When anxiety is running very high, patients are so disordered that they "cannot think straight."

Some strategies that have been helpful with these clients include counting details in the environment (e.g., the number of pieces of molding in the room, the number of parallel lines in a paneled wall, or how many people are wearing a red object), or reciting, either mentally or out loud (e.g., the multiplication tables, a song, slogan, etc.).

ACTIVITY

Two of the most widely assigned homework activities in RET are risk-taking and shame-attacking. Although these exercises are often interchangeable, they can be distinguished on the basis of the client's underlying fear. *Risk-taking* encourages patients to reevaluate their definition of certain behaviors as terribly dangerous, when in fact they are not. In such assignments, clients try to be more assertive and to push themselves to take risks, particularly social risks, that they may have been avoiding. A unique aspect of risk-taking assignments is that many times the exercises are designed to *have patients experience failure,* especially in cases of perfectionism or fear of failure. As we mentioned earlier, people learn by experience: if they have never experienced failure, they will be unlikely to change their IB's about it and their avoidance of it. Thus, it is difficult to work on the fear of an aversive event unless the client actually experiences it.

Consider the case of a young man with dating anxiety who, after some social skills training, is instructed to make three social contacts in the next week. If he is successsful he may miss an important lesson, since the probability is that he will not *always* be successful. He will not have been immunized against the stress of failure and may continue to be vulnerable to it. The rational–emotive therapist may instead suggest that the client go out and collect three *rejections* in the next week. Such a suggestion may bring a twinkle to the client's eye and, by itself, produce a change in attitude. Note the win–win nature of this assignment, since the client will succeed even as he fails. If his social overtures are accepted, he has made progress toward his goal, and if they are rejected, he has succeeded in doing his homework and can bring in these incidents for analysis in therapy. Thus, the therapist may prescribe failure experiences for two reasons: they are instructive, and they allow for desensitization, because if the client is afraid to fail, he will probably not try in the first place.

Risk-taking assigned by the rational-emotive therapist often has a paradoxical quality, encouraging clients to do what they view as a bad behavior, *and* simultaneously to work at not catastrophizing or putting themselves down. The insomniac may be instructed to try to stay awake all night, the obsessive to obsess 100 times per day, the impotent male to not get an erection (Fay, 1978). Being given the assignment to do the very thing that troubles them often removes the "horror" of the behavior, and clients commonly report, with surprise, that they found the assignment difficult to accomplish.

Consider the case of a certified public accountant who had a dread of making errors—a serious case of perfectionism. His assignment was to deliberately make mistakes and to practice accepting himself nonetheless. Although the client insisted that he made mistakes routinely and did not have to try, when he came back the following week he reported that in fact he had made no mistakes. As the therapist had predicted, he was extremely fearful of what was in reality a low-probability event. In the ensuing weeks the assignment was continued, and the client forced himself to make an occasional error. He reported experiencing a revelation: an error was not a catastrophe, and he was not a failure for making one.

Shame is a form of self-downing, and *shame-attacking* (Ellis, 1973b, 1977b) is designed to teach clients that if they actually perform a silly or foolish act, even in public, their world will not come to an end and they needn't denigrate themselves. The central tenet is to teach clients to discriminate between their behavior and their worth as a human being. Clients thereby learn to rate their behavior, not themselves.

Shame-attacking assignments are also designed to challenge our dire need for conventionality. We often exchange conformity for approval, which is a strong social control device but which can also be unnecessarily stifling if we punish ourselves with anxiety and shame. What might happen if we challenge conformity? People might think poorly of us: people might frown. But people's thoughts and facial expressions cannot hurt us; often, however, we *believe* they can. Shame-attacking exercises help patients to challenge this belief. In addition, these exercises are fun and can help clients to take social disapproval less seriously.

Here are some examples of shame-attacking exercises often used in RET:

Go up to a stranger and greet him or her warmly. Ask about his or her health. Be effusive.

Stand on a busy street corner. Stretch out your arms and say, five times, "Your messiah has come. Follow me."

In a restaurant, go up to an attractive person's table and inquire if the meal is satisfactory and if you can bring him or her anything.

Go to three nearby shopping centers and try to sell someone a copy of yesterday's newspaper.

Go to a store and announce to the salesclerk that you are a transvestite or a fetishist. Buy something typical of the opposite sex (e.g., high-heeled shoes or sexy men's briefs).

Go into a large department store and announce the time, five times, by saying, "Ladies and gentlemen, the time is now 1:15 . . . 1:16 . . . 1:17 . . ." etc.

Tie a long red ribbon around a banana and "walk" it down a busy street.

Ride a crowded elevator standing backward (facing the rear).

Yell out five successive stops in the subway or on the bus.

Go to the local library and, in a strong voice, ask the librarian to see two books: *The Illustrated Version of the Marquis de Sade* and *Sex and Perversion in Contemporary America*.

Find a restaurant that offers "two eggs any style." Ask your waiter for one fried and one scrambled.

If clients are being seen in a group, shame-attacking assignments can be given to all group members and often can be done in the group setting. For example, clients can be asked to sing a song, do a dance, or perform a "spotlight" act.

Clients can adopt one of these stock assignments or, preferably with the help of the therapist, design one that is more personally relevant. For example, one client claimed that she could not be assertive with her mother for fear of harming her mother's health, which would in turn lead others to conclude that she was a bad daughter. Her homework assignment was to tell her friends that "dear old mother has had a nervous breakdown because of my bad behavior"; she was to watch their reactions and practice accepting herself nonetheless.

An *important warning* about shame-attacking exercises: be certain that the client is not planning to do an exercise that will result in the loss of a job, expulsion from school, or arrest. If the consequences of his or her behavior could be disadvantageous, the assignment will be harmful, not helpful. It would not be wise to do a shame-attacking exercise, such as wearing a pillow on your head, in front of the boss who is likely to decide about your promotion. There would be fewer practical negative consequences if the pillow were worn while walking down the street. Also, we do not encourage clients to act in ways that are likely to alarm or unduly inconvenience other people.

Thus, shame-attacking assignments accomplish two goals. The first is to help clients behaviorally dispute their sense of shame. In order to achieve this goal, it is necessary to do the exercises as prescribed. Cognitive rehearsal and an A-B-C-D analysis may prepare clients to perform them properly.

The second goal is to help clients evaluate the accuracy of their predictions of how the world will react to them. Most of us overestimate the extent to which others care about or even notice our behavior. For example, Ellis tells of one of his clients who, for weeks, tried to find the courage to call out the stops in a New York subway. Finally he succeeded in calling out one stop and saw that nothing disastrous happened. The next week he gave himself the assignment of yelling out each of the seven stops between his home and his work. What happened? No one on the subway said anything to him—except some teenagers who came over and inquired, "What's the next stop, Mister?"

Other kinds of activities are also assigned by the rational-emotive therapist. The married couple caught in a spiral of getting-even behaviors may be instructed to do three caring acts for each other during the next

---

To persuade the reluctant client to do a shame-attacking assignment, the therapist may set an example. For example, the therapist might go out on the street with the client and model unusual behaviors to show the client that people are more tolerant of our behavior than we think. Could you do this?

We suggest that new rational-emotive therapists follow the training example at the Institute for Rational-Emotive Therapy and set themselves the task of doing a series of shame-attacking or risk-taking assignments. Pick from the list in the text or design your own project, and *do an exercise this week yourself.* In fact, it is a good idea to schedule a shame-attacking exercise for yourself at periodic intervals to keep up your skills.

week. The reluctant job seeker may be asked to write up a résumé. The woman experiencing guilt about being "selfish" may be told to do something nice for herself before the next session. The sexually troubled couple may be given sensate focus assignments. The client with a poor self-image may be instructed to look in the mirror for ten minutes each day and practice self-acceptance while acknowledging realistic physical defects. The list of assignments is long and varied, but in all of them the therapist encourages the client to *behave differently in order to think and feel differently*.

Happiness Assignments

One additional bit of homework, not often mentioned in the formal RET literature but which we find very important, are assignments that focus on pleasure, happiness, and joy. To shift from a purely problematic focus to a more positive one, it may be useful to have clients write down a list of things that they enjoy during the day—focusing on the small sensual pleasures of everyday experience, such as the smell of coffee or a good sandwich. This assignment can remind patients of the pleasant practical realities of life. Some of these pleasant moments will be interpersonal: Who smiled at me today? Who did I enjoy seeing? What positive moment did I share with my spouse?

Encourage fantasies about upcoming positive activities and past positive events. Mental activity can be playful as well as aimed at disputing negative or dysfunctional thinking habits. Developing the habit of playful thinking can also be equally salient to feeling better. Our job, as therapists, can be viewed as not merely working to dispel misery, but actively working to *promote happiness*.

Another route to happiness is to develop the habit of doing nice things for other people. In depression, for example, the patient's focus is narcissistic and negatively self-focused. Reminding oneself to focus outward, and especially to do something for another person that has no immediate payback to oneself, may redirect and energize the client.

Trouble-shooting Homework Problems

When your clients return to therapy each week, be sure to check their homework assignments first. Unless clients bring up a new issue which is clearly of greater importance or they are in obvious emotional distress, following up on old assignments provides you with a systematic way to integrate therapy visits.

Patients may expect their homework assignments to change each week, as they do in a classroom or in a physician's office when medication or dosage level is adjusted. In fact, however, the client may work at a behavioral assignment for a number of weeks before cognitive or emotional change occurs. Be sensitive to your client's expectations; if uncorrected, they may lead to depressive cognitions (e.g., "Oh Lord, I'm not making progress") which can increase the client's distress.

What do you do if clients have failed to do their homework assignments? You investigate; such failures often provide valuable diagnostic information about clients' belief systems. The uncompleted assignment may be treated as a new activating event which may have resulted in additional emotional stress to the patient. Thus, the therapist may ask the following useful series of questions.

T: How do you feel about not doing the assignment?
C: Terrible.
T: Terrible? In what way?
C: I feel guilty. I should've done my homework.
T: You believe you should have done it? Well, why did you *have to?*
C: Because I feel so terrible about not doing it.
T: Do you think you'd feel differently if you didn't say *should've?* Try it now: "It would have been nice if I did it, but I didn't. Too bad. I'll do it next week."
C: I didn't do it. Too bad. I'll try it again next week.
T: Do you think you'd feel better if you just stuck to that belief?
C: Yes; it would be better if I thought about it that way.
T: Well, can you remind yourself to think that way?
C: How?
T: What would you do if you wanted to be sure to remember to buy milk at the store?
C: I'd write it down! I'm going to do that now. Now, what was it we just said? . . .

Depressive cognitions may follow the failure to do a homework assignment, as in the example above, or may be the cause of the failure. Thus, the patient may have been stopped by the cognition, "It's hopeless—why try?" Typically, the patient will not have answered this question, and the therapist may then help the patient to challenge the notion of helplessness and to review the reasons why the situation is not hopeless.

How do *you* feel when your patient fails to do a homework assignment? Do you find yourself getting angry? If so, it would be wise to examine your own musts and dispute them. Or do you feel somewhat anxious or depressed? Look for cognitions such as, "If I were a good therapist, he'd have done his assignment," and challenge them. Homework assignments can indeed be diagnostic tools.

Don't be afraid to confront your client and ask why the assignment was not completed. Why was it so difficult to accomplish? One hypothesis is that the client defined the required step as *too large*. As we stated earlier, rational-emotive therapists tend to follow a flooding model, urging clients to take large rather than small steps. Although the theoretical model is clear, the practical reality is that it is often desirable to go down the hierarchy of difficulty a step or two in order to find a task that the client is willing to confront. Remember that the goal is to get clients to carry out their behavioral challenges, and a little patience and creativity in breaking down difficult assignments into smaller steps may be important in accomplishing this goal. Thus, if the client is a dependent adult who has always phoned her mother every day and yet wants to loosen this attachment, she may be unwilling to refrain from calling her mother for a week but agree to a two-day hiatus at first. Success at an easier task makes it more likely that she will attempt more difficult tasks later.

Similarly, the therapist will want to investigate the *response cost* of the assignment. Perhaps the client is more likely to listen to a tape than to read a book. Perhaps an adolescent is more willing to read a smaller book than a larger one. Perhaps a woman will practice relaxation exercises twice a week but "cannot find the time" to do them nightly. While the therapist will want to continue to urge the client to work steadily and with increasing effort, it is wise to praise the client for any accomplishments at first; learning is, after all, a gradual procedure. The therapist may still confront clients with the reality that the less they do, the more slowly they will improve. Clients always have a choice, but the therapist can be sure that they understand the consequences.

A common problem encountered among patients who do not do their homework is the "mañana contingency" (Ellis and Knaus, 1977). The patient continually makes excuses for not beginning the assignment and ardently vows to begin it tomorrow; when tomorrow comes, the cycle is repeated. For example, "Today is too hectic—I'll relax tomorrow" or "I'm too anxious to study today—I'll really buckle down tomorrow."

A related problem is the *double-bind contingency* (Ellis and Knaus, 1977). Here are some examples. An anorexic client complains that she has no friends. Although her stated goal is to cultivate a friendship, the therapist finds out that she has turned down two invitations from a fellow bridge player to visit her home after the bridge game. Why? Food might be served at the other woman's house and, being anorexic, the patient believes that she is overweight and needs to lose ten pounds. A more common illustration is the smoker who wants to give up cigarettes and also lose some weight. Neither goal is accomplished because he fears that if he gives up cigarettes, he will eat more; and if he diets, he will smoke more.

Problems such as those just described illustrate a philosophy of low frustration tolerance and are best treated by direct confrontation, a determined course of action, and perhaps a program of external contingencies. It might be pointed out to the smoker, for example, that he has three choices for change: he could stop smoking and not worry about his weight for the first few difficult weeks of withdrawal, he could work very hard at losing ten pounds and then begin his smoking cessation program, or he could do both at the same time, which is *merely harder*. Thus, the patient is confronted with the fact that the two problems can be treated independently. Once a goal is selected, a strategy can be outlined.

Doing the homework is critical for the therapeutic process to be effective. It is particularly important that clients understand this fact. Whenever possible, rewarding contingencies can be established for the successful completion of homework. This does not mean that clients have to succeed in the homework by getting what they want, but rather "succeed" in the sense of doing what they have been assigned. It is even desirable, when clients repeatedly avoid doing their homework for reasons of low frustration tolerance, to make the next appointment contingent upon the client's completion of the homework assignment. Of course, the use of clinical judgment is necessary here; certainly this strategy would be contraindicated with a depressed patient or others whose problems require regular attention.

Phasing Out the Therapist

A goal prior to terminating therapy is to have clients function independently and to acquire the cognitive and behavioral skills necessary to be their own therapist. To achieve this goal, the therapist can gradually fade out his or her role as the active agent in assigning homework projects and encourage clients to develop their own assignments. Thus, when clients report on their previous week's progress, the therapist can ask, "What could you do next week to follow up on that?" By gradual shaping and fading out of directiveness, clients will acquire the ability to design their own self-help work.

15 Comprehensive Rational-Emotive Therapy

The early writings of Ellis focused almost exclusively on the *elegant solution* and a logical, persuasive model of therapy. In fact, it is this focus on philosophical content that distinguishes RET from other cognitive and cognitive-behavioral systems of therapy. You will recall, from our discussion on page 78, that an elegant solution assumes that the activating event is true and will remain so or could occur ("assuming the worst") and encourages clients to change their evaluation of the given reality. In Ellis' subsequent writing (1973a, 1977b, 1979b), he expanded his theory to include both elegant and inelegant solutions, recognizing that clinical realities may require the use of both to maximize therapeutic effectiveness. *Inelegant solutions* are attempts to help clients change their misperceptions of A and, if feasible, to change A.

Up to this point, you have been guided through the process of an elegant disputation, and you are probably aware that your client may require additional therapeutic help. Therefore, we now turn our attention to other therapeutic modalities used by the rational-emotive therapist.

After reviewing the psychotherapy literature, we have discovered that cognitive-learning therapies appear to fall into four categories:

- Elegant RET, with its emphasis on a philosophical solution.
- Self-instructional training programs, which attempt to directly guide clients' behavior by teaching rational self-statements and establishing a mediating influence between internal self-talk and behavior.
- Analyses of clients' perceptions of reality, with efforts to help them develop more realistic schemas about themselves, others, and the world.

- Helping clients develop more efficient problem-solving skills so that they may more effectively deal with their world.

Rational-emotive therapists utilize all four modalities of cognitive-learning therapy. This chapter briefly describes the work in each of the three areas not covered so far. It is not meant to be all-inclusive of other cognitive-learning therapies but to provide what, in our estimation, are examples relevant to RET.

Self-Instructional Training

The client may not understand or profit from the disputation phase of therapy. Some reasons for this difficulty may be that the client is too young, is intellectually limited, is overwhelmed by anxiety and unable to think clearly, or has an underlying psychotic thought disorder. Another case in which a formal disputation may not prove practical is with impulsive behaviors, such as striking in anger, succumbing to an addiction, or fleeing in panic. In these cases a strategy is needed to stop the impulsive act when you do not have the luxury of time to do a disputation. In other instances, the RET therapist may simply see that disputation is not working and the client is failing to reach the elegant solution; the reasons for this failure may not be obvious. When progress has not occurred or seems unlikely to occur, or when the problem behavior is aggression or impulsivity, the rational-emotive therapist may turn to *self-instructional training* as an alternate solution.

Self-instructional training is a procedure developed by Donald Meichenbaum (1985) in his work with test-taking and public-speaking anxiety. Other examples of self-instructional training include Novaco's (1975) work on anger control, Camp's (1975) work with hyperaggressive children, and Maultsby's (1975) work in rational behavior training. Essentially, clients are asked to imagine troublesome situations, to experience their emotional impact, and to recite coping self-statements. In Meichenbaum's therapist manual (1973), for example, three types of coping self-statements are outlined.

Confronting and handling the stressor. These self-statements help the client to focus on the task rather than on the anxiety. The principle is that task-relevant cognitions are incompatible with anxiety-producing ones. For example:

What is it I have to do? Just think rationally.

Don't worry; worry won't help anything.

I'm not sure how to begin. Well, I'll just get started and maybe it'll become clearer as I go along.

Coping with the feeling of being overwhelmed. These self-statements are designed to help the patient understand anxiety and reinterpret it. The message is that anxiety itself is not awful. For example:

Don't try to eliminate the anxiety totally; just keep it manageable.

This is the anxiety I thought I'd feel. It's a reminder for me to cope.

Slow down a little. Don't rush and get all in a panic.

I'll label my anxiety from 0 to 10 and watch it change. There, now I'm in better control.

Reinforcing self-statements. These coping sentences are an important component because the processes the patient is using are internal, and others may not be able to reward the patient for small increments of control. Examples are:

It's working; I can control how I feel.

I did it!

I'm in control. I made more out of my fear than it was worth.

It's getting better each time I try these procedures.

Here is the procedure for doing one form of self-instructional training. First, the client learns relaxation techniques. While this skill is being developed, client and therapist construct a hierarchy of anxiety-provoking situations from least to most threatening. For example, for a test-anxious student, the lowest item on the hierarchy may be "sitting in class when the instructor announces that a test will be given in two weeks." The highest item on the hierarchy might be "taking the exam and seeing other students finishing and leaving the room." Hierarchies typically consist of at least ten items, arranged on spatial, temporal, or thematic dimensions. When the patient is relaxed, each hierarchy item in turn is presented imaginally, and the patient practices reciting aloud, and later covertly, self-statements from each of the above three coping categories.

The RET therapist may add another element to self-instructional training. The technique of coping self-statements does not provide the

Relaxation training, like any other behavioral skill, is taught with the emphasis on changing *thinking*. In addition to mitigating anxiety directly, it can be used to change cognitions that result in anxiety.

When teaching relaxation, emphasize its use as a *coping* rather than a mastery skill. Its use will not preclude anxiety episodes but can help to manage them. In the relaxation instructions, stress self-efficacy. For example, "Notice the sensation of relaxation that *you* are bringing forth . . . notice what *you* can evoke in yourself."

Imagery can add to the experience. Before inducing relaxation, you may ask clients to think of an image or scene in which they feel totally relaxed and safe. Almost all clients will be able to provide an image that has a great deal of personal meaning for them. Ask the client to use all sensory modalities in describing the scene in detail—the colors, sounds, smells, and so on.

Other procedures that may deepen the state of relaxation include the following:

Ask the client to say the word "relax," perhaps 50 to 100 times in a row (without actually counting), as the client exhales, which establishes a rhythm. This strategy helps to make the word "relax" a discriminative stimulus for the state of relaxation.

Have a client with good imagery skills imagine the word "relax" in the form of a neon sign, blinking on and off rhythmically.

Remind the client to focus on the breathing, making sure it is slow and deliberate.

Toward the end of the process of inducing relaxation, say, "Soon, I'm going to count to ten. Even though you are now relaxed, when I get to ten, you will be *profoundly* relaxed." Then count slowly to ten, intermittently directing the client to notice and deepen the state of relaxation.

patient with a philosophic understanding, but instead provides descriptions of adaptive behaviors. It may be obvious that these techniques are derived from a behavioral model and treat covert stimuli, responses, and reinforcers in the same manner as external stimuli, motoric responses, and externally applied reinforcers. Meichenbaum's procedures place less emphasis on thinking and logical analysis than does RET, and behavior change may, therefore, be less likely to generalize across problems. The RET therapist may add self-statements that include rational thoughts and emotional scaling down.

For example, if the problem is aggression and the patient has a tendency to hit before thinking, Meichenbaum might suggest self-statements such as:

> "Don't do anything.
>
> Count to ten.
>
> There! I'm walking away."

The rational-emotive therapist might add:

> "I can stand criticism.
>
> That's the way he [or she] is . . . he's just doing his usual routine.
>
> I can tolerate this discomfort.
>
> I don't have to get upset, and I don't have to act impulsively."

Case Example. Helen was an obese twenty-year-old woman who avoided all contact with men. She had had a traumatic upbringing with an alcoholic father and had been raped by a stranger at the age of fourteen. Initial attempts at RET helped her to feel less depressed and guilty about the rape experience, but her fear in the presence of men continued unabated. A fear hierarchy was constructed: The first item was walking alone on a beach and seeing a man about 200 yards away; across items, the man was imagined to come closer and closer. The highest item was sitting in a school cafeteria, talking to a man. After relaxation training, each item was imagined and paired with the following self-instructional statements: "This man is unlikely to hurt me. There I go again, overgeneralizing. All men aren't the same. I'm tense, but I can stand it. What could I say to introduce myself? I'm doing fine. Isn't it great that I'm in control?" After five sessions, the client was able to have lunch with men in the school cafeteria with minimal anxiety.

You might try to suggest some coping statements, utilizing Meichenbaum's three categories, for clients with the following types of problems:

> A married individual afraid of dealing with an argumentative spouse.
>
> A child afraid of sleeping alone in the dark.
>
> A man afraid he won't be able to satisfy his sex partner.
>
> An employee who is afraid to disagree with her supervisor.
>
> The problem of a client you are presently treating.
>
> See answer key, p. 370.

A less elaborate version of Meichenbaum's procedures used by rational-emotive therapists is the "rational barb" (Kimmel, 1976), in which the therapist deliberately recreates specific activating events. To illustrate this technique, consider the case of a child who becomes upset when her schoolmates call her names. The therapist might ask the child to practice some name calling on him; the therapist can then model both coping self-statements and the absence of emotional overreactivity. The therapist may then tell the child that he will call her a name (i.e., give her a "barb") so that she can practice the same responses (e.g., "Well, you might think I'm a four-eyes, but that doesn't make me a bad person").

Dealing with A

If clients have understood and profited from a disputation, yet perceive that their world contains many unpleasant activating events, the work of therapy is not completed. They may feel sad (rather than depressed), annoyed (rather than angry), and apprehensive (rather than anxious), but have these feelings a substantial portion of the time. In such cases, even though clients think rationally and feel an appropriate level of emotion, certain aspects of their lives are still unpleasant and worthy of psychological intervention. Two major procedures to which the rational-emotive therapist may turn are helping clients to (a) examine the accuracy of their perception of A, and (b) develop strategies to change those A's that can be changed.

INTERPRETATION OF A

In drawing the distinction between elegant and inelegant solutions in Chapter 6 (p. 78), we used the example of a male client who believed that everyone in his office hated him. Using the elegant solution, we assumed that his perception of A was correct and attempted to de-awfulize his evaluation of this situation. Even if the disputation were successful, however, the client would be left with unpleasant emotional effects and undoubtedly be uncomfortable when he went to work every day. This negative affect would be needless if the client were misperceiving the situation; other procedures would be warranted to correct his misperception. An additional task of RET, therefore, is to encourage the client to be more scientific in his examination of data and his conclusions from them.

Psychologists such as Kelly (1955) and Wegner and Vallacher (1977) believe that we function as scientists in our approach to the world around us, although we may be unaware of performing this role. Scientists are interested in the classification, prediction, and control of events in the physical or social environment. All persons are interested in the same phenomena but may not know how to function as scientists. Without careful monitoring, we can easily slip into habits of poor observation, inaccurate classification, incorrect predictions, and inept attempts at control. These errors can produce the problems that bring patients to the psychotherapist's office. Thus, one way to conceptualize the therapist's role is as a teacher of scientific methodology.

One of the first axioms in the philosophy of science is that there are no immutable facts; all facts are viewed as hypotheses. In the logic of science, an hypothesis can never be confirmed; data that fail to disconfirm the theory provide support for it but never proof of it. The scientist recognizes that even repeatedly observed events occur in a world of change; thus, even scientific "laws" are regarded as temporary and subject to revision. Scientists, therefore, are prepared to *change their minds* as they adapt their beliefs and behavior to changes in reality (Johnson, 1946). Now, let's see how these principles apply to therapy.

One of the first principles to teach the client is the distinction between facts and hypotheses. In working with the hypothetical male client discussed above, we would first challenge his notion that it is a fact that no one likes him; this "fact" is merely hypothesis. If our client is willing to accept this view, his job is to determine the validity of the hypothesis by gathering data and drawing appropriate conclusions from them. These steps are precisely the ones used by therapists such as Raimy (1975), Maultsby (1975), and Beck (1985) in their cognitive therapy. In this work, therapist and client search for two major kinds of cognitive errors: errors in gathering data and errors in drawing conclusions.

A scientist gathers data impartially, attempting to observe and report his or her observations objectively and accurately. The scientist's precise use of language, therefore, is of the utmost importance. In therapy, the patient in our example would be asked for data to support his hypothesis that no one likes him, and the therapist would listen carefully to these reports. How does he know that no one likes him? Clients typically respond to this question with a list of persons whom they believe dislike them. This evidence, however, is not objective; rather, the client simply *assumes* that these individuals do not like him. The same question deserves to be repeated, therefore: How do you know that she or he doesn't like you? How do you determine who *does* like you? What criteria do you use in making these determinations? In other words, the therapist is teaching the client to report the data objectively before he evaluates them.

Beck (1976; Beck et al., 1979) has indicated two primary ways in which patients distort data: selective abstraction and magnification or minimization. *Selective abstraction* "consists of focusing on a detail taken out of context, ignoring other more salient features of the situation and conceptualizing the whole experience on the basis of this element" (Beck et al., 1979, p. 7). *Magnification/minimization* "is reflected in errors in evaluation that are so gross as to constitute a distortion" (p. 8). In both types of cognitive errors, patients ignore certain features of the world around them, so that they are gathering biased data. In selective abstraction, clients focus on one category of data and ignore others; in magnification/minimization, clients ignore information within a category.

For example, our hypothetical client may selectively attend to only certain features of his co-workers' behavior; perhaps he ignores their greetings, their nonverbal cues of approval when business is being discussed, or the times they seek his professional advice. He may inaccurately discount these data as being irrelevant to his hypothesis. In addition, the client may minimize when he states that he is never asked out to lunch; in fact, he may have been approached one or two times over the past six months. Statements such as "They always avoid me" indicate maximization.

If your job as a therapist is to teach the client to gather more accurate data, what techniques do you use? For one thing, you and the client had better agree on which data are relevant to the hypothesis, thus avoiding selective abstraction (e.g., eye contact, greetings, minutes spent in conversation, relaxed intonations in speech). Second, frequency counts in log books will help the client keep accurate records and avoid the problem of magnification/minimization.

If the client returns to therapy with more accurate data, he may be able to report that, in fact, four co-workers made good eye contact with him while two did not, verbal interchanges were very brief with three of the first group and longer with the remaining three, and he was invited to lunch once in the past week by one co-worker. With such specific data, the client may already have abandoned his hypothesis that *no one* likes him; but if he still believes it, he is making logical errors in drawing conclusions from his data.

If the frequency of social interactions is low, many hypotheses could be entertained as an explanation. For instance, the client may behave unsociably in the office, and his co-workers may believe that *he* doesn't like *them*. Another possibility is that the client's role in the office may preclude social invitations from others—because of differences in status, for example. Other hypotheses include an office norm of minimal social interchange set by the pressures of the work itself or by administrative fiat. The behaviors of the clients' co-workers may have more to do with their own intrapsychic problems than with personal dislike for the client. In other words, the therapist can help the client generate numerous alternative hypotheses to account for the objective data, and in doing so the client learns to make a habit of generating hypotheses.

Beck has outlined three errors in inductive logic commonly made in drawing conclusions from data. Induction is a tricky process because to make an accurate judgment, it is necessary to examine every instance of a particular phenomenon from which the conclusion is being made. For example, if you hypothesize that all little red hens have high IQ's, it is logically necessary to examine the IQ of each and every little red hen. Since such a task is impossible, conclusions drawn inductively are usually based on a sampling procedure, subjected to inferential statistics, and accepted within probability limits, and therefore are always tentative. Clients, however, rarely follow these canons of science.

The errors of conclusion drawing to which Beck refers are:

Arbitrary inference—drawing a conclusion in the absence of supporting evidence or in the face of contrary evidence.

Overgeneralization—drawing a general conclusion on the basis of a single incident.

Personalization—relating external events to oneself when there is no basis for making such a connection.

You can easily see that the hypothetical client above was making these kinds of logical errors about the behavior of his co-workers.

One way to teach the client to view his cognitions as hypotheses to be tested is for the therapist to model this behavior. Beck and colleagues (1979) suggest that therapists offer their own interpretations of the client's behavior as hypotheses to be tested. With the client above, for example, the therapist has hypothesized that the client tends to draw a conclusion ("no one likes me") when certain social interchanges at work fail to take place. This theory can be tested by having the client record how often he makes this conclusion in the actual situation. Thus, the therapist's conclusion is subject to testing, and at the same time, the client's cognitions are objectively validated. The point of these procedures is to train the client to objectively test his perception of A in a much more rigorous fashion than he is likely to have done prior to therapy.

In summary, two major procedures are to train the patient to (a) objectively collect and accurately label data outside the therapy session, and (b) question his or her automatic conclusions from these data. The first procedure evaluates whether A as reported by the patient is true or has been cognitively distorted. Consider the following hypothetical examples.

First example. The client, Georgina, reports that she acted very selfishly. First, the therapist examines what the client actually did. A useful discussion might involve asking the client to define *selfishness* and to distinguish it from *self-interest*. It might be pointed out to her that selfishness implies total disregard for other human beings, whereas self-interest implies simply choosing to put oneself first, even if others are temporarily inconvenienced. Discriminations such as these encourage clients to carefully examine their perception of A (in this case, their own behavior) and to determine whether they have correctly labeled it.

Second example. The client, Bill, who works in the art department of a large New York City advertising agency, claims, "I'm no good at snappy conversation!" Is this statement correct? If so, his perceived deficiency may be the result of inborn or acquired tendencies. Another possibility, since he views this lack of ability as awful and is anxious, is that he is editing out his verbal repartee. More likely, however, the client is misperceiving his level of ability in this area. He may be better than average but does not notice it, because he is comparing himself against a talented reference group—New York ad men, who make their living with their verbal skills.

Third example. The patient, Ron, reports that someone criticized him, and he accepted the other person's evaluation as fact. There are two parts to this challenge: determining if the other person's comments were indeed critical, and if they made sense as statements of fact. In the first instance, for example, the patient might say that someone insulted him; questions the therapist could use as challenges include, "What actually happened?" "How was that an insult?" In the second instance, the therapist might consider using the following analogy:

> "Suppose a little child came in at 4 PM and began whining for cookies, but his mother told him "No." The child threw himself on the floor and began screaming, "You're a bad mother . . . you're mean . . . you're stupid!" That's an activating event. Do you think mom will react badly to it? Probably not, because she knows differently. In fact, isn't she being a good mother by restricting sweets just before dinner so he won't spoil his appetite? Now, let's see if what Mr. X said to *you* made sense."

The second procedure, questioning the patient's conclusions drawn from the data, is best done by Socratic dialogue. As early as 1946, in Wendell Johnson's work on semantic therapy, it was pointed out that two important questions for the therapist are "What do you mean? and "How do you know?" These questions are embedded in the following transcript, in which the client is a young woman obsessed by jealous feelings for her husband.

T: Just because he meets her for lunch, does that mean they're having an affair?

C: Well . . . no.

T: There's no way you can hang onto a lover and not have him enjoy members of the opposite sex in any way—can you?

C: I can expect him not to have sexual relations!

T: OK, but if you're going to suspect that's so every time he talks to a woman, what's going to happen to you? You'll constantly be on guard, won't you?

C: Yes, I guess so.

T: And it *is* possible that an affair might happen. What does one sexual encounter mean?

C: That he doesn't care for me anymore.

T: Does it really mean that? If I say "blue means green," does that make it true?

C: But if he has an affair, that means I'm not enough for him.

T: No, that's your perception of what you think it means. Just because you believe it, that doesn't make it true. You're assuming that he can only love one person at a time, and can only have sex with someone he loves, and will not love you if he's having sexual relations with someone else. All of these assumptions are in your thinking.

C: It could mean he didn't think enough of me to abide by my wishes and not have outside sex.

T: Right. It could also mean that he thought he could get away with it!

C: I want him to be only mine.

T: I would like that too with my mate. Maybe that's not possible. It doesn't mean we can't enjoy our mates at all.

C: But if he does that, I'm going to be very upset.

T: I think it's appropriate for you to be disappointed, but do you have to be really upset?

C: I don't want him to do it!

T: You didn't answer my question.

C: I don't have to be very upset, but so far I've been doing that.

T: What do you think would happen if you weren't so upset?

C: Maybe he wouldn't be so careful—maybe he wouldn't do what I want him to.

T: How would that happen?

C: He won't take any chances—he knows I'll get really upset.

T: You know that?

C: He takes me seriously because he knows I'll get really upset.

T: You're repeating your position, but you still haven't told me how you know that. Have you tried out both ways of responding?

C: No, but I just don't want him to.

T: From what you've told me, it sounds like you're upset most of the time, and your upset seems to result from some of these unwarranted assumptions that you're making. Let's go back and talk about some of your assumptions again in detail.

Most rational-emotive therapists seem to engage in procedures such as those outlined above, perhaps not realizing that they are working in a very similar style to Beck, Johnson, and others. We hope that this description will make clear what they are doing, as well as inform the new therapist how to go about clarifying perceptions of A more efficiently. The process of correcting misperceptions of A is also used in challenging irrational ideas about B, namely, posing this question to the client in many different forms: "Where is the evidence that what you believe is really true?"

CHANGING THE A

When you have helped the client examine the accuracy of his or her perception of A, it will be clear that A's are rarely black-and-white issues. Absolutist hypotheses (always, never, everyone, nobody, etc.) are rarely confirmed. Thus, our client may discover that although some people in his office like him, the percentage is lower than he would like. A psychological intervention is then appropriate. Helping the client change those A's that can be changed is a legitimate and important endeavor for the rational-emotive therapist. This concept is taken from Ellis, who in his therapy groups spends a significant portion of time helping clients develop social survival skills. Attempts to change A are of two basic types: (1) attempts to change the environment in which the patient operates, and (2) attempts to change personal aspects of the client.

Changing the World

Clients frequently experience real-life adversities that can be changed. There may be severe financial, legal, in-law, medical, educational, career-related, and marital or family problems. In dealing with these issues, the rational-emotive therapist fills two basic roles: giving information where appropriate and, more important, teaching problem-solving skills.

Perhaps one of the first skills clients may profit from is discrimination training, that is, learning when they have reached the limits of their knowledge and need to consult an outside expert. Seeking advice may be difficult for some clients; they may not even know that there are resources to which they can turn. We recommend that all therapists develop a resource list of specialists (medical, legal, financial, etc.) for handy reference.

The second skill clients may profit from is maintaining a *coping* frame of reference. By this phrase we mean three important cognitive realizations:

- Helplessness is not helpful; it is possible to do something about an adverse situation. As we stated earlier, rational living entails neither passive acceptance of unfortunate or unpleasant events nor endorsement of them. If it is not possible to directly change an unpleasant situation, one can at least selectively encounter it. For example, although pollution can't be removed from the air in New York City, one can choose not to live there. Similarly, we may never change obnoxious behaviors in (say) our in-laws, but we can at least limit our contact with them.

- In many instances only limited change is likely within a particular period of time. Holding unrealistic expectations and awfulizing when these deadlines are not met can be detrimental to one's mental and physical health.

- There are no perfect solutions, merely better or worse alternatives.

Many of the difficult A's that patients present are approach–avoidance conflicts. Conflict resolution training utilizes many elements of rational-emotive therapy. Difficulties clients have in resolving conflicts or reaching decisions include failure to take risks, a need for certainty, a desire to predict the future, and awfulizing about making the wrong decision. These concerns are dealt with by disputing the underlying irrational beliefs. Even when clients have learned that there is no such thing as a perfect solution, no guarantee of a given outcome, and no shame in making a wrong decision, they may lack the ability to draw up what Ellis calls an hedonic calculus.

An *hedonic calculus* is a fancy way of saying that rational decision making consists of listing all the elements that enter into the decision, their relative value to the patient, and the probability of various long- and short-term consequences; tallying up the pro's and con's; and then being brave enough to act upon these data. Each of these steps may involve elaborate discussion between the client and therapist, the client and outside experts, and the client and others involved in the decision.

For instance, suppose the client is a divorcee with two children who is considering marrying a man who lives in another city several hundred miles away. In addition, the prospective spouse is a workaholic with a medical disability. The contemplated marriage involves changing the client's residence, leaving a stable job, and disrupting the children's schooling. These negative factors are balanced by her affection for the man, their shared professional interests, their sexual compatibility, and his excellent rapport with her children. In drawing up her hedonic calculus, she discussses with her therapist the relative probabilities of various outcomes, such as the effects of remarriage on the children, the level of commitment by her partner, her need for guaranteed longevity in the relationship, and so forth. With her physician, she discusses the import of her partner's medical disability; with her children, she discusses their reaction to the contemplated union; and with others in her profession, she investigates the chances of finding remunerative employment in the new location. Once the data are amassed, she and the therapist work on the hedonic calculus until it becomes clear that greater happiness may be achieved on taking the risks of entering into the marriage.

A major change strategy which clients can be taught in order to make their world a little brighter is the use of principles of *contingency management*. Many interpersonal difficulties can be helped by the judicious use of contingency management to shape new behaviors and extinguish or punish undesired behaviors. Parents may find lessons in behavior modification helpful in reducing conflicts with their children, and children can profit from the same principles in attempting to change interaction patterns with their parents, teachers, and siblings. In other words, learning to establish reinforcement systems may be useful for clients of any age in almost any interpersonal situation. If you have not yet been trained in these basic behavioral systems, helpful references are available in Chapter 18.

Here is an illustration of the use of RET which includes behavior modification (as RET usually does, since it's orientation is cognitive, emotive, *and* behavioral). In this case, the client was a young mother of three children who was recently separated from her husband. Among her emotional complaints were depression, guilt about the dissolution of the marriage and its possible negative effects on the children, and increasing anger at the children as they began to misbehave more frequently. As she and the therapist began to explore and sample her child-rearing skills, it became apparent that although she was a warm and caring parent, she had begun to refrain from punishing or containing the children's unwanted behaviors. The motivation for this change in her behavior appeared to be avoidance of guilt, and the guilt, in turn, resulted from some irrational cognitions she held. For example, she implicitly believed that she had to provide twice as much love for her children since her husband was no longer living at home. Her definition of love apparently meant that she must not disapprove of her children's behavior and certainly should not yell at or punish them. As might be expected, the children got more and more out of hand until, in exasperation, the mother lost her temper. She immediately chastised *herself* for being a cruel witch. The client was therefore "doing herself in" by an unfortunate choice of an interpersonal and intrapsychic system;

A special case: therapists who work predominantly with women and children are dealing with a relatively unempowered population. A common error of new rational-emotive therapists who work with these clients is to fail to stress that the goal is not merely to tolerate being an underdog. Having a low position or being underpaid in the workplace, or being verbally abused by a domineering spouse, are not situations in which a rational thinker would choose to be resigned. *Acceptance of reality is not equivalent to resignation.* Women specifically may need empowerment lessons from the therapist in order to effect change in their A's.

Children may be less fortunate. If twelve-year-old Johnny is living with a verbally abusive dad, there may be little he can do about it, except to plan for his escape at age eighteen. For the time being, Johnnie's best option may be to reduce his own emotional distress and learn to cope with his unfortunate reality, consider the reasons for his father's difficult behaviors and not feel responsible for them, and protect himself from his father as best he can. If there are certain behaviors that Johnnie knows are likely to "set his father off," such as coming home late, Johnny can work at avoiding those behaviors *for his own sake,* as self-protection. The therapist will want to exercise caution, however, that Johnny understands that his behavior is not the cause of dad's verbal abuse.

she was punishing herself instead of appropriately disciplining the children.

The rational-emotive therapist helped her to cognitively explore her definitions of concepts such as "love," "punishment," and "mothering"; it soon became clear to her that good mothering included not only demonstrations of affection but also appropriate limit-setting. It was in her children's best interests to be temporarily discomforted by parental control if they were to learn important behavioral lessons. After all, for example, one would immediately scold a young child for crossing the street without looking for oncoming traffic. Similarly, teaching social behaviors may occasionally require a firm hand. It is an act of a loving parent to take the responsibility and risk of confronting a child's misbehavior, giving direct feedback, and implementing a contingency to change it. Once the client had thus given herself permission to manage her children, she and the children, with the help of the therapist, worked out a constructive set of mutual responsibilities with appropriate reward and penalty arrangements to deal with specific problems. The children's allowance, instead of being doled out, was made contingent upon desired behaviors. A potent penalty turned out to be the loss of TV privileges for a specified number of hours. Even after her cognitive challenges, however, this mother remained a "softie" and became uncomfortable with the prolonged penalties she had assigned. Accordingly, an amendment to the system was added whereby the children could work off some of their penalty time with additional constructive behaviors, such as helping around the house or doing something nice for someone else in the family.

To summarize, attempts to change external factors of a client's A may be accomplished by teaching the client (a) problem-solving skills, such as gathering information, weighing consequences, and choosing a course of action; and (b) by sharing information with the client, such as the use of operant technology to attempt to change the behavior of others in the environment. Another major aspect of changing the client's A is changing the client's own behaviors so that his or her world will react differently to him or her.

Changing the Client

If your clients are performing poorly in some life endeavor and are deprecating themselves for their poor results, the first order of business in therapy, as we have said, is to work on the self-downing. If the work of therapy were to stop there, however, clients might well accept themselves but remain what Goldfried and Davison (1976) have labeled "relaxed incompetent[s]." The question the therapist will want to ask is, "Is my client investing significant effort and does he or she have sufficient skills to change a poor performance?" Let's examine some common skill deficits that may hinder the client from achieving desired goals.

A primary area of concern is often a deficit in *social problem-solving skills*. A number of researchers and therapists have worked in this area (e.g., Allen et al., 1976; D'Zurilla, 1986; Mahoney, 1977; D'Zurilla and Goldfried, 1971), but we will focus primarily on the work of Spivack, Platt, and Shure (1976) of the Hahnemann Medical School. These researchers indicate that there is no correlation between the ability to solve interpersonal problems and the ability to solve practical problems (such as the one presented in the previous section) or those involving inanimate objects. Thus, one may be a brilliant research physicist and yet be unable to figure out how to get along with the department secretary. Social problem solving is not correlated with IQ, but has been shown to correlate with other measures of psychopathology and poor social adjustment. Deficits in social problem-solving skills may also be present when there is no strong emotional component. Clients may not be upset about their behavior, but they may continue to behave in a self-defeating and inappropriate manner.

Spivack describes an encounter with a youngster that inspired him to investigate the role of social problem-solving skills in behavioral disorders. While Spivack was employed as a psychologist in a residential treatment facility, one of his patients went AWOL late one night and walked to the nearby town. Spivack was summoned to help find the child; after a search by the police, the boy was discovered walking down the railroad tracks at 11 PM near the center of town. The following day, Spivack discussed with the child his reasons for the trip. As an analytic psychologist, he had many hypotheses to explain the child's aberrant behavior. Possibly the boy was behaving masochistically and wanted to be punished for his behavior, or he was acting out his anger toward his caretakers. As the therapist proceeded to gather information in support of these notions, he asked the child many questions about his behavior. The boy reported that he was going to town to buy an item that he had seen in one of the stores. The therapist asked if he didn't realize that the store would be closed at that hour of the night. The child responded that he hadn't thought of it. Didn't he realize that he was breaking a rule? The boy responded that he hadn't thought of it. Didn't he realize the consequences of his actions—that the staff would be angry with him and that his privileges would be curtailed? The boy responded that he just hadn't thought of it. Didn't he realize that there were other ways to get the desired item? The boy responded again that he just hadn't thought of it. At this point, Spivack reported having a dramatic insight. Perhaps his own hypotheses concerning the child's behavior were wrong, and the child's were correct. Was it possible that instead of some intricate masochistic motivation the child *simply didn't think?* The simpler hypothesis subsequently led Spivack and his co-workers to conduct a large research project investigating cognitive factors in perceiving problems and related problem-solving skills.

The results of Spivack's studies suggest a number of hierarchically developed cognitive skills that, when absent, lead to psychopathology. The first skill, of course, is the ability to recognize that a social problem exists; that two or more people are in conflict. This skill includes the ability to interpret others' feelings from their verbal and nonverbal cues. The next skill is the ability to stop and think—for example, "OK, here is the problem, now what am I going to do about it?"). Another skill is the ability to distinguish facts from opinions. A fact is an observable or verifiable phenomenon or act which can be agreed upon by at least a majority of those who observe it. Finally, a related skill is the ability to recognize that others will have different opinions than oneself about the same facts.

Once the problem is identified, the first step in dealing with it is *alternative-solution thinking,* or the ability to generate (not merely recognize) a number of possible solutions. The more alternatives the client can devise, the more likely he or she is to function adaptively. Consider the example of a child who sees another child playing with a toy that he or she wants. Spivack's research showed that a socially well-adjusted child could generate many alternative courses of action to cope with the situation; for example, he or she could ask the other child for the toy, trade a different toy for the desired one, hit the other child and grab the toy, ask to play with it when the other child is finished, play with something else, and so forth. A less socially adept child is more likely to simply grab at the toy. The suggestion is that this child has not learned the cognitive skill of considering alternative courses of action. Don't be misled into assuming that when you have cleared up a client's irrational beliefs, more appropriate behaviors will follow. Spivack's notion questions this assumption and points out that alternative thinking is a skill that the client may need to acquire and practice. It is akin to what has been called brainstorming. The therapist encourages the client to suggest as many alternative behaviors as possible, without censoring or evaluating them. Crazy, silly, impractical, and imperfect ideas are all encouraged before the therapist leads the client to the next step in the hierarchy.

The second step in developing problem-solving skills is *consequential thinking.* This term refers to the ability to predict the consequences of one's behavior, particularly its effects on other people. Will the other person respond positively or negatively? How is the other person likely to feel: Will he or she be angered by the behavior? Is the behavior likely to elicit compliance? Will the behavior get you what you want? Consequential thinking thus involves making predictive inferences about the relationship between social behaviors and social consequences. The therapist's knowledge of behavioral principles may also provide useful data to help the client make these predictions. For example, consider the case of a mother who is trying to decide how to react to her son's persistent habit of whining. Among the behavioral alternatives she generates is the idea of simply ignoring the child when he whines, thus using the concept of extinction. What might be the consequences of her action? The literature on operant extinction clearly suggests that the *immediate* effect of this procedure might well be an initial increase in the very behavior the mother dislikes. Another possibility is that the mother might not be entirely consistent in her plan, and intermittently attend to the child when he whines. It could be pointed out to the mother that intermittent reinforcement significantly increases a behavior's resistance to extinction, thus prolonging the problem. Thus, in consequential thinking, the patient is essentially evaluating the benefits and disadvantages of each of the alternatives previously generated.

After the client has evaluated the various alternatives and selected one(s) that appear(s) to have the best probability of success, the next step is to do *means–end thinking*. The client analyzes the sequence of events that are likely to happen, identifying the process step-by-step that is required to achieve the goal. The mother in the example above cognitively rehearses exactly how she would implement her extinction plan and how she would respond if her child escalated his whining. For example, how could she cope with the whining if she were in a public place with her child?

Finally, the client learns the skill of *verifying the solution*. The plan is implemented and its effects are evaluated. How did it work? What went wrong? Can it be fixed? If the results are negative and the plan appears to be ineffective, the client is led back again to alternative-solution thinking, to generate new approaches to the problem.

A theory of psychopathology that focuses only on cognitive elements that inhibit or interfere with appropriate functioning assumes that more appropriate responses are available to the individual. If the client thought rationally and were freed from inhibiting processes, he or she would, theoretically, be able to behave competently. The work of Spivack and his colleagues points out, however, that learning problem-solving skills may be necessary to add appropriate, adaptive behaviors to the client's repertoire. This model suggests that dysfunctional behavior can be caused by the absence of appropriate cognitions as well as by the presence of dysfunctional ones.

Many elements of Spivack's training program in social problem-solving skills overlap with rational-emotive theory. For example, differentiating facts from opinions, stopping to think before acting, and identifying problems are routinely taught by rational-emotive therapists. It is unfortunate that the RET literature has neglected to report the social skills training that rational-emotive therapists have done with clients over the years. In particular, Ellis has conducted a workshop called "Creative Contacts for Singles," one of the most popular ones given at the Institute for Rational-Emotive Therapy. In this workshop he first helps people identify and challenge their inhibiting thoughts and then teaches them how to practice the social skills needed in making contact with members of the opposite sex. Since the literature on RET has been imprecise in specifying the steps entailed in social problem solving, the work of Spivack, Platt, and Shure provides a significant complement.

When rational-emotive therapists teach problem-solving skills, however, they go one step further and also teach the client *how to cope with failure.* On many occasions clients will find that they have only a choice of very imperfect alternatives, that each solution has a probability of producing undesirable consequences, or that the problem is simply unsolvable. Cold reality sometimes thwarts the best problem solvers. When this is the case, finding the elegant solution (e.g., anti-awfulizing) is an indispensable tool.

ASSERTIVENESS TRAINING

One behavioral skill that can help the client adapt to the environment is *assertiveness,* or the appropriate expression of feelings and desires. Deficiencies in this area may result from lack of verbal and nonverbal repertoires or cognitive factors that impede the expression of these behaviors, or both. In addition, you may recall that deficiencies in assertiveness may be situation-specific. Thus, a client may be quite assertive with employees at work, yet timid with family members at home. The assertive female professional may fall into unselective sexual encounters because she "cannot say no." A client may be quite adept at expressing negative feelings, but tongue-tied when it comes to expressing tender, gentle, or loving thoughts. Changing this aspect of the client's behavior, therefore, may also help to change the client's A's as long as two anti-absolutist notions are kept in mind:

- Behaving assertively is no guarantee that the client will get what is wanted, although it may increase the probability of a favorable outcome.
- If the client knows how to behave assertively, that does not mean that he or she must behave this way all the time. In some instances,

discretion may be the better part of assertion. In other words, the skill of consequential thinking is relevant.

The first step in teaching the client to behave more assertively is to outline the differences in assertive, nonassertive, and aggressive behavior. *Assertive behavior* is characterized as a statement of a preference or a request for change from another person, which is communicated directly, but without hostility or defensiveness. *Nonassertive behavior* is characterized by indirect communication, inhibition, and anxiety, and perhaps by not attempting to get what one wants at all. *Aggressive behavior* typically communicates demands rather than preferences, is righteous or hostile, and has the intent of punishing the other person.

A second task in assertiveness training may be to correct the client's irrational self-statements: notions that lead to unassertive, hostile, or aggressive responses; or ideas with which the client punishes himself or herself for inept assertive responses, for assertions that don't prove immediately successful, or for failures to respond at all.

An eye-opening step for clients is to perceive their *right* to be assertive. What are their rights as human beings? What are their rights in specific social roles—as spouse or as parent? Such questions often provide a provocative homework assignment. The following suggestions may help clients get started: "I have the right to have feelings and express them, including complaints and criticisms. I have the right to set my own priorities. I have the right to say no without feeling guilty."

Assertiveness training also entails assessing the clients' strengths and weaknesses in assertive communication and developing training procedures to bridge the gaps in their skills. The following checklist is adapted from one prepared by Janet Wolfe.

Guidelines for Behaving Assertively

When refusing, express a decisive "no"; explain why you are refusing, but don't be unduly apologetic. When applicable, offer the other person an alternative course of action.

Give as prompt and brief a reply as you can, without interruption.

Request an explanation when asked to do something unreasonable.

Look directly at the person you're talking to. Check your body language for postures that might convey indirectness or lack of self-assurance (e.g., hand over mouth, shuffling feet). Watch your vocal inflection, making sure that you speak neither too loudly nor too softly.

When expressing annoyance or criticism, remember to comment only on the behavior; avoid a personal attack.

When commenting on another person's behavior, try to use "I" statements. For example, instead of saying, "You rat—you made me so mad!" try, "When you keep cancelling out on social arrangements at the last minute, it's extremely inconvenient and I feel really annoyed." Whenever possible, offer an alternative behavior: "I think we'd better sit down and try to figure out how we can make plans together and cut down on this kind of inconveniencing."

Keep a log of your assertive responses. Review them and talk them over with a friend. Observe role models. Remember that you don't unlearn bad habits or learn new skills overnight.

Reward yourself in some way each time you've pushed yourself to make an assertive response, whether or not you get the desired results from the other person.

Don't berate yourself when you behave nonassertively or aggressively; rather, try to figure out where you went astray and how to improve your handling of the situation next time.

A useful model for constructing an assertive communication that is found in the self-help literature is DESC, a four-step communication package:

Describe—the client is trained to briefly and objectively describe the troublesome A, without editorializing, personalizing, or elaborating.

Emotion—this is simply stated, using "I" language.

Specify what you want—the client makes a request (not a demand), and does so with clarity, concreteness and specificity.

Consequence—the communicator spells out to the listener the positive consequences that may accrue if the request is met.

An example will probably make this model clearer. The speaker is a noncustodial father speaking to his ex-wife:

D—When you make plans to do things with our son on my visitation days, without discussing it with me . . .

E—I feel annoyed and disappointed. I miss my son when I don't get to see him.

> As a training exercise, try to compose two DESC communications, one for a positive emotion or request and another for a negative emotion or request. Perhaps the positive DESC could include a request for a change in a sexual behavior with one's sex partner or an increase in social activity.

S—I would be willing to rearrange my schedule if you called me several days beforehand. I could see him on a different day.

C—This way we could both do the things we want to with him.

The preceding list and model are intended merely as a synopsis; they do not provide sufficient guidance if assertiveness training is new to you. A more extensive bibliography is provided in Chapter 17. Remember, assertiveness training is one technique that you can use in helping clients to change their A's.

GIVING PRACTICAL ADVICE TO HELP A CLIENT CHANGE THE A

Suppose you, as a therapist, think that the client could make some changes in physical appearance to improve his or her chances of reaching certain goals. Would you feel comfortable with giving your client honest feedback or initiating such discussions?

For example, suppose your client is an older woman who is looking for a mate, yet has allowed herself to become a bit dumpy and dresses in a dowdy fashion. Wouldn't you be irresponsible if you withheld practical advice that might be relevant? How could you tactfully suggest changes that might enhance her chances of reaching her goal? You might say something like, "You know, Mary, it's been my experience that a woman has a better chance of getting into a relationship if she loses some weight, gets a new hairstyle, and learns what she can about putting her best foot forward. Does that sound like anything that would appeal to you?" or "Is that something you'd be interested in?" In other words, without being critical, you can make suggestions in the third person, not directly aimed at the client. The suggestion implies, "You can do what you wish, but this might be helpful," and allows the *client* to make the decision to change.

If the client accepts the suggestion, be sure to reinforce any positive

How would you feel about confronting and openly discussing any of the following topics with a client?

Homeliness
Obesity
Physical deformities
Body odor
Breaches of etiquette
Psychotic speech

Do you give yourself the freedom to tell your clients that some aspect of their behavior or appearance is socially unacceptable or goal-defeating? Be alert to whether you are avoiding such topics because they are uncomfortable for you. Are you afraid of your client's reactions? If so, is your hesitancy based on rational reasons or on an irrational need for your client's approval, or belief that your client would be harmed by such feedback?

changes that you observe from week to week. For example, "Mary, what an attractive dress you're wearing!" or "I like the way you've done your hair; it's very flattering." The changes made may also begin pleasing the client herself.

In other cases, feedback may be more direct. More seriously disturbed clients may be grossly unaware of the effects of their appearance or behavior on others, and your confrontation therefore will be more forceful and persistent. Remember that few people, if any, in the patient's life have been brave enough to provide such feedback; your timidity in the guise of "unconditional acceptance" is counterproductive.

In a recent example, the client was a young anorexic woman whose emaciated appearance immediately struck the therapist. The presenting problem given by the patient was her lack of friends, about which she was puzzled and depressed. One symptom of anorexia is a distorted body image; the skinnier such patients get, the more acceptable they appear in their own eyes, even when their physical state has deteriorated so much that hospitalization is required. The therapist in this case example confronted the client with his own reaction to her appearance: discomfort of the same sort he might feel upon visiting someone wasting away from a terminal disease—hardly the sort of reaction a young woman in search of friends would desire. At first the patient vehemently denied that her appearance played any role in her social difficulties, but with repeated and vigorous challenges by her therapist, she finally recalled a recent interaction with a co-worker. The other woman had timorously inquired whether the patient was suffering from leukemia. In the ensuing weeks, with continuing persistent confrontations by the therapist, the patient began clearly to realize the impact of her appearance on others, and although she preferred her cachectic state, she became determined to make some changes in her diet and choice of clothing.

The psychotic patient may similarly be unaware of the social discomfort of others in responding to his or her peculiarities of speech, movement, or appearance. In fact, some psychologists refer to psychotic behavior as "disturbing" rather than "disturbed." Obviously, such behaviors are socially detrimental to the patient in many areas of life. You may serve three important roles here. First, the therapy session, as it progresses, provides a training ground for social interaction, with the therapist giving immediate feedback regarding undesirable behaviors. You may work out a signaling system with the patient; for example, you may snap your fingers every time the patient mumbles, goes off the topic, or inappropriately breaks eye contact. Second, you can train the patient to more carefully observe the reaction of others. Reports of these verbal and nonverbal reactions to inappropriate behaviors can then be discussed in therapy. Finally, you can train the patient to use some self-statements that will reduce the discomfort of others as well as self-instruct the patient. Meichenbaum (1977) has reported successfully using phrases such as, "I'm not making myself understood." or "It's not clear; let me try again."

In summary, in addition to the elegant disputations and philosophical restructuring used by the rational-emotive therapist, many other skills and techniques may be helpful. Among these, we have considered the use of coping statements (or self-instructional training), improving the client's distorted perceptions of A, and helping the client to change those A's that can be changed. In the last category we discussed techniques for helping clients to change their world (e.g., problem solving and contingency management) and techniques for helping clients to interact more favorably with their world (e.g., social problem solving, assertiveness training, and providing direct feedback). In touching upon these varied techniques drawn from the work of therapists such as Beck and Meichenbaum, we realize that we have not been able to do them justice, but we do want you to understand how rational-emotive therapists incorporate their work. We suggest that readers familiarize themselves more thoroughly with these other techniques, by exploring the list of recommended readings in Chapter 18.

16 The Course of Therapy and Beyond

Let us review what we have learned so far. The therapist has identified a problem situation (A), a distressing emotion (C), and the irrational concepts held by the patient (IB) and has attempted to dispute these irrational notions. Of course, clients will typically have more than one A or C on which to work. If you have seen Ellis' demonstrations of therapy, you may have an oversimplified impression of the process of rational-emotive therapy, for in these demonstrations Ellis purposely focuses on only one or two problems. In ongoing therapy, it is also appropriate to focus on one problem at a time, but clients typically have multiple problems. An error that the novice rational-emotive therapist may make is to try to condense the client's problems into one. Instead, we recommend that you work on each problem separately but develop a treatment plan to assure that you don't neglect any problems or become mired in the client's complaints.

Treatment plans are frequently used at mental health clinics and psychiatric hospitals; they are also likely to be required by many third-party payment systems and appear to be an inevitable consequence of professional peer review systems. Treatment plans are best developed from a problem-oriented record system such as the one outlined below. Realize that not every therapist constructs treatment plans, nor will it be necessary to do so for each of your clients. We offer this model to help you understand the ongoing therapeutic process and as a guide for satisfying formal requirements to document treatment.

To begin a treatment plan, list each of the client's dysfunctional emotional reactions, behavioral excesses, and behavioral deficits; these are the emotional and behavioral aspects of the C. Look for relationships among these components and among the C's and their accompanying cognitions.

A Sample Treatment Plan

Table 16.1 provides a problem list that was developed over the first several sessions of assessment with a client. The next step is to arrange these problems in order of priority, which can best be done in consultation with the client. For each problem identified, plan behavioral and cognitive strategies. In addition, we recommend that you try to plan ahead for your next three sessions with the client, organizing how you will utilize your therapy hour in blocks of time. Keep your plan flexible, so that you remain

Table 16.1   Sample Problem List

Problems	Emotions	Cognitions	Behaviors
1. Relationship with boss	Anger, anxiety	He mustn't criticize me. It would be terrible if the boss doesn't like me.	Talking angrily to boss. Inefficiency at work due to time spent catastrophizing. Lack of assertive responses in repertoire.
2. Problems in dating	Anxiety	No one will ever like me. It's awful to get rejected.	Avoidance of social contact. Lack of social skills.
3. Relationship with mother	Guilt	I should visit my mother more often. I'm not a good son	Undesired daily phone calls with mother. Undesired Saturday night dinners at mother's house.
4. Obesity	Agitation when not eating, depression after eating	I've got to have what I want (LFT). It's hopeless; I'll never control it. I'm no good.	Overeating.

sensitive to your client's immediate concerns; yet be alert to and guard against distractions. If your client brings in a new problem every week, you may lose sight of your original goals. Another purpose of a treatment plan, therefore, is to help the therapist and client remain on track.

The following treatment plan was constructed after four sessions with the client whose problem list is presented in Table 16.1. You may find this plan useful as a general model.

Session 5

Problem 1

1. Check on homework assignments from previous week.
2. If client was successful, reinforce him; if unsuccessful, trouble-shoot.
3. Continue disputing the irrational demands creating anger at client's boss.
4. Dispute awfulizing about obtaining boss's approval.
5. Teach and role-play some assertive responses for client to use at work.
6. Give homework assignment: (a) read *Your Perfect Right* (Alberti and Emmons, 1974), (b) implement the behavior rehearsed in session with the boss, (c) monitor work efficiency, and when off-task, use as a cue to do A-B-C-D homework sheet on catastrophizing.

Problem 2

7. If time permits, begin inquiry into client's anxiety in social situations.

Session 6
Problem 1

1. Check on homework assignments from previous session; reinforce or trouble-shoot.
2. Review disputation of IB's leading to client's anger or anxiety in work situation.
3. Role-play assertive responses in different hypothetical work situations to increase generalization.

4. Give homework assignment: (a) continue to read *Your Perfect Right* and begin *Overcoming Frustration and Anger* (Hauck, 1974), and (b) do homework sheets on anger and anxiety when work efficiency drops.

Problem 2

5. Dispute awfulizing about rejection.
6. Give homework assignment: do A-B-C-D homework sheet disputing fears of rejection.
7. Summarize major points in session and review homework assignments for coming week.

Session 7

Problem 1

1. Review homework assignment; reinforce or trouble-shoot.
2. Briefly review disputation of anger-producing beliefs.
3. Homework assignments: (a) continue monitoring work performance and do homework sheets as needed, and (b) continue trying to implement new assertive responses as needed.

Problem 2

4. Check homework sheet disputing fears of rejection. Reinforce or trouble-shoot.
5. Do rational-emotive imagery in dating situations to uncover anxiety, and do in-session disputing.
6. Begin social skills training: role-play asking a woman for a date.
7. Homework assignment for risk taking: attempt to elicit three rejections this week; if distressed, do homework sheet(s).

Session 8

Problems 1 and 2

1. Review and check on progress. Put problems 1 and 2 on working agenda for the session if needed.
2. Assign relevant homework.

Problem 3

3. Dispute beliefs about self-worth causing guilt.
4. If client appears to understand the disputation, check veracity of perception of the A.
5. Summarize major points of session and review homework assignments for coming week.

After reading this treatment plan, as a new rational-emotive therapist you may find it overwhelming. Is therapy so tightly organized, do therapists accomplish that much in every session, and do clients really move that quickly? Rest easy; the sample above is somewhat exaggerated and was designed to make three major points:

• It is important to work *consistently* on each of the problems outlined by the client. Notice how the therapist continues to work on the first problem across sessions. Although the percentage of time spent on this problem is reduced over sessions, therapeutic follow-up is built into the system. Therapist attention to this problem is faded slowly, principally by assignment and review of homework tasks, as the client improves.

• New problems are introduced *systematically* into treatment as the more significant problems show improvement.

• Note also the *multiplicity* of treatment strategies implemented. (Some of these strategies will be discussed below.)

While all of these steps might be taken in therapy, the number of steps per problem, number of problems per session, and number of sessions required to accomplish each goal varies widely from client to client and for the same client at different points in therapy.

Note that each session begins with a review of homework (usually a written disputation by the patient) and a review of a previous disputation in session; in both instances the therapist is checking to see if the client has thoroughly understood the D. If your client has not comprehended the D or is having problems with the homework sheet, trouble-shooting is called for (see p. 208).

New therapists frequently experience impatience or even anger at the client who makes mistakes. Monitor your reactions in this situation. If you are impatient, look for your own irrational beliefs—specifically, that the client *should* have felt better or at least have performed better. Be careful that you are not rating *yourself* by your client's behavior. Disputation involves subtle and sophisticated philosophical points and taps skills that clients ordinarily do not use. Give yourself and your client permission to be beginners.

If your client has successfully worked out a homework sheet and has experienced a reduction in emotional stress during an in-session dispute, you may recognize one of two possible outcomes at this point:

> The client may continue to experience the old C somewhat regularly and will use this as a cue to utilize his or her rational-emotive skills as modeled in therapy. Disputation thus serves as a coping technique.
>
> A new C may emerge. If the patient has truly been able to replace the old IB's with more rational philosophies, the original A's will automatically be followed by more appropriate emotional reactions. When well practiced, the new RB's will tend to become as automatic to the client as the original IB's were.

Expanding the Focus of Therapy

Question: Who are the most depressed people in America?

Answer: Women, especially married women.

Answer: Women, especially married women.

Question: What happens when they go into therapy for their depression?

Answer: They get better, but their husbands (or their marriages) may get worse!

When a person starts to change, it is important to recognize that the change may have implications—provide activating events—for other family members. They may be happy to see the change or become distressed about it, find it threatening, and even attempt to sabotage it. You will want to assess any ripple effects of the psychotherapy in the family.

Thus far we have written about RET as if it were only conducted in the context of individual therapy. What we would like to suggest at this point, however, is that RET and the host of cognitive-behavioral strategies incorporated under it may appropriately be used for couples, families, or groups. As your skills in managing the RET model grow, we recommend that you *plan* to invite family members into the sessions. In this

Can you see how it might be helpful for the wife of a man with erectile problems to be present in sessions—to share the process as an observer? What benefits might accrue as she watched the therapist work with her husband? List three.

_____

_____

_____

Would the issues be different if the husband were watching the therapist work with his wife on her depression?

way, you can independently assess the changes in your client and how this change affects others, perhaps thereby forestalling negative reactions from the family. You may be able to teach family members what you and the client are working on. In fact, with your client's agreement, it may be very helpful to conduct some therapy *in the presence* of family members or the client's spouse, as long as the "other" can remain a largely silent observer.

It is possible to do individual RET within a family context, by having other family members present as participant-observers, and with the therapist actively coaching helpful responses and modeling therapeutic interactions. Often, other issues will come up in a family meeting that expand the individual's psychotherapeutic work.

Comprehensive family therapy within an RET context is beyond the scope of this book, but you will find helpful reading suggestions on such topics in Chapter 18.

If family members are not available for sessions, some therapists make use of an "empty chair" strategy: as an issue is being discussed, the therapist might say, "What do you think your husband would say to this if he were sitting right over there?"

Continuing Therapy

In many cases, after the client's presenting problem has been resolved, the patient will continue to make appointments or request a continuation of therapy. What do you do then? You listen. Very often the behavioral changes made in therapy will provide clients with new social opportunities which they may not have the skills to handle. For example, the formerly obese man may now find himself confronted with new dating issues or find that colleagues at work have higher expectations of output from him. A formerly nonassertive, reclusive housewife may encounter new problems as she finds a job and adjusts to the working world. In other words, although there may no longer be evidence of psychopathology, the client may profit from continued therapeutic work.

In other instances, clients may bring up new problems when they experience some relief from the original ones. This pattern may be viewed as a figure-ground effect; as the primary problem (figure) gets resolved, it recedes and minor problems (background) come into relief. This is *not* an example of *symptom substitution,* a term which implies that curing one problem leads to an increase in or the development of other problems. Rather, the client may now have the time and energy to focus on less pressing issues. With low socioeconomic status clients, who seem to live by "crisis management," a new "figure" may be presented to the therapist each week.

When clients do bring in new problems they may, at some point in therapy, become discouraged, making dire predictions of a gloomy future filled with problems for which they must continue to get professional help. At such times, it is useful to have patients recollect their earlier problems, now in the background; point these out to them and reinforce your patients lavishly for the progress they have already achieved. An analogy such as the following one may also be helpful: "If you go to your physician with fourteen splinters in your hand, even after five are out, your hand may still hurt because nine more remain. It just takes more work." Remember that your patient's confidence in allowing you to go on removing "psychological splinters" may waver unless you point out that five have already been removed. Pointing out the figure-ground analogy discussed above might also be useful. If you have a minor cut on your finger, sore feet, and a pounding headache and then receive a punch in the nose, you probably won't notice the first three troubles until the pain of the last one recedes.

Is RET a short-term therapy? This question is asked by patients (e.g., "How long will I have to be in treatment?") as well as by insurance companies.

The cognitive-behavioral therapies in general, and RET in particular, are known to be fast-acting, and we have seen patients catapulted into positive changes in mood and behavior in just a few sessions. However, it would be foolhardy to conclude that *all* patients are or *should* be able to respond so quickly.

Under what conditions do clients tend to remain in therapy for longer periods of time? The following list, although not complete, provides some answers to this question.

Protracted A's, such as a difficult divorce

Chronic, albeit intermittent conditions, such as physical disability, or certain affective illnesses

Axis I conditions compounded by an Axis II diagnosis

Behaviorally undefinable goals, for example, existential dilemmas or self-actualization issues

Clients' narcissistic entertainment in hearing themselves talk, and enjoying the therapy hour for this reason alone

Periodic progress reviews are recommended as a routine part of therapy. Patients come to therapy because they are in pain, and as soon as it is alleviated they tend not to think about it or how the relief was accomplished. We all tend to forget the stone that was in our shoe yesterday. If patients are made aware of the pain reduction and how it was accomplished, they will be more likely to use the same techniques in the future. If you think that patients have made gains which are not clear to them, you needn't hesitate to point these out and show how you think they were accomplished.

Also, ask your clients for periodic feedback on the therapy experience. They can usually recall what preceded an "Aha!" reaction, and this feedback may be a rich source of information for you. In addition, their comments may reinforce your therapeutic interventions. Ask the following kinds of questions: "How did I help you?" or "How could I have helped you more?" and "Was there anything I did that interfered with my helping you?" Some therapists (e.g., Beck et al., 1978) ask these questions

Beginning therapists have a high probability of being assigned patients who are chronically disturbed, characterologically disordered, and minimally motivated—that is, those patients least likely to participate actively in therapy and profit greatly from it. The novice therapist may erroneously end up concluding, "RET really doesn't work" or "I'm no good as a therapist." As the therapist gains experience, he or she learns to set very limited goals for such patients and to be pleased with small changes.

at the end of every therapy hour, not only for personal feedback but also to identify any lingering irrational beliefs or to correct misperceptions.

The periodic review may also help prepare for the client's termination. Terminating is often uncomfortable for clients; for example, they may feel that they need an excuse to terminate, or that they will be unable to function independently after therapy has ended. When it is time for a review, therefore, you may also ask, "How are we doing in getting you closer to your goals? How much longer do you want to work together? When shall we schedule our next review?"

Termination of Therapy

In a sense, therapy provides ongoing preparation for termination. RET in particular, following an educational model, attempts to teach the client rational self-analysis skills which, hopefully, can be generalized to new problem situations. As the client improves, the therapist can do less of the disputing in the session and leave more of it to the client. We recommend that as sessions progress, you remain active but shift the content of your speech.

In early sessions, you will talk more about the IB's and why they are irrational. Toward the final sessions, you will comment more about how well your clients are disputing their own IB's. Thus, by the end of therapy, most patients have acquired some basic understanding of the theory of emotional disturbance and have learned some skills to combat it, so that you can merely guide them through the application of RET to specific problems.

When patients announce that they feel ready for termination and you agree that the goals outlined at the beginning of therapy have been met, you may wish to inquire if they have any new goals or issues that they wish to discuss. Such an invitation may be helpful to clients who feel inhibited about bringing up what they view as minor or unrelated problems. Occasionally, you may believe that clients are terminating before they are ready; the original goals may have been met, but the clients have a number of other significant issues with which you can help. By all means, bring these to their attention; however, if clients do not contract to work on them, you may be making an ethical error in insisting that they remain in therapy.

You may have to deal with your own perfectionist standards. Do you have an absolute "should" about how clients will perform at the end of therapy? Clients will not always arrive at the end points you'd prefer, and little will be achieved by pestering them or worrying whether they've gotten their money's worth. It is possible and acceptable for therapy to terminate before all goals are accomplished. In fact, some clients report that major gains occurred after therapy was terminated; there may be a significant lag time between learning the principles and deciding to implement them wholeheartedly. Of course, you may suggest to clients that you perceive them to be selling themselves short, and the merits of working on further problems can be discussed. Ultimately, however, it will be the client's choice.

WHEN IS THERAPY COMPLETED?

The question of when therapy is completed is frequently asked of us when we do supervision training. Poignantly, it is asked also by patients in the process of therapy. Clearly, there are no hard-and-fast rules to answer this question, and sometimes the end of therapy occurs for practical or financial reasons that are extraneous to the process. Nonetheless, there are some general criteria to offer the student or client in making the decision to terminate therapy.

Among these criteria, we have found ourselves discriminating between *necessary* and *sufficient* criteria; that is, some outcomes clearly seem to be important for termination, but perhaps are not sufficient for us to feel comfortable that the patient's gains can be maintained. One such criterion is *insight*. In the process of therapy, it is hoped that clients will understand the basic principles of RET. Either in the form of an "Aha!" or by gradually discovering a new idea that makes sense, we expect the client to understand the B–C connection that links thoughts to moods. If our goal is for clients eventually to function as their own therapist, they will need to

When is therapy done?

Have I acquired some new behaviors? Are they permanent habits?

Are my emotional responses more adaptive?

Am I able to laugh at myself and not take myself so seriously?

Am I able to tolerate frustrations better?

Am I coping by doing, instead of by avoiding?

Can I manage my own A-B-C's? Am I productively challenging my distressing cognitions?

Have I stopped blaming others and taken responsibility for my own misery?

Do I have fewer problems to work on?

Do I just feel better, or have I genuinely gotten better?

be able to analyze their problems, catch their self-talk, and recognize their own variations of common irrational beliefs. Insight may be necessary, but typically is not sufficient for successful termination.

The box on this page contains a list of possible criteria for termination, stated as questions, that you may find helpful to share with your clients when they express confusion about how they will know when it is time to end therapy. The list may be prepared as a handout, which will initiate discussion and exploration between the two of you.

New Habits

In one sense, therapy is *never* done. We may stop going to visit our therapist, but the process of managing our moods and behaviors is ongoing. We easily understand that we cannot make ourselves thin this year and then coast through the rest of life, eating whatever we want. We accept that we cannot get in shape with an exercise program and maintain our fitness without continued effort. In a similar way, cognitive therapy or rational-emotive living skills require maintenance.

Therapy is a prevention program for the rest of our lives. As Ellis (1975) has pointed out, we have a natural tendency to think irrationally. In RET, patients acquire new philosophies, and new philosophies, like other new habits, require maintenance work. As RET *therapists,* we get to practice these philosophies almost every day in our work with patients. Therefore, we might be the least likely to backslide—and yet we do! It is difficult to live rationally, and none of us are likely to be perfect at it. Even if the skills acquired in therapy have been neglected, however, we probably won't slide back to zero but with a little practice our unused skills will come back again fairly readily.

As we suggested above, insight is a necessary precursor to ending therapy, but not sufficient without behavior change. If one continues to behave in self-defeating ways, understanding why and articulating how one gives oneself permission to go on doing so is mere sophistry. Ideally, we would like our clients' changes in behavior to be stable across various situations and so automatic that they can be called habits. Even habits are fragile at first, however, and if not practiced will often be lost. If therapy ends before behavior change is stabilized, the outcome may be less than desirable, although not terrible. Clients can always return to therapy for booster shots and further practice if needed.

Even if termination occurs before the behavior seems to be habitual, the work may not have been a waste, although neither therapist nor client may realize it at the time. Many therapists have had the experience of hearing from a client, months or years after what seemed to be a relatively unsuccessful therapy, that the client was finally able to put into practice what were only words before. What happens in these cases is uncertain. Perhaps the client is in some way eventually ready to use the material. Perhaps the stimulus constraints are changed so that the client can hear the therapeutic messages better. Perhaps understanding occurs gradually, as in some of the maze learning studies from earlier decades in which animals that had not yet solved the maze were nonetheless outperforming naive animals. The learning may be incremental; working with some patients is like pouring materials through a sieve in which additional little pieces get caught each time the pouring is repeated. Some patients will learn quickly or experience sudden changes, and others may not complete the process while they are in therapy with you. Ideally, we would like to work with each client until behavior change is stabilized into new habits.

Emotive Reduction

Some schools of therapy seem to deal with intense emotion by encouraging the patient to deny or suppress it, or act as if the affect were not there. Other forms of therapy encourage expression of the emotion, as if emotions operated on a hydraulic model in which letting off steam was useful. Unfortunately, it is usually not healthy either to hold in emotions or to irresponsibly ventilate them. RET reminds us of a third, often forgotten option, which is to uproot the troublesome emotion and replace it with a different one. RET takes emotional distress as its starting point. It is the distressing affect and consequent disrupted behavior that bring patients to us in the first place.

When therapy gets bogged down, it is often because the patient is *not* bringing in affectively loaded material. In fact, some of the more prolonged courses of therapy have been with clients who were raised in families in which feelings were considered unseemly, uncomfortable, or at best, unnecessary. Often the first step in therapy with these clients is to help them to acknowledge their intense feelings and to share them in the safety of the therapeutic relationship.

The successful completion of therapy, therefore, does not mean that the patient is devoid of feelings, but rather that intense affect has become the trigger for practicing RET. In some instances, clients report that the A's that formerly set off distress are so well worked through that the clients' response is now emotionally neutral. More typically, however, the emotions are modulated in frequency, intensity (for both negative and positive feelings), and duration.

Laughing at Oneself

Various schools of therapy seem to hold divergent views on what might be called the "essence of man." Carl Rogers, for example, teaches that man is inherently loveable and deserves unconditional positive regard. Freud seemed to stress our evil nature and the necessity of developing adequate superego and ego strength to keep the "lid on the id." The broad position of cognitive therapy might be stated as follows: humans are not, in essence, any *one* thing; in other words, we are far too complex to be viewed simplistically. The *RET position* is basically in agreement, but adds that humans are merely fallible and full of imperfections—about which we would do well to hang onto our sense of humor!

Part of ending therapy is the recognition that we're more like other

Ask yourself: Would you want to advertise *everything* you did, thought, or felt each day?

Ask yourself: Deep down, what age do you really feel yourself to be?

We suspect that most people would report that inside, they feel a lot younger, sillier, and "crazier" then they may appear to others.

---

people than unlike other people. RET does not promote the idea that we are special because of our uniqueness as individuals. Rather, our *kinship* renders none of us special. The awareness of our kinship with others has a number of benefits, including reduction of personal perfectionism and the lessening of humiliation (e.g., "So, I goofed. We all do, from time to time"). It may also bolster our frustration tolerance ("It's not only hard for me; it's hard for everybody") and tolerance of others ("You won't believe what he did!" "Oh yes I would; we all do foolish things!"). Every human, by definition, is vulnerable to feeling, thinking, and behaving in a foolish or self-defeating manner.

Finally, from an aerial, if not existential, perspective we find it helpful to remind ourselves to look at the relative significance of life events. If you were observed from an airplane, you'd be only a speck on the map, and as the airplane passed by, your speck would be there for only an instant. The significance of our goofs and our accomplishments begins to recede, so that a more rational, light-hearted, and hedonic focus is possible. That is an elegant stance from which to consider termination of therapy!

Higher Frustration Tolerance

The client who is preparing to end therapy will no longer be surprised by frustrations, but will come to expect them. For example, one client concluded that if he didn't have at least ten frustrations in a day, it was because he probably hadn't yet gotten out of bed!

When something unfortunate happens, we may always say, "Oh, rats!" (or some more colorful expletive). When we've really learned our RET lessons, what happens next is where we really see the difference. We no longer get swept away by an emotional tide, but instead bring our skills into play.

Some of us can do even better than that. One colleague had a sibling and then a son diagnosed as having diabetes. Over the years, he gradually turned his reasearch and clinical interests to the topic of coping with diabetes. When congratulated on how elegantly he made "lemons into lemonade" he demurred, "It's funny. I don't even think of it as 'lemons'; it's just What Is." He had gone beyond frustration tolerance to a more advanced stage: acceptance.

Coping by Doing

By writing out A-B-C's, by talking them through, by going to therapy, the client is problem solving and actively trying to make changes. "Doing," in a behavioral paradigm, means actively searching for reinforcers, rather than settling for the avoidance of pain.

We have two choices in dealing with problems: we can either do nothing or do something. We can function as fighters or flee-ers, and RET tends to turn us into fighters. Why? When we remain anxious or depressed, we feel like powerless victims. Even when we function like "survivors," we are hunkering down; "standing it." The RET stance, by contrast, is exemplified by the person who says, "I can stand any problem until I solve it and work out a better plan." RET does not recommend mere stoicism, rationalizing, or passivity.

A passive stance doesn't teach us anything useful that we can generalize from one problem to the next. The passive person flees down a narrow path that leads to denial or dissociation. By contrast, the mental set of a do-er is more of an open field: "I won't necessarily do the same thing every time I have a problem, but I will *change the conditions* so that something else can happen." If we make errors, they are ones of commission, not omission; in that way, we see the problem as a challenge that will at least bring about a new set of conditions.

PREMATURE TERMINATION

Some clients come in after just a few sessions announcing complete success. In these instances of "flight into health," it is extremely important to ask the patients how they account for the change. Have they improved because they've applied RET principles? Have they changed for the wrong reasons (e.g., to please the therapist)? Have they improved because the obnoxious A's in their lives are less frequent? As a check on clients' improvement, you may ask them to think of examples of problems that they used to upset themselves over but now do not, and to explain *why*. The last part of this question highlights cognitive change and enables the therapist to evaluate whether clients are in fact thinking more helpfully.

If a client terminates abruptly, without notification, what is the appropriate course of action? Many clinics send the client a letter noting the failure to keep an appointment and offering further treatment if desired. A phone call by the therapist is acceptable in most cases; although more intrusive, it may also be more informative to the therapist and helpful to the client. If you do not know the client well, however, a phone call may not be desirable. For example, some patients may have kept their foray into therapy a secret from family members; leaving a message may prove awkward, and even if the patient is at home, he or she may not feel able to talk openly. In any case, it is recommended that you contact no patient more than once, since doing otherwise may legally be viewed as harassment.

In many instances, because of external factors, clients terminate therapy before either they or you feel they are ready. It would be helpful for you to stop and ask yourself, "This may be my last session to work with the patient. How can I structure the session so that it will be of maximal value to him [or her]?" Here are some suggestions:

1. Ask the client what he or she wants to accomplish in the final session(s).

2. Try to elicit a recapitulation of the therapy: why the client originally came to treatment, what has been learned, and what the client still wants to change. You may then compare your own ideas on these three questions and share them with the client.

3. Suggest a continuation of behavioral assignments to fill the gap after therapy ends. Assignments may also serve as a reminder of the concepts you have taught the patient.

If clients are terminating therapy because of a geographical move, you can discuss whether they plan to resume therapy in the new location. It may be possible for you to make a referral to another RET professional or to suggest how patients can go about locating a new therapist. The Institute for Rational-Emotive Therapy has a referral list of RET therapists in the United States and abroad.*

It is also helpful to point out to clients that the move itself may be a life stressor. In this way, patients may be prepared for backsliding, if it

---

*This list may be ordered by writing to the Institute at 45 East 65th Street, New York, NY 10021, and sending three dollars to cover mailing costs.

occurs, and be given a non–self-blaming *attribution* for it. Otherwise, they may view any new emotional distress as evidence that they are *never* going to get better, which may induce further panic and depression, or a decision to stop working at therapy. Understanding and accepting their backsliding may help patients to move forward in their future work with therapy.

At termination, some patients may not readily discuss their reactions to this change but instead act in a depressed manner. In this instance, you would respond to body language and voice inflection cues and comment on this behavior. Later in the sesssion, you may wish to add, "You know, if you hadn't been my patient, I have a feeling we could have been good friends. I feel badly about not seeing you in the future. How do you feel about our terminating?" If you avoid such a confrontation, patients may never receive this message or have the opportunity to discuss what may have been a very significant relationship in their lives.

Enhancing Treatment Benefits after Termination

It is helpful to send clients off with some final recommendations for how to continue to profit from therapy after regular therapy sessions have ended. The task is to maximize generalization from therapy to real life, and thus extend the results of treatment over time and new life issues. The following list of suggestions, adapted from the work of Norma Campbell, may be prepared as a handout for patients. Go over it carefully with them, and urge your clients to refer to it often.

How Can I Enhance the Benefits of Therapy?

Read—Keep your texts handy, read new RET books and articles, reread helpful passages.

Think—Rehearse your RET skills; try keeping a "healthy self-talk" journal; use pencil and paper to dispute when you feel yourself getting upset.

Practice—Every day, practice increasing your frustration tolerance. Do something hard. Scary. Boring. With no immediate pay-off. This exercise will build your frustration tolerance, help you control your temper, and lead to honestly earned self-respect and pride.

Build—Empathy and tolerance can be built by trying daily to do something kind: pay a compliment, listen to the other side, give a gift of time or interest—with no payoffs.

Prevent—To avert a return of perfectionism and grandiosity, every day do one of these: yield gracefully, apologize and admit your mistake, laugh at yourself when you goof, make a mistake on purpose, ask yourself, "So what if I goofed? How terrible is that?"

Promote—Happiness. Every day, do something fun. When you have a good time, remember it and tell someone else about it.

Ellis (1984, p. 3) adds two more good points:

> Try to keep in touch with several other people who know something about RET and who can help go over some of its aspects with you. Tell them about problems that you have difficulty coping with and let them know how you are using RET to overcome these problems. See if they agree with your solutions and can suggest additional and better kinds of RET disputing that you can use to work against your irrational beliefs. . . .
>
> Practice using RET with some of your friends, relatives, and associates who are willing to let you try to help them with it. The more often you use it with others, and are able to see what their IB's are and to try to talk them out of these self-defeating ideas, the more you will be able to understand the main principles of RET and to use them with yourself. When you see other people act irrationally and in a disturbed manner, try to figure out—with or without talking to them about it—what their main irrational beliefs probably are and how these could be actively and vigorously disputed.

BOOSTER SHOTS

After your clients have terminated therapy, they may occasionally find reasons to call for an appointment or to resume therapy for a brief period. Before terminating, therefore, be sure they understand that there is no stigma to coming back for further work, which you might suggest is analogous to getting immunization booster shots. The future probably holds new challenges that they may want to discuss with you, and it would be incorrect to assume that no further problems will emerge or that clients who have successfully learned RET principles will henceforth be *absolutely* rational.

Many therapists find, in fact, that a particularly satisfying aspect of their work is serving as the family psychologist. New therapists who train with Dr. Ellis soon realize that he often has a multigenerational portrait of a given client because he recalls working with the client's mother or other relative. Communicate that it is not only OK for the client or his or her family members to return for help as needed, but welcomed by you.

Part VI
Training

17 Supervision and Further Training

We hope that you have not been working through this book purely at an intellectual level, but that you have been practicing RET skills on yourself and on your clients. Learning to do therapy is much like learning to sew or ski or perform any complex skill: reading about it simply doesn't do the trick. At one level, RET is easy to learn, but as almost all of our students have discovered, it is a difficult therapy to do, especially artfully. The best way to acquire and polish your skills is to get some supervision and feedback.

One student, midway through a year-long training program in the cognitive therapies, described it very well: "Learning to do cognitive therapy is like trying to find the starting place on a new roll of plastic kitchen wrap. Just when you think you have it, it eludes you again—it's simple, but not easy!"

What if I don't have a client? If you are not working in a clinical setting you can practice your therapy skills on yourself or on a friend. The only caveat we would offer is that you'll need to find a friend who is willing to present a Real Problem. Too often we have found that if a friend is simulating a patient, the absence of a true state of affective distress means that you will have a hard time targeting B's. In order for RET to work, the underlying assumption must be met: the patient has emotional distress. If not, the experience is not likely to be a good learning exercise for either of you.

There are a variety of ways to obtain supervisory feedback, including self-supervision, peer supervision, finding a certified local RET supervisor, mailing in tapes to an RET supervisor, or enrolling in a training program in your geographic area or at the Institute in New York City.

No matter what form of supervision you choose, prepare yourself by doing your homework (see below, "How to prepare for supervision"), and more important, by getting your ego off the line; accepting this as a learning experience, accepting yourself as an RET beginner (although you may otherwise be an experienced clinician), and accepting that a modicum of concern or tension is normal in a training situation. If your anxiety level begins to soar before sessions or your mood plummets afterward, be sure to capture that mood and the attendant cognitions as grist for your own therapy mill. Conquering your supervision anxieties is a great way to practice and master RET.

Self-Checking Supervision

Actively begin supervising yourself. One way to monitor your progress in learning to do RET is to evaluate your sessions on a regular basis and to have your patient do the same. Checklists are useful as standards against which to compare your work. Here are some suggested items:

Was the session actively structured?

Were you able to specifically elicit the client's thoughts and feelings?

Could you identify any major irrational beliefs? Automatic thoughts? Underlying assumptions?

Were these IB's, automatic thoughts, and underlying assumptions challenged?

What were the results of the challenge?

Were homework assignments given?

Did you help the client to stay on task?

How did you feel about the therapist–client relationship?

Who was leading the session, you or the client?

Did you feel you were offering advice? Was it appropriate?

Did you do any problem solving? Was it effective?

Was there closure at the end of the session?

A somewhat more elaborate checklist, used at the Institute for Rational-Emotive Therapy in New York, is the "Session Notes" in Appendix A. As you practice using this form for each therapy session, you will find that it also begins to function as a cueing device to remind you of strategies to implement.

A "Patient's Report of Therapy" has been used in some training programs in cognitive-behavior therapy. A helpful form of feedback in your personal training may be to have your patients fill out a form of this type.

Obtaining Supervision

Our experience as training supervisors has led us to the firm conviction that the expedient way to do supervision is when we can work from a videotape or audiotape of your work with clients. Process notes, used in supervision in other forms of psychotherapy, are not as helpful because we cannot get "on line" data about the content or the form of the therapist's intervention, and of course we miss the nuances of the patient's communications. We strongly urge, therefore, that you begin taping your sessions with patients in preparation for work with your supervisor.

Preparing the patient. The American Psychological Association committee on professional ethics and conduct states that *during the onset of a professional relationship with a client, the client should be informed of the psychologist's intended use of supervisors.* Patients should be told the general nature of the information that will be disclosed. Failure to do so violates the client's right to privacy. Even if the client's name or other personal information is not revealed, the psychologist should obtain informed consent in writing prior to discussing the case with a supervisor or a peer.

If you are going to record sessions, we suggest that you prepare a written consent form for the patient to sign, and that you keep a copy and give one to the supervisor as well. Here is a sample consent form used in one training program:

Don't forget that many patients also profit enormously from listening to the recordings of the sessions. Try to assess whether your patient would also like to review the tapes.

I understand that my therapist, Dr. _____, will be studying princi-ples of cognitive therapy and rational-emotive therapy and will be having his or her work supervised. The purpose of the supervision will be for the further development of my therapist's skills; the super-visor will have no responsibility for the management of my case.

I further understand that my therapist may play segments of audiotapes of my therapy sessions for purposes of supervision. I freely consent to allowing my therapist to play tape segments and/or discussing our work with a supervisor.

Preparing yourself. Relax. Remember, supervision is a learning experience, not an attempt to evaluate you personally. You may become aware of conflicting desires in yourself, that is, the desire to receive suprvisory help and at the same time to impress your supervisor with how little help you need! You may simultaneously experience the desire to improve your skills and the desire to deny any lack of competence.

These conflicting desires or the presence of performance anxiety pro-vide you with an opportunity to do your own RET. Pull out your pad of paper and write out your A-B-C's, do your disputation work, and see if you can construct some more helpful beliefs—and then make this work the first item on your agenda to review with your supervisor. You'll be surprised how much you can learn from this little exercise.

Preparing your tapes. This may sound obvious, but it bears repeating: spend some time doing audio checks before you tape your sessions. Make sure that the tape recorder's microphone is sensitive enough to pick up both your voice and that of the client, even when the client is speaking in a muffled or emotional voice. Sometimes it helps to invest in either an external or plug-in microphone, or in external speakers for playback. Certainly it is worthwhile to invest in voice-quality audiotapes. There is nothing more frustrating to the student and the supervisor than to dis-cover that the tapes are not audible.

Decide which tape to play, and listen to it once through, noting on your tape recorder's counter the segments that might be relevant for su-pervision. Then select one or two such segments to play for your super-visor. You will probably only be able to play ten to twenty minutes of tape, because you'll want to allow enough time for questions and discus-sion. As a point of etiquette, therefore, it is a good idea to have your tape cued up and ready to play back.

Ask yourself: "What do I want the supervisor to listen for? What do I

Helpful therapy is not the same as good therapy. "Good" therapy is what the therapist does, not how well the client responds to it. Be sure to present "good" and "bad" sessions. You may not recognize errors in the former or the good work in the latter (especially if you cop out by not playing the latter!).

want help with? Do I want feedback on what I think is 'good work' or do I want help with my problem moments?"

Decide whether you want to obtain case management supervision, skill acquisition supervision, or both. Write down any specific questions you have for your supervisor. If you don't have a tape to play, these questions become particularly important in helping you to maximize your supervision time.

Do try to *actively use* the feedback you get from the supervisor. If your supervisor has given you a suggestion to implement, try to do so in your next session with the client. You might even tell the client that the strategy was suggested in your supervision work. Be sure to tell the supervisor if his or her suggestion was useful. Supervisors need feedback, too.

Locating a supervisor. If you are not in one of the formal training programs available (see below), you may want to purchase individual supervision hours with a local RET supervisor in your community. To find out if such a person exists, you can write to the Institute in New York City, where a list of certified RET supervisors is maintained. Alternatively, you can request that this list be sent to you and then write to a supervisor of your choice and arrange to do your tape supervision by mail. In the latter case, it is useful to send the supervisor (a) a brief write-up on the patient, the point in the session at which the tape is cued for feedback, and any questions you have formulated; (b) a blank tape for the supervisor to record feedback; and (c) a prestamped, self-addressed envelope to ensure rapid return of your work.

Although your supervisor can probably review your therapy tape without any preliminary information, you both will profit more from the work if you provide some background about the case. Here are the instructions for presenting client tapes used at the Institute for RET in New York.

Be prepared to quickly describe:

1. Identifying data: first name, age, sex, marital status, and ethnic group.
2. Social history: brief overview of the client's social, family, and love relationships, past and present.
3. Work history: brief description of educational background, and current and past enployment.
4. Previous treatment history.
5. Presenting problems as the *client* sees them.
6. Client's irrational beliefs as *you* see them.
7. Behavioral excesses and inhibitions.
8. Affective state (e.g., depressed, anxious, flat, manic, euphoric, normal range).
9. Client's fears and goals.
10. Major coping strategies used in the past. For example: How does the client handle anxiety? Mention passivity, hyperactivity, drug or alcohol abuse, overeating, promiscuity, isolation, and so on.
11. Physical problems, such as illness, deformities, or chronic medications.
12. Any family history of serious psychological disturbance.
13. Purpose of presenting this segment of the tape.
14. Your diagnosis, treatment recommendations, and assessment of work in progress.
15. Reinforcers of inappropriate behavior.
16. Homework assignments given.
17. Summary of your current assessment of the problem(s).

In addition, you will find it helpful to organize your thoughts on the following topics.

Goal of the particular session

Problems and good points in this session

How you feel about this client: issues of transference or countertransference

What your goals are from the supervision

If you have a local supervisor. You could consider inviting one or more colleagues to share supervision time with you. Many students have found that in addition to lowering the cost of supervision, the benefit of listening to the work of others is an effective way to learn concepts and skills.

If you are doing supervision in a small group, there are a number of formats that may be useful. Discuss these with the supervisor and other supervisees, and consider experimenting with them to see if they meet your educational needs. Here are some group supervision formats that we have found helpful.

Round robin—Each student comes perpared with an issue to put on the group's agenda; typically, the student will play a segment of tape for specific feedback. The focus may be case management, basic clinical skill development, or specific RET skill development. A description of this model is given in Wessler and Ellis (1980).

Problem focus—Either the student or the supervisor may select the problem focus for the session. It may be general in nature or follow from a difficult case. For example, the meeting may focus on how to manage suicidal patients, establish a working alliance with a hostile or suspicious client, or motivate the reluctant client to do homework. One or two such items can fill the agenda for a one- to two-hour supervisory session. A description of this model may be found in Childress and Burns (1983).

Apprenticeship model—The supervisor may elect to offer individual students the opportunity to come into his or her practice and work with a patient directly in co-therapy. Alternatively, one supervisee may role-play therapy as a co-therapist with the supervisor in the supervision group. This strategy is very powerful and can provide an active forum for learning. Details of this model can be found in Moorey and Burns (1983).

Whatever the group format, keeping members actively involved will help your learning. Some suggestions for doing so might include:

Selective listening—One person listens to the tape for automatic thoughts, another for the presence of client affect, another for therapist affect, another for collaborative set, and so forth.

"Pitch in"—Each member of the group is asked to come up with one suggestion for how to handle an issue. For example, "What could you say if your client says or does . . . ?"

Feedback—Have the group listen to a sample of work in which the novice therapist is trying to follow suggestions from a previous supervision meeting. Group members can offer constructive criticism or positive feedback to what they hear.

Monitor the case—Group members can examine the case in terms of case management or research issues, or similarities to cases in their

A positive aspect of doing rational-emotive therapy is that the therapist can get some fairly direct feedback that it is working. The client may experience a momentary or sustained feeling of relief, a look of insightful recognition, or a changed philosophy, or may begin to laugh at himself or herself. Experienced clinicians can often tell within the first session or two whether the client is a good candidate for RET and if it will be an *effective* and *sufficient* tool. As a beginner, you will certainly want to be cautious in making such judgments, but if you have done six to eight sessions with your client and your work has had no impact, you would do well to stop and take stock.

You may need to get some supervision to find out whether you are (a) using RET appropriately with this client, (b) assuming that your client is motivated when, in fact, he or she is unmotivated or has motives counter to therapy, or (c) are making a diagnostic error. For example, you may be trying to do RET with a client who needs antidepressant, antipsychotic, or antianxiety medication in addition to psychotherapy.

own experience, or reading assignments to help the presenting supervisee.

Role-playing—The supervisor can role-play the patient and one or more supervisees can act as the therapist. Other group members can be asked to discuss what the pair is doing and why.

Modeling—The supervisor models as the therapist and one group member models as the client; then the group discusses what was done and why.

HOW YOUR WORK IS RATED

At the beginning level, your supervisor will evaluate your tape with a simple "yes" or "no" decision on the following five items:

1. Identified the activating event
2. Identified the emotional and/or behavioral consequences
3. Identified irrational beliefs
4. Disputed philosophically
5. Assigned homework

If your tape were being rated as part of the Primary Practicum training program (see the "Training Program" section which follows), the supervisor would also rate your general knowledge of RET and your potential as a rational-emotive therapist (A = excellent; B = very good; C = average; D = inadequate). More elaborate ratings are done at the advanced training levels (see "Fellowship," below).

Some common errors that new therapists make are:

Telling the client what to do—Lecturing encourages passivity rather than active learning on the part of the client.

Arguing—Arguing with the client is not the same as persuading, either in tone or content, and may reflect the therapist's impatience.

Judging—The client is concerned that he or she had done something wrong, and the therapist says, "There's nothing wrong with that!"

Mind-reading—The client is concerned about her son's behavior, and the therapist says, "Maybe he was just angry."

Banal advice-giving—For example, "Look out for Number 1."

Being sarcastic—Especially in the early stages of therapy when the working alliance is somewhat fragile, humor should be used carefully or it may be misunderstood.

Making irrational demands of the client—For example, the therapist may go too quickly, assuming that if the client can do one A-B-C that she has mastered the disputation.

Being passive—The therapist may tend to support rather than confront the client, listen too much, or generally avoid taking a direct approach.

Not using RET tools—The therapist may not adequately know or believe the theory, not fully try the therapy, or even suffer from the same irrational beliefs as the client!

Training Programs

THE INSTITUTE FOR RATIONAL-EMOTIVE THERAPY

The Institute offers two categories of training programs: basic *Practica* and the more in-depth *Clinical Fellowship* and *Internship* program. The practica are available at three levels: Primary Certificate, Advanced Certificate, and Associate Fellowship. The practica are brief one- to two-day training programs for which no certificate is awarded, but satisfactory completion of a two-and-a-half to three-day program results in the awarding of a *Primary Certificate* in RET. Primary Certificate programs are available in New York City and other sites; for example, three-day programs were recently scheduled in Las Vegas, Chicago, and Tampa.

The next level of training is the Advanced Program. Candidates complete a five-day Advanced Practicum (typically held twice a year in two locations), consisting of special-topic seminars, and are supervised on at least five tapes of cases from their caseload. Successful completion of this program results in an *Advanced Certificate*.

Once these two certificates have been earned, trainees may go on to the Associate Fellowship program, which is the highest level of external training provided by the Institute. During a twelve-month period, candidates submit twenty sessions for individual case supervision. Ten tapes are evaluated in twenty-minute segments, and ten are full-session evaluations. One additional tape is then submitted to the International Training Standards and Review Committee for final evaluation. Successful completion of the training makes the candidate eligible for *Associate Fellowship membership* at the Institute.

The two most comprehensive programs of study offered by the Institute are the Fellowship and Internship programs. Each is an eleven-month part-time program; the Fellowship is a two-year course and the Internship is one year. In addition to more in-depth training in RET and cognitive-behavioral methods, the trainees serve as therapists in the Institute's clinic. They co-lead a therapy group with Albert Ellis, conduct their own (group) therapy sessions, and participate in four-and-a-half hours of individual and group supervision per week. Supervision rating forms for work performed at the fellowship level are given in Appendix B. Upon completion of the training, graduates may be eligible for fellowship status at the Institute and be invited to join the treatment center as staff psychotherapists or faculty members.

Finally, the Institute sponsors Advanced Training Practica in Supervision as well as Advanced "Refresher" Practica. A catalogue entitled "Professional Training Programs," which also includes a list of books, tapes, pamphlets, software, and even T-shirts, is available from the Institute by phoning (202) 535–0822 or writing to the Institute for RET, 45 East 65th Street, New York, NY 10021–6593.

OTHER PROGRAMS

In addition to courses and workshops in RET available at affiliate centers in the United States and abroad (e.g., Mexico, Italy, and Australia), training is available at the center for Cognitive Therapy at the University of Pennsylvania, affiliated with the Department of Psychiatry under the direction of Aaron T. Beck, M.D. The Center has an intramural fellowship program (one year) and an extramural program, in which participants visit the Center three times a year for weekend workshops and receive weekly supervision either in person or by telephone from tapes mailed to the supervisors. Further information can be obtained from the Center for Cognitive Therapy, 133 South 36th Street, Suite 602, Philadelphia, PA 19104.

18 Readings

This chapter presents an annotated bibliography of books, articles, and tape recordings that the rational–emotive therapist-in-training may wish to either draw upon when confronted with specific clinical problems or recommend to clients. In fact, one of the great strengths of RET is the availability of resource materials for clients and therapists, in print and on tape. Although this resource list is far from complete, we hope it will provide a basis for the continued study of cognitive-learning therapy.

The chapter is organized by major topics. Under each heading, we provide a list of professional references, followed by materials appropriate for clients to listen to or read. Some of these materials (especially the pamphlets and tapes) can be purchased directly from the Institute for Rational-Emotive Therapy at 45 East 65th Street, New York, NY 10021; many of the books are also available at bookstores or through direct mail.

Introductory Materials: RET and Other Cognitive Therapies

FOR THE PROFESSIONAL

Cognitive Therapy and the Emotional Disorders, by A. Beck. New York: International Universities Press, 1976. This is Beck's first major text, and it traces the development of his cognitive approach to psychopathology and psychotherapy, which in many aspects is parallel to RET. Beck discusses how cognitions relate to emotions and deals specifically with depression, anxiety, phobias, obsessions, and psychosomatic disorders.

The Essential Albert Ellis: Seminal Writings on Psychotherapy, edited by W. Dryden. New York: Springer Publishing, 1990. This book contains Albert Ellis' most important theoretical and clinical writings on rational-emotive therapy. In the theory section Ellis' views are presented on the theory of personality, the biological basis of human irrationality, the RET view of the self, the construct of discomfort anxiety, and the constructivist underpinnings of RET. The clinical practice section includes papers on intimacy in RET, the use of rational humorous songs in psychotherapy, the importance of force and energy in behavior change, the value of efficiency in psychotherapy, and three articles on failure and resistance to change in RET. Each section is introduced by an up-to-date view on the general theory and basic practice of RET.

Handbook of Rational-Emotive Therapy (Volumes I and II), by A. Ellis and R. Grieger. New York: Springer Publishing, 1977 and 1986. Together these two paperback volumes constitute the most comprehensive collection of papers on RET. Each volume has the following major sections: theoretical and conceptual foundations of RET, dynamics of emotional disturbance, primary techniques and basic processes in RET, and specialized applications of RET (e.g., group therapy, women's issues, children's therapy, and family therapy). Contributors include Arnold Lazarus, Aaron Beck, Michael Mahoney, Donald Meichenbaum, and other prolific RET writers.

Cognitive-Behavioural Approaches to Psychotherapy, edited by W. Dryden and W. Golden. London: Harper & Row, 1986. This book looks at different approaches to cognitive-behavior therapy. Chapters are structured around discussions of theory, major assumptions, the etiology and perpetuation of emotional disturbance, and therapeutic style and major strategies. Each chapter also includes a case study.

Overcoming Resistance, by A. Ellis. New York: Springer Publishing, 1985. Ellis outlines common forms of client resistance and their determinants, making an important distinction between healthy and unhealthy resistance. He enumerates many cognitive, emotive, and behavioral methods that therapists can use to help clients overcome their unhealthy resistance, including the use of "force," energy, and vividness. A particularly interesting chapter focuses on the resistances of therapists, which can lead the helping professional to be his or her own "most difficult client." We think this is the best of Ellis' recent books for practitioners; it provides many explicit clinical interventions.

Pamphlets and Journals

The following series of pamphlets published by the Institute for Rational Living offers guidance to therapists in handling specific questions about the principles of rational-emotive therapy.

"An Answer to Some Objections in Rational-Emotive Psychotherapy," by A. Ellis (originally appeared in *Psychotherapy: Theory, Research and Practice,* 1965). This paper may be particularly useful before you face your first client or first class in which you try to defend RET.

"Showing Clients They Are Not Worthless Individuals," by A. Ellis (reprinted from *Voices* and originally appeared in 1965) outlines Ellis' position on human worth.

"The Neurotic Agreement in Psychotherapy," by Paul Hauck (originally appeared in *Rational Living* in 1966). This paper is particularly good reading for the new therapist. The neurotic agreement to which Hauck refers is the psychotherapist's irrational notion that all of his or her patients must get better swiftly, a belief that the author disputes nicely.

"What Really Causes Psychotherapeutic Change?" by A. Ellis (originally appeared in *Voices,* 1968).

For the student who plans to become a serious scholar of RET and cognitive-behavioral therapy, we recommend subscribing to the two major journals in this topic area.

Journal of Rational-Emotive and Cognitive-Behavioral Therapy, edited by R. Grieger and P. Woods, published by Human Sciences Press. This journal publishes research, theoretical discussions, descriptions of clinical procedures, and case studies, as well as brief book reviews. In recent years, the journal has published special-topic issues, for example, women's issues, medical problems, and couples therapy.

Journal of Cognitive Psychotherapy: An International Quarterly, edited by T. Dowd (consulting editor, W. Dryden), published by Springer Publishing. This journal provides a forum for theoretical, case study, and research articles on all types of cognitive behavior therapies, as well as for articles promoting the integration of cognitive psychotherapies with other systems.

FOR THE CLIENT

A New Guide to Rational Living, by A. Ellis and R. Harper. North Hollywood, CA: Wilshire Books, 1975. This is the granddaddy of self-help books in RET. Ellis and Harper introduce rational-emotive theory and explain how the techniques can be used by nonprofessionals to solve their own emotional problems. Included are such topics as "how far you can go with self-analysis, how you create your own feelings, recognizing and attacking neurotic behaviors, overcoming the influences of the past, controlling your own destiny, and conquering anxiety." This is probably the most commonly recommended self-help book used by rational-emotive therapists.

A Guide to Personal Happiness, by A. Ellis and I. Becker. North Hollywood, CA: Wilshire Books, 1982. This self-help book emphasizes not only how to use RET to relieve emotional disturbance, but also how to increase your happiness, sense of well-being, and satisfaction with life. Included are chapters on overcoming shyness and feelings of inadequacy, coping with depression and low frustration tolerance, overcoming sex problems, and dealing with work problems. An important feature of the book is its appendix, which provides numerous suggestions for enjoyable pursuits.

Think Your Way to Happiness, by W. Dryden and J. Gordon. London: Sheldon Press, 1990. This is the first RET self-help book written by British authors. It deals in a clear, no-nonsense fashion with the following emotional problems: anxiety and worry, depression, guilt, anger and hostility, love, shame and embarrassment, and self-discipline. It shows how the irrational beliefs that underlie these problems can be identified, challenged, and changed. The final chapter shows how to stay emotionally healthy and avoid backsliding.

A Rational Counseling Primer, by H. Young. New York: Institute for Rational Living, 1974. A useful, very brief introduction to the basic concepts of RET, often prescribed by rational-emotive therapists as preliminary reading. Adolescents in particular find its style and illustrations quite interesting. The book is also an important resource for adult clients whose reading skills are limited.

Any book by Paul Hauck. He writes in a particularly simple style that many clients appreciate. Therapists often find that they get the best rates of compliance with reading homework when the selections are from Hauck's repertoire. Included in Hauck's work are: *Overcoming Worry and Fear, The Three Faces of Love, How to Stand Up for Yourself, Marriage Is a Loving*

Business, Overcoming Procrastination, Overcoming Anger, and *Overcoming Jealousy and Possessiveness.* All are very good, and can be ordered from the Institute.

Pamphlets and Tapes

For clients who want a very brief introduction to RET, we recommend a pamphlet entitled, "The Essence of Rational Psychotherapy: A Comprehensive Approach to Treatment" by A. Ellis, or the still more brief "RET in a Nutshell," in a cartoon format. Another pamphlet which we have found useful is "Techniques for Disputing Irrational Beliefs (DIBS)," by A. Ellis. It helps clients to prepare written homework assignments by providing models for filling out a self-help form and beginning a disputation. All of these pamphlets and the following tape are sold by the Institute.

A tape that has been very popular at the Institute is "What Do I Do With My Anger: Let It Out or Hold It In?" by R. DiGiuseppe (1989). Most people justify their irrational anger-producing philosophies by citing the importance of letting their anger out and the problem of holding it in. In this tape the justifications for holding onto anger are reviewed and disputed, and alternatives to expressing anger are suggested.

Problems of Love, Sex, and Relationships

FOR THE PROFESSIONAL

Rational-Emotive Couples Counseling, by A. Ellis, J. Sichel, D. DiMattia, R. Yeager, and R. DiGiuseppe. New York: Pergamon, 1989. A rational-emotive perspective on romantic relationships and therapeutic strategies to help couples cope with the trials of love and living together is provided in this clinician's guidebook. In addition, the RET approach to couples counseling is compared with other theoretical systems.

The Civilized Couple's Guide to Extramarital Adventure, by A. Ellis. New York: Pinnacle Books, 1972. This classic book, available only through the Institute, is probably the most sensible exposition in print on what is often a crushing problem in marriage: infidelity. Ellis does not recommend extramarital adventuring, but rationally discusses its advantages and disadvantages in various settings. The book describes how to handle some of the problems that may arise from extramarital sexual encounters, as well as how a couple can be happily monogamous in a basically non-monogamous world.

Love Is Never Enough, by A. Beck. New York: Harper & Row, 1988. This is an accessible book to both professionals and couples. Descriptive chapters include "the power of negative thinking, silent thoughts, static in communication, and tricks of the mind." Therapy chapters include "reinforcing the foundations, tuning up the relationship, changing your own distortions, the art of conversation, and working together." The book may help save a failing marriage or be used to make a good relationship even better.

FOR THE CLIENT

Intimate Connections, by D. Burns. New York: Signet Books, 1985. This paperback book focuses on issues of shyness and loneliness. Written in an engaging style, the five major sections are "the good news about loneliness, self-love comes first, making connections, getting close, and making love." Included are chapters on "how to radiate an irresistible glow" and "your rags-to-riches social program." Clients almost invariably react positively to this self-help text.

Marriage Is a Loving Business, by P. Hauck. Philadelphia: The Westminster Press, 1977. This little book shows what marriage can be when both husband and wife understand it as a partnership. Hauck describes the real reason why people form such a partnership and what pitfalls the couple is likely to encounter. The book includes many case histories and examples drawn from Hauck's private practice and is written in an easy-to-read style that makes it accessible to a wide range of couples. (See also *The Three Faces of Love*).

Marital Myths, by A. Lazarus. San Luis-Obispo, CA: Impact Publishers, 1985. Lazarus explodes twenty-four myths commonly held in our culture, including "husbands and wives should be best friends," "romantic love makes a good marriage," and "extramarital affairs will destroy a marriage." The book includes a marital satisfaction questionnaire and some self-help suggestions.

Tapes

"How To Be Happy Though Mated" is a recorded lecture given by Dr. Ellis at the Institute. He rationally evaluates the advantages and disadvantages of being mated, and points out cognitive blocks to happy mating and some solutions to those blocks. He provides valuable insights and practical solutions to the myriad communication problems that beset the mated or about-to-be-mated.

Problems of Children and Adolescents

FOR THE PROFESSIONAL

Rational-Emotive Therapy with Children and Adolescents, edited by M. Bernard and M. Joyce. New York: Wiley, 1990. This is the most scholarly and complete text available on the application of RET with children and adolescents. The book focuses on developmental issues in understanding children's feelings and thoughts, and how the stages of development impact on rational-emotive theory and therapy. Chapters on both treatment and prevention provide many clinical intervention strategies.

FOR THE CLIENT

The Rational Management of Children, by P. Hauck. New York: Libra Publishers, 1967. This classic book, available at the Institute, is a good resource for the parent. The book discusses techniques of child management, habits of kindness and firmness, and discipline. It includes five chapters on the fears of people, failure, injury, rejection, and ridicule. Additional chapters deal with anger, worry, and depression. The book presents, in clear language, parenting methods for the most commonly encountered problems of early childhood through the teens.

Feeling, Thinking, Behaving and *An Emotional Education Curriculum for Children,* both by Ann Vernon. New York: Research Press, 1989. These two books, one for elementary and the other for high school students, provide specific exercises that can be used in classrooms or groups to teach the concepts of RET. The material is culled from years of experience in teaching RET to children and incorporates the best features of all the work in this area that has appeared in the past. These books can be used for both therapeutic and prevention programs.

Pamphlets and Tapes

Rational Stories for Children, by Ginger Waters. New York: Institute for RET, 1980. This series of pamphlets is designed to be used by parents with their children. Each constitutes a little RET lesson and has two parts: a fairy tale to be read to the child by the parent, and a parent's RET instruction manual. Each understandable yet entertaining tale is about a common problem of childhood and presents a rational philosophy of coping.

You Can Do It, a videotape by M. Bernard (1990) that is available through the Institute, is made for children who are having trouble in school. This upbeat and professional video is designed to help kids accomplish more and feel better about themselves in the process.

Women's Issues

Pamphlets

There are several items published by the Institute for Rational Living that will be useful to therapists with an interest in feminist therapy and how RET relates to women's problems. The first is a pamphlet by J. Wolfe entitled "Rational-Emotive Therapy as an Effective Feminist Therapy" (1975). In this delightful paper, Wolfe analyzes some of the problems that prevent women from maximizing their happiness in love and sexual relationships. A second pamphlet by Wolfe is *"How to be Sexually Assertive"* (1976). The author discusses the specific irrational beliefs that prevent women from assuming responsibility for their own sexuality, their sexual pleasure, and their orgasms. It is very helpful for women with concerns in this area.

Family Therapy

FOR THE PROFESSIONAL

Rational-Emotive Family Therapy, by C. Huber and L. Baruth. New York: Springer Publishing, 1989. This text integrates rational–emotive and family systems therapy. It presents these paradigms as complimentary rather than competing, stresses the advantages of work with families to solidify change, and suggests that irrational beliefs may be the mechanism whereby family systems provoke resistance. This is an excellent book for all practitioners who work with children or couples.

Cognitive-Behavioral Therapy with Families, edited by N. Epstein, S. E. Schlesinger, and W. Dryden. New York: Brunner/Mazel, 1988. This is one of the first books published on the use of cognitive behavioral therapy with families. The book is divided into two sections. The first section focuses on theory and methods; the second section considers specific family problems from the cognitive behavioral perspective, including child abuse, physical aggression in marriage, conduct-disordered children and adolescents, and adult sexual dysfunctions.

Problems of Anger

FOR THE PROFESSIONAL AND CLIENT

How to Live With and Without Anger, by A. Ellis. New York: Reader's Digest Press, 1977. Ellis outlines the rational-emotive theory and therapy for anger control, comparing this technique to other points of view and thus giving a comprehensive and critical analysis of the problem of anger. Chapters include "looking for self-angering philosophies, disputing your self-angering philosophies, acting your way out of your anger, ripping up your rationalizations for remaining angry, and accepting yourself with your anger."

Dealing with Anger Problems: Rational-Emotive Therapeutic Interventions, by W. Dryden. Sarasota, FL: Essential Professional Resource Exchange, 1990. This short guide considers the rational-emotive approach to dealing with clients' anger problems. After introducing the basic principles of RET, Dryden outlines how rational-emotive therapists conceptualize clients' anger problems. He distinguishes eleven different types of anger and illustrates each one with case vignettes. In the final part of the volume, Dryden presents twelve steps of rational-emotive treatment and illustrates these steps with verbatim excerpts from case histories.

Overcoming Frustration and Anger, by P. Hauck. Philadelphia: Westminster Press, 1974. An easy-to-understand explanation of the A-B-C's of angry emotions, and the thinking processes that comprise the common denominator of anger. Hauck points out that by blaming people or events and reacting with anger, hostility, and rage to frustration, reactions backfire and are ultimately self-destructive, preventing one from handling the problem and producing emotional distress. The book presents RET techniques for correcting blame cognitions, and suggests techniques for coping with frustration and how to be firm without being angry.

Problems of Anxiety

FOR THE PROFESSIONAL

Anxiety Disorders: A Rational Emotive Perspective, by R. Warren and G. Zigourides. New York: Pergamon, 1991. This is the most up-to-date book on the use of RET with the entire spectrum of anxiety disorders. The book's strength lies in the integration of cognitive and behavioral interventions.

Anxiety Disorders and Phobias, by A. T. Beck and G. Emery. New York: Basic Books, 1985. In Part I, Beck outlines the phenomenology and an explanatory model by which to understand the cognitive, emotive, and behavioral aspects of generalized anxiety and panic disorder, phobias, agoraphobia, and the evaluation anxieties. In Part II, Emery describes a cognitive-behavioral program for treating these disorders, based on the theoretical model outlined. Cognitive restructuring, relaxation, distraction techniques, exposure therapy, and activity scheduling are among the clinical strategies discussed.

Hope and Help for Your Nerves and *Relief from Nervous Suffering,* as well as any other books by Claire Weeks. Clients and therapists can profit from these books, although there is less emphasis than RET practitioners might like to see on the nature of catastrophizing as a key cognitive distortion in panic and anxiety.

FOR THE CLIENT

How To Master Your Fear of Flying, by A. Ellis. New York: Institute for Rational Living, 1978. This small book, available at the Institute, is a favorite of some RET practitioners, because it deals with existential issues. The author describes how he overcame his own fear of flying, thus providing a useful model for the application of RET to a specific fear. A particularly important contribution of this book is a discussion of anxiety about death and dying.

Overcoming Worry and Fear, by P. Hauck. Philadelphia: The Westminster Press, 1975. This book gives practical techniques for relaxing and learning to take problems in stride. Hauck explains RET and how fears and worries are generated by irrational beliefs. In the case of fear, the major irrational belief that is challenged is that if something is dangerous or fearsome, one ought to dwell upon it endlessly, and never let it out of one's mind. The book gives numerous examples of persons who have learned to question their faulty philosophy and to handle situations with a feeling of calmness and accomplishment. The book is useful for both therapist and client.

Pamphlets and Tapes

The following two items are available at the Institute and continue to be popular with clients. One is a paper for students who suffer from test anxiety, *"Overcoming Test Anxiety"* by R. Oliver (reprinted from *Rational Living*). Oliver discusses and disputes irrational beliefs that maintain test anxiety and gives both cognitive and behavioral techniques to overcome it. The paper is easy to read and well organized, with subheadings that make the major points clear to the student. The second item is a tape by Ellis entitled "Twenty-one Ways to Stop Worrying." Ellis reviews a large number of techniques to stop worrying, some more helpful than others— all, however, temporary and palliative. He then discusses a more elegant series of procedures that the anxious individual can use to diminish anxiety and teaches the listener how to engage in anti-awfulizing cognitive and behavioral strategies.

Problems of Depression

FOR THE PROFESSIONAL

How To Cope with Depression, by J. R. DePaulo and K. R. Ablow. New York: Fawcett Crest, 1989. The authors take the position that a "powerful and useful way to understand severe depression and manic-depressive disorder is to recognize them as diseases." They also outline the "personality perspective," the cognitive-behavioral perspective, and the "life story" perspective, as well as various treatments, including drug and other somatic therapies as well as psychotherapy. Available in paperback, this is an important book for professionals as well as depressed clients and their families to read.

Cognitive Therapy of Depression, by A. T. Beck, A. J. Rush, B. F. Shaw, and G. Emery. New York: Guilford Press, 1979. Recommended for therapists working with depressed clients. Chapter headings include, "the therapeutic relationship, the initial interview, session-by-session treatment, application of behavioral techniques, cognitive techniques, specific techniques for the suicidal patient, homework, and termination of therapy." This detailed manual provides many concrete suggestions for the therapist, including segments of therapist–patient dialogues.

FOR THE CLIENT

Feeling Good and *The Feeling Good Handbook,* by David Burns. New York: William Morrow, 1980 and 1989. As Walen commented on the dust jacket of the original hardbound copy of *Feeling Good,* "This is one of the happiest books on depression I've ever read. It will be a staple in my clinical cupboard." These two books, the second containing many self-help exercises, continue to be best sellers in the self-help literature. They are clearly and dynamically written and teach step-by-step procedures for combating depression. Highly recommended.

Overcoming Depression, by P. Hauck. Philadelphia: The Westminster Press, 1976. This book portrays three main reasons for emotional depression and what the reader can do about them. The first reason is self-downing, the second is self-pity, and the third is other-pity. Hauck discusses techniques for attitude change, including ways to correct these three erroneous beliefs and thereby reduce depression. An excellent and readable text for clients.

Other Applications: Assertiveness

FOR THE PROFESSIONAL

Responsible Assertive Behavior: Cognitive-Behavioral Procedures for Trainers, by A. Lange and P. Jakubowski. Champaign, IL: Research Press, 1976. This book continues to be an excellent resource for the therapist who wants to learn more about problems of nonassertiveness and the therapeutic techniques for dealing with them. Chapter headings include "structured exercises, cognitive restructuring procedures, behavior rehearsal procedures, modeling and behavioral rehearsal, planning and conducting stages in the life of an assertiveness training group, theme-oriented assertiveness groups, assertiveness training and consciousness-raising groups, specific applications of training groups, assessment procedures, and ethical considerations." The book is unusually comprehensive and well organized.

FOR THE CLIENT

I Can If I Want To, by A. Lazarus and A. Fay. New York: William Morrow, 1975. Lazarus and Fay discuss a number of erroneous ideas with which individuals block their assertiveness and outlines a readable, three-step program of change: understanding basic mistakes that ruin your life, understanding the faulty assumptions underlying these mistakes, and applying techniques to combat the mistakes by changing one's thinking and behavior. The book is concise and well organized for quick reference.

Problems of Procrastination

Overcoming Procrastination, by A. Ellis and W. J. Knaus. New York: Institute for Rational Living, 1977. The authors define procrastination and its main causes, and teach a rational approach to overcoming the problem. Chapter headings include "overcoming procrastination resulting from self-downing, low frustration tolerance, hostility, and other emotional problems; and impediments to overcoming procrastination." The book concludes with a verbatim psychotherapy session. In our opinion, this book may be as useful for the client as it is for the professional.

Habit Control and Addiction

FOR THE PROFESSIONAL

Rational-Emotive Therapy for Alcoholics and Substance Abusers, by A. Ellis, A. McInerny, R. DiGiuseppe, and R. Yeager. New York: Pergamon, 1988. This practical book is the first professional text to provide a rational-emotive perspective on understanding addictions. It is easily incorporated into twelve-step programs and provides specific interventions for disputing the "stinking thinking" underlying substance abuse. Two important chapters are on helping enablers and therapists deal with the frustration of clients dropping out and relapsing.

FOR THE CLIENT

Under the Influence, by J. Milam and K. Ketcham. New York: Bantam Books, 1981. The main tenet of this book, which is available in paperback, is that the physiology of the alcoholic, not psychological makeup or cultural background, is the chief determinant for this disease. This biological perspective can go a long way toward destigmatizing the condition and reducing guilt in the sufferer and anger in family members. It can set the stage attitudinally for a course of cognitive-behavior therapy.

The Small Book, by J. Trimpey. Lotus, CA: Lotus Press, 1989. Although self-help groups like AA have helped many people, a substantial number of clients with addiction problems as well as many RET therapists are unhappy with the religious slant of the twelve-step programs. *The Small Book* introduces an RET self-help approach to dealing with addictions and an alternative to AA: *Rational Recovery.* This group model combines the principles of RET with the fellowship concept of AA to help those with addictive problems. A growing number of RR groups are forming around the country, and further self-help materials for addictive problems are emerging from this movement.

Tapes

For the individual who is trying to give up a bad habit, whether smoking, drinking, overeating, and so on, a tape which is a best seller at the Institute will be very helpful. *"I'd Like To Stop, But . . ."* by A. Ellis deals with the need for immediate gratification, overcoming the "mañana (tomorrow)" and "I deserve to have it easier" attitudes, and how not to denigrate oneself for one's bad habits. Both cognitive and behavioral procedures are described.

Appendix A:
Session Notes

Session:_____ Date:_____

1. Assessing the presence of dysfunctional emotions or behaviors.
2. Exploring the adaptability of the client's emotions and behaviors.
3. Assessing the presence and type of dysfunctional cognitions.
4. Exploring the adaptability of the client's belief system.
5. Clarifying the activating events.
6. Offering the client a hypothesis about what irrational belief the client is holding.
7. Teaching the B—>C connection.
8. Teaching the difference between irrational and rational beliefs.
9. Offering alternative rational beliefs to replace the client's irrational beliefs.
10. Philosophical disputing.
11. Rational–emotive imagery.
12. Assigning homework.
13. Assessing the client's emotions, thoughts, and behaviors which occurred when the client tried to implement a homework assignment.
14. Empirical disputing.
15. Instruction for rehearsal of self-statements.
16. Helping the client generate alternative solutions to practical problems.
17. Helping the client evaluate the effectiveness of alternative solutions.
18. Behavioral rehearsal of new solutions to practical problems.
19. Relaxation training or relaxing imagery.

Rate the client's attempts to complete homework from the last session.

1	2	3	4	5
Made an attempt at the homework	Made a partial attempt at the homework	Completed some of the homework	Completed most of the homework	Completed all of the homework

Comments:_____

_____

Homework:_____

_____

Appendix B:
RET Supervision Form

Therapist's name:_____   Date:_____
Client:_____   Session:_____

Please circle the appropriate choices and record the score at the end of each item.

I. General Therapeutic Behaviors

1. Was it clear that the therapist was working toward a particular target or goal in the session (i.e., changing a specific cognition, emotion, or behavior)?

1	2	3	4	5	N/A_____
Not at all		Somewhat, but not adequately		Yes, goal clearly noticeable	

2. Was the session goal a clinically appropriate and relevant one?

1	2	3	4	5	N/A_____
Not at all		Somewhat		Yes, appropriate	

3. Did the client and therapist have the same agenda, or did they clash over different agendas?

1	2	3	4	5	N/A_____
No		Not clear		Yes, clearly	

4. Was the therapist's language appropriate for the client's ability to understand (i.e., was the client tuned in with the therapist as opposed to being "left in the dust" of the therapist's brilliant didactics and disputations)?

1	2	3	4	5	N/A_____
Not at all		Somewhat		Very appropriate	

5. Did the therapist focus and use time well rather than digressing on peripheral and tangential material such as background/historical data or activating events?

1	2	3	4	5	N/A_____
Did not use time well		Fair use of time		Efficient use of time	

6. Was one target focused on at a time rather than switching or jumping from one target to another?

1	2	3	4	5	N/A_____
Scattered		Somewhat focused		Well focused	

7. Did the therapist overly lecture or question and not allow the client to speak?

1	2	3	4	5	N/A_____
Too much lecturing		Some unappropriate lecturing		Appropriate use of lecturing to clarify RET concepts	

8. Did the therapist summarize periodically or when necessary to ensure that the client understood?

1	2	3	4	5	N/A_____
Did not summarize		Summarized, but inappropriately		Summarized important points appropriately	

9. Did the therapist ask the client to summarize periodically to ensure that the client understood the therapy procedures?

1	2	3	4	5	N/A_____
No		Insufficient summarizing		Appropriate requests for summaries	

10. Did the therapist use a style or strategy that would likely enhance the therapeutic alliance (rapport) given the characteristics and expectations of the client?

1	2	3	4	5	N/A____ _
Did not develop rapport		Partial rapport		Developed good rapport	

II. Diagnosis and Conceptualization

1. Did the therapist work to explain the B—>C connection; or if not, is it clear that the client and therapist are working at changing beliefs (IB's)?

1	2	3	4	5	N/A_____
Not working on showing B—>C, or not working on B's		Inadequate explanation of B—>C; insufficient work on B's		Clearly working on B's or illustrating B—>C	

2. Did the therapist clearly and specifically identify the negative emotional and behavioral consequences (C's)?

1	2	3	4	5	N/A_____
Did not work well		Some identification of C's		Worked well	

3. Did the therapist work to assess relevant irrational beliefs?

1	2	3	4	5	N/A_____
No assessment of IB's		Some assessment of IB's		Good assessment of IB's	

III. Disputation/Intervention and Homework

1. Did the therapist work to help the client become somewhat aware of the dysfunctional nature of his or her self-defeating emotions and/or behaviors (C's); i.e., did the therapist do "pragmatic disputing"?

1	2	3	4	5	N/A_____
Did not use pragmatic disputing		Used pragmatic disputing		Used pragmatic disputing well	

2. Did the therapist use "functional or pragmatic disputing," i.e., demonstrating to the client that his or her irrational beliefs lead to dysfunctional emotions and behaviors?

1	2	3	4	5	N/A_____
Did not use dysfunctional disputing		Used dysfunctional disputing		Used dysfunctional disputing well	

3. Did the therapist show good judgment by focusing disputations on the client's irrational beliefs?

1	2	3	4	5	N/A_____
Showed bad judgment		Showed some judgment		Showed good judgment	

4. Did the therapist dispute irrational beliefs on a philosophical level, rather than solely focusing on empirical inferences, automatic thoughts, or activating events?

1	2	3	4	5	N/A_____
Did not dispute		Disputed, but only empirically		Effectively disputed on a philosophical level	

5. Were the therapist's interventions vague or unstructured without targeting specific interventions?

1	2	3	4	5	N/A_____
Unstructured style		Some attempt at structure		Clear and targeted interventions	

6. Did the therapist use appropriate examples, metaphors, and analogies in disputing?

1	2	3	4	5	N/A_____
Inappropriate		Somewhat appropriate		Very appropriate	

7. Did the therapist use emotive, evocative, or stimulating techniques such as rational role reversal, imagery, changes in voice tone, and the like?

1	2	3	4	5	N/A_____
Monotonous or nonevocative		Used some evocative procedures and variations in style		Very evocative in style and strategy	

8. Did the therapist provide rational alternative beliefs or help the client generate them when appropriate?

1	2	3	4	5	N/A_____
Never		Occasionally		When appropriate	

9. Did the therapist adequately assess whether the client completed the previous homework?

1	2	3	4	5	N/A_____
No		Yes, but inadequately		Very well done	

10. Did the therapist dispute the client's irrational beliefs in both an abstract and concrete (specific) way, or at only a concrete or abstract level? (I.e., abstract disputing, "Why must people like you?"; concrete disputing, "Why must your mother like you?")

1	2	3	4	5	N/A_____
Did not use either abstract or concrete disputes		Insufficient attempts to use concrete or abstract disputes		Used both abstract and concrete disputes well	

11. If the homework was completed, were the client's efforts reinforced and praised by the therapist?

1	2	3	4	5	N/A_____
Not praised at all		Some praise		Appropriate praise	

If the homework was not completed, were the client's reasons, irrational beliefs, automatic thoughts, and feelings about the homework assessed and discussed?

1	2	3	4	5	N/A_____
Not discussed		Inadequately discussed		Adequately discussed	

12. Did the therapist show skill in assigning or negotiating a new homework assignment?

1	2	3	4	5	N/A_____
Unskilled or no homework		Homework assigned, but with some lack of skill		Skilled and appropriate, considering implicit or explicit therapy goals	

13. If a new homework assignment was accepted, did the therapist help the client achieve an understanding as to its relevance toward his or her goals and well-being?

1	2	3	4	5	N/A_____
Not at all		Somewhat or not applicable		Very well	

14. Was the homework assignment specific as opposed to vague?

1	2	3	4	5	N/A_____
Vague		Not applicable		Clear and Specific	

15. Did the therapist assess and dispute the potential reasons why the assignment might not get completed?

1	2	3	4	5	N/A_____
Not at all		Somewhat or not applicable		Very well	

IV. Additional Comments and Recommendations

V. Score = Total Points/Possible Points x 100

Supervised by_____

Glossary

Activating events: An external or internal event or a set of stimuli that a person reacts to emotionally.

Appropriate emotion: An emotional reaction that, although negative, is appropriate and not disturbed, does not involve suffering, and leads to adaptive behavior.

Awfulizing: A type of irrational belief that involves an exaggerated negative evaluation of an event. Awfulizing involves believing that events are more than 100 percent bad and arbitrarily defining them as awful.

Catastrophizing: See "Awfulizing."

Dichotomous thinking: A type of irrational belief that characterizes the world in terms of bipolarity. Things are good or bad, black or white. There is no acknowledgment of a middle position or "gray area." This type of thinking also denies the fact that things could be partly good and partly bad.

Discomfort anxiety: The emotional state that one experiences when one is fearful or anxious about an anticipated discomfort or difficulty.

Disputing: The process of challenging an irrational belief and replacing it with a more adaptive rational belief.

Demandingness: An irrational belief that involves thinking or commanding that the world should comply with one's wants. Demandingness may occur when word such as "must," "ought," or "should" are used.

Elegant solution: A therapeutic strategy aimed at changing the irrational beliefs of demandingness, awfulizing, LFT, and self-rating, instead of challenging the inference behind these IB's. The elegant solution helps the client cope with negative reality or the worst thing that could happen, instead of convincing the client that reality is better than it appears.

Emotional solution: A therapeutic strategy that aims at changing a person's emotional reaction to an event, instead of either changing the event itself or helping the person find a way to avoid or escape from the event.

Hypothetico-deductive assessment: An assessment strategy in which the therapist shares his or her hypotheses with the client and asks the client for feedback on the accuracy of these suggestions. This strategy can be used to assess emotions or beliefs.

Inappropriate emotion: A disturbed negative emotion that leads to pain, suffering, and inappropriate, maladaptive behavior.

Inference: The thought a person generates when emotionally upset that refers to a negative prediction, or inaccurate description, about reality.

Inference chaining: A strategy used to assess irrational beliefs that involves hypothetically positing the client's inference and then asking the client what would it mean if the inference were true. This strategy is repeated until the therapist discovers an irrational belief.

Inelegant solution: A therapeutic strategy aimed at changing the client's inference that the world is bad in some regard. An inelegant solution is less generalizable than an elegant solution, because the client has not learned how to cope if the inference turns out to be accurate.

Irrational belief: A thought that is logically incorrect, inconsistent with empirical reality, or inconsistent with one's long-term goals.

Long-range hedonism: The philosophical position that a person attempts to maximize his or her happiness in life by planning the activities that will be rewarding in the long term. This position supports investing in the future and doing things that are difficult in the present because of the pay-off in the future. RET maintains that people attain happiness through long-range hedonism.

Love slob: A person who maintains the irrational belief that he or she must be loved and approved of by everyone. As a result, the person frequently tries to please people and may become upset by the slightest criticism.

Low frustration tolerance (LFT): An irrational belief that an event or task is too difficult for a person to endure. LFT beliefs usually include statements to the effect that the person is too weak and will perish because of the difficulty involved in a task.

Practical solution: A therapeutic strategy aimed at teaching skills to clients that will help them change, avoid, or escape from negative events.

Rational barb: A therapeutic technique designed to increase the client's skill at coping with stressful interpersonal situations. The therapist role-plays a person who is insulting or provocative to the client, and the client practices responding with rational coping statements.

Rational belief: A thought that is logically correct and consistent with both empirical reality and a person's goals.

Rational-emotive imagery: A therapeutic technique designed to help clients practice rational thoughts. There are two different approaches to this task. In one version clients imagine an upsetting situation and feeling the disturbed emotion they usually experience in the situation. They then try to imagine changing their emotion to an appropriate one and explain how they have caused the change in their emotion. In the second version, clients imagine themselves in a stressful situation while making rational coping statements and experiencing an appropriate emotional reaction.

Rational role reversal: A therapeutic technique designed to increase clients' skill at disputing irrational beliefs. The therapist role-plays a client with a similar problem to that of the client; the client role-plays the therapist and attempts to dispute the irrational belief.

Risk-taking exercise: A behavioral homework assignment. The client chooses to behave in a manner that he or she was previously afraid of and which involves negative consequences. For example, the client may decide to risk asking someone for a date, applying for a new job, or asking an employer for a raise in pay.

Shame attack: A homework assignment in which the client deliberately behaves foolishly in public so that others will notice and think poorly of him or her. This procedure is a form of behavioral flooding for social disapproval.

Short-term hedonism: A philosophical position advocating that one maximize one's satisfaction in the present. Rational–emotive theory maintains that short-term hedonism results in disturbance.

Self-acceptance: The rational belief that one is a worthy person just because one exists, and despite one's faults. Self-acceptance replaces self-pride in RET theory.

Self-rating: The process of irrationally evaluating one's total self based on one or more aspects of one's behavior.

Socratic method: A style of questioning clients that attempts to have clients discover the answers by themselves. The therapist asks questions that bring out information the client already knows but has not assimilated.

Secondary disturbance: A client's irrational beliefs about a disturbed emotion that he or she is experiencing. These irrational beliefs lead to additional (secondary) disturbed emotions.

Bibliography

Allen, G., Chinsky, J., Larcen, S., Lockman, J. and Selinger, H. (1976). *Community Psychology and the Schools: A Behaviorally Oriented Multilevel Preventive Approach*. Hillsdale, NJ: Erlbaum.

Araoz, D. (1985). *The New Hypnosis*. New York: Plenum.

Beck, A. T. (1976). *Cognitive Therapy and the Emotional Disorders*. New York: International Universities Press.

Beck, A. T., and Beck, R. W. (1972). Screening depressed patients in family practice: A rapid technique. *Postgraduate Medicine, 52,* 81–85.

Beck, A. T., and Emery, G. (1985). *Anxiety Disorders and Phobias*. New York: Basic Books.

Beck, A. T., Rush, A. J., Shaw, B. F., and Emery, G. (1979). *Cognitive Therapy of Depression: A Treatment Manual*. New York: Guilford.

Beck, A. T., Steer, R., and Garbin, M. G. (1988). Psychometric properties of the Beck Depression inventory: Twenty-five years of evaluation. *Clinical Psychology Review, 8*(1), 77–100.

Bernard, M. (ed.) (1991). *Using Rational-Emotive Therapy Effectively*. New York: Plenum.

Bernard, M. E., and DiGiuseppe, R. (1989). *Inside Rational-Emotive Therapy: A Critical Appraisal of the Theory and Therapy of Albert Ellis*. New York: Academic Press.

Bowlby, J. (1980). *Attachment and Loss. Vol. 3: Loss: Sadness and Depression*. New York: Basic Books.

Burns, D. (1980). *Feeling Good*. New York: William Morrow.

Burns, D. (1989). The New Mood Therapy. Talk presented at Taylor Manor Hospital, Ellicott City, Maryland, November.

Camp, B. (1975). Verbal mediation in young aggressive boys. Unpublished manuscript, University of Colorado School of Medicine.

Carkhuff, R. (1969). *Helping and Human Relations: A Primer for Lay and Professional Helpers*. New York: Holt, Rinehart and Winston.

Childress, A. R., and Burns, D. D. (1983). The group supervision model in cognitive therapy training. In A. Freeman (ed.), *Cognitive Therapy with Couples and Groups*. New York: Plenum.

Davison, G. C., and Neale, J. M. (1990). *Abnormal Psychology*, 5th ed. New York: Wiley.

DePue, P. (1987). The General Psychological Well-Being Scale. In I. McDowell and C. Newell (eds.), *Measuring Health: A Guide to Rating Scales*. New York: Oxford University Press.

Diener, E., Emmons, R. A., Larsen, R. J., and Griffen, S. (1985). The satisfaction with life scale. *Journal of Personality Assessment, 49,* 71–75.

DiGiuseppe, R., Leaf, R., Exner, T., and Robin, M. (1988). The development of a measure of irrational/rational thinking. Poster session presented at the World Congress of Behavior Therapy, Edinburgh, Scotland, September.

DiGiuseppe, R., and McInerney, J. (1991). Models of addiction: A rational-emotive perspective. *Journal of Cognitive Psychotherapies: An International Quarterly*.

DiGiuseppe, R., Robin, M., and Dryden, W. (1991). On the compatibility of rational-emotive therapy and Judeo-Christian philosophy: A focus on clinical strategies. *Journal of Cognitive Psychotherapy: An International Quarterly*.

Dryden, W., and DiGiuseppe, R. (1990). *A Primer on Rational-Emotive Therapy*. Champaign, IL: Research Press.

Dryden, W., Ferguson, J., and McTeague, S. (1989). Beliefs and inferences: A test of a rational-emotive hypothesis. 2: On the prospect of seeing a spider. *Psychological Reports, 64,* 115–23.

D'Zurilla, T. (1988). Problem-solving therapies. In K. S. Dabem (ed.), *Handbook of Cognitive-Behavioral Therapies*. New York: Guilford.

D'Zurilla, T., and Goldfried, M. R. (1971). Problem-solving and behavior modification. *Journal of Abnormal Psychology, 78,* 107–26.

Ellis, A. (1958). Rational psychotherapy. *Journal of General Psychology, 59,* 35–49.

Ellis, A. (1962). *Reason and Emotion in Psychotherapy*. Secaucus, NJ: Lyle Stuart.

Ellis, A. (1971). *Growth Through Reason*. North Hollywood, CA: Wilshire Books.

Ellis, A. (1972a). *Psychotherapy and the Value of a Human Being*. New York: Institute for Rational-Emotive Therapy.

Ellis, A. (1972b). *How to Master Your Fear of Flying*. New York: Institute for Rational-Emotive Therapy.

Ellis, A. (1973a). *Humanistic Psychotherapy*. New York: McGraw-Hill.

Ellis, A. (1973b). How to stubbornly refuse to be ashamed of anything (cassette recording). New York: Institute for Rational-Emotive Therapy.

Ellis, A. (1973c). Twenty-one ways to stop worrying (cassette recording). New York: Institute for Rational-Emotive Therapy.

Ellis, A. (1974a). The treatment of sex and love problems in women. In V. Franks and V. Burtle (eds.), *Women in Therapy*. New York: Brunner/Mazel.

Ellis, A. (1974b). *Techniques of Disputing Irrational Beliefs*. New York: Institute for Rational-Emotive Therapy.

Ellis, A. (1975a). *How to Live with a "Neurotic,"* rev. ed. North Hollywood, CA: Wilshire.

Ellis, A. (1975b). RET and assertiveness training (cassette recording). New York: Institute for Rational-Emotive Therapy.

Ellis, A. (1976a). The biological basis of human irrationality. *Journal of Individual Psychology, 32,* 145–68.

Ellis, A. (1976b). Conquering low frustration tolerance (cassette recording). New York: Institute for Rational-Emotive Therapy.

Ellis, A. (1976c). *RET Abolishes Most of the Human Ego*. New York: Institute for Rational-Emotive Therapy.

Ellis, A. (1977a). *Anger—How to Live with and without It*. Secaucus, NJ: Citadel Press.

Ellis, A. (1977b). The basic clinical theory of rational-emotive therapy. In A. Ellis and R. Grieger (eds.), *Handbook of Rational-Emotive Therapy*. New York: Springer Publishing.

Ellis, A. (1977c). Fun as psychotherapy (cassette recording). New York: Institute for Rational Living. Also in A. Ellis and R. Grieger (eds.), *Handbook of Rational-Emotive Therapy*. New York: Springer Publishing.

Ellis, A. (1978). I'd like to stop, but . . . (cassette recording). New York: Institute for Rational-Emotive Therapy.

Ellis, A. (1979a). Discomfort anxiety: A new cognitive behavioral construct. *Rational Living, 14,* 3–8. Also in A. Ellis and W. Dryden (eds.), *The Essential Albert Ellis*. New York: Springer Publishing, 1990.

Ellis, A. (1979b). *The Intelligent Woman's Guide to Dating and Mating*. Secaucus, NJ: Lyle Stuart.

Ellis, A. (1979c). A note on the treatment of agoraphobics with cognitive modification versus prolonged exposure in vivo. *Behavior Research and Therapy*.

Ellis, A. (1979d). Rational-emotive therapy. In R. J. Corsini (ed.), *Current Psychotherapies,* 2nd ed. Itasca, IL: Peacock.

Ellis, A. (1980). Psychotherapy and atheistic values: A response to A. E. Bergin's "Psychotherapy and religious values." *Journal of Consulting and Clinical Psychology, 48*, 635–39.

Ellis, A. (1983a). *The Case Against Religiosity*. New York: Institute for Rational-Emotive Therapy.

Ellis, A. (1983b). The philosophic implications and dangers of some popular behavior therapy techniques. In M. Rosenbaum, C. Franks, and Y. Jaffe (eds.), *Perspectives on Behavior Therapy in the Eighties*. New York: Springer Publishing.

Ellis, A. (1984). How to maintain and enhance your rational-emotive therapy gains (pamphlet). New York: Institute for Rational-Emotive Therapy.

Ellis, A. (1985). *Overcoming Resistance: Rational-Emotive Therapy with Difficult Patients*. New York: Springer Publishing.

Ellis, A. (1987a). Integrative developments in rational-emotive therapy (RET). *Journal of Integrative and Eclectic Psychotherapy, 6*, 470–79.

Ellis, A. (1987b). Religiosity and emotional disturbance. *Psychotherapy, 24*(4), 826–27.

Ellis, A. (1987c). A sadly neglected aspect of depression. *Cognitive Therapy and Research, 11*, 121–46.

Ellis, A. (1988). *How to Stubbornly Refuse to Make Yourself Miserable about Anything—Yes, Anything!* Secaucus, NJ: Lyle Stuart.

Ellis, A. (1989). Comments on my critics. In M. E. Bernard and R. DiGiuseppe (eds.), *Inside Rational-Emotive Therapy: A Critical Appraisal of the Theory and Therapy of Albert Ellis*. New York: Academic Press.

Ellis, A. (1990a). Albert Ellis live at the Learning Annex (cassette recording). New York: Institute for Rational-Emotive Therapy.

Ellis, A. (1990b). Special features of rational-emotive therapy. In W. Dryden and R. DiGiuseppe (eds.), *A Primer of Rational-Emotive Therapy*. Champaign, IL: Research Press.

Ellis, A. (1991a). Achieving self-actualization. In A. Jones and R. Crandall (eds.), *Handbook of Self-Actualization*. Corte Madera, CA: Select Press.

Ellis, A. (1991b). The revised ABC's of RET. *Journal of Rational-Emotive and Cognitive Behavior Therapy, 9*, 139–72.

Ellis, A. (1991c). Unconditionally accepting yourself and others (cassette recording). New York: Institute for Rational-Emotive Therapy.

Ellis, A., and Abrahms, E. (1978). *Brief Psychotherapy in Medical and Health Practice*. New York: Springer Publishing.

Ellis, A., and Becket, I. (1982). *A Guide to Personal Happiness*. North Hollywood, CA: Wilshire Books.

Ellis, A., and Bernard, M. (1986). What is rational–emotive therapy (RET)? In A. Ellis and R. M. Grieger (eds.), *Handbook of Rational-Emotive Therapy*, vol. 2. New York: Springer Publishing.

Ellis, A., and Dryden, W. (1987). *The Practice of Rational-Emotive Therapy*. New York: Springer Publishing.

Ellis, A., and Dryden, W. (1990). *The Essential Albert Ellis*. New York: Springer Publishing.

Ellis, A., and Grieger, R. (eds.) (1977, 1986). *Handbook of Rational-Emotive Therapy* (2 vols.). New York: Springer Publishing.

Ellis, A., and Harper, R. (1975). *A New Guide to Rational Living*. Englewood Cliffs, NJ: Prentice-Hall.

Ellis, A., and Knaus, W. (1977). *Overcoming Procrastination*. New York: Institute for Rational Living.

Ellis, A., McInerney, J., DiGiuseppe, R., and Yeager, R. (1988). *Rational-Emotive Therapy with Alcoholics and Substance Abusers*. New York: Pergamon.

Ellis, A., Sichel, J., Yeager, R., DiMattia, D., and DiGiuseppe, R. (1989). *Rational-Emotive Couples Therapy*. New York: Pergamon.

Ellis, A., and Velten, E. (1992). *When AA Doesn't Work For You: A Rational Guide to Quitting Alcohol*. New York: Barricade Books.

Fay, A. (1978). *Making Things Better by Making Them Worse*. New York: Hayworth Press.

Freud, S. (1965). *New Introductory Lectures on Psychoanalysis,* ed. and trans. by J. Strachey. New York: Norton.

Goldberg, D. P. (1972). *The Detection of Psychiatric Illness by Questionnaire: A Technique for the Identification and Assessment of Nonpsychotic Psychiatric Illness*. New York: Oxford University Press.

Goldfried, M. R., and Davison, G. C. (1976). *Clinical Behavior Therapy*. New York: Holt, Rinehart and Winston.

Goldstein, A. J., and Chambless, D. L. (1978). A re-analysis of agoraphobia. *Behavior Therapy, 9,* 47–59.

Guidano, V. F. (1988). A systems, process–oriented approach to cognitive therapy. In K. S. Dobson (ed.), *Handbook of Cognitive Behavioral Therapies*. New York: Guilford.

Harlow, H. (1958). The nature of love. *American Psychologist, 13,* 673–85.

Hauck, P. (1972). *Reason in Pastoral Counseling*. Philadelphia: Westminster Press.

Hauck, P. (1974). *Overcoming Depression*. Philadelphia: Westminster Press.

Hauck, P. (1985). Religion and RET: Friends or foes? In A. Ellis and M. Bernard (eds.), *Clinical Applications of Rational-Emotive Therapy*. New York: Plenum.

Horney, K. (1945). *Our Inner Conflicts*. New York: Norton.

Johnson, W. (1946). *People in Quandries*. New York: Harper & Bros.

Kelly, G. (1955). *The Psychology of Personal Constructs*. New York: Norton.

Kimmel, J. (1976). The rational barb in the treatment of social rejection. *Rational Living, 11*, 23–25.

Kohlberg, L. (1976). Moral stages and moralization: The cognitive developmental approach. In T. Leckona (ed.), *Moral Development and Behavior: Theory, Research, and Social Issues*. New York: Holt, Rinehart and Winston.

Kübler-Ross, E. (1969). *On Death and Dying*. New York: Macmillan.

Lange, A., and Jakubowski, P. (1976). *Responsible Assertion Training*. Champaign, IL: Research Press.

Lazarus, A. A. (1972). *Behavior Therapy and Beyond*. New York: McGraw-Hill.

Luria, A. (1969). Speech and formation of mental processes. In M. Cole and I. Maltzman (eds.), *A Handbook of Contemporary Soviet Psychology*. New York: Basic Books.

Mahoney, M. (1977). Personal science: A cognitive learning therapy. In A. Ellis and R. Grieger (eds.), *A Handbook of Rational-Emotive Therapy*. New York: Springer Publishing.

Mahoney, M. (1991). *Human Change Processes*. New York: Basic Books.

Marks, J., Boulougouris, J., and Marset, P. (1971). Flooding vs. desensitization in the treatment of phobic patients. *British Journal of Psychiatry, 119*, 353–75.

Maultsby, M. (1975). *Help Yourself to Happiness*. New York: Institute for Rational Living.

Maultsby, M., and Ellis, E. (1974). *Techniques for Using Rational-Emotive Imagery*. New York: Institute for Rational Living.

Meichenbaum, D. (1973). Therapist manual for cognitive behavior modification. Unpublished manuscript, University of Waterloo.

Meichenbaum, D. (1985). *Stress Innoculation Training*. New York: Pergamon.

Millon, T. (1987). *Millon Clinical Multi-axial Inventory-II*, 2nd ed. Minneapolis: National Computer Systems.

Millon, T. (1988). *Manual for the MCMI-II*. Minneapolis: National Computer Systems.

Moorey, S., and Burns, D. D. (1983). The apprenticeship model: Training cognitive therapy by participation. In A. Freeman (ed.), *Cognitive Therapy with Couples and Groups*. New York: Plenum.

Novaco, R. (1975). *Anger Control: The Development and Evaluation of an Experimental Treatment*. Lexington, MA: Lexington Books.

O'Leary, D., and Borkovec, T. (1978). Conceptual, methodological, and ethical problems of placebo groups in psychotherapy research. *American Psychologist, 33,* 821–30.

Protinsky, H., and Popp, R. (1978). Irrational philosophies in popular music. *Cognitive Therapy and Research, 2,* 71–74.

Rachman, S., Marks, I. M., and Hodgson, R. (1973). The treatment of obsessive-compulsive neurotics by modelling and flooding in vivo. *Behavior Research and Therapy, 11,* 463–71.

Raimy, V. (1975). *Misunderstandings of the Self: Cognitive Psychotherapy and the Misconception Hypothesis.* San Francisco, CA: Jossey-Bass.

Rogers, C. (1951). *Client-Centered Therapy.* Boston, MA: Houghton Mifflin.

Sampson, E. E. (1989). The challenge of social change in psychology. *American Psychologist, 44,* 914–21.

Schwartz, R. M., and Gottman, J. M. (1976). Towards a task analysis of assertive behavior. *Journal of Consulting and Clinical Psychology, 44,* 910–20.

Sichel, J., and Ellis, A. (1984). *RET Self-Help Form.* New York: Institute for Rational-Emotive Therapy.

Sobel, H. (1978). Panel discussion, Presented at the Second National Cognitive-Behavior Therapy Research Conference, New York.

Spivack, G., Platt, J., and Shure, M. (1976). *The Problem-solving Approach to Adjustment.* San Francisco, CA: Jossey-Bass.

Styron, W. (1990). *Darkness Visible: A Memoir of Madness.* New York: Random House.

Tosi, D. J., and Reardon, J. (1976). The treatment of guilt through rational stage-directed therapy. *Rational Living, 11,* 8–11.

Trexler, L. D. (1976). Frustration is a fact, not a feeling. *Rational Living, 11,* 19–22.

Vygotsky, L. (1962). *Thought and Language.* New York: Wiley.

Walen, S. (1983). Phrenophobia. *Journal of Cognitive Therapy, 6*(4).

Walen, S., Hauserman, N., and Lavin, P. (1977). *A Clinical Guide to Behavior Therapy.* New York: Oxford University Press.

Walen, S., and Rader, M. (1991). Depression and RET: Perspectives from wounded healers. In M. Bernard (ed.), *Using Rational-Emotive Therapy Effectively.* New York: Plenum.

Wegner, D. M., and Vallacher, R. R. (1977). *Implicit Psychology: An Introduction to Social Cognition.* New York: Oxford University Press.

Wessler, R. A., and Ellis, A. (1980). Supervision in rational-emotive therapy. In A. K. Hess (ed.), *Psychotherapy Supervision: Theory, Research, and Practice.* New York: Wiley.

Wessler, R. A., and Wessler, R. L. (1980). *The Principles and Practice of Rational-Emotive Therapy*. San Francisco, CA: Jossey-Bass.

Wolfe, J. L. (1975). Rational-emotive therapy as an effective feminist therapy. *Rational Living, 11,* 1–6.

Wolfe, J. L. (1980). Woman: Assert yourself (cassette recording). New York: Institute for Rational-Emotive Therapy.

Yankura, J., and Dryden, W. (1990). *Doing RET: Albert Ellis in Action*. New York: Springer Publishing.

Answer Key

Chapter 6

I did poorly on that exam.
> *Activating event.*

Oh, I'm such a failure.
> *Self-evaluation.*

No one talks to me.
> *Activating event.*

I just can't stand being so alone.
> *Hedonic evaluation.*

My mother's always picking on me. I know she hates me.
> *Activating event (no evaluation stated.).*

Doctor, the most terrible thing happened last week.
> *Evaluation of activating event.*

My wife told me she wanted a divorce.
> *Activating event.*

I ate like a pig.
> *Activating event.*

You see, I know now that I'm really no good.
> *Evaluative conclusion about self.*

I only make $40,000.
> *Activating event (the word "only" implies an evaluation, however).*

Do you call that success? How can I be satisfied with that?
> *Evaluation of activating event expressed as rhetorical questions.*

I'm on top of the world when I'm with George.
> *Activating event.*

It makes me feel so important that he loves me.
> *Self-evaluation.*

Chapter 8

All statements in the exercise are *rational beliefs*, expressing an evaluation but not an absolutist demand.

Chapter 12

Sample cognitions leading to *depression:*
> I'll never be able to get what I want.
> Others have it better than I.
> I can't cope.

Sample cognitions leading to *pity:*
> How awful not to get what I want!
> Poor me!

Sample cognitions leading to *mirth:*
> It's great to be alive!
> What a wonderful time I had!

Chapter 14

Activating event: I went for a job interview *and* was turned down.
> (Client incorrectly included part of the A as a rational belief.)

Rational belief: I did not like getting turned down. I wanted the job.
> (Incorrectly stated by the client; the therapist provides a likely guess.)

Irrational belief: It is horrible that I didn't get the job.
> (Correct. There may be others, but additional irrational beliefs can be sought later.)

Emotional Consequence: I felt depressed.
> (Correct. The emotion appears to be appropriate to the activating event and irrational belief. There may be other feelings, but these can be sought later.)

Disputing: Why is it *horrible* that I didn't get the job?
> (The client's statement, "I don't care that I didn't get the job," is a rationalization, not a disputational question. Depression often follows frustration unless

the client questions the "horror" of the frustration. The resulting beliefs, at E, would probably be something like the following statement.)

New effect: It is unfortunate that I didn't get what I want, but it is clearly not horrible. There is no evidence that it is more than unfortunate and disappointing. I'd better look for another job rather than indulge in self-pity.

Chapter 15

Sample *coping* statements:

Dealing with an argumentative spouse—

> Yelling won't help anything. Try to state your ideas clearly without yelling and sounding angry.
>
> Calm down a little. When I raise my voice, it's a sign I'd better calm down.
>
> It's working! I'm not escalating the argument.

A child afraid of the dark—

> There is nothing here that can hurt me. Pretending that there is won't help anything.
>
> I feel afraid but I can cope with that. It's OK for me to feel that way; it's not so bad.
>
> I feel better now. I can do it!

A man afraid of being unable to satisfy his sex partner—

> Don't worry. Worry won't help anything. She will probably be satisfied if I take my time and learn what she likes.
>
> This fear is what I expected. It reminds me to focus on enjoying myself and my partner, and not on what she might think of me.
>
> It's working! I can control how I feel! And the more I relax, the sexier I feel.

An employee afraid of disagreeing with her supervisor—

> I'm not sure how to begin. Just speak up as best I can. The worst that can happen is that she might fire me, and I can cope with that.
>
> I can feel anxious about disagreeing with her and still speak up.
>
> My anxiety won't stop me unless I let it.
>
> It's getting better each time I try. I'll probably feel even more in control next time.

Index